ALEPPO

It is incredible to think that there has never been a one volume history of Aleppo before. Burns' *Aleppo* will join its companion, *Damascus: A History*, as an excellent introduction to the subject for students and anyone interested in the history of this fascinating city and, it is much to be hoped, will one day become a guide for future visitors.

Professor Emma Loosley, *University of Exeter, UK*

Aleppo is one of the longest-surviving cities of the ancient and Islamic Middle East. Until recently it enjoyed a thriving urban life – in particular an active traditional suq, with a continuous tradition going back centuries. Its tangle of streets still follow the Hellenistic grid and above it looms the great Citadel, which contains recently uncovered remains of a Bronze/Iron Age temple complex, suggesting an even earlier role as a 'high place' in the Canaanite tradition.

In the Arab Middle Ages, Aleppo was a strongpoint of the Islamic resistance to the Crusader presence. Its medieval Citadel is one of the most dramatic examples of a fortified enclosure in the Islamic tradition. In Mamluk and Ottoman times, the city took on a thriving commercial role and provided a base for the first European commercial factories and consulates in the Levant. Its commercial life funded a remarkable building tradition with some hundreds of the 600 or so officially declared monuments dating from these eras. Its diverse ethnic mixture, with significant Kurdish, Turkish, Christian and Armenian communities, provides a rich layering of influences on the city's life.

In this volume, Ross Burns explores Aleppo's rich history from its earliest times through to the modern era, providing a thorough treatment of this fascinating city, accessible both to scholarly readers and to the general public interested in a factual and comprehensive survey of the city's past.

Ross Burns worked in the Australian Department of Foreign Affairs for thirty-seven years until his retirement in 2003, with roles including Ambassador to Syria and Lebanon (based in Damascus) from 1984 to 1987, as Minister in Paris (and Ambassador to UNESCO) and as Ambassador in South Africa (1992–95), Athens (1998–2001) and Tel Aviv (2001–03). After his retirement, he completed a PhD at Macquarie University in Sydney on 'The Origins of the Colonnaded Axes of the Cities of the Near East Under Rome'. He is the author of *Damascus* (Routledge, 2004) and *Monuments of Syria* (3rd edition, 2009).

CITIES OF THE ANCIENT WORLD

Cities of the Ancient World examines the history, archaeology and cultural significance of key cities from across the ancient world, spanning northern Europe, the Mediterranean, Africa, Asia and the Near East. Each volume explores the life of a significant place, charting its developments from its earliest history, through the transformations it experienced under different cultures and rulers, through to its later periods. These texts offer academics, students, and the interested reader comprehensive and scholarly accounts of the life of each city.

DAMASCUS – *Ross Burns*
MILETOS – *Alan Greaves*
ALEPPO – *Ross Burns*

Forthcoming:

CÁDIZ – *Benedict Lowe*
EBLA – *Paolo Matthiae*
CARLISLE – *Mike McCarthy*
PALMYRA – *Michael Sommer*
ELIS – *Graham Bourke*
CARTHAGE – *Dexter Hoyos*
MEMPHIS, BABYLON, CAIRO – *David Jeffreys and Ana Tavares*
PAPHOS – *Scott Moore*
ANTIOCH – *Andrea De Giorgi and Asa Eger*
SALAMIS – *Giorgos Papantoniou*

ALEPPO

A History

Ross Burns

Routledge
Taylor & Francis Group

LONDON AND NEW YORK

First published in paperback 2018

First published 2016
by Routledge
2 Park Square, Milton Park, Abingdon, Oxon OX14 4RN

and by Routledge
711 Third Avenue, New York, NY 10017

Routledge is an imprint of the Taylor & Francis Group, an informa business

British Library Cataloguing-in-Publication Data
A catalogue record for this book is available from the British Library

Library of Congress Cataloging-in-Publication Data
Names: Burns, Ross, author.
Title: Aleppo : a history / Ross Burns.
Description: New York, NY : Routledge, [2016. | Series:
Cities of the ancient world
Identifiers: LCCN 2016001815| ISBN 9780415737210
(hardback : alk. paper) | ISBN 9781315544076 (ebook)
Subjects: LCSH: Aleppo (Syria)—History.
Classification: LCC DS99.A56 B87 2016 | DDC 956.91/3—dc23
LC record available at http://lccn.loc.gov/2016001815

ISBN: 978-0-415-73721-0 (hbk)
ISBN: 978-0-8153-6798-7 (pbk)
ISBN: 978-1-315-54407-6 (ebk)

Typeset in Times New Roman
by Swales & Willis Ltd, Exeter, Devon, UK

MIX
Paper from
responsible sources
FSC   FSC™ C013985
www.fsc.org

Printed in the United Kingdom
by Henry Ling Limited

CONTENTS

FIGURES

Note: All figures by the author unless otherwise credited in captions

PREFACE

This book was written as the terrible history of Syria's disintegration into war was unfolding.

Some of the background as to why the present tragic confrontation in Syria has raged so intensely lies hidden in Aleppo's past. Yet the city's history also teaches us that the sectarian and ideological tensions that might at any point have torn the city apart were never allowed to get out of hand as they have now. The explanation for how a well-tempered society that usually found a way through the worst of crises found itself today caught in the most murderous turmoil that has ever been visited upon it is not the subject of this book. What I hope to convey, though, is some sense of Aleppo as it was in the hope that it helps inspire a new phase of regeneration in the future.

Much of the present conflict in that city has centred on built heritage. Amidst concern for the monuments of Aleppo, however, we should not forget the people. They have been the real tragedy of the conflict, one that has engulfed most of Syria. The Postscript gives a provisional tally of the destruction of major monuments but this should be seen in the context of whole suburbs of civilian housing that have been blasted to rubble, not only denying Aleppines their homes but also forcing a large percentage of the population to become refugees outside Syria.

Damage to monuments should therefore be seen in the context of a massively destructive conflict across much of Syria, of the huge toll it has taken in human lives (over 250,000 at the time of writing) and of the lost opportunities for the country's next generation who must despair of any hope of a future as they languish in refugee camps or temporary accommodation abroad.

Buildings are not just pretty facades. They are part of the fabric of history and their loss matters. This chronicle of Aleppo's history will frequently pause to look at the buildings that serve as milestones along its path. Today, when self-proclaimed 'Islamic state' (IS) is busy destroying all it can get its hands on which remind us of a past they would like to see forgotten, it is all the more important to reassemble these milestones in some semblance of order. While documentary, numismatic and archaeological material often give us the precise raw data on a city's history, it is the building record which can give physical form to the narrative. You only have to consider, for example, the central role that the great

Citadel of Aleppo serves in today's events as it looms over the *suq*s, mosques and *madrasa*s of the city's burnt out central area to understand how vital it has been in the evolution of the city going back many thousands of years. Ironically it is the destructive urge of the followers of various Islamist groups which shows how important buildings are as embodiments of memory.

In 2014, Islamist forces (followers of another organisation, 'Islamic Front') turned to dust the unassuming mosque that housed the burial chamber of the great Ayyubid leader of Aleppo, Sultan al-Zahir Ghazi, the most successful of Saladin's sons. Islamist Front dug a tunnel under its structure, packed it with explosives, scurried out and then lit the fuse.[1] Virtually all the building, except for its outer entrance gate, was either turned into a huge dust cloud or sucked into the resulting crater. The Islamists were attacking not just an obstruction cluttering their free fire zone beneath the Citadel but also the physical memory of a successful Aleppan ruler of the late twelfth/early thirteenth century. During Sultan Ghazi's reign and that of his sons – and through the inspiring tutelage of his widow, Dayfa Khatun – a series of buildings was erected in Aleppo which testify to the spiritual and political fruit of a period of remarkable stability. Confident in the thought-world of their own Sunni beliefs, the leaders of Aleppo in these decades produced two of the most significant buildings of Syria, both models of restraint and harmony in their proportions and sober taste in decoration: Dayfa Khatun's Paradise Madrasa and the Mashhad (shrine) of Hussein.

As the Syrian conflict at the time of writing has coalesced around a central theme of a supposed millennial sectarian struggle between Sunni and Shi'i versions of Islam, reading these buildings right becomes even more important. Dayfa Khatun's Paradise Madrasa is an incomparable statement in stone of the calm and repose which comes through Sunni Islam's search for a paradise not through the suicide vest but through spiritual renewal. The Mashhad al-Hussein directed its message to the residual Shi'i community in thirteenth-century Aleppo, conveying respect for the twelve Shi'i imams and so reminding all Muslims of the need to soften if not reconcile their differences.[2]

Dedication

I wrote this book because of a promise to an old friend, John Iremonger, a leading figure in Australian publishing who had been through all the fascinating zigzags of a history degree at Sydney University with me. He and his wife, Jane Marceau, fell in love with Aleppo in 2000, perhaps more so than most visitors. He told me I had to put down a record of its wonderful history. Two years later, John died not long after holding me to my promise. I feel now I have done something to let him know that all that fascination with history that he helped inspire in me did come to a good end.

This book is also dedicated to the Aleppines who have loved their city and sought to convey its unique qualities of hospitality, its traditions and their pride in the co-existence it espoused. Many have through their own research sought to bring their city to a wider audience. This book has gained immensely from the inspiring efforts of Abdullah Hadjar to catalogue the city's monuments for the visitor. Many other Aleppan and foreign researchers laboured over the past century; so many that their best tribute lies in the Bibliography where their devoted research is recorded. There you will see that Henri Sauvaget, Jean-Claude David, Anne-Marie Eddé, Julia Gonnella, Ernst Herzfeld, Carole and Robert Hillenbrand, Bruce Masters, André Raymond, Soubhi Saouaf, Yasser Tabbaa are some of the names whose contributions span many productive years. All of them have pushed new barriers in reaching our understanding of one of the most complex and fascinating of cities. One of the challenges for the next generation, however, would be to progress our knowledge of the rich Arab sources which have been left without new critical editions and translations since the pioneering work of the nineteenth-century *savants*.[3]

Other friends and scholars have contributed in many other ways including the panel of 'readers' who were suborned into giving their opinions or informed comments on the text or parts thereof.

This book would never have taken root without the people of Aleppo whose hospitality and pride in their city lured me back to the place innumerable times over three decades. This book, in a small way, seeks to remind us what can be saved. It can, however, never fully capture the generosity of the people of that great city before they were crushed under the weight of events on a destructive scale possibly exceeding the last Mongol invasions six hundred years ago. No city has ever deserved the fate Aleppo is experiencing now; least of all Aleppo.

Notes

1 This and other tunnels were dug in the first half of 2014, shortly after the 'Islamic Front' was formed from six smaller groups to revitalise the Aleppo frontline with Saudi funding. It also received supplies and facilitation from Turkey, according to media reports quoting German intelligence sources.
2 We will return to the Mashhad al-Hussein in the Postscript.
3 A work such as Ibn al-'Adim's *Everything Desirable about the History of Aleppo* is so far only available in two facsimile editions of the Arabic manuscripts found in Turkish libraries. A critical edition with translation would be immensely enlightening to a wider audience. So far Ibn al-'Adim has been mined for translated extracts relating to the Crusaders' adventures prepared 150 years ago providing us with only a selective picture of what was happening on the Arab side during the Crusades. David Morray, however, has provided us with an excellent summary of the picture it presents of the world of Ayyubid notables in Aleppo.

ABBREVIATIONS

d. died

ed. editor

EI2 Encyclopaedia of Islam (second edition)

EI3 Encyclopaedia of Islam (third edition)

r. years of reign

trans. translator

As there is no clear rule for the use of a noun or adjective referring to Aleppo and its people I have used a rule of thumb: 'Aleppan' for the adjective ('Aleppan food') and 'Aleppine' for the people ('the Aleppines resisted'). I have followed the transliteration system used by the *International Journal of Middle East Studies* as follows – Shi'i (noun + adjective), Shi'a (plural), Shi'i Islam, Shi'ism.

1

SETTING THE SCENE – BRONZE AND IRON AGES

Early Bronze Age – *c*.3600–*c*.2000 BC
Middle Bronze Age – *c*.2000–1600 BC
Late Bronze Age – *c*.1600–*c*.1200 BC
Iron Age – *c*.1200–*c*.539 BC
Persians – 539–333 BC

Aleppo must have one of the most mundane settings for a major city. Many travellers in the past have noted that it fails to announce itself. This was put in a characteristically blunt style by an Australian officer, Hector Dinning, at the end of 1918. He had been one of the celebrated Light Horsemen whose mounted charge at Beer Sheba the previous year had helped bring the collapse of Ottoman Arab empire. Sent north at the end of the war to join the British occupying forces in Syria, he noted:

> If you look at Aleppo from a great height . . . you will see little of natural beauty. You will see nothing but a flat sea of house-tops with the bare island of the citadel rearing somewhat uncouthly from the midst. That is all – excepting the scanty orchards that lie on the fringe of the desert.[1]

It is undeniable that Aleppo lacks a defining context, stranded on a corner of the dusty north Syrian plain and too far from the highlands of eastern Anatolia to the north to benefit in terms of distinctive geographical features. It is only as you descend the bowl of low hills forming a perimeter that the striking profile of the great medieval Citadel rears, competing today with graceless skyscrapers in your line of sight but still commanding attention.

Aleppo's only water resource was the Quweiq River, a small, 130 kilometre-long stream that flowed out of the hills around Aintab (modern Gaziantep) to the north in Turkey. The river fed a thin band of grain cultivation, orchards and kitchen gardens supplying just enough to attract settlement in an area otherwise deprived of water needed to supplement the low seasonal rainfall. Though the flood plain of agricultural land reached by the river widened as it flowed past Aleppo, the Quweiq could not in itself support a major population centre. What little the stream can muster today is siphoned off well before it reaches Aleppo, surviving only as a storm-water drain through a modern city park. Thirty or so kilometres south of Aleppo, the river gave up the struggle against the harsh reality of the Syrian steppe and evaporated in marshes to the south.[2]

Most major historic urban centres that survive through to modern times have an obvious asset that would have recommended them to their founders. The vigorous Barada River supplies Damascus with its snow-fed flow even during the summer months and sustains an extensive oasis in what would otherwise be desert. In the case of Antioch, 100 kilometres to the west near the Turkish coast, the city founded by one of Alexander the Great's successors was fed by the waters of the Orontes. That river brought the inland run-off from the Lebanon and Syrian coastal mountains and bounced along with such enthusiasm that it earned itself in the past the Arabic nickname 'the rebel'.

Stripped of the accumulated over-burden of more than five thousand years, it is hard to identify what Aleppo offered its first settlers. This corner of the steppe lies at around 400 metres above sea level. To the southeast, the land stretches for

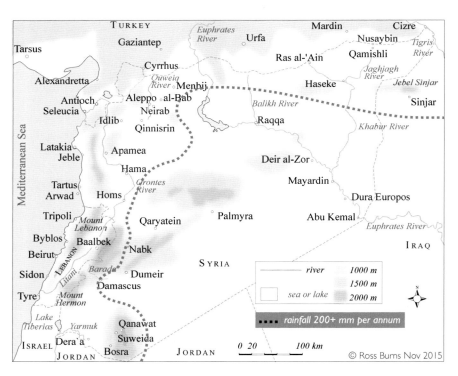

Figure 1.1 Syria, geography

2

hundreds of kilometres towards the deserts of Arabia. To the north, the ground rises slowly until it meets the southern limit of the eastern Anatolian highlands and the Anti-Taurus Mountains. As the terrain reaches around 450 metres in elevation, it forms an ideal corridor bordering the foothills providing easy access from west to east, the historical route along which much of the contact between the civilisations of the Mediterranean and the great cultures of Mesopotamia and Iran flowed. It first passed into written records as the 'Royal Road' that bound the Persian Empire, linking its royal centre, Susa in modern-day Iran, as far west as the Aegean Sea. Aleppo, however, lies some way south of that corridor.

The easiest and shortest connection from the Mediterranean to the basin of the Euphrates and Tigris rivers is the inland road from Orontes mouth at Samandağ. Aleppo is less than 100 kilometres from the coast. After traversing Antioch (modern Antakya), the route heads inland through a convenient gap in the range of mountains that sweeps south from the Anti-Taurus Range petering out in the Sinai. Another 50 kilometres brings it to Aleppo and from there the shortest connection to the Euphrates lies across featureless, dry agricultural land. The Aleppo route provides virtually an open door to the great agricultural spread of the Land of Two Rivers or Mesopotamia.

If there is any advantage in Aleppo's situation, it lies in its proximity to the point where the route inland from Antioch flexes northeast to join the corridor of

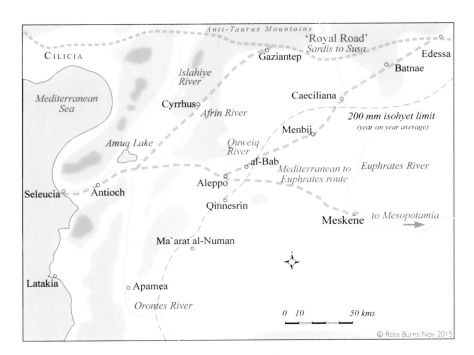

Figure 1.2 Routes from Antioch to Edessa with staging posts

the ancient Royal Road. Stretching from Sardis in western Anatolia, the Royal Road provided the great trunk route between the Aegean and Persia, notably in the Achaemenid and Hellenistic periods. On the other hand, if the traveller's destination is Mesopotamia, landing at the port of Antioch (ancient Seleucia) and choosing the inland route via Aleppo allows easy passage across relatively flat country – by far the fastest way of reaching the next opportunity for water-borne traffic, the Euphrates. It is therefore not the immediate benefits of Aleppo's topography but its access to two nearby key communication routes that have sustained the city's historical role. As the long-distance trade in such key commodities required by ruling groups across the Fertile Crescent grew, Aleppo's territory stood alongside a web of routes transferring precious metals, copper and wood especially to Mesopotamian markets deficient in these essentials. Even when at least the domestication of the camel in the early first millennium made the cross-desert route to the lower reaches of the Tigris-Euphrates viable, Aleppo still offered the greatest choice of access to long distance trade flows.

Environment

While Aleppo's environs lack perennial streams, the city lies within the 200 iso-hyet rainfall zone, usually enough to ensure adequate grain supply and pasture across the flat open countryside. The stonier limestone country to its west and north is less favourable to broad-scale agriculture but can support grazing and the growing of olives and fruits on the slopes or in pockets of relatively rich soil trapped between rising country.

The climate of inland northern Syria is relatively harsh. Long cloudless summer months offer temperatures around 35–40 degrees with no rain. In winter, minimum temperatures often descend to just above freezing (occasionally diving to minus ten) and the city experiences a variable pattern of rain arriving in cloudbursts with occasional snow. The unequal distribution of rain throughout the year brings a reliance on adequate water storage. The run-off from the higher land to the north cannot be counted on for the rest of the year and subterranean capture is limited. The variety of crops grown is therefore limited to those that can avoid or endure the long rainless summers. More intensive zones of fertility can be found in the shallow valleys fed by streams, including the Quweiq, but they are often very seasonal in their flow. Even water for domestic use could be problematic. The city's fresh water was supplemented by channels bringing water from the springs at Hilan in the hills to the north. This supply was delivered by aqueduct from the Roman period. Much of the water was then stored under the city in domestic cisterns, many of which survive to this day.

Besides grain (traditionally corn and wheat), fruits and nuts, Aleppo lies in country best suited to the raising of sheep and goats, usually grazing between seasonally productive agricultural areas. Aleppo largely learned about trading the hard way, through millennia of experience of buying in supplies and processing and trading products to surrounding markets, especially to the north.

However, in periods of longer-term stability, Aleppo moved to a new level of prosperity. Its access to long-distance trade with regions far to the north, east and southeast, tapped markets ranging as far as Baghdad and Basra down the river system of the Tigris-Euphrates, Persia to the east and Asia Minor to the north and west.

A high place

If Aleppo had nothing much to offer to attract a permanent population of any size, what accident of history led to its steady rise to urban status and eventually to its rank as the most populous of the major cities of Syria? It had one small feature that other centres lacked: an elevated rocky outcrop on the edge of the steppe which could readily house an important defensive or religious centre. Prominent man-made mounds or *tells* dot the countryside of northern Syria, marking population centres that died out millennia ago leaving behind the accumulated detritus of their houses and contents. Aleppo's central mound, today occupied by the magnificent Citadel of the Islamic Middle Ages, has long been a feature that defined the city's profile and provided it with a major defensive asset.

Unlike the customary mound (or *tell*) left by layers of human occupation, Aleppo's Citadel rise is a largely natural rock feature, though to some extent its features have been rounded off by the shaping of the material remains of many centuries. A medieval visitor from al-Andalus, Ibn Jubayr, marvelled at the claim that the rocky rise had its own natural spring that permanently assured a supply of water but it is more likely that the early inhabitants relied on two deep caverns serving as cisterns topped up by the winter rains.

If we look further at the terrain beneath the centre of the modern city, the reasons for its early rise to fame might become a little more apparent. Figure 1.3 shows the ground underneath the historic walled city of Aleppo and marks the perimeter of the historic walled area. For the moment we are concerned only with two underlying features. The first (marked on the right of Figure 1.3 below) is already apparent from historic engravings – the Citadel hill that rises to 437 metres above sea level (and thus almost 40 metres above the level of the plain). There is, however, a second elevated feature on the western side of the historic city centre, the Aqaba Quarter (in English, 'the slope'). Not noticed by most visitors, this hill is lower, rising only some 20 metres above the city's average.

This prominence lies on the northwestern edge of the area later defined by the ancient and medieval city grid which would fill the area between the Citadel hill and the Aqaba Quarter. Attention was drawn early last century to this area as the location of an early settlement. The presence of a Mamluk mosque (Mosque al-Qiqan) which included reused Late Bronze Age material presumably found on or near the site gave the clue. The incorporation into the mosque's walls of a stone in Luwian hieroglyphic script (see Figure 1.5 p.7) referring to the dedication of a temple indicated the site was used for religious purposes from the period of Hittite domination into the Iron Age.[3]

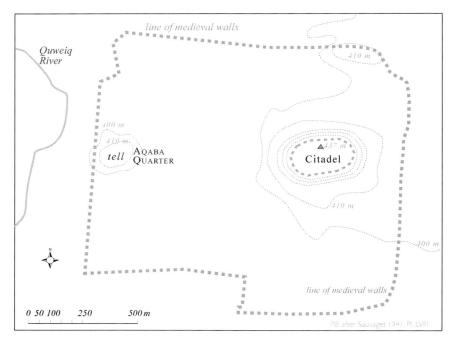

Figure 1.3 Topography beneath the ancient city

The western mound in the Aqaba Quarter would appear to represent the remains of an early human settlement on a site near the Quweiq River and its flood plain, thus close to food gardens and water. This largely artificial *tell* on the western side of the later walled city was barely 100 metres square, a fraction of other *tells* of the north Syrian steppe. It marks a small population centre on the edge of a rather meagre river, typical of the period.

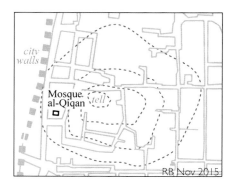

Figure 1.4 Western *tell* of the old city

6

It is the more prominent rise under the present-day Citadel that might better convey the significance of the site. We have noted already the likely defensive role of such a natural feature, a place of retreat for the inhabitants of the village in times of invasion. But it may have had an even more significant second purpose which would better account for Aleppo's later fame.

Curiosity about the likely original use of the Citadel hill began to develop in modern times, giving rise to the temptation to explore beneath its jumbled remains of many centuries. The use of the hill as a military base as late as Ottoman and French Mandate times ruled this out for many decades, though interest in the area had risen with the discovery during the French Army's occupation of the site in the 1920s of blocks with remarkable relief panels (see Figure 1.9 on page 15). It was only in the 1990s that German and Syrian excavations near the highest natural part of the rise were authorised to investigate further. The excavations revealed a large temple spanning many centuries of occupation going back to the Early Bronze Age (2500 BC) but whose surviving elements largely date from the Late Bronze Age and Iron Age.

Nothing in the few indications of Aleppo's origins outlined so far account for its later rise to prominence. The temple, however, might provide important clues. To understand its significance, we have to look more generally at the context in which Aleppo was flourishing in the northern Syria region, the role of such temples on 'high places' and the extent to which the religious and political life of the time was dominated by cult centres (see 'The Storm God' on page 13).

Figure 1.5 Mosque of Qiqan, Luwian inscription

Bronze Age (*c.*3600–*c.*1200 BC)

Amorites (c.2000–1595 BC)

Our picture of northern Syria in the Bronze and Iron Ages is still developing. The Old Testament is little help to us as Aleppo (though later associated with legends of Abraham's journey from Mesopotamia to Jerusalem, to be examined later, page 134) fails to rate a mention. The first archaeological material from Aleppo emerges only in the second half of the second millennium with the discovery of the temple just described. Before the recent excavations on the Aleppo Citadel, no opportunities had arisen to explore what lies beneath Aleppo. First references to Aleppo are therefore documentary and emerged in archives dating from *c.*1700 to 1600 BC discovered at the site of Alalah, on the Amuq Plain 55 kilometres west of Aleppo. The texts are in the form of cuneiform tablets written in Akkadian and date from the period of Amorite dominance in northern Syria. We still lack precise information on the origins of this previously nomadic group but Jebel al-Bishri in northeastern Syria, west of the Euphrates, is recorded as the 'Land of the Amorites' (Amarru) in contemporary Akkadian records.

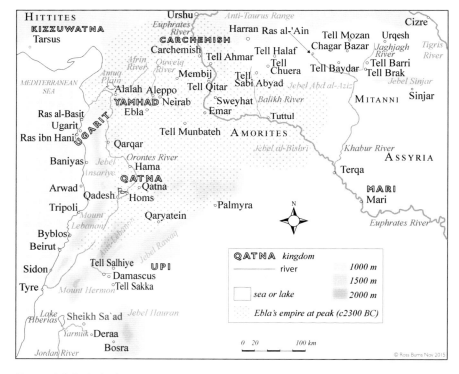

Figure 1.6 Syria in the Bronze Age, 3600–1200 BC

8

The Amorites were able to wield power over a large part of northern Syria, eastern Turkey and northern Iraq where they formed the first Assyrian kingdom and brought to an end the initial phase of Mari, the great centre on the mid-Euphrates whose power had extended over much of northern Syria east of the Euphrates. Their rise to dominance in northern Iraq coincided with the end of the Third Dynasty of Ur, the prelude to the rule of Hammurabi of Babylon (1792–1750 BC). While centralised control of the Amorite lands probably did not exist, one of the centres where an Amorite dynasty held sway was at Aleppo, capital of the kingdom known as Yamhad.

The Amorite dynasty based on Aleppo became the major power in northern Syria during the period 1800–1600 BC. Its rule extended at times to the Euphrates and as far west as Alalah. Yamhad's power was checked to the south by a new kingdom based at Qatna, near modern-day Homs in central Syria. The third great power in Syria at this time was the regenerated kingdom of Mari. A young son of the dynasty, who had been sent as a child to Aleppo, was brought back to Mari to restore the dynasty's claim to the throne. His name was Zimri-Lim and his thirteen-year rule (1774–62) represented a high-point in Mari's history as many of the tablets of this period as well as remains of the dynastic palace (perhaps) sacked by Hammurabi of Babylon in 1762 BC have been uncovered by the French excavations at Mari.

Hammurabi's sacking of Mari meant that Yamhad, the Amorite centre already allied with Hammurabi, was unchallenged as the 'dominant power in northern Syria'.[4] The archives of Alalah have given us one of the rare documentary insights into the affairs of the time and give some indication of Aleppo's strength, seen as rivalling even the great empires of Mesopotamia. One tablet, an intelligence report sent in by an agent at Mari on the Mid-Euphrates, recorded as follows:

> There are ten or fifteen kings who follow Hammurabi of Babylon and ten or fifteen who follow Rim-Sin of Larsa but twenty kings follow Yaram-Lim of Yamhad'.[5]

Going by The Book

As we move into the later second millennium BC, the problems of interpretation of evidence multiply as sources become more varied. Even scientific researchers have been preoccupied by the Western fascination with accounts of the area given in the Old Testament. The dominance of the Bible narrative has meant that for a long time everything turned up in archaeology had to be fitted into the account of the region's affairs as related in the books of the Prophets and where possible aligned to the king lists and other records that emerged from the plundering of Mesopotamian sites since the late nineteenth century. In the process, a pseudo-science of 'Biblical archaeology' emerged that put little store by what was happening, for example, in the large zone between the Tigris-Euphrates basin and the Palestinian coast.

'Biblical archaeology' has taken a considerable battering in recent decades as scientific results put more and more distance between verifiable facts and the Bible

Figure 1.7 Central citadel at Ebla, seen from the west

narrative. Northern Syria was the 'black hole' at the centre of this zone and the assumption that its culture and economy were largely determined outside was difficult to budge. The picture was partly corrected by the discoveries made during the eight decades of French excavations at Mari on the Middle Euphrates and by the unearthing of Ugarit, a major Bronze Age trading centre with strong ties to Egypt and to the Aegean world. Both sites, however, were on the fringe of the black hole and had their own links to an outside world more familiar to Western audiences. There is, however, a good deal of other corroborative evidence that the political and religious role of Aleppo in this period spread much wider than expected.

In particular, the long-standing assumptions that events in northern Syria were largely determined by cultures further south or abroad have been discredited by the results of the excavations since the 1960s by the Italian researchers at Ebla (principally under Paolo Matthiae). Ebla lies 55 kilometres south of Aleppo at a site known as Tell Mardikh. This vast doughnut-shaped mound had long evoked curiosity given its size but only with the commencement of the Italian excavations did the real significance of the site emerge, enabling new insights into the 'black hole'.

Extensive archives of clay tablets were found in several locations in the complex of buildings in the central Citadel area revealing a monarchical society which attained its zenith in the second half of the third millennium BC when it controlled most of northern Syria and extending into modern Lebanon (see Figure 1.6). The late third millennium archives, written in a combination of Sumerian and Eblaite languages (the latter the first documented Semitic language and akin to Akkadian), provided a name for the Bronze Age city – Ebla. The records revealed a rich culture, an empire intensely oriented towards international trade (notably through the export of textiles) with links spreading from Cyprus to the lower Euphrates as well as extensions north and south.

Ebla's kings had strong associations with Ugarit on the coast and with Mari. The existence of such a powerful and populous centre close to Aleppo might lead us to think that Aleppo was only a minor tributary of the Eblaite empire. The references to Aleppo in the Ebla tablets, however, have provided an unexpected twist. While Ebla had temples of its own dedicated to a range of gods and goddesses, Aleppo was the cult centre whose drawing power in the region was extensive, often embracing or even supplanting Ebla, as seen in the adoption by Ebla of Aleppo's Hadad as a patron deity after 1750 BC. Aleppo's Citadel housed a pilgrimage centre whose links drew in devotees from afar – a city whose religious role probably considerably outweighed its economic significance at the time. To what purpose did the visitors flock to Aleppo? Before returning to look for the answer on the Aleppo Citadel, we need to sketch the changing historical scene in northern Syria.

Hittite dominance (Halab, 1595–c.1200 BC)

Aleppo in the early second millennium BC, as noted earlier, had been the capital of the important kingdom of Yamhad. Yamhad's supremacy in the region was clipped by the rise of the Hittites whose empire at its peak from the mid-fourteenth through much of the thirteenth centuries was to dominate the affairs of the Late Bronze Age Near East. It was the Hittite king Hattusili I (r. *c.*1650–*c.*1620)[6] who first made inroads into northern Syria from his base in central Anatolia to the northwest. These moves reflected ambitions for wider empire and more specifically Hattusili's aim to secure a dominant trade role controlling the supply line for tin from Iran and Afghanistan, an essential element in bronze making. Hattusili's first objective became Aleppo in order to benefit from Yamhad's strategic position straddling trade lines, particularly for tin and copper.

Aleppo's prominent Citadel had ensured that the city did not fall to the invaders on this the first of probably a number of attempts by Hattusili. However, Aleppo's importance in the Hittite scheme of things was illustrated by the creation of a temple to Aleppo's Storm God (whose cult is examined below) in the Hittite capital Hattusa following Hattusili's campaign. Eventually, the city known to the Hittites as Halab was taken by Mursili I, the successor and probably the grandson of Hattusili, in *c.*1595. The taking of Halab marked the end of the kingdom of Yamhad but the beginning of a prominent role for Aleppo in the Hittite empire, marking the beginning of the Hittites' wider designs not only on Syria (where they sought to block inroads from Egypt to the south) but also on Mesopotamia. Babylon fell in the same year, bringing to an end the Old Babylonian Kingdom, Babylon's first flowering in the Near Eastern world.

Mitanni, Hittite kingdom and Egypt (c.1500–1274 BC)

In the wider region on which the Hittites were now encroaching, the dominant power was that of Mitanni, a Hurrian-speaking confederacy in northeast Syria probably centred on the upper Khabur River. While the Mitanni had a common interest with the Hittites in ensuring that the Egyptian New Kingdom did not take a permanent hold in northern Syria, ultimately the Mitanni represented a greater threat to Hittite ambitions in Syria than the Egyptians. This three-way contest for Syria between the Hittite kingdom, Mitanni and Egypt was one of the defining features of the Late Bronze Age in Syria, inevitably drawing in Aleppo which lay at the point of convergence of the three powers.

The extension of Hittite dominance across northern Syria had only brought a temporary end to Halab's monarchy which had been re-established under Mitannian sovereignty. A line of fifteenth-century puppet kings was installed in Aleppo by the Mitannian king Parrattarna. Halab was again recorded as a client of the Kingdom of Mitanni in the fourteenth century and attempted a new assertion of Aleppan local dominance in northern Syria under Mitannian tutelage. Aleppo then ranked possibly as a temple-estate under the authority of a Mitannian viceroy at Alalah.

Aleppo normally succeeded in remaining beyond the reach of Egyptian ambitions to extend its influence into northern Syria in the Late Bronze Age. Egyptian attempts to gain a foothold on the plain around Aleppo had begun in the fifteenth century by engaging Alalah as its vassal but were only temporarily successful. In the three-way pattern of rivalry between Egyptians, Hittites and Mitanni, Aleppo usually only had to find a modus vivendi between the Hittites and the Mitanni, though a tentative renewal of Egyptian moves into northern Syria was made by Thutmosis III (Battle of Megiddo 1458 BC) campaigning as far as the Euphrates. Egyptian treaties with several of the states under Mitannian dominance, however, only temporarily held off a resurgence of Mitannian power.

Renewed Hittite interest in the region resulted in a campaign under King Suppiluliuma I (r.1350–1322) to end Mitannian supremacy in northern Syria. Halab was chosen as the residence of a Hittite viceroy, Suppiluliuma's son Telipinu, after 1327 BC – one of only two such vice-regal seats in Syria. The continued prestige of the Weather God Temple on Aleppo's Citadel is underlined by the appointment of Telipinu as high priest of the cult that was honoured in both Syria and Anatolia. The next Hittite-appointed king, Talmi-Sharruma, is the last recorded in Bronze Age records. It is clear from the Hittite records that Talmi-Sharruma was not a powerful ruler and from the reign of Mursili II, Carchemish was recognised as the dominant Hittite centre in the region. Instructions issued to Talmi-Sharruma from the Hittite capital make it clear that he was not to extend his influence regionally at the expense of Hittite imperial interests.

This renewed expression of Hittite interest in Syria in the fourteenth century inspired Egypt to return to the Syrian game, particularly to counter the Hittite 'New Kingdom' leader, Tudhaliya (first half of fourteenth century). An uneasy

Hittite–Egyptian line of control across central Syria prevailed for the next century with Mitannian influence confined further east.

Among the powers contending for Syria, however, there appears to have been an expectation, certainly between the Hittites and the Egyptians, that this tacit division had to be finally decided in battle. The stage was set near the central Syrian town of Qadesh, a little southwest of modern-day Homs. By the mid-thirteenth century, the greater Syrian ambitions of the Nineteenth Dynasty pharaohs prompted Aleppo to contribute its forces to the Hittite-sponsored confederation which countered Ramses II at the Battle of Qadesh in 1274 BC.[7] While the battle for the Egyptians was at best a draw (or possibly a rout), it provided copious material for Ramses II's self-promotion programme in Egypt (featuring five times on billboard-like battle scenes on Egyptian temples). In the longer term, though, it was certainly a bloody nose for Pharaonic Egypt. Attempts to sustain control so far north in the Levant had proven difficult and New Kingdom Egypt did not seek to test its Syrian ambitions while the Hittites remained.

The Storm God

While Aleppo's political role largely succumbed to the 'great power' game being played out in Syria, its religious importance was still significant. One insight that the Old Testament has given us is the importance in Bronze and Iron Age Syria/Palestine of the worship on 'high places' – usually mountain tops which brought the worshipper closer to the heavens, providing a more direct link with the deity controlling rainfall and thus fecundity. At times, the Old Testament seems obsessed with the lingering influence of high places, with over fifty references to such cult centres as anathema to the followers of the monotheistic cult of Yahweh. Northern Syria, in particular, is dotted with elevated platforms apparently devoted to the cult of the Storm God, Hadad, in most sources. In Iron Age central Syria and the coast, the god is given the title Baal ('lord'), often with different local combinations such as Baal-Shamin. His various manifestations amounted to one of the most widespread cults in the ancient Near East and thus the great adversary of the Hebrew Yahweh. In centres with multiple temples, Baal/Hadad is usually given first billing in the Phoenician tradition (e.g., Ugarit) and his influence prevailed inland, as at Damascus where he would later be loosely assimilated to the Roman Jupiter.

Most of the 'high places', at least originally, were simply adapted from natural formations with a bench and lustral basin carved into the rock and no superimposed structures. Other sites were later given conventional temple buildings. It therefore came as no surprise that the temple unearthed in the 1990s on the Aleppo Citadel proved to be honouring the Storm God (Addu in his local designation). The first indication that an important religious complex might exist in this area had come with the discovery in 1930 of a basalt relief slab (mentioned earlier).

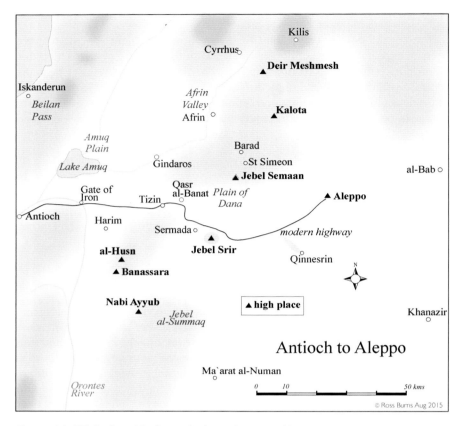

Figure 1.8 'High places' in the Antioch to Aleppo corridor

Dated to the ninth or eighth centuries BC, two genii are depicted under a crescent moon framing a radiating sun, indicating a cult associated with the heavens.

The excavations begun in 1996 and directed by Kay Kohlmeyer revealed a building of massive proportions, possibly 35 metres wide and 26 deep. Figure 1.10 provides some perspective on the excavations, showing the temple forecourt and the entrance to the main shrine (part of which lies under the modern concrete outdoor theatre, see Figure 1.11). While the excavators faced numerous challenges in exposing the site, one of the deepest soundings of any urban dig in Syria, from it has emerged one of the most important temple structures of the Bronze Age Middle East.

The temple was in use almost continuously from the Early Bronze Age to the Iron Age – *c.*2500 to the ninth century BC, surviving across numerous cultures. We have seen above the importance attached to the temple as a cult centre of regional significance for the Hittites. This reflected what was already a long tradition. The

14

Figure 1.9 Basalt panel from the Temple of the Storm God on the Aleppo Citadel

Figure 1.10 Excavations of the Temple of the Storm God on the Aleppo Citadel

first references to the king of Ebla journeying to worship at the Aleppo temple originated *c*.2500 BC. The Middle Bronze Age building comprised a large hall 20 by 17 metres oriented west–east with the main shrine on the middle of the north side, approached by the southern door leading in from an equally broad porch. The god's cult figure is described in documents from Mari as a 'huge seated figure in the round with a smaller sun god on his knees'.[8] The major reconstruction phases of the temple in the Late Bronze and Iron Ages have provided the bulk of the present remains, beginning with the shrine as reconstructed under the kings of Yamhad when the shrine is mentioned in tablets from Mari.

Transition to the Iron Age (*c*.1200–900 BC)

Within fifty years of the great battle at Qadesh, the slate of Middle Eastern affairs was virtually wiped clean. From around 1200 BC, the Levant experienced widespread disruption, the causes of which are still difficult to identify. The mysterious incursions of the 'Sea Peoples', first noted in Egyptian temple records in the

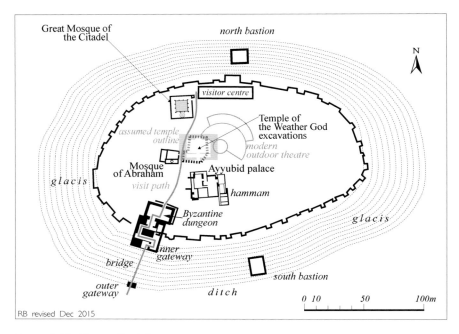

Figure 1.11 Aleppo Citadel

late thirteenth century BC, turned the region upside down, bringing the end of the old empires such as that of the Hittites or even of a major trading city such as Ugarit and leaving few if any of the population groups of the Late Bronze Age still intact. This disruption brought new population movements, possibly in some cases peaceful or quietly absorbed over a number of years.

Our picture of events in northern Syria in the transition from Late Bronze to Early Iron Age is still being assembled. Until recently it was commonly assumed that virtually all the Bronze Age societies vanished in this series of population movements. Egyptian and Ugaritic records described the arrival of the 'Sea Peoples', who appeared to have had their origins in Anatolia to the north. The new excavations on the Aleppo Citadel, however, have contributed to a new perspective. The fact that there is no evidence of disruption on the Aleppo Citadel mound (and possibly at other inland centres) suggests that the 'Sea Peoples' (probably more a series of 'domino effect' population movements rather than a concerted wave), may be more a coastal phenomenon, with limited secondary effects inland. A recent survey of the evidence of collapse sees no single cause as responsible for such widespread disruption but rather a range of factors that occurred during the first half of the twelfth century – a 'systems collapse intensified by a "multiplier effect," in which one factor affected the others' which it took some decades to recover from.[9]

'Aramaean' and 'Neo-Hittite States' (c.1100–c.900 BC)

The traditional picture had also assumed that the end of a 'golden age' of Late Bronze Age trade and prosperity was linked in the inland centres to the arrival of a new population group, the Aramaeans. The people labelled 'Aramaeans' assumed power in a series of cities of the Syrian inland by 1000 BC. Recent research, again based partly on the findings on the Aleppo Citadel, has brought a corresponding

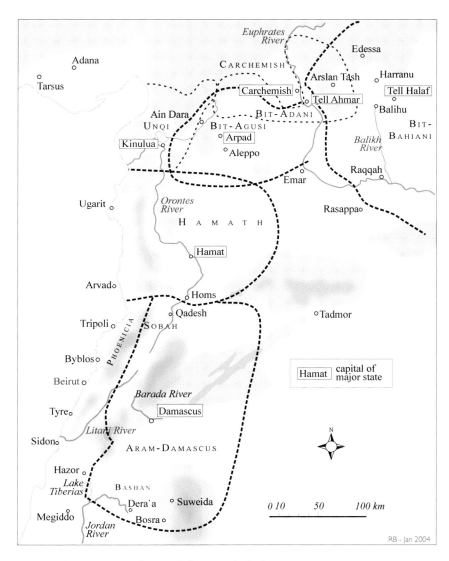

Figure 1.12 Aramaean and Neo-Hittite states in Syria

17

revision of traditional assumptions. The fact that the transition seems to have occurred without major destructive evidence at Aleppo in the period 1200–1100 BC (previously written off as a forgotten 'dark age') has upset many received views.

In northern Syria, in this confused phase after 1200 BC, there seem to be two major influences at play. Trevor Bryce notes that there had already been a considerable shift of ruling elements from the Hittite realm into northern Syria in the last centuries of the Late Bronze Age, evidenced in the creation of vice-regal presences at Carchemish and Aleppo. Some Luwian-speaking elements of this shift survived and formed 'Neo-Hittite' princely houses in the Early Iron Age. At the same time, a more prominent role in the region developed around several centres identified with Aramaean newcomers.

Alterations to the Aleppo Storm God temple, a cult whose fame had already spread as we have seen to the Hittite capital, perhaps reflect this pattern of change within continuity. Under Hittite domination, the Aleppo temple's orientation had been changed from its broad temple plan common in northern Syria with the main cult figure opposite the southern doorway to a plan focusing attention to the east in the Hittite tradition. In the temple's last phase (post-1100 BC), the plan was switched back to the north–south orientation when a local dynast, King Taita, renewed the emphasis on the central niche along the north wall.[10] This phase saw a rearrangement of carved stone panels both new and from earlier phases (Late Bronze and Iron Ages) and would appear to be evidence of a willingness to refer back to older traditions. In the final arrangements, the selections varied from the familiar theme of the Storm God wielding his axe or club to weird mythical figures such as the male shrink-wrapped in the scales of a fish (a Mesopotamian theme) or human heads on the bodies of griffins or bulls.

Who were the Aramaeans who now became the dominant culture? People described under variations of the name 'Aramaean' had appeared in written records from as early as the mid-second millennium. Recent research indicates that there was a considerable increase in the number of settlements in the Iron Age compared to the Late Bronze Age but that initially the new settlements were small 'indicating a "dispersal" of the population into small, rural settlements' lacking at first any unified political structure (Niehr 2014: 17). This suggests there was no massive new influx into northern Syria but a process by which small Aramaean-speaking communities, previously nomadic, settled down and became the nucleus of a new leadership element as the predominant influence of the Hittites and their Luwian-speaking allies began to wane.

These Aramaeans, speakers of a Semitic language, may have originated in north-eastern Syria through the consolidation of pastoral communities who turned to a settled way of life. However, we have no evidence that they had assumed an identity based on a common 'Aramaean' *ethnos*. Rather they were an amalgam, probably peacefully achieved, of existing population groups with the addition of new elements and through the adoption of a new common language. The new states went on to become a rallying point amid the disruptions of the coming centuries and their language would endure even to the time of Christ when it provided a lingua franca to the wider region.

While it is now clear that the population movements triggered by the Sea Peoples along the coast did not affect all of northern Syria directly, the widespread disruption may indirectly have stifled trade and the ability of traditional powers (notably the Hittites, the Egyptians and the powers-that-be of Mesopotamia, the Kassite kingdom) to play a direct role in the area. This uncertainty in the period 1200–1000 BC appears to have given new opportunities for groups already partly resident in the region to assert a leadership role without necessarily displacing the existing population groups. As Aramaean rulers began to consolidate power

Figure 1.13 Relief panels from the Temple of the Storm God: King Taita (right) facing the Storm God

at several centres by the early first millennium, they erected buildings that signalled societies which had assumed roles beyond that of a subsistence economy. Much of the existing material culture simply continued, in some cases, under these new rulers who often sought to emulate their predecessors. They adapted the imagery of the previous dominant imperial presence in the area, the Hittites, and have thus been given the label of 'Neo-Hittite' in recent decades. While some dynastic offshoots from the Hittite/Luwian-speaking dynasties of earlier times survived in the area alongside the Aramaean rulers, the term 'Neo-Hittite' would be misleading, though, if taken to imply a resurgence of centralised Hittite identity or political power. Rather, in many cases, all that was involved in a centre like Aleppo was a simple merging of earlier imagery with elements from Assyria to the east which was soon to seek a dominant role in Syria in the ninth century.

To summarise the evidence sketched above: Aleppo, now reborn as an Aramaean-age centre, was still drawing on many of the old trappings of the Hittite era. It may have come under the principality Bit-Agusi whose capital, Arpad, was probably Tell Rifaat not far to the north, an Aramaean kingdom. Aleppo seems to have fallen in prestige. Possibly it retained local importance as the major centre for agriculture along the river. It was the temple, however, which continued to attract patronage from local dynasts who sponsored the renewal of much of its basalt relief panelling but arranged the new and the old relief figures in imaginative new combinations. The eleventh-century ruler of Unqi, King Taita, now controlled Aleppo from his base in the Amuq Plain, Kinulua.[11] The king was displayed presenting tribute to the Storm God, Hadad, confecting a new tribute scene by repositioning an earlier relief of the god beside a new panel depicting the king.

Trade

While it is difficult to be definitive about the evidence for the ethnic composition of the new entities in northern Syria, it seems clear that the region benefited greatly from several developments that greatly promoted new trade links across political borders. Two breakthroughs were particularly important. The development of techniques for the production of iron introduced agricultural tools, providing ways to cultivate soils once seen as too hard to work. Second, the domestication of the camel meant that trade could span longer distances without access to water, thus opening up faster routes across the Syrian Steppe, particularly to the southeast. Aleppo must have benefited greatly from both developments. New trade routes were most easily accessed from Aleppo's commanding position and its region found new opportunities to develop agricultural products for export. The trading energy generated by the Phoenician coastal communities also played into a burgeoning economic picture inland and the demand for the cedar of Mount Lebanon brought a new emphasis on longer distance trade, particularly into Iran.

Art

The art of the Aramaean period in Aleppo is known to us now by the relief decorations used to adorn the Weather God temple, complementing the other scattered finds from the region around Aleppo. The style is common to numerous 'Neo-Hittite' sites across northern Syria and northwest into the Anatolian mountains. Depictions of gods, kings, mythical figures and beasts are often stiff and stylised, borrowing some thematic elements (without the scale) from the massive relief panels found in contemporary Mesopotamia but notably more human and intimate in some instances – for example, the superb relief panels from Neirab (15 kilometres southeast of Aleppo) now in the Louvre.

A more awkward attempt at the gargantuan was found early last century at the site of Tell Halaf (ancient Guzana) well to the east of Aleppo alongside the line of the Ottoman railway to Baghdad. These huge orthostats show mythical

Figure 1.14 Relief panel from Neirab near Aleppo depicting a priest of the Moon God (seventh century BC, Louvre, Paris)

Figure 1.15 Sculptural pieces from Tell Halaf guarding the entrance to the Aleppo
Archaeological Museum

beasts guarding the palace of the local Aramaean ruler, an attempt to terrify rather
than impress. Most of the basalt pieces were taken to Berlin where they suffered
severely in a British bombing raid in 1945. Some, however, survived better in the
Aleppo Museum where reconstructed versions of the palace guardians still play
their customary role protecting the main entrance in formidable array.[12]

Neo-Assyrian dominance (883–612 BC)

By the ninth century BC, the two centuries of consolidation in north Syria were
disturbed by another intrusion from the Mesopotamian world to the east. The rise
to regional dominance of Assyria represented a revival of the ambitions of the
second millennium Assyrian empire. This time the Neo-Assyrian push to the west
sought to extend their control from their northern Iraq base (in modern terms)
as far as the Mediterranean by co-opting or absorbing the small Aramaean and
Neo-Hittite states. The latter were too tiny and disunited to meet the challenge on
their own but occasionally managed to form loose confederations among themselves and with the Biblical states to the south. The first signs of Assyrian ambitions to incorporate the Aramaean and Neo-Hittite kingdoms into the structure
of Assyrian provinces occurred when the two entities east of the Euphrates, Bit-
Bahiani and Bi-Adini, were taken into the Assyrian sphere in the first half of the
ninth century BC. The Neo-Assyrian drive westwards became more aggressive

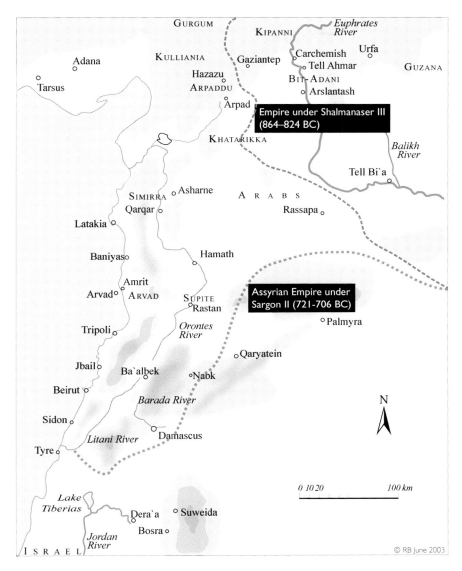

Figure 1.16 Neo-Assyrian and Persian rule in Syria, 883–330 BC

under Ashurnasipal II (883–59) who campaigned fourteen times in his attempts to expand his empire. Neo-Assyrian control was frequently challenged by the Aramaean and Neo-Hittite states. In 853, a confederation led by the king of Hamath and joined by Ahab, king of Israel, met the Neo-Assyrian forces under Shalmaneser III outside the city of Qarqar on the Orontes.

Shalmaneser had arrived via the northern route, taking Aleppo on the way where continuing respect for the Storm God required him to make offerings at his temple. At Qarqar one of the reputedly great battles of the ancient world said to involve prodigious numbers on both sides in fact seems to have yielded uncertain results. The Assyrian king was forced to campaign for another decade to put down rebellions. Shalmaneser III's taking of Damascus in 841, for example, prompted Hazael of Damascus to recover much of central Syria and it took another hundred years and a second battle outside Qarqar (720 BC) to produce a decisive victory for Assyria.

By then Neo-Assyrian sway extended even as far as the Phoenician coast (modern Lebanon). The Phoenicians, successors of the Canaanites, had established a wide-ranging network of commercial and colonising enterprises as far as North Africa and Spain. The Assyrians largely saw advantage in allowing a

Figure 1.17 Statue of Shalmaneser III in the Istanbul Archaeological Museum (from Assur)

higher degree of autonomy to the Phoenicians to maximise their own commercial advantage. Much of the drive behind the Neo-Assyrian imperial project was thus commercial with the western provinces in Syria exploited through the massive export of commodities, especially timber and slaves. The empire was never fully established on a sustainable basis and periods of military aggression were interspersed with loss of control, particularly in areas neighbouring the Neo-Hittite or Phrygian states to the north or the Egyptian/Nubian kingdoms to the south.

Neo–Babylonian and Persian rule (612–333 BC)

The Neo-Assyrian Empire thus easily fell prey to the ambitions of the next wave of rulers who established themselves in Iran and swept through the Neo-Assyrian domains in Mesopotamia. The Neo-Babylonian ruler Nabopolassar (r.626–605 BC) captured and sacked the Neo-Assyrian capital, Nineveh, in 612 BC. His son, Nebuchadnezzar, was appointed to lead a campaign that took Carchemish in 605 BC in order to fend off an Egyptian attempt under the Pharaoh Necho to move back into Syria.

The Neo-Babylonians ruled in alliance with the Medes, a group who had moved their power base from the Zagros Mountains of Iran to the southwest. The Neo-Babylonian Empire increasingly succumbed to the ambitions of the Medean Persian side of the alliance, who in 559 BC struck westwards to realise their earlier ambitions to establish a state of their own under the Achaemenid dynast, Cyrus II ('the Great'). Cyrus had virtually unlimited ambitions, extending Persian control from Central Asia and as far west as the Mediterranean. The next generation of Achaemenid rulers pushed as far as Cyprus, Egypt and into the western reaches of Asia Minor, pressing against the Greek-speaking states around the Aegean. In 538, Syria became one of the satrapies of the empire under a system that gave considerable autonomy to local communities and under which the retention of Aramaic as the everyday language of communication was encouraged. Persian ambitions peaked under Darius I (522–486), who campaigned on the Greek mainland while controlling (for a time) regions as far east as the Sind (modern Pakistan).

We have no reminders of these troubled centuries under the Neo-Assyrians, the Neo-Babylonians or the Achaemenid Persians in the rare pre-Classical finds that have emerged from Aleppo or its environs. Generally, these empires left little for the benefit of the Syrian population, preferring to take Syria's wealth, manpower and skills to adorn their homeland, including under Darius the new ceremonial capital at Persepolis. A few hints of Achaemenid influence, however, are found 200 kilometres to the southwest of Aleppo on the Syrian coast, near Tartus. Here the site of Amrit, lying opposite the Phoenician settlement on the island of Arwad, gives a few indications of the blending of Achaemenid and Phoenician influences in the architecture of the Temple of Melqart and a small group of funerary towers.

Aleppo, however, was barely a way-station at this time. The Persian satrap (governor) of the region was stationed not at Aleppo but at a nearby town, al-Bab, now a dusty way-station on the route to the Euphrates and the Jazira. Aleppo was not noted in any of the written records of the Iron Age. It still enjoyed a certain religious fame through the Weather God temple. On the Citadel hill, the memory of the palaces of the Hittites' client kings and the Aramaean princes perhaps lingered but the village itself was barely distinguished from a number of other small inhabited centres clinging to the narrow fertile band along the Quweiq.

Alexander (333–323 BC)

Since the fifth century, the Persian Empire of the Achaemenids had long taunted the Greek states by seeking dominance in the Aegean. Alexander, the young son of Philip II of the northern Greek kingdom of Macedonia, grew up amid vivid tales of the fifth-century battles which had turned back aggressive Persian campaigns at Thermopylae, Marathon and Salamis. Driven, according to Classical sources, by a mission to liberate the Greeks of Asia Minor from Persian rule, Alexander's army crossed the Hellespont to the Asian shore in 333 BC. As he pursued his campaign against Persia, the revenge motive assumed wider dimensions that were to culminate in widespread carnage and the burning of the Achaemenid ceremonial capital at Persepolis in 330 BC, settling the score after the fifth-century sacking of Athens by the Persian army.

As Alexander pursued his campaign to the east, the first major battle against the Persian forces under Darius III was in 333 BC at Issus, not far from Aleppo but on the Mediterranean side of the coastal range just near the later Greek-founded city, Alexandretta (today Iskanderun). Darius suffered a disastrous defeat but escaped east towards his homeland. Alexander decided not to set off in pursuit but took the Persians' disarray as an opportunity to divert south down the coast. His first objective was to seize the Phoenician cities so important in the region's trade flows and to capture their fleet. His second was to press on into Egypt, there to explore his possible deification by consulting the oracle at the Temple of Amun in the oasis of Siwa in the Western Desert.

Alexander's ten-year campaign then resumed its path towards Iran. The fortuitous death of Darius, who had fled as far as northeast Iran in an attempt to rally forces to his failing cause, meant the Achaemenid Empire after two further decisive losses passed to the Greeks. Alexander's efforts to pacify and reorganise this huge domain was cut short by his death in Babylon in 323 BC. The first challenge facing his followers was to settle Alexander's inheritance among his generals. The span of the new empire from Greece to India was too much for one ruler to control and a series of conflicts over succession saw the territory divided by 301 BC between three dominant figures drawn largely from his generals – Antigonus in Syria and Mesopotamia; Ptolemy in Egypt; and Cassander and Lysimachus dividing western Asia Minor and Greece. Lesser princes or satraps ruled in the constellation of small principalities distributed as far as modern Karachi in Pakistan. Many areas along the seams between these kingdoms, however, were contested. Syria, in particular, was uneasily partitioned between Ptolemy and Antigonus. The vague line of control initially ran across modern southern Syria but wavered during the wars of succession that marked the third century BC. Aleppo, however, remained securely on the Seleucid side.

Antigonus died in battle in 301 BC (Ipsus) and the western parts of his kingdom (Anatolia and Syria) fell to Seleucus I Nicator, who, as satrap in Babylon, had already conducted a fierce and prolonged campaign to prevent Antigonus from usurping his command. Seleucus now joined Syria to his former domain which had nominally covered Babylonia, all of Iran and the empire to the east. Seleucus was a determined leader who appreciated that after the constant wars between Alexander's generals he needed to provide the enormous spread of his realm with a viable structure through a clear chain of command and an impregnable base. Seleucus decided to fashion such a structure around two capitals – Antioch in northern Syria and his old command, Babylon (later moved to nearby Seleucia on the Tigris) in Mesopotamia.

The arrival of the Greeks in Syria brought an end to centuries of control of northern Syria from Mesopotamia or Iran and gave the region a new orientation – towards the Mediterranean and with a focus on Hellenic civilisation. This was to influence Syria's choices for the next thousand years.

Notes

1 Dinning 1920: 167.
2 The Quweiq formed part of the survey by a British team reported in Mathers (1981, I and II). The lack of a broader survey of the environs of Aleppo is to be addressed by a new project outlined in Del Fabbro (2012).
3 Herzfeld 1955: 277 for foundation inscription; Sauvaget 1939. The Luwian stone was identified as early as 1870 and later became an important clue in tracing the development of Indo-European languages and their spread from Central Asia. On the significance of the use of Luwian in Aleppo, see the particularly interesting contribution by Aro (2010).
4 Bryce 2012: 22.
5 Woolley 1953: 65. Woolley believed that the presence of the archives at Alalah perhaps indicated that the king of Yamhad had adopted Alalah rather than Aleppo as the kingdom's functional capital while retaining Aleppo's formal status.
6 On problems relating to the chronology of the Hittite period, see Bryce 1998: 408–15.
7 There are at least two Bronze Age chronologies in the Near East depending on the methods used to reconcile astronomical and literary evidence – 1274 is the date now more generally accepted, the fifth regnal year of Ramses II.
8 Kohlmeyer 2009: 191.
9 Cline 2014: 165.
10 On Taita, see Hawkins 2009: 169; Hawkins 2011. An interesting comparison with the Aleppo temple is provided by another temple structure 60 kilometres to the north, at ʿAin Dara in the Afrin Valley. The ʿAin Dara temple followed a similar plan. The first version probably dates to around 1300 BC though the existing remains are largely Iron Age.
11 The location of Taita's capital is not certain but may have been at Tell Taʿyinat on the Amuq Plain east of Antioch (Hawkins 2009: 169).
12 The result of a remarkable project by the Vorderasiatisches Museum in Berlin to reconstruct the pieces from fragments is documented in Cholidis and Martin (2010).

2

GREEK AND ROMAN ALEPPO

Hellenistic period 300–31 BC
Roman period 31 BC–AD 353

So far we have had few clues as to how Aleppo housed its inhabitants. The only hints to its layout we have discerned have been the Citadel hill to the east and the smaller rise now covered by the intra-mural quarter of al-Aqaba at the western end of the cross-city axial route. While the Citadel was a largely natural feature providing a prominent position both for a palace for the local sovereign and for a religious centre devoted to the Storm God, the lower rise to the west was primarily the place where the population lived close to the Quweiq River and its gardens. That picture did not fundamentally change during the centuries of rule by Aramaean, Neo-Assyrian, Neo-Babylonian and Achaemenid Persian rulers. It seems likely that although Aleppo at times was still ruled by local princes serving as clients to kings elsewhere, its wider regional role was defined by its residual religious influence resulting from the fame of its now 2000-year-old cult centre – still one of the pre-eminent 'high places' in a region studded with such shrines.

The Greeks, too, have left us with no evidence of their settlement of Aleppo beyond that perennial device for a managerial makeover – a name change. The city had long been known (as it is today in Arabic) by a variant of the name first recorded in the early second millennium BC, Halab حلب.[1] The Seleucids established one of their kingdom's capitals less than 100 kilometres away at Antioch in order to stamp a Greek imprint on the area. It had become the habit of the Hellenistic kingdoms to chose place names referring to their Macedonian origins, honouring the origins of the Diodochi (Alexander's generals) or other regime figures and their wives, mothers or sisters. This applied both to the many new foundations – meant to implant a Hellenised identity in an area through Greek language, education and political institutions – and to existing towns which were simply 'rebadged'. Aleppo was in the last category. Thus Halab became Beroia, a reference to the Macedonian city, Βέρροια, second most important of the cities of the Macedonian kingdom after Pella but today a minor

28

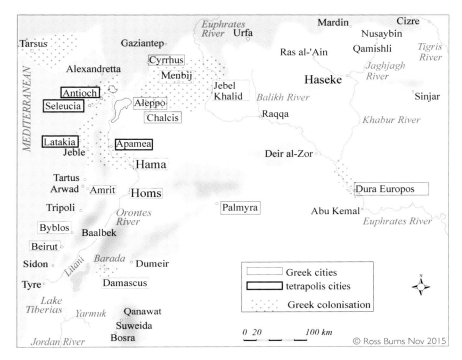

Figure 2.1 Greek colonisation in Syria

town (often rendered as Veria in English) 75 kilometres southwest of Thessaloniki in northern Greece.

Seleucus I Nicator was reported in later Classical sources as the founder of Beroia.[2] Born to an aristocratic Macedonian family, Seleucus had been steeped in the atmosphere of Hellenism as a boy when he shared the young Alexander's lessons under Aristotle. He served loyally in Alexander's expedition to the East and his flexibility of spirit persuaded him not only to join in the mass marriage ceremony arranged by Alexander at Susa but also to remain with his chosen bride, an Iranian princess, Apama, who was to produce his heir Antiochus I.

Seleucus' policy of enlightened Hellenism recognised the need for an amalgam of Greek and Persian traditions. This, however, did not rule out the conferral of dynastic names on most of the major towns of Syria. These towns were given implantations of colonies of Greek settlers though often the Greek element was housed in separate quarters established alongside the existing Iron Age centres. Even smaller centres and many rural areas received Greek colonies, often retirement schemes for members of the army at the end of their careers but with the dual purpose of planting Greek control through the institution of the city (*polis*), regarded by the Greeks as the essential framework underpinning civilised values.

Figure 2.2 Coin depicting Seleucus I Nicator (Seleukos I Nikator AR Tetradrachm. Sardes mint, Wildwinds)

If we look at the map of northern Syria under the Greeks in Figure 2.3, the pattern of the contribution the network of cities made to the maintenance of a Greek identity is clear. It is a remarkable tribute to the Greeks' capacity to identify locations essential in implanting a Greek identity on the region that virtually all of the first-rank centres chosen as Greek urban centres remain major cities to this day. In northern Syria, only a few of the second-rank towns were deserted in the post-Classical period, such as Cyrrhus and Chalcis (Qinnisrin).

Moreover, the word *polis* (plural *poleis*) applied to the new and adopted cities was more than just recognition of a city's precedence as an urban centre. It denoted too that it possessed the institutions that the Greek found essential to their

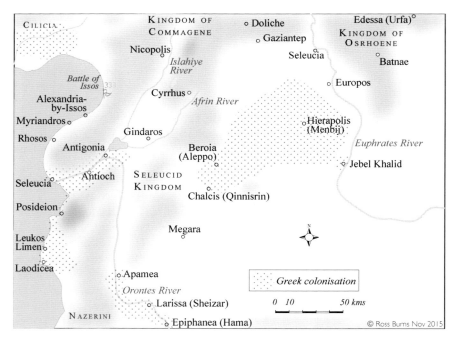

Figure 2.3 Hellenistic north Syria

30

way of life – an assembly of elected citizens or *boule*, occasional gatherings of the *demos* defined as those people educated in the Greek language and to a syllabus that reflected Hellenised values. Classical notions of Athenian democracy might have fitted awkwardly with Seleucus' ideas of an over-arching monarchic structure but it did leave the administration of cities largely in local hands, a practice that was to survive well into Roman times. This 'guided democracy' became a way of unleashing the energies of a community and brought a sense of healthy competition between urban centres.

It is difficult to discern how local non-Greek inhabitants of a city might access these institutions. Perhaps at least one generation was required to gain the familiarity with Greek as a language to enable Syrians to gain admission, if at all. As the centuries passed, though, the degree of convergence between Syrian local identity and the advantages of a common system based on Hellenised values seems to have been broadly accepted.

Seleucus' *tetrapolis*

By far the most important of the new cities in Syria was Antioch. A new foundation on virgin ground, within three centuries it rose from nothing to become one of the great *metropoleis* of the classical world – the 'third city of the world' in Josephus' euphoric description (in the late first century AD).[3] Its rise was not quite as spectacular as that of the Ptolemaic capital at the mouth of the Nile, Alexandria, which could draw on a court society endowed on an extravagant scale by Egypt's annually renewed fecundity and by the memories of the splendours of the Pharaohs. But Antioch was not a poor second. The Orontes was not the Nile but Antioch could draw on a hinterland with considerable agricultural riches and access to trade routes almost as bountiful as Egypt's. It spawned many other small poleis in its neighbourhood but none of them (except perhaps Apamea) would rise above a moderate population level, at least during the Greek period. Aleppo/ Beroia's proximity to Antioch may have brought the same disadvantages that many Nile Valley settlements faced with the competition from Alexandria. The burgeoning metropolis simply sucked much of the urban life out of its hinterland – everyone wanted to be where the action was; where it all came together.

As Seleucus Nicator began to lay down the Greek colonial presence in northern Syria, he must have been conscious of some compelling strategic needs. With a vast kingdom that stretched from Iran to Anatolia and with two capitals a thousand kilometres apart to straddle, he needed a strong base from which to operate. Access to communications and victualling, animal transport for his army and a reliable supply of manpower were all vital. To cover these essential needs he chose four nodal points to form a secure base area for the colonial localities scattered across his vital communications route between Syria and Mesopotamia – Antioch to Seleucia-on-the-Tigris. This *tetrapolis* became the western buttress of his empire. The strongpoints created *c*.300 BC were Antioch itself, its port at Seleucia (a little to the north of the mouth of the Orontes and within easy reach of the capital), Laodicea (modern Latakia, on the coast 85 kilometres south) and Apamea (these locations are marked on Figures 2.1 and 2.2). The four points of this tetrapolis in northern Syria comprising two ports and two inland centres for assembling, provisioning and indoctrinating the empire's strategic forces not only gave him a base area straddling two major lines of communication but also offered relatively easy access to the Mediterranean, still the heart of Hellenic civilisation.

Hellenistic Aleppo (Beroia)

Aleppo – slightly outside the tetrapolis – does not figure in a major way for the next few centuries. Written sources that refer to it are limited and although it was close to some of the key communication routes, it was outclassed by other sizeable secondary cities in the region – Cyrrhus, Hierapolis, Chalcis, Apamea – which lay right on the lines of communication or in more productive agricultural areas.

We do know, though, that Aleppo/Beroia was chosen to receive an implanted colony of Greek veterans. The direct literary or archaeological evidence of this is fragmentary[4] but it is impossible to ignore the corroboration provided by Jean Sauvaget, the French historian who spent much of his distinguished career puzzling the evolution of Classical cities in Syria. Using mostly deductive reasoning based on the city's modern streets, he reconstructed the evolution of the city's street plan, noting that the western side of the existing walled city bore clear traces of a grid pattern characteristic of the Hellenistic era and found at numerous contemporary cities around the eastern Mediterranean.[5]

The thoroughfares show the streets, surviving in the modern layout which conformed to the grid, clearly orientated to the compass points. The full extent of the grid, based on standard city blocks (*insulae* to use the more common Latin term) each 114 by 47.2 metres did not continue as far as the Citadel to the east.[6] It also seems to have occupied no more than two insulae on either side of the main east–west axis, considerably smaller than the later walled city. The grid suggested a profile for the Hellenistic city as seen above. If the missing streets are restored to the plan (see Figure 2.4), it further suggested a pattern typical of the period with a wide central axis linking the ancient tell to the west with the Citadel area on the eastern edge – an aspect to be discussed further in the next chapter. Over the centuries, the Greek grid elements or insulae have been broken up through the creation of laneways and informal structures blocking earlier thoroughfares but the origins of the pattern as a grid are incontrovertible.

The date of this implanted Greek city that filled in the space between the Citadel hill and the original settlement on the Aqaba tell is not known. The dimensions of the new city were 550 metres north–south and 780 east–west, thus enclosing just over 40 hectares but not all the planned area was necessarily settled *ab initio*. As to the date of the new foundation, we cannot assume that all the new Greek settler colonies in Syria date from the early Seleucid years. Even if two later classical sources ascribe Aleppo's re-founding to Seleucus I Nicator, it is possible these

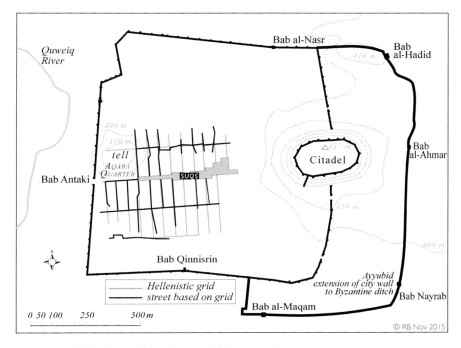

Figure 2.4 Hellenistic grid in Aleppo, with later survivals

are simply foundation myths conveying the most prestigious origins. In fact, for the first Greek century (300–200 BC) Seleucid rulers were preoccupied with the struggle for control of Syria. Only with the opening of the second century after southern Syria/Palestine was taken from the Ptolemies in 198 BC by Antiochus III ('the Great' – r.223–187 BC) did the Seleucids manage to enjoy a few decades of stability. Many cities, including Dura-Europos on the Euphrates, Damascus and possibly Apamea, did not receive an expanded Greek presence until the second half of the second century BC).

Hellenisation

The Seleucid Greeks, following Alexander's lead, were relatively accommodating towards 'native' religious and political traditions. The exception was in Palestine where the two-tiered policy based on an assumed process of convergence clearly failed. The revolt of the followers of Judas Maccabeus in 167 BC challenged the Greek attempts to develop a state based on a loose religious structure assimilating indigenous gods into a Greek pantheon. This contrasted with the tight definition of the Jewish religious code favoured by their priests. To the Maccabees, the worship of the old Canaanite/Aramaean gods was anathema, particularly Baal (loosely

Figure 2.5 Coin showing Antiochus III 'the Great' (uncertain Mesopotamian mint, courtesy Classical Numismatic Group)

equivalent, as noted earlier, to Hadad and the Storm God) still widely honoured through the 'high places'. The Seleucids responded to the Maccabean revolt with a more aggressive policy of 'Hellenisation', especially under Antiochus the Great's successor, Antiochus IV (r.175–164 BC). The fiery temper of the unstable younger Antiochus was legendary and he sought to use aggressive Hellenisation as a vehicle for restoring political control.

It was possibly during this phase that Beroia was among those cities selected for replanning along more organised (i.e., 'Greek style') lines. In other cities, such as Damascus, we know that the cult of Hadad was loosely associated with the supreme god in the Greek pantheon, Zeus, whose temple became one of the focal points of the city's grid plan. Under Antiochus IV's policies, it is possible that Aleppo's great cult centre to the Storm God/Hadad also took on the same association. Its continued dominance of the urban landscape of Aleppo was certainly enhanced when the temple was selected as the visual end-point of the cross-city axis of the replanned city.

A new city centre

One other aspect of the Greek city plan deserves examination. We look now more closely at the mid-point along this cross-city axis, the zone occupied today by the Aleppo Great Mosque. This central area spreads across three or four of the insulae blocks in the city centre. Such a zone combining several blocks for civic use is common in Greek-founded cities in the region. Sometimes the purpose was to provide more space for commercial as well as civic activities (*agora*) and possibly to accommodate an important shrine in its environs.

Given the 'continuity of use' principle, such spaces would often remain dedicated to religious use across future centuries even if the change from paganism to Christianity to Islam would later raise sensitivities regarding the reuse of physical structures consecrated under earlier creeds. This is an issue that will be explored later but what should be noted now is the likelihood that the 'continuity of use' rule suggests that the insulae occupied by the present-day Great Mosque also once housed the principal temple of the lower city of Aleppo with additional space used as a forum or garden area. We have no enlightenment from inscriptions,

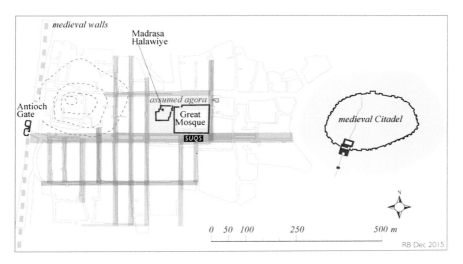

Figure 2.6 Assumed agora and Great Mosque

coins or written descriptions as to the deity who might have been honoured in this space. The gods who gained city-centre billing in the region tended to be among the top-rating figures of the pantheon. Hadad was already honoured in Aleppo as he would have been loosely equated with Zeus or Jupiter on the Citadel hill but other favoured deities in the region include Atargatis (Hadad's consort) at nearby Hierapolis (modern Menbij) or Zeus at Apamea.[7]

The Syrian Goddess

The cult that had the most spectacular reputation in northern Syria was Atargatis, the 'Syrian Goddess'. She was the consort of Hadad as the north Syrian storm god and her cult too went back well into the pre-Hellenistic period. Given the region around Aleppo lay so close to the great military routes to the east, an emphasis on cult centres favoured by the military could be expected. Her temple at Menbij lay 90 kilometres northeast of Aleppo, directly on the campaign route crossing the Euphrates and joining the old 'Royal Road' into Iran. Today the only sign of her temple is a slight depression on the western side of the modern town centre, just the right size for a football field and probably the residual imprint left by the sacred lake that was such a feature of Atargatis' cult.

On a platform edging the lake, fearsome sacrifices were practised. This rather frenetic cult is described in obsessive detail in a racy almost mocking style in the work of the second-century Roman author of Syrian origin, Lucian – complete with a long description of self-castration, of rituals involving sessions over several days perched on phallus-shaped poles and of human sacrifice including babies

35

Figure 2.7 Coin showing Atargatis issued at Ascalon under Demetrios III (wikipedia.de)

stuffed into bags and tossed into the lake. The lake's waters were then annually drained through a deep fissure in the earth presumably to appease the goddess.

Collapse (*c.*100–65 BC)

By the beginning of the first century BC, the Seleucid kingdom began to fall apart. The growing power of Rome in the eastern Mediterranean was a factor in the new forces pressing on Syria in the second century. Seleucid ambitions to assert their power as far as Greece had already been crushed by Rome's victory over Antiochus III's army at Magnesia in 190 or 189 BC. Other pressures came from Armenia and the Pontic region of Asia Minor. By the mid-second century BC, the

Figure 2.8 Remains of the southern enclosure wall of the Temple of Atargatis, Menbij

eastern empire from Babylonia east had fallen to the Parthian dynasty sometimes labelled Arsacid after its founder, Arsaces (r.247–217). The latter had rebelled against Greek rule in Iran in the mid-third century BC and succeeded in splitting off Iran under a separate dynastic name.

By 100 BC, the Seleucid monarch in Antioch controlled little beyond the confines of the Orontes Valley perhaps including Latakia, thus the original tetrapolis. Seleucid Syria began to break into fiefdoms held by local dynasts, of which one was based on Aleppo. In 96 BC, the Seleucid king, Grypos, was murdered by his army commander and chief minister, Herakleon, who made an unsuccessful bid to take the throne. Grypos fled to his home town of Aleppo and ruled it as a separate principality. In 88 BC, the Seleucid king, Demetrios III, besieged Aleppo, by then ruled by Herakleon's successor Strato. However, Aleppo appears to have withstood the siege and survived as a city-state independent of the Seleucids for another twenty years.

The implosion of northern Syria, however, was an open invitation to trouble with so many ambitious powers already eagerly gathering around the fragmented kingdom. Even the Parthians, who had seized the former Seleucid domains in Iran, were by 88 BC as close as the Euphrates crossing at Zeugma when they sent a contingent to the aid of Strato, helping him to withstand the siege by Demetrios III. In 84/83 BC, the last Seleucid ruler died. The Antiochean elders met not to decide on a successor but to select an outside protector of the residual empire. They eliminated the Pontic king Mithradates (r.120–63 BC) as too likely to provoke Rome's hostility due to a long-standing rivalry in western Anatolia but chose Tigranes, the king of Armenia (r.95–56 BC).

Tigranes' takeover of Syria was apparently largely peaceful. At least nominally, Tigranes retained the Seleucid arrangement of a constellation of poleis rather than a tightly managed kingdom and Aleppo remained a city-state under a Herakleonid prince.

Tigranes' overlordship of the wider region which had extended as far south as Damascus and the Palestine coast was to last not much more than a decade. He nevertheless awarded himself the title of 'King of Kings' with a new capital befitting his empire at Tigranocerta, northeast on the Upper Tigris. By 68 BC, his base was threatened, as Roman leaders advanced further into Asia Minor to address the convoluted rivalries in the area, not least for the opening they offered for an extension

Figure 2.9 Coin of Demetrios III, minted in Damascus (courtesy of selukidtraces. comDE3-AR-01)

Figure 2.10 Tetradrachm of Tigranes II the Great, possibly Seleucia on the Tigris mint (commons.wikimedia.com)

of Parthian power. Suppression of the ambitions of Tigranes was seen as the only way order could be made to prevail. Tigranes surrendered to the Romans under Gnaius Pompeius (Pompey 'the Great') in 66 BC and Tigranes' son, who had already defected to Rome, was installed as a client king. Rome had initially been reluctant to move further and enter Syria. Pompey's commission from the Roman Senate had been limited to the elimination of the pirate hideouts of the eastern Mediterranean that were threatening Roman shipping. It became increasingly clear to leaders in the field such as Pompey, however, that as neither the Greeks nor the Armenians could be entrusted to maintain a newly stabilised order, Rome must.

Enter Rome (64 BC)

By 64 BC, the overly ambitious empire of the Seleucids had been further reduced to a sliver of territory from Antioch to Aleppo. Pompey entered Antioch without the slightest resistance. He faced a threshold decision. Should he, as he had done with the Pontic and Armenian kings, let the Seleucid, Antiochus XIII ('Asiaticus' 69–64 BC), wither on the vine; or dismiss the dynasty's claim to be capable of governing the region effectively and abolish it?

End of the Seleucids

Tigranes' son was allowed to stay on as Rome's client and Mithradates, who had escaped to the Crimea, conveniently suicided. Pompey, however, chose a more interventionist solution for the Seleucids.

> Pompey . . . when he had overthrown Mithradates, allowed Tigranes to reign in Armenia and expelled Antiochus from the government of Syria, although he had done the Romans no wrong. The real reason for this was that it was easy for Pompey, with an army under his command, to rob an unarmed king, but the pretense was that it was unseemly for the Seleucids, whom Tigranes had dethroned, to govern Syria, rather than the Romans who had conquered Tigranes.[8]

The last Seleucid monarch put in a bid to have himself confirmed king but Pompey's answer was to arrange his murder by one of the Seleucids' Arab allies, Samsigeramus I.[9] Syria was simply too important to be left to a young dynast's whims and was declared a Roman province with its governor answerable only to the emperor. The new province's capital remained Antioch, which had all the necessary facilities of a major administrative centre. Antioch was conveniently buttressed by the Seleucid tetrapolis, a base still essential to Rome's new role. The inhabitants of Antioch were of many origins and the arrival of a new ruling caste made little difference. A new era for the dating of events was declared, originating not with the year of Seleucus' foundation of the city but the date of Pompey's victory over Tigranes – underlining that the takeover of Syria had been on the Roman commander's mind since that time and was no rush of blood to the head.

Aleppo is not mentioned in the accounts of these tumultuous events. Antioch was by now a great metropolis of the East, third in rank around the Mediterranean (second until Alexandria was brought into the empire in 30 BC with the demise of Cleopatra VII, the last ruler of the Ptolemies). Nothing in northern Syria could match Antioch in size or importance. The region was prosperous and vital for Roman control but Aleppo was just one of many burgeoning cities that sustained the booming economic activity under the Pax Romana.

Parthia – threat or opportunity?

The importance of northern Syria in facilitating massive military deployments to the East was to be even more obvious under Rome. The Parthian threat did not go away; at times it could even be reinvented. In 53 BC, the Syrian governor Marcus Crassus, in an attempt to follow Pompey's example and use an Eastern war to claim a higher political profile in Rome, sought battle with the Parthians at Carrhae not far to the northeast of Aleppo outside Edessa (modern Sanliurfa in Turkey). He suffered a devastating defeat, was forced by his own troops to surrender his seven legions' standards and was later killed by a Parthian officer. The disaster was to resonate through Roman history for decades. The distraction of the Civil Wars that brought the Roman Republic to an end seemed to be a further invitation to the Parthians to probe deep into the new Roman province of Syria. Antony, Caesar's rival for control, followed Crassus' example and saw a campaign against the Parthians as a means of buttressing his claim to leadership. Antony's appointee, Ventidius, met the Parthians in battle in the region around Cyrrhus north of Aleppo in 38 BC. A Roman victory paved the way for Antony's move into the Levant that would be decisively brought to an end with his suicide at Alexandria a year later following Octavian's victory at Actium.

However, Octavian (after 27 BC given the title Augustus) followed a new approach. Augustus' adopted son, Tiberius, was sent in 20 BC to the East to redress the humiliation of Carrhae and found the Parthians amenable to compromise. Prisoners were exchanged, hostages sent westwards and the standards of Crassus'

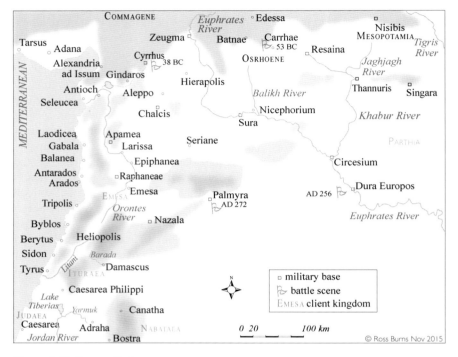

Figure 2.11 Roman Syria

legions returned. Both sides would choose to let the Euphrates remain the dividing line between the two empires, a situation symbolised with a ceremony on the
river twenty years later. As far as we know, the situation in the north settled down
without complications. In southern Syria, by contrast, residual banditry and the
quarrels within the royal family of Judaea presented serious distractions to be
addressed for some decades.

Roman Beroia

The groundwork for the Roman city of Beroia had been laid in the Greek period.
No physical remains of this phase have come down to us but some clues can be
inferred from the way the city evolved on its footprint. On the Citadel rise to
the east, the landmark Weather God temple was now probably identified with a
Roman counterpart deity – perhaps Jupiter given the close link that seems to have
prevailed between Jupiter and the Weather God, Hadad, in Damascus. Spreading
from the foot of the hill towards the west, the city of the Hellenistic period under-
went major changes while retaining in the central area the old grid dimensions.
We can assume that the insulae covered by the Great Mosque of the present city

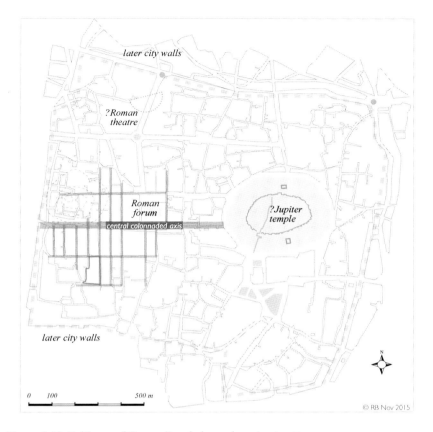

Figure 2.12 Evidence of Roman Beroia in modern street pattern

continued to be the focus for the major civic institutions inherited from the Greek city, a central forum replacing the Greek open space or *agora*. (The development of this area will be examined in the next chapter where remains of its Byzantine redevelopment give further clues.)

It also seems likely that the Romans greatly extended the area covered by the original city grid. The recent researches of Giulia Neglia indicate that a second grid following the same compass alignment extended the city to the north, south and east of the original Greek footprint.[10] The new blocks differed from the narrow Greek insulae and allowed for more spacious housing.[11]

Possibly another decision taken during this phase of expansion of the city's footprint to accommodate the new era of prosperity was the conversion of the wide central avenue stretching from the western gate (today's Bab Antaki or Antioch Gate) to the foot of the Citadel. Other east–west streets on the Hellenistic grid measured no more than 5 metres in width but this central axis spanned 25 metres.[12] Like most Greek cities, Hellenistic Beroia had made few concessions to monumentality. This was now corrected with an apparent decision to give to the city's spine a new visual emphasis.

We owe the identification of this axis to Sauvaget who noted that amid the pattern of streets of the central bazaar area three narrow west–east alleys ran closely in parallel interrupting the uniform grid. He assumed that this marked a band where originally a wide central street had formed the city spine in the manner of other Macedonian settlements including Alexandria. Though we have no physical evidence of how Aleppo's axial street was treated, it is tempting to assume that the wide central avenue of the Hellenistic plan was upgraded in the second century AD with colonnades on each side, as was the case in virtually all the mid-ranking Roman cities of the Levant, apparently following the lead of Antioch. The most spectacular nearby example is the main avenue through Apamea where the broad central street was later colonnaded and can still be seen today. The pattern Sauvaget had identified can be demonstrated by overlaying on the present-day passages of the Aleppo suqs (in grey in Figure 2.13) the template of a typical colonnaded street plan.[13]

In his study of Aleppo, Sauvaget saw in the Classical period the true foundation of Aleppo as a city of prestige and influence.[14] The physical structure endowed by its Greek and Roman rulers initiated a concept of urban development that was to continue through the centuries to this day. His vision of Aleppo may owe too much to the French fascination with the *urbanisme* of the inter-war period and lacked the appreciation we have today that the city's prestigious role stretched back as early as the Late Bronze Age. More questionable is Sauvaget's assumption that only Greek and Roman values could endow a city with greatness; everything after that was decline.

Most cities of reasonable size in Provincia Syria had a theatre and perhaps other manifestations of Classical culture including a hippodrome, amphitheatre or gymnasium. No remains of a theatre have been identified in Roman Beroia, though in her recent study, Giulia Neglia has carefully analysed the detailed cadastre of Aleppo before its post-Second World War redevelopment and has noted a semicircular outline preserved just within the medieval northern walls

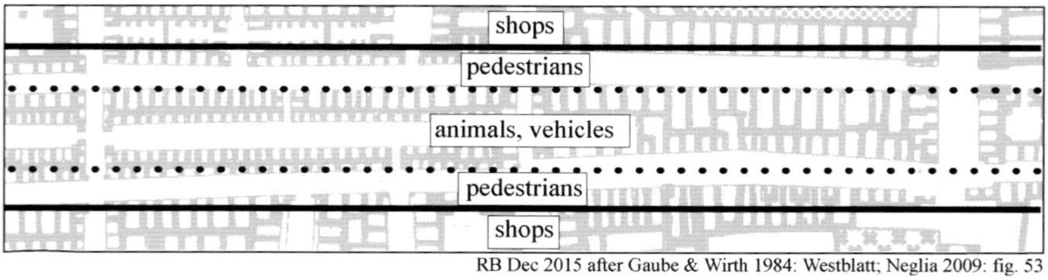

RB Dec 2015 after Gaube & Wirth 1984: Westblatt; Neglia 2009: fig. 53

Figure 2.13 Remains of the triple passages of the colonnaded street (black), reflected in the street pattern southwest of the Great Mosque (grey)

(see Figure 2.12). The area was heavily reconfigured in an ill-conceived urban development project in the 1970s and is now bisected by Abdel Mounem al-Riad Street separating the Bahsita and Bandara Quarters. Neglia estimated the theatre as roughly 100 metres in diameter, which would indicate it needed to cater for a population of the size of Damascus or Bostra.[15]

It is possible that the civilian population of the Roman city was protected by walls extending from the Citadel but there is no firm indication of an initial Roman phase in the remains of the lower city walls visible today – including at those points where the city's Classical circumference can be assumed to have been reflected in later Islamic defences.

It would seem that Beroia continued to be overshadowed by Antioch and Apamea. It gained virtually no profile among ancient writers familiar to us from the surviving contemporary sources. Its cult centres in Roman times lacked the wider fame of Hierapolis and certainly Baalbek. The latter was a relatively small city, a centre for Roman veterans that happened to have been favoured with a complex of temples that still impress with their eye-watering scale. Aleppo could not even match the reputation of the temples of Jupiter Damascenus, of Elagabalus at Emesa (Homs) or of the Jupiter Dolichenus shrine to the north (Doliche outside modern Gaziantep in southeastern Turkey). The latter shrine was a favourite of Roman soldiers en route to campaigns in the East. Even the shrine of Atargatis at Hierapolis now enjoyed empire-wide fame far exceeding the temple of her old consort, Hadad, at Beroia and like Doliche attracting throngs of cult followers from the Roman military.

Beroia's coins, usually a mark of a city's trading prowess and economic influence, were a minor short-lived series in bronze confined to the reigns of Trajan and Hadrian. Most of the currency circulated throughout Syria originated in Antioch or Seleucia. Their prolific numbers issued in these centres reflected their importance as the sources of major trade and military movements as well as the availability of excavated material remains.[16]

The reality was, though, that Beroia was simply one of the mid-ranking cities on an inner orbit governed by Antioch's gravitational pull. Within a 100 kilometre circle centred on Aleppo one could count nine such cities. The prosperity of the area depended not just on its agricultural resources but on the flow of long-distance trade through the region, visits by imperial officials including emperors, the constant deployment of army units and their demand for replenishment. The whole region flourished in the demand economy of the Roman imperial system as it lay in the zone of intersection of most of the vital routes. Some of the remaining client kingdoms to the north were brought under direct Roman rule. Commagene, the kingdom whose ruler had erected at Nemrut Dag a striking emblem of the spiritual unification of the Hellenised and Persian worlds, was absorbed in AD 72. In the period 107–13, Cappadocia was transferred to a new province of the same name incorporating the Pontus region. From Antioch all the way along the Euphrates bend or north to Armenia and the Black Sea direct Roman rule now prevailed, though Edessa remained an exception.

Figure 2.14 Coin of the Trajanic era, minted in Beroia and found at Zeugma (courtesy Wildwinds)

Wider challenges

The Euphrates, easily fordable once the post-winter snow melt passed, proved a fragile line of separation from Rome's foe to the east in Parthia. Greater Armenia (today's northeastern Turkey, extending to the Caspian Sea), while theoretically a Roman ally, often proved less than trustworthy when it came under Parthian pressure. After more than a century of 'live and let live', by the early second century AD Rome started to explore again a more aggressive approach beginning with Trajan (r. AD 98–117).

The Judaean experience

Rome's new policy reflected the experience over the previous thirty years of the challenges to Rome's authority emanating from southern Syria, specifically Judaea. Judaea had been a troubled but relatively loyal client of Rome under Augustus, given the close understanding in the first half of Augustus' rule between himself and the Judaean client king Herod the Great. Herod had been an enthusiastic adherent in the Roman new order but ten years after Herod's death Judaea's heartland had been placed under direct rule in the form of a local Roman-appointed *procurator* in AD 6.

The old tensions in Judaea over religious issues in fact had never entirely disappeared. Jewish difficulties with alien rulers who favoured a plethora of gods rather than one were smothered for a time by Herod's spectacularly generous endowment of major projects to appease the Jewish community including a huge new temple complex in Jerusalem. In AD 66, the tensions that had persisted below the surface in Judaean society between secular and religious currents exploded in the event known as the First Jewish War. Rome had been caught napping; now it was faced for the first time in the empire with a 'full scale popular rebellion'.[17] The relatively sparse local forces it had kept in southern Syria[18] were not enough to stifle the uprising which quickly spread. The last of the Herodian rulers still in power supported Rome. This was Agrippa II who since AD 53 had ruled a collection of southern Syrian districts from Chalcis in the Beqa'a Valley as well as carrying the role of high priest of the Jewish temple in Jerusalem. However, it required the deployment of four additional legions, under the command of the Roman general Vespasian, and four hard years of campaigning to bring the situation in this relatively small corner of the Eastern empire under control. With the bloody taking of Jerusalem in AD 71, the Jerusalem temple was destroyed to prevent it serving again as a rallying point for Jewish defiance of Rome. It took another three years for the last resistance in the rest of Judaea to be overcome.

Thirty years later the lesson of these events would not have been lost on Trajan, who had been commander of the X Fretensis Legion in the Judaean campaign: any challenge to Roman authority in the East simply could not be allowed to fester. The preceding decades had been marked by a build-up of Roman units and by the end of the first Jewish rebellion, one quarter of all the empire's forces were stationed in greater Syria. Though some were later redeployed or returned to their normal stations, a considerable militarisation of the region had taken place. At the civilian level, a tightening of the administrative structure had also been implemented. By the early second century, with most of the 'client kings' gone, Edessa remained the last client kingdom after Nabataea was incorporated as the Province of Arabia in AD 106.

Military build up

In northern Syria, the earlier incorporation of Emesa, Commagene and Cappadocia also required a strengthening of Roman legionary resources. This military build up corresponded with a growth in the status of Antioch and with it the region which sustained what had become the third 'capital' of the empire often now serving as a temporary imperial seat. Roads were improved, notably those communicating to the East or across the steppe to the southeast of Aleppo. For the first time, the mid-Euphrates east of Aleppo was endowed with military fortifications.

The logic of Trajan's decision to undertake aggressive campaigning to the East would later be severely discredited by the decision of his successor Hadrian to abandon the terrain taken by his adoptive father. At one level, it can be explained as a policy of deterrence that responded to events in the wider Syria region following the Jewish rebellion. Previously most campaigning towards the East had involved marching via what is now southeastern Turkey and northern Mesopotamia. The absorption of most client kingdoms in the area strengthened Rome's hand along this strategic corridor, though the problematic status of Armenia, nominally allied to Rome but with Parthia in effect nominating its preferred ruler, remained of concern. From the second century, however, the focus would also have to swing southeastwards down the Euphrates valley and into the Syrian steppe. This deflection of the Roman war effort would have required Beroia's increasing involvement in Roman plans.

Trajan's immediate objective had been to attempt the first Roman bridgehead in Mesopotamia. For the first time, too, an emperor was to involve himself directly in the acquisition of territory in the East. Like many such 'bold' decisions by a chief executive, it was badly conceived but perhaps no one dared tell him so. If it was meant to push the frontier further away from settled Roman-controlled territory and thus provide Syria and eastern Asia Minor with a greater buffer, it failed badly. Once again, it was the inability to read what was happening in the Armenian kingdom that distorted Rome's assessment of its options. Armenia's Parthian-nominated king had taken office without waiting for Rome's endorsement (as required by the Roman-Parthian treaty), a display of independence which alarmed the Roman leadership. Trajan's initial move was to annex Armenia in AD 113 by armed intervention. In 115, he moved into Mesopotamia and proclaimed it a Roman province but quickly found he could not sustain a Roman presence there and withdrew, a situation formalised under his successor Hadrian.[19]

For the cities of the northern Syria region, one outcome of this series of eastern campaigns was the exposure they now enjoyed on the circuit of the imperial court. Emperors who had gone no further than Greece, Gaul, Britain or Germany in the past, usually as military commanders before higher office, now visited with the full panoply of imperial authority. The cities quickly appreciated that the way to catch the emperor's eye was to present a splendid cityscape preferably with a striking central axis adorned with colonnades and beautiful religious or civic buildings in the imperial style. Trajan spent three years in the eastern provinces, admittedly on military duties in remote places, but he also spent considerable periods in Antioch. His nephew and successor Hadrian was in his entourage in Antioch in AD 115 when they experienced a catastrophic earthquake that affected the whole region as far as Apamea (and thus necessarily Aleppo). We know from later literary accounts that in both Antioch and Apamea they gave considerable support to the cities to restore public buildings and colonnades, though there is no specific mention of Beroia.

A new Persian threat

The next (third) century was marked by new tensions with the Persians to the east. The Achaemenid Persians, although hostile to Rome as the successor to its traditional enemy the Greeks, had not allowed this hostility to prevent them from emulating many aspects of Classical art and architecture. In 224, they were overthrown by a new dynasty based in the south, the Sasanians, more aggressively intent on reviving the achievements of Persian civilisation. Though his campaign up the long Euphrates Valley should have given plentiful notice of his intentions, the new Sasanian monarch, Shapur I, arrived without warning at the upper defences of Antioch in 252 while the complacent townspeople were attending the theatre on the lower slopes.

Shapur's forces then fanned out to take control of much Roman territory west into Asia Minor. Aleppo/Beroia was on a long list of other cities claimed in Shapur's inscription at Naqsh-e Rustam near Persepolis. The city's sense of security that had marked early Roman Syria was shaken to the core. Though the invaders were driven out by 257, further blows to the Roman foothold in Syria followed. Dura Europos on the Euphrates had fallen in 256 to the Sasanians and was abandoned as a Roman defensive post that had protected the trade route to the Persian Gulf.

On this occasion, the Sasanians do not appear to have sought more permanent control of territory. In a later phase of the invasion, Rome suffered the catastrophic blow in 260 of seeing their emperor, Valerian, taken prisoner and marched off into humiliating captivity in Persia. It was forces raised by the Palmyrene ruler, Odenathus, who rallied the residual Roman units and chased the Sasanians from Syria. A little over a decade later, under Odenathus' widow (Zenobia), Palmyra itself challenged Rome's supremacy when she attempted to wrest from Roman control a large swathe of territory from Egypt to Asia Minor. A Roman army had to be deployed to put down her rebellion and to see her taken off to Rome in chains. These turbulent decades were symptomatic of a crisis of authority throughout the empire in which strife among the contenders for leadership in Rome was matched by ferment on the margins of empire where new external forces sought to test Rome's ability to hold territory stretching from Spain to Syria.

From pagan to Christian – the Byzantine Transition

It is always difficult to find a logical point at which to divide the Roman from the Byzantine periods in what continued to be known as the Roman Empire. For our

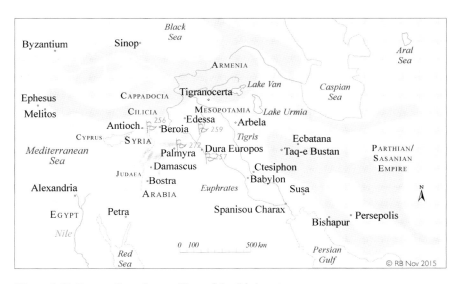

Figure 2.15 Roman-Sasanian conflicts of the third century

47

Figure 2.16 Portrait head of Emperor Julian (Athens National Museum, courtesy Jona
Lendering (Livius.org))

purposes, I arbitrarily nominate the visit of Emperor Julian to Antioch and Aleppo
in 362. Though this came a few decades after Constantine's decision to move the
empire's capital to Byzantium (renamed Constantinople) in 330, it does mark the
last attempt to arrest the swelling support for Christianity. Constantine (r.305–37)
had endorsed Christianity as the imperial faith early in his reign. This was confirmed under his son Constantius II (r.337–61) but the subsequent accession of
Julian (r.361–3), a fervent and militant pagan, initiated a brief interlude in which
the new emperor sought to restore the traditional cults. While the interlude lasted
less than two years, Julian's reign was marked by a campaign against the Sasanian
ruler, Shapur II, whose long rule (r.309–79) had brought a sustained attempt once
again to extend Persian control as far as the Mediterranean.

Julian's decision to embark on a new Persian campaign was taken after
spending nine months in Antioch in 362–3 where he tried unsuccessfully
to turn back the city elders' growing attachment to Christianity by seeking
to promulgate enthusiasm for an ascetic form of Hellenism. His attachment

to this austere reading of paganism encountered a reception that veered between ridicule and indifference. Having decided to press on with his eastern campaign, he departed for Aleppo in March 363 leading his campaign force of 80,000–90,000 troops.[20]

Failed mission

We have not had a chance to examine what might have happened to the site of the Weather God temple on the Aleppo Citadel hill in the Classical centuries. The recent German excavations on the temple site found 2 metres of post-Iron Age debris above the 'neo-Hittite' layers but no sign of later in situ structures. This probably reflects subsequent disturbance of the site over the following centuries, though one of the excavators has noted that there appeared to be evidence of a Roman-era structure of considerable size to the northeast of the Weather God footprint.[21] This would locate part of the structure under the outdoor theatre erected in the 1970s and forming a concrete sarcophagus preventing further exploration. It would appear that the temple on the Aleppo Citadel remained in service or accessible throughout the Classical centuries, for Julian sought to mark the continued validity of the old cults by ascending to the shrine and offering a white bull as a sacrifice to Zeus.

Julian wrote a brief account of the Aleppo experience from his next stop, Hierapolis (Menbij). It is worth quoting, both as one of the few accounts we have of Aleppo in the Classical period and as an indication of the struggle Julian's difficult, remote and exacting personality had in seeking to reverse the trend towards Christianity:

I proceeded to Beroia and there Zeus, by showing a manifest sign from heaven, declared all things to be auspicious. I stayed there for a day and saw the Acropolis and sacrificed to Zeus in imperial fashion a white bull. Also I conversed briefly with the senate about the worship of the gods. But though they all applauded my arguments very few were converted by them, and these few were men who even before I spoke seemed to me to hold sound views. But they were cautious and would not strip off and lay aside their modest reserve, as though afraid of too frank speech. For it is the prevailing habit of mankind, O ye gods, to blush for their noble qualities, manliness of soul and piety, and to plume themselves, as it were, on what is most depraved, sacrilege and weakness of mind and body.[22]

It is tempting to wring too much out of this brief reference to classical Aleppo in a single written source but I will venture a few insights that may be worth noting.

First, Julian clearly chose to visit the Aleppo Citadel temple as representing a site continuously devoted to the worship of Zeus on a 'high place'. It

Figure 2.17 Mount Casius seen from the west

is worth remembering that he had just come from Antioch. During his visit to that region, he had ascended the most elevated and celebrated of the high places, Mount Casius (today on the Syrian-Turkish border). This symbolic gesture seeking Zeus' blessing for his Persian campaign had significant precedents. The founder of the Seleucid dynasty and emperors Trajan and Hadrian had all ascended to the windswept and featureless summit to add their sacrifice to the pile of desiccated bones that provided about the only commemorative mark on its 1740-metre-high bare profile. Hadrian's gesture, also seeking Zeus' intervention in his campaign against the Persians, had been particularly momentous. As he prepared to offer his sacrifice on the summit, according to the *Augustan*

History, lightning struck as if to underline that the Storm God had not lost his powers of intervention.[23]

Second, the fact that Julian travelled via Beroia to seek out its Zeus temple and to try to convince the city fathers to restore the traditional cults indicated that the rise of Christianity had already made considerable inroads in the city and that the ancient temple, though still preserving the old rites, was in need of a symbolic boost. Julian's lengthy visit to Antioch had inspired a new phase of animosity between Christians and pagans in a city where paganism was still avidly promoted by the emperor's friend, Libanius. Julian, however, had failed in his mission to reverse the increasing ascendancy of Christianity in the eastern capital. The emperor's austere interpretation of Hellenism had put off the more sybaritic pagans among the city fathers of Antioch whose lax observance of the rites of the old temples inspired their indifference to Julian's mission.

While Beroia might not have been the most prosperous or strategically important city in the region, it retained a considerable status for its religious role and as a base for the continuing tradition of Hellenism. We have no physical record of Aleppo's Zeus temple in the version that Julian visited. It clearly remained one of the religious high-points of the area, though probably long overshadowed by the more salacious reputation of Hierapolis. After Beroia, Julian went on to honour the Hierapolis temple before crossing the Euphrates and heading east from Carrhae. While his eastern campaign nominally succeeded in defeating the Sasanian army outside Ctesiphon, Julian's forces though sizeable lacked the capacity to control such a huge expanse of land. Their retreat

Figure 2.18 Julian's corpse crushed by Shapur II's foot on a relief at Taq-e Bustan in Iran (Philippe Chavin, Wikimedia Commons)

towards Roman-controlled territory became the opportunity the Sasanians had hoped for to pick off his forces as he sought refuge via the northern route. He was killed when his column was intercepted by a Sasanian detachment north of Sumere (Samarra) in Mesopotamia. His humiliating demise is depicted in a low-relief insertion on the triumphant rock relief of Shapur II at Taq-e Bustan in Iran (see Figure 2.18).

Julian's visit to Beroia was a final and apparently feckless attempt to rally the residual forces of paganism. The long supremacy of Hellenism in the city, effectively dating from 300 BC, was already over. There had always been at Aleppo, as at other major cities of the region, an undercurrent of a Semitic-based culture that had not died out. While many among the city's prosperous classes had aspired to Greek culture as a means of gaining the favour of the rulers, underneath an Aramaised culture survived, though it would be another three hundred years before the old Semitic name, Halab, resurfaced. The Romans had sanctioned a blend of local and Classical religious traditions, witnessed in the merger of Zeus' primacy with the cult of the Weather God. Classical myths and art still graced material culture but such traditions, while surviving as decorative themes or secularised myths, no longer enjoyed a religious dimension.

Now, after Julian, there would be but one God.

Notes

1 *EI2* 'Halab'; Rabbath 1935b: 21.
2 Cohen (2006: 154 and note 2) lists the sources. Grainger (1990: 52) is sceptical.
3 Josephus 1927: 3.29.
4 Appian 11 57, Strabo XVI 2 7, Stephen of Byzantium, Pliny V XIX.
5 Sauvaget's seminal works on this subject are Sauvaget 1935 and 1941.
6 Neglia (2009: 88) gives these dimensions. Sauvaget (1941) has 124 by 48 metres.
7 This brief list omits the constellation of cults at Antioch, all of whose temples are lost to us.
8 Appian 1912: ch. 49, n.p.
9 Initially *phylarchs* in the Seleucid system, the dynasty was installed by Rome in the central Orontes Valley with its first capital at Arethusa (Rastan), later Emesa (Homs). It was quietly absorbed into the Roman province of Syria in the second century AD.
10 Neglia 2009: 120–2, esp. fig. 57.
11 Neglia's study based on cadastral records also speculates on a third extension of the Roman grid related to the terrain surrounding the city. As the city expanded over the centuries, this broader grid is seen as influencing the alignment of streets and buildings on a bearing rotated 18 degrees clockwise from the previous celestially oriented grids.
12 Sauvaget's figure (1941: 42). Neglia estimates 22.18 metres between the shop frontages or 13 metres between the columns. For comparison, the magnificent central axis of Apamea was even larger – 37.5 metres maximum in total width, of which the roadway itself was up to 21 metres.
13 In this plan, Neglia's assumptions on the original Roman street pattern (reflecting Sauvaget's idea) is overlaid on the modern city plan prepared by Gaube and Wirth (1984). See also Neglia (2009: fig. 53). A schema tracing the process of transformation into medieval times is given in Figure 4.07 (page 81).
14 Sauvaget 1941: 33–68.

15 Neglia 2009: 124–5, fig. 58 and note 17. The Roman theatre in Damascus, funded by Herod the Great, was also less than 100 metres wide and was also first detected in the layout of the street pattern.

16 Butcher 2013: 18, 32 (catalogue C131); 2004: 157–63, 439. Samples of coins that come from the Dura Europos and Antioch excavations as well as a private collection of 1404 coins purchased on the Aleppo market are surveyed in Seyrig 1958. While these samples are too small to be authoritative, the evidence certainly suggests that the main trade flows via Aleppo were to Zeugma and Edessa rather than down the Euphrates. Butcher (2004), for example, records only one (Trajanic) Beroia coin found in recent excavations at Zeugma. For the Trajanic type, see Figure 2.14. It is also relevant that both Trajan and Hadrian were active in Eastern campaigns, a factor which would have increased the level of Roman military activity in northern Syria.

17 Millar 1993: 69.

18 Millar (1993: 68) notes that Rome had no legion specifically stationed in Judaea on a permanent basis before the war. Forces loyal to Rome were confined to auxiliary units under the procurator stationed in Caesarea (Millar 1993: 69).

19 Millar (1993: 100–2) notes that Trajan's concept of 'Mesopotamia' was probably a geographically minimalist one, confined to northeastern Syria from Mardin in modern Turkey to Singara on the western edge of Iraq, rather than the larger extent of central and northern Iraq.

20 For a vivid account of Julian's stay in Antioch, see Bowersock (1978: 94–108).

21 Gonnella et al. 2005: 16.

22 Julian the Apostate (Works vol III, #58, W. C. Wright trans. 1923).

23 Anon. *Lives of the Later Caesars (the Augustan History)*. London. 1976: 72.

3

IN ANTIOCH'S ORBIT –
BYZANTINE ALEPPO IN A
WORLD OF CHURCHES AND
MONASTERIES (353–637)

Byzantine period AD 353–637

If the reader imagines that the adoption of a single faith under imperial patronage would now simplify things, nothing could be further from the truth. Constantine's shift of the political capital of the empire to Byzantium/Constantinople transferred imperial affairs to an environment which would be riven by new tensions between the traditional cultures of the East and the strictly defined orthodoxies sanctioned by the new Rome.

Bidding for God

Like most other Eastern centres, Beroia had lived comfortably enough under the vaguely 'Hellenised' culture sponsored by Rome which had been tolerant of gods other than the Greek and Roman pantheon. Christianity, however, was an Eastern faith and had only one God, intolerant of competitors. The early mission-ary Paul had come to Antioch in the forties of the new era to spread the message of Christ as it had emerged from a Jewish environment in Jerusalem. He recognised, however, that the new faith could only acquire a 'universal' appeal if it were intelligible also to gentiles. His travels in Asia Minor and Greece pursued that theme further and by the end of the first century, Christianity had begun to make inroads into numerous communities around the Mediterranean. As the movement acquired an ecclesiastical structure, not all the tensions between the traditions of the East and the Hellenised societies of the West were set aside. This would result in religious divisions that will take on worrying proportions in our later narrative but for the moment we should turn to the pattern through which Christianity was spread in the region of northern Syria from the fourth century onwards when the first evidence of the Christian presence emerges.

We noted earlier (page 43) the role of pilgrimage centres in the Roman period not only as religious gathering points but also as a means of reinforcing the mes-sage of Roman prosperity under the 'new order'. Huge complexes had grown up at centres including Baalbek, Damascus, Jerash or Palmyra to accommodate the crowds assembling on festival days. The role of such centres was not lost on the early leaders of the church. As the old gods were stood down, in some cases corresponding Christian pilgrimage centres sprang up, sometimes on nearby sites. Once the legalisation of Christianity had made possible the building of churches as conspicuous structures, they were built not only to cater to the local Christian communities but also to provide larger complexes which had the dual purpose of honouring a figure of considerable ascetic prowess or a martyr who had resisted Rome's sporadic persecution of Christians as well as serving as processing centres for conversion and baptism.

As we have seen in the last chapter, the competitive environment that prevailed between pagans and Christians in Antioch and Aleppo was further provoked by Julian's visit in 362–3. Within fifty years of Constantine's endorsement of the new faith, Christianity had already made considerable inroads. Antioch, as one of the first objectives for Jesus' followers and a major metropolis, was a particular hotbed of competition. So it should not be surprising if the battle for souls was also particularly fierce in the hinterland of the great city.

Between Aleppo and Antioch lies the belt of high limestone formations known popularly since last century as the 'Dead Cities', a label inspired by the hundreds of deserted stone villages whose remains dot the countryside and which in the nineteenth century were inhabited only sparsely. Today repopulated (and more often cited by the more matter-of-fact title, the Limestone Massif), this elevated zone stretches for over 140 kilometres divided into several hilly zones (Figure 3.1). In the early Roman period, this region had been neglected, probably long regarded as inhospitable due to its prominent rock outcrops that allowed fertile soil to collect only in pockets and made communications difficult. As Antioch grew, however, the city's inhabitants required new sources of food, particularly olive oil so essential to a 'Mediterranean diet'. The Limestone Massif could cope with small olive plantations between the swathes of rock and could access the main road that crossed the Massif by the pass between Antioch and Aleppo. From the second century AD the wealthier farmers of the area were building stylish houses using the readily available stone and by the fourth century agriculture based around the pockets of arable soil had become noticeably more intense.

More than any other region of the empire, this zone of once-'dead cities' gives us a relatively unspoilt picture of life on the fringe of a major urban centre. When the oil-based industry of the region collapsed by the tenth century, reflecting the decline of Antioch, the deserted structures avoided being cannibalised by later settlers.

A world of churches

What is most striking in our picture of the Aleppo hinterland in its most prosperous phase, from the fourth to the seventh centuries, is the intensity of the religious dimension to community life. Virtually none of hundreds of communities lacked a church. In some villages, up to four or five are found. In no other period of the history of the region was such an investment put into religion. In addition, many villages included monastic complexes usually on the fringe of the inhabited area and often with facilities for visitors, indicating that pilgrims were coming from afar. In the opening century of this new presence, the emphasis was on conversion to the new faith. This conversion process seems to have taken at least a century and often required a deliberate emphasis on spectacular feats of self-privation to advertise the heroic status of the saints who drew crowds from distant, often still pagan, communities to the major monasteries.

The monastic tradition had spread in the fourth century from Egypt, where it began as a quest to be as close to God and as far from distractions as possible. In the case of northern Syria, however, the emphasis is rather on giving witness to the community. Monastic centres were to be visited, their locations often chosen for their proximity to routes and to former cult centres that had handled the masses of the past. Most importantly, they had facilities for processing large-scale baptisms. Those visitors who arrived through curiosity would have found themselves swept up by the religious fervour of the crowd. Claims of miracles or interventions by saintly figures renowned for their ability to withstand prodigious privations reinforced the message. When the church began by the 380s to persuade the authorities to adopt measures discouraging and then banning pagan practices, the push to conversion became all but unavoidable.

Beroia lay on the fringe of this zone of mass conversion. Though we have little evidence of any surviving Byzantine religious structures in Beroia at this time (there is one significant exception, discussed on page 60–64), there is no reason to believe that the city avoided this headlong abandonment of paganism that Julian had so fruitlessly tried to arrest. A few of Aleppo's mosques were later built on the remains of, or recycled *spolia* from, Byzantine churches, so we know the location of some of the churches from the evidence of later centuries.

Church of St Simeon

However, it is largely the ecclesiastical buildings of the surrounding countryside to which we must turn for a picture of Byzantine life in the region. The most magnificent of the great pilgrimage churches was that of St Simeon the Stylite. 'Stylite' refers to Simeon's habit of living on top of a column or pillar, safely isolated from the distractions of everyday life but visible to the crowds of visitors. To trace the significance of the pilgrimage complex built in Simeon's honour after his lifetime, however, we need to go back to Roman times. Among the 'high places' mentioned earlier in Chapters 1 and 2 was the mountaintop noted as Jebel Sheikh Barakat.

Though not as high as Mt Casius on the coast near Antioch, this prominent peak towers over the Beroia/Antioch highway in one of the breaks between hilly outcrops of the Limestone Massif. While the origins of cult practices on the summit of Jebel Sheikh Barakat probably went back well into the Iron Age, the first formal structure on the peak was a small temple to Zeus Madbachos and Selamenes dating from the late first century.[1]

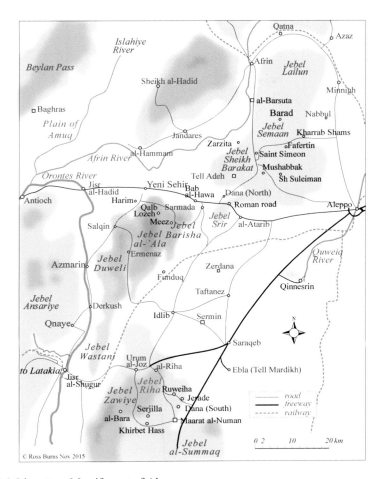

Figure 3.1 Limestone Massif, west of Aleppo

A little way to the north of the mountain stands the Church of St Simeon with a nearby pilgrimage and monastic dormitory settlement known as Deir Semaan. While the origins of the monastery precede the church, clearly the decision to link this monastic complex to a new cult centre on a magnificent scale was no accident. Whereas most monastic or church projects were local initiatives using local funds, this complex was different. The Byzantine authorities directed the operation to perpetuate the saint's memory, beginning with the seizure of the body after his death atop the column in 459, its removal to Antioch and finally to Constantinople. Emperor Xeno (r.474–91) fifteen years later found funds to commemorate the saint's career by erecting four basilicas radiating from a central courtyard enclosing the column. Only the eastern basilica served as a church, the

Figure 3.2 Jebel Sheikh Barakat seen from the south

other three formed massive crowd-control spaces to handle the press of visitors. Perhaps even more significant was the building of a baptistery south of the church at a point where visitors, on ascending the ridge, could be channelled via a chamber which housed at its centre a baptismal font sunk in the floor with steps on two sides to process the stream of converts.

The Church of St Simeon was basically a facility to process converts en masse, possibly concentrating on those visiting from the steppe to the east where paganism still held some sway even in the fifth century. However, there was another factor to explain the sudden decision of the Byzantine ruler to involve himself in the commemorative complex – the need to divert the faithful away from heretical readings of the Christian message and to bombard them with the Constantinopolitan or Orthodox version. The issue was basically not deeply doctrinal but concerned nuances in the interpretation of the relationship between Christ's nature as both man and God. The dual aspects of Christ were accepted by both sides but the Eastern church officially adopted the ruling of the Church Council held at Chalcedon in 451 which argued that Christ's two natures were inseparably united in the son of God become man ('in two natures without confusion') while the Eastern churches (today's Coptic, Syrian and Armenian Orthodox communities) believed in a single nature after incarnation, at once both human and divine.

Today it is hard to believe that this level of nuance could fuel fierce popular controversy. It is also not clear whether the good Simeon himself advertised his affiliations either way. More likely, the whole debate that raged in the Eastern

Figure 3.3 Church of St Simeon, south narthex and entrance

cities was driven more by a subterranean level of tension that had not been resolved within communities. This agenda involved not only Christian beliefs but went back to deeper issues of identities inherited from the past. In Byzantine times (as indeed today) people sought explanations for their origins which ignored most of the complexities of thousands of years of invasions, ethnic blending, inter-marriage, educational indoctrination, language modulation, enforced population movement and conversion. Whereas the Hellenised elites of Antioch or Aleppo might feel an attachment to a metropolitan interpretation of Christianity, many of their counterparts in Syria preferred to listen to those bishops whose faith found its centre of gravity further east even if the distinction claimed at the theological level is essentially meaningless to us today.

These anti-Chalcedonian forces (today's Eastern Orthodox churches) were once described as 'Monophysite' (a term that has fallen out of favour). Their approach to the debate over the nature of Christ partly reflected the experience of the churches in the Eastern regions in an era when paganism (for which read polytheism under a 'Hellenised' guise) was receding. This version of Christianity represented a faith that had deeper roots not in the Hellenised world around the Mediterranean but in the recesses of the interior. Here Aramaic, other Semitic tongues including proto-Arabic and the influence of the major civilisations of the East, notably Sasanian, survived to varying degrees. This was relayed back into Byzantium as a debate over the nature of orthodoxy which made about as much sense as does unreasoned commitment these days to football teams.

Whatever the merits of the rhetoric, it reflected the environment in the wider region in which Beroia existed. By the end of the fourth century, there were few pagans left, though pockets survived into the next century. The temples had been closed to sacrifice, then closed altogether and in some cases dismantled. Now towns, villages and even remote caves in the steppe were studded with churches, chapels, monasteries and aesthetes' towers. Some were built, as we have seen at the Church of St Simeon, to profit from the old pilgrimage centres but they were spread much more thickly around the region than the relatively limited number of temples had been.

The favoured form for the churches had moved beyond the house-churches which had marked the two centuries or so in which Christian group worship was banned. Nor did it choose to evoke the form of temples. Instead the legalised church quickly favoured the basilica, in its origins an often mundane hall-like building used by the Romans for general administrative purposes. Basilicas were given a semicircular apse at one end (often a feature that had its origins in a frame for the local magistrate presiding over his court) now invariably positioned towards the rising sun. As church architecture became bolder in the fourth century, more flamboyant decorative styles were tried out. In some cases, particularly where the church was built to mark an important commemorative purpose, a centralised form was preferred usually with either round, square or octagonal outer walls. Baptisteries were included at times either within or outside the church structure and sometimes a *martyrion* to house the remains of an honoured bishop or saint.

Hundreds of such churches can be found in the Limestone Massif outside Aleppo, perhaps the greatest concentration of Byzantine remains found anywhere. The decoration of the churches borrowed heavily from the Classical repertoire but with many new flourishes. The Limestone Massif remains an inexhaustible repository of architectural styles, partly generic to the Byzantine world at the time but also showing a lively degree of local inventiveness. The use of decorative bands linking doors, window frames and the outside of *chevets* (the external wall of the eastern apse) are especially remarkable.

Cathedral of St Helena

While Constantine's personal faith may be difficult to appreciate (he was not baptised until shortly before his death), his mother, the formidable Helena, took upon herself a major project to implant respect for the new religion. In 327, she travelled to the East and sought out places that could be identified with the life of Christ. Her celebration of such sites as the place of Christ's crucifixion and burial in Jerusalem launched the Christian travel industry on an epic scale; one that continues to this day.

Though Aleppo/Beroia had no direct association with Helena as far as we know, she was commemorated in the city with a splendid new cathedral, possibly as early as the fifth century. The first version of this structure may have been destroyed

Figure 3.4 Church at Qalb Lozeh in the Limestone Massif near Aleppo with decorated
door frame and 'Syrian arch' above

in the Persian invasion in 540, described later (page 66). Shortly afterwards, the
cathedral was rebuilt in a style reflecting the confidence and flamboyance of the
architecture of the time. By an extraordinary fluke of history, this version of the
Cathedral of St Helena partly survives in that part of central Aleppo where we
located earlier the city's original agora and possibly a major temple structure.

The remains of the cathedral are preserved in a medieval madrasa or Islamic
religious school, the Madrasa Halawiye, located on the western side of today's
Great Mosque (Figure 2.6, on page 35). Entry is from the lane running alongside
the mosque from where a narrow passage leads into a sunken courtyard and pool
in the Ayyubid style. On entering the prayer hall, the *madrasa* presents a cluster of classical-style columns with capitals in the Corinthian order arranged in a

Figure 3.5 Remains of the Cathedral of St Helena in the Madrasa Halawiye

semicircle against the western wall. Against the eastern and southern walls of the prayer hall are more columns. The layout is awkward for the purposes of Islamic prayer as the *mihrab* indicating Mecca lies in the southern alcove to the left of the semicircular row of columns which thus provide a redundant focal point.

The madrasa and its Byzantine remains have sparked a debate over the origins of the building going back to the period immediately before the First World War. If this were part of a Christian basilica church, the design was clearly wrong. No Christian buildings were known with an apse at the western end. The first solution was proposed in 1914 by Samuel Guyer, who suggested the church had two apses with a deeper eastern one framing the altar. Guyer's plan (Figure 3.6) shows the surviving structure in hatched shading, superimposed on his imagined plan of the cathedral assumed to have been a basilica (shown as unfilled black lines) with three domes over the nave and an elongated apse extending its eastern end. Guyer's proposed trio of domes over a nave and an apse at both ends were simply without precedent in the Byzantine architectural canon, which followed a fairly standardised range of plans.

The French architect-historian, Michel Ecochard, provided a better informed solution in 1950. Further research had emerged on centralised Byzantine church plans in the Syria/Palestine area. Ecochard noted a remarkable fit in an example from Bosra in southern Syria of a centralised church with four apses facing a central domed space – the Church of Saints Sergius, Bacchus and Leontius, dated 512–13. The plan of the Bosra centralised church's central piers and western

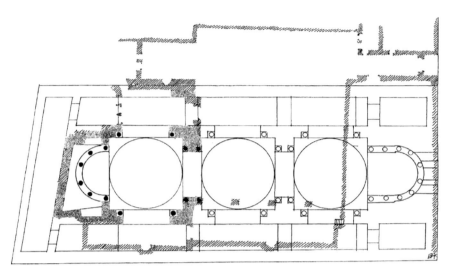

Figure 3.6 Guyer's reconstruction of the Byzantine Cathedral of St Helena (1914: pl. IV)

semicircular colonnade virtually overlapped with their counterparts at Aleppo (Figure 3.7). If the plan of the Aleppo remains is superimposed on the Bosra equivalent (prepared by the British expert, Crowfoot), the fit is uncannily precise.

The remains of Aleppo's Cathedral of St Helena also gives us an important clue to the development of the area around the forum of the Roman city which later written accounts described as lying under the present-day Great Mosque. It seems probable that the church was not placed directly on one of the blocks reserved for the forum but immediately to the west. The forum itself (which may once have housed a Roman shrine) was referred to as a garden area in later Arab accounts of this zone, indicating that the pagan shrine had disappeared under the Byzantines and a garden occupied the open space.

We will look later (Chapter 6) at the circumstances that led to the seizure of the remains of the Helena church and its conversion to a madrasa in the twelfth century. For the moment, though, we have in the Madrasa Halawiye a snapshot of a monumental Byzantine religious structure of the sixth century. One point to note is that the style of the capitals has considerably evolved from the strictly Classical form of previous centuries. The design of Corinthian capitals is based essentially on bunched acanthus leaves shaping the transition from the round form of the column to the square impost supporting an entablature. The Byzantine artists by the sixth century had begun to play with these architectural shapes, often introducing basket forms to mask the transition from round to square. In this north Syrian example, however, a local adaptation had crept in. (It was already found at the Church of St Simeon constructed a century earlier.) The acanthus leaves

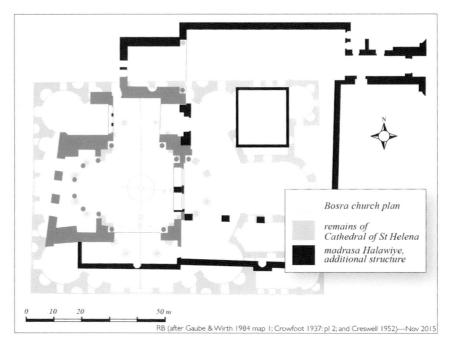

Figure 3.7 Remains of the Cathedral of St Helena in the Madrasa Halawiye
(superimposed on plan of a church in Bosra by Crowfoot 1937: pl. 2)

sweep around in a twisted pattern as if moved by a powerful wind. (We will see later how local fascination with this device continued as late as the Arab Middle Ages when it became a favoured decorative detail on mosques.)

The Bandara Synagogue

There is one more building which carries memories of Byzantine Beroia; another remarkable survival story. In the 1970s, Aleppo was involved in an exercise in 'urban renewal' designed partly to improve traffic flows and to make some of the older quarters more accessible. Over-enthusiasm, however, brought plans to bulldoze significant areas of the old northern quarters within the medieval walls including an area known as al-Bandara, already partly dilapidated due to riots in the Jewish Quarter in 1947 protesting the planned establishment of the Israeli state (see page 277). After prolonged resistance and protests, most of the urban renewal project was abandoned in the 1980s. One building spared was the building that had long served as the Great Synagogue of the Jewish community.

The Bandara Synagogue, though often later reported to have been 'destroyed', in fact survived the 1948 riots in a gradually deteriorating state. Some restoration was done in the 1990s with the support of the World Monuments Fund. It is a

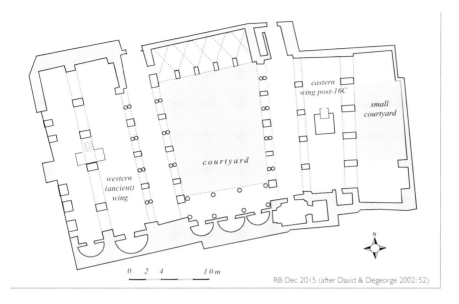

Figure 3.8 Bandara Synagogue (after David and Degeorge 2002: 52)

building of singular interest but has not been the subject of a detailed technical study to determine the origins of the complex of spaces, including two prayer halls and two courtyards. Clearly, however, it preserves remains of numerous eras in the city's history though it is difficult to say how much has been recycled from previous structures on this spot and how much gathered from the environs. Sauvaget believed that parts of the masonry of the north and west walls dated to the Byzantine period but the elements recycled in the internal structure include capitals and columns ranging from the Byzantine period to the Arab Middle Ages. Along the south wall are five alcoves that once housed the Torah scrolls and a small chamber leading down to a subterranean space described as 'the cave of Elijah'. While it would be misleading to attribute the entire building to the Byzantine period, it does appear to represent a medieval reconstruction of earlier (Byzantine) remains possibly mainly derived on site including in situ wall sections.[2]

Fortress City

We noted in the last chapter indications that the military role of the Aleppo region became increasingly important after the second century AD. Efforts to counter the Persian threat by military operations across the Euphrates necessarily engaged a greater role for Beroia as a secure base inland from Antioch. Though there is no physical evidence in the present circuit of walls around the Citadel of any Byzantine phase of construction, written references to Beroia at the time (examined below) underline that the Citadel offered a secure refuge for the inhabitants of the city in times of siege. We know from these written sources that Beroia also possessed city walls around the civilian-occupied town but that they were not in good condition. Although the city's western town walls were necessarily determined by the river and probably correspond with the alignment of today's western walls, it seems likely that in other directions the city was only now beginning to extend beyond the original grid area of the Hellenistic/Roman periods. Immediately north of the central grid, the quarters of Bahsita and of Bandara have names of Syriac origins probably indicating they were conferred before the Islamic conquest (637), an assumption consistent with the possible date of the first structure of the Bandara Synagogue.

Underneath the present Citadel, just inside the inner gate entrance structure, lies a series of underground spaces which may also have Byzantine origins. These have served many purposes in the past including as cisterns for water storage and as formidable prison spaces. The style of construction, however, indicates Byzantine origins given the mixture of stone pillars supporting arches constructed in flat fired bricks. Such spaces in Byzantine times were used for the collection of water against periods of conflict or drought.[3]

The Eastern threat

Beroia, lying on the path leading to Antioch, was threatened several more times by Sasanian incursions. As related in the last chapter, though the campaign along the

Figure 3.9 Byzantine cisterns under the Aleppo Citadel

Figure 3.10 Antioch from the upper fortification walls on Mount Silpius, the vantage point seized by Shapur I in 252

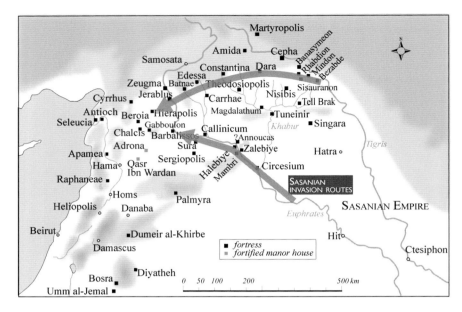

Figure 3.11 Byzantine fortifications in northern Syria under Justinian

Euphrates by the Sasanian ruler Shapur I should have given plentiful warning of his intentions, in 252 he had arrived at the upper defences of Antioch while the complacent townspeople were attending the theatre on the lower slopes (see Figure 3.10).

Almost three hundred years later during the reign of Justinian (r.527–65), another Sasanian king, Chosroes I, besieged Aleppo in 540 as part of a long campaign, entering Syria along the Euphrates Valley and departing via the foothills skirting Mesopotamia to the northeast. Most cities along his path surrendered after only a nominal resistance (usually agreeing to provide hostages or a ransom). Only at Beroia and Antioch was a full siege required. Chosroes' siege of Aleppo had to be pressed for some weeks.

We have a detailed account of the sequence of events in the work of the Byzantine court historian Procopius on the Persian wars of the 540s.[4] The citizens of Beroia had initially decided that the price they had to pay to be spared Chosroes' siege and likely reprisals was too high and planned to withstand the Persian assault. In Procopius' account, however, Aleppo's inhabitants changed their mind and lost confidence in their dilapidated city walls. While acknowledging that they might have no option but to meet Chosroes' demands, they first tried to buy more time by paying half the ransom demanded (two thousand pounds of silver) and joined the Byzantine military in carrying on resistance from within the upper (Citadel) walls.

Chosroes, however, had made his own calculations and realised the defenders were ill prepared. The Citadel enjoyed only one water source and the Aleppines

Figure 3.12 A coin of Chosroes I (Classical Numismatic Group, via Wikipedia)

had unwisely brought their animals and horses into the fortress, obliging all to share drinking water with consequent risks to hygiene. Assessing Beroia's capacity to hold out as limited, Chosroes pressed the siege when the citizens refused to pay the rest of the ransom. He easily took the lower city. Furious at the townspeople's treachery in reneging on the ransom agreement and irritated at the momentum he had lost in reaching his main objective at Antioch, Chosroes set fire to Aleppo's lower town and razed its remains. While the Citadel for a time held out, according to Procopius, the determination of the Byzantines rapidly collapsed, beginning with the army: 'The majority (of the soldiers) came as willing deserters to Chosroes, putting forth as their grievance that the government owed them their pay for a long time; and with him they later went into the land of Persia.'[5] Accordingly, Bishop Megas had little option but to agree to hand over the second ransom (ten *centenaria* of gold) as payment for the Sasanians' lifting the siege and sparing the citizens.

Chosroes moved on to Antioch and quickly camped against its walls on the Orontes side. This time, he was in no mood to entertain more trickery on the part of the Antiocheans, assessed even by Procopius as 'not seriously disposed but . . . always engaged in jesting and disorderly performance'.[6] Chosroes did not hesitate to press the attack and Antioch quickly fell. Again, as at Beroia, it was the townspeople, not the military, who put up the stiff resistance, setting aside their reputation for frivolity. After a short but fierce struggle, the city again was put to the flames, in response to what Chosroes judged to be Byzantine treachery in breaking the peace Justinian had signed.

The 540 campaign by the Sasanians was only the start of a pattern of repeated incursions, to a large extent motivated by booty and profits from ransom as much as by the ancient Persian ambitions of extending their empire to the Mediterranean. The Sasanian king returned on annual excursions, sometimes concentrating on parts of the eastern frontier's necklace of forts, sometimes aiming directly at the Byzantine eastern capital. If we look at this pattern of Byzantine fortifications east of Antioch (Figure 3.11), we can see that Beroia stood now at the apex of a formidable range of walled cities or fortresses stretching along two axes (the Anatolian foothills to the north and the valley of the Euphrates) which came together just east of Antioch. Defences were also built up to the southeast of Beroia to prevent access via the Syrian steppe. One of the oldest was at Qinnisrin (ancient Chalcis), a Greek foundation that became an important way-point on the Roman road network. Later, other defences included a system of manor houses or settlements on the estate of a landed proprietor who raised militia units from his tenant farmers. (A superb example can still be seen today at Qasr Ibn Wardan east of Hama.) However, whereas the late third-/early fourth-century line of Roman forts across the steppe and its western edge had focused on blocking direct entry from Mesopotamia, the more dispersed Byzantine defences largely ignored possible invasion routes crossing the steppe. Perhaps it was assumed that the Byzantine's semi-nomadic allies, the Arab tribes federated under the Ghassanids, would look after the interior. The disastrous consequences of this assumption will be seen later.

Sasanian occupation (AD 611–28)

The pattern of Persian/Byzantine wars of the sixth century reached a climax in the seventh. The most disastrous of the invasions was in 611 when Chosroes II (r.590–628) occupied Syria in a sustained campaign. This time, the Sasanian Persians stayed on, preferring not to return home with their booty after the annual campaigning season. The Persian occupation lasted for almost two decades and had brutal results. Many towns were razed again. It should be no surprise that we have few standing remains of the Byzantine centuries from any of the main urban centres of northern Syria.[7] Even a major centre such as Apamea only preserves little more than the foundations of its important churches and bishop's complex. One surviving gem of ecclesiastical architecture of the early Byzantine period is the baptistery of the cathedral complex at Nisibis well to the east on the Syrian/Turkish frontier near the Tigris (today preserved as the Church of St Jacob). Except for the remnant of the Cathedral of St Helena in Aleppo, virtually all other Byzantine remains have disappeared from the cities, victims of the depredations of the Persians while later earthquakes or invaders removed what else might have remained.

Nevertheless, there was one outcome of the seventeen years of Sasanian occupation worth noting. Many Christians might well have felt some relief to be spared the harassment waged by the Byzantine authorities towards the churches that had remained loyal to the anti-Chalcedonian (i.e., Monophysite) bishops. The Sasanians were more tolerant of this version of Christianity whose spread straddled Sasanian territory. Not all Christians enjoyed a sense of liberation, therefore, when the Byzantine emperor Heraclius (r.610–41), who had come to power just before the Persian invasion, managed to bring about the invaders' departure. In a hard-won series of campaigns which probably did much to deplete further the resources of the eastern provinces, he pushed back the Persian presence during the years 622–8, reaching as far as the Sasanian capital at Ctesiphon (near modern Baghdad). In the process, he regained the great symbol of Christian faith, the True Cross, in 630 and restored it to Jerusalem.

It was, however, a battered and exhausted set of Eastern provinces that Heraclius regained. Two years after Heraclius received the True Cross (ironically at the deeply pagan cult centre, Hierapolis near Aleppo), an even more momentous event occurred well to the south, in a world that lay beyond the Byzantines' horizons. Muhammad, the Prophet of Islam, died after a life spent defining and spreading a new revelation he had received from God.

Notes

1 Selamanes or Saramana is a reference to an Assyro/Babylonian god, depicted like the Weather God armed with an axe and sometimes identified with Reshep (Coulter 1999: 413).
2 Remains of another ancient (possibly Byzantine) synagogue were incorporated in the al-Hayyat Mosque in the fourteenth century.
3 Sauvaget (1941: 64) on the Byzantine cisterns. There may be another segment of Byzantine construction surviving in the Citadel enclosure walls. Sauvaget, in a footnote (1941: 64 note 174), reported that on the defences immediately outside the Great Mosque of the Citadel, a small section of wall could be reached via the mosque's north portico. This incorporated three firing points, apparently from the original Byzantine wall.
4 Procopius 1914: II, vii, 5–20. Much the same narrative is contained in Procopius 1971: II, vii, 5–13.
5 Procopius 1914: II, vii, 37.
6 Procopius 1914: II, viii, 5–6.
7 This observation excludes, of course, the larger towns (some the seats of bishops) in the Limestone Massif such as Barad, Bara, St Simeon, where major cathedral-like structures survive with recognisable walls.

4

TRANSITION TO AN ISLAMIC ORDER – ALEPPO ON A NEW FRONTIER (637–947)

Early Islamic and Umayyads AD 638–750
'Abassids and Tulunids 750–944

A soft transition

In 637 (or early 638), Aleppo peacefully opened its gates to its Muslim conquerors.[1] Few epoch-making transitions have been marked so uneventfully. The first Islamic units entered the city by the Antioch Gate where today's Bab Antaki marks the western extremity of the main columned axis. The gates were opened following an agreement between the Muslim army's northern commander, Abu 'Ubayda, and the Bishop of Beroia. These days we are keen to identify 'turning points in history'. Our perspective on the past is plagued with a surfeit of them. In the late 630s, Syria truly went through such an experience but few living at the time may have identified it as an epochal event given the relatively peaceful way it unfolded.

The first incursions into settled Byzantine lands had come a few years after Muhammad's death in 632 when Muslim forces burst out of the remote reaches of Arabia. By 636, Byzantine resistance to the new pressures from the Islamic forces reaching Syria from both the south and the east (modern Iraq) had collapsed. At the Battle of Yarmuk (on the northern side of the river which today forms the frontier between southern Syria and Jordan), Muslim forces brought together elements from both invading armies. In a sequence of encounters spread over five days, a huge Byzantine field army was masterfully out-manoeuvred by Islamic units never previously tested in major formations. After several days of skirmishing, the Byzantines were driven in flight from the field, many perishing on the steep flanks of the Yarmuk Gorge, others managing to flee via the Palestine coast or through the Beqa'a Valley of modern Lebanon.

The Emperor Heraclius had preferred to wait out the campaign in Emesa (Homs). After Yarmuk, he saw no point in rallying his remaining forces. In spite of his long and successful campaign against the Persians eight years previously, there was no fight left in the remnants of his army. Heraclius assessed that further

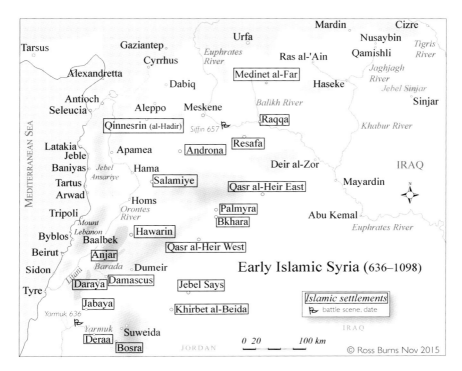

Figure 4.1 Umayyad Syria, 638–750

battles would prevent his remaining forces consolidating for the defence of the Byzantine heartland in Anatolia beyond the Taurus. He withdrew north via Edessa leaving the cities of Syria to their fate, instructing them not to resist further with officials to remain at their posts.

The exact sequence of the subsequent Islamic conquest of Syria still lacks clarity on certain points. However, it seems likely that left to their own devices the citizens of Byzantine Syria were too disillusioned to mount their own campaign to impede an easy Islamic victory after Yarmuk. One after another the towns of the Syrian interior and coast came under Islamic rule peacefully and without reprisals. Even the great metropolis of Antioch succumbed quietly: 'There was more to be lost than gained in defending Antioch to the last man.'[2] The arrival of Islam was just another transformation in a world that had faced massive upheaval since 608, this time without the violence and destruction that had marked the Persians' arrival. Two factors conditioned the Syrians' response to the Islamic takeover. In 628, the return of Byzantine rule had come after a period of Persian control which had proved relatively benign for the Monophysite communities of Syria who had resented the heavy-handed Byzantine attempts to impose orthodoxy. Moreover,

73

the idea of Arab forces visiting from the steppe and deserts to the south and east was not new and many had already peaceably settled in parts of Syria during the Roman and Byzantine centuries when some of the major 'client kingdoms' had been Arab in origin.

Consolidating Islamic rule

The Islamic conquest rolled methodically and inexorably over Syria.[3] It took up to two years to reach Aleppo. The first step was the signing of a ceasefire between Byzantine leaders and Muslim commanders in late 637 at Qinnisrin. Residual Byzantine forces had time to evacuate and destroy their defences before their retreat, even laying waste much of the countryside as if it were already enemy territory and leaving an 'empty zone' between Muslim forces and the Byzantines' new line in Anatolia.[4] When the ceasefire expired, Islamic forces received the surrender of other northern cities, though some coastal centres did not go over until 640.

Those Arab forces that entered Aleppo in 637/8 unopposed arrived via the Antioch Gate (Bab Antaki). Though some construction work to repair the dilapidated Byzantine city walls had been done by the Persians, the fortifications had been badly affected by an earthquake before the Arabs' arrival. A medieval account recorded that the Citadel walls too were in no fit state to face a siege at this time. The city thus passed under Islamic rule without opposition. The first

Figure 4.2 Antioch Gate (Bab Antaki) as rebuilt under the Ayyubids and Mamluks

prayers were offered by the Islamic military leader Abu 'Ubayda just inside the Antioch Gate. The spot is still marked by a mosque popularly known by the picturesque title of the Mosque of the Mulberry Tree (al-Tuteh, Figure 4.3) but in more scholarly sources as al-Shu'aybiye. We will look again at this curious little mosque later (pages 131–2) but note for now that it lay at the western end of the cross-city axis. In later accounts, the memory of the first Islamic prayer was to be the reason why Nur al-Din chose this site for a commemorative mosque, a new construction (1150) replacing the first mosque to be built in the city.

Qinnisrin

There is one curious mystery relating to the first Islamic presence in the Aleppo region. We have noted earlier the series of fortifications on the edges of the steppe to the south that had come to play a role in a Byzantine defensive perimeter guarding Antioch against the rising pressure of the tribal groups of the interior to the southeast (69–70). Nominally, many of the Arab groups had been joined under the leadership of the Ghassanids, an Arab confederation loosely affiliated with

Figure 4.3 Mosque al-Shu'aybiye from inside the Antioch Gate

the Byzantines but at times not entirely compliant with the objectives of the New Rome. Most of the tribes grouped under the Ghassanids were partly nomadic but tended to congregate at times of festivals or to find water and pasture for their flocks. One of those gathering points was at Resafe, 160 kilometres southeast of Aleppo where the robustly constructed Ghassanid audience hall still stands outside the remains of the Byzantine walled fortress city.

Qinnisrin was probably another such gathering point, closer in to the more fertile region around Aleppo but a useful base for retaining contact with the desert groups. Here a fortress had stood since Hellenistic times (hence its Macedonian place name, Chalcis). The settlement was expanded under the Byzantines to embrace a considerable hill site. Beyond Chalcis' southeast walls, al-Hadir was an area apparently reserved as an encampment for visiting Arab groups. (The Arabic *al-hadir* is a generic name for a major gathering point.) The proximity of Qinnisrin to the desert and the expansion of its citadel reflected the city's rising importance vis-à-vis Aleppo by the seventh century and it was a natural choice for the point at which the Islamic forces halted to negotiate a ceasefire for the whole region.[5]

The puzzle, though, is why Qinnisrin not Aleppo was then chosen as the capital of the northern-most district (*jund*) of the province of Syria-Palestine. Possibly the choice can be explained by Qinnisrin's easier access to the steppe. The district

Figure 4.4 Shepherds breakfasting amid remains of the Byzantine city at Qinnisrin (Chalcis AD Belum)

surrounding the new capital, however, carried the name Aleppo (reverting in Arabic to the Semitic root, Halab). Certainly Qinnisrin offered more accessible pasture, room for tent encampments and water in the form of the last of the Quweiq's flow before the stream petered out on the desiccated steppe. The fact that Aleppo, as we will see, would lie so close to the line of confrontation with the Byzantines in decades to come may also have dictated the continued preference for Qinnisrin as the initial Arab administrative base.

Aleppo too received an Arab presence though the influx was limited and confined to an area southwest of the walled city. It is unclear what use the new rulers made of Aleppo's great Citadel still battered by a recent earthquake, though the medieval Arab chronicler Ibn al-Shihna notes that the Islamic military leader Abu ʿUbayda rebuilt the tumbled masonry but 'without care for solidity'.[6] What tiny glimpses we have of the use of the area in Umayyad times is limited to a segment examined during the Weather God temple excavations. This showed continuous use of the area but no distinctive structures.[7] Sauvaget believed that as Muslim numbers in the city grew, the first area selected for congregational prayer was at the foot of the Citadel. This area, now marked by the esplanade in front of the later gateway to the Citadel served in the early Islamic period as a *musalla* or outdoor space for worship, a feature found at many centres.[8]

Rightly Guided Caliphs (640–60)

During the period in which Islam developed more formal structures of leadership (the period of the 'Rightly Guided' or Rashidun Caliphs, 632–60), Aleppo found itself almost in a dead zone between the Arabs and the Byzantines. The Byzantine withdrawal to Anatolia, having laid waste much of the country north of a line between Antioch and Aleppo, had seen the former rulers consolidate in Cilicia and in the recesses of eastern Anatolia. The Christian and Muslim forces clashed along a broad frontline running close to Aleppo through Cyrrhus and Menbij. The uplands north of Aleppo became subject to attempts by both sides to penetrate the other's territory through campaigns and raids that kept the area depopulated. This also deeply affected the viability of agriculture in the Limestone Massif to Aleppo's west where the rapid decline of Antioch once it fell into Muslim hands brought a collapse of the main market for the area's produce.

The Umayyads 661–750

To the south, Damascus became the new focal point of the Islamic world when it was chosen as headquarters for the first of the Caliphs from the Umayyad faction who had long made their fortunes in the trade between the Hijaz and southern Syria. In 639, Muʿawiya Ibn Abi Sufyan had been appointed Governor of Syria based in Damascus. An effective governor, he used Syria as his base to claim the position of Caliph in 661 in the aftermath of the first civil war initiated when followers of Muhammad's son-in-law 'Ali assassinated Caliph 'Uthman in 656. Mu'awiya led the call for revenge against the followers of 'Ali, thus touching off centuries of rivalry undiminished to this day.

While the world ruled from Damascus soon extended from Spain to Central Asia, Aleppo's concerns were closer to home. For the next several centuries, Aleppo's focus would be fixed on the lands to its east and northeast. Figure 4.5 summarises the picture in the centuries between the highpoint of Byzantine control in the area (AD 600, broken grey line on right) to the line of confrontation in the century immediately after the Islamic conquest (c. AD 750, broken black line at left). Aleppo was now at the centre of the contested zone.

Figure 4.5 also illustrates a classic case of fighting a new war with the strategy of the last. All the great forts erected by the Romans and the Byzantine extension of the line to the east and along the Euphrates had proved useless. The new enemy arrived largely from the south. They found the south entrance open and free of geographical impediments. They were certainly not interested in being trapped into long sieges of fortress cities.

After the taking of Syria, however, the Arabs found their further progress blocked by the Byzantines' ability to hold on in the Anatolian highlands, by supply difficulties on extended campaigns through hostile territory and by the fact that the Byzantine capital at Constantinople was just too far away to be threatened by the occasional long-distance Arab campaign. Even the Arabs' resorting to sea

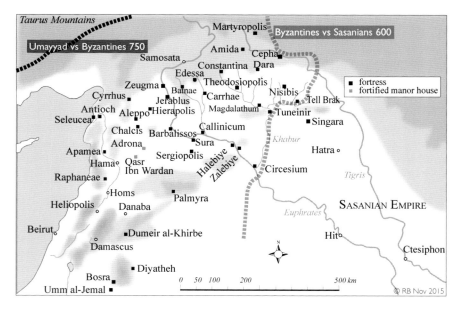

Figure 4.5 Byzantine eastern frontier, 600–750

power (with the help of numerous Christians from Syria) could not shake the Byzantine Asia Minor base. It was in the bad lands between the Taurus Mountains and the Syrian plains that the tensions were to be played out for the next few centuries.[9]

Aleppo's economy would suffer from this endemic uncertainty in the region, from the decline in Antioch's population and from the disruption caused by constant jockeying for advantage by internal Islamic forces each lacking the strength to maintain a dominant position in northern Syria. The jund of Aleppo took a triple battering from these tensions but it is difficult to determine the kaleidoscopic sequence of events since our sources, either written largely from a later perspective or archaeological evidence, are both poor and inconsistent.

The Aleppo Great Mosque

As the Umayyads' efforts to extend the new Arab world empire slackened, Aleppo felt more keenly the consequences of losing the attention of Umayyad rulers in Damascus. The citizens of Aleppo nevertheless saw the need to try to emulate the splendid new monuments being constructed in the south. The Damascus Great Mosque had set the trend in Syria. The reality was, however, that the smaller centres lacked the resources that the capital of an extensive empire could call upon. Whereas the Damascus mosque's builder, Caliph al-Walid I (r.705–15), had even managed to inveigle the Byzantine authorities into sending craftsmen to complete its huge glittering mosaic panels, smaller centres relied mainly on local resources and talent.

In Aleppo's case, however, we have to reserve judgement for the mosque known to have been completed in Aleppo by Suleiman, the brother of Caliph al-Walid and his successor in 715, is lost to us except perhaps in its broad outline plan. It was built in a brief period of great confidence in the Umayyads' annals when their forces managed to take the fight as far as the Byzantine capital only to be forced to make a hasty retreat. Enough resources were found to build a beacon for the new faith in Aleppo which sought to emulate the imperial template at Damascus. The pattern of prayer hall and courtyard with its surrounding colonnaded porticos or *riwaq* continued the plan originally set by the Prophet's house-mosque in Medina but recreated in Damascus on an extravagant scale. How much Aleppo might have sought to emulate the Damascus mosque's example cannot be determined as so much of the original project has been lost but the choice of a sizeable area of land for the project made its ambitions clear (Figure 2.6). Arab accounts also refer to the fact that the new mosque in Aleppo reused some of the columns from the great cathedral at Cyrrhus to the north underlining the original scale.

As in Damascus, the Umayyads consciously adopted a space associated with pagan and Christian worship for centuries but in this case rather than incorporate existing remains they appear to have adapted an area which at least in part was not built upon. In his account, the Arab historian Ibn ach-Shihna al-Shina tells us that the northern side of the site was a cemetery, not a religious building. For reasons explained earlier (page 63), the western part of this central group of *insulae* of the Classical city also appears to have been a garden area on which the Christians had built their cathedral (possibly to keep it separate from the ruins of the pagan temple). The long neglected temple enclosure was then reused as the site of the mosque. As we will see later, the original mosque was destroyed by fire in 1169 but this was not the only disaster to overtake it. The 'Abassids would strip it of its decorative mosaics to spite the Umayyads; the Byzantine emperor Nicephorus would burn the mosque in 962; it would be sacked during the Fatimid occupation of the mid-eleventh century. After considerable rebuilding in the Seljuk period, it was subsequently rebuilt in an austere Zengid style under Nur al-Din, though much of his work was in turn replaced by his Ayyubid and Mamluk successors after further fire damage. Though a few fragments of a pre-twelfth-century wall may survive, almost everything else is Ayyubid or later.[10]

Perhaps the closest insight into the original Aleppo mosque can be seen at the town of Ma'arat al-Nu'man (ancient Megara) 70 kilometres south of Aleppo on the Damascus road. This complex has never suffered the pain of beautification which has affected many other congregational mosques over the centuries. While there has been some reworking of the initial building, the design of the original is still apparent in all its sobriety – a prayer hall to the south, an open courtyard but without the surrounding colonnades forming a riwaq. Never subjected

Figure 4.6 Courtyard of the Great Mosque at Ma'arat al-Numan

to an architectural study, its prayer hall evidently dates from Ayyubid or Mamluk times with simple cross-vaults supported on robust square piers but much of the stone is clearly recycled from a Classical building on the site. A few Classical or Byzantine columns from the preceding temple and church are used to emphasise the most significant parts of the building. They support two simple domed structures in the courtyard providing the mosque's treasury (following the Damascus example) and protection for the ablution fountain. Some of the treasury capitals show the 'windswept acanthus' style so popular since its use on the facade of the Church of St Simeon.[11] The Ma'arat Mosque is one of the most striking examples of the principle of 'continuity of use' at a religious centre, particularly notable for the conscious way in which the Classical elements are used to adorn and give status to the Islamic project.

From forum to suq

It is typical of early Islamic times to find a close association between a congregational mosque, intended to gather the faithful on a Friday, and the city's commercial heart. This tradition was clearly observed in Aleppo where until 2011 the shops of the suqs closely enfolded the central mosque to form the heart of the city. The demands of commerce and the likely need to reconstruct areas which had been affected by earthquakes or invasions had seen a considerable refashioning of the great colonnaded axis which had run immediately to the south of the temple, now mosque. However, we can see that although the overall grid dating back to Hellenistic times was retained, there was much 'in-filling' over the centuries, especially on the broad east–west central spine.[12]

This pattern of in-filling in Aleppo was first identified by Sauvaget and taken by him as a prime example of the decline of the streetscape of Roman/Byzantine cities as they adapted to Early Islamic and later patterns of use.[13] Figure 4.7 provides a schema of the way in which over the centuries the wide central axis of the city was divided into several parallel lanes occupying the broad avenue in

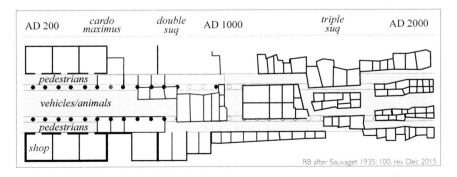

Figure 4.7 Evolution of a colonnaded street from Roman to medieval times

a somewhat erratic pattern. The main thoroughfare with sidewalks, demarcated by rows of columns supporting a protective roof and shops behind, now became a straggling series of lanes with smaller booths and narrow pedestrian passages.

Sauvaget's ingenious description of the evolution of the street plan has largely retained its validity but one detail is still unclear. When did this happen? Sauvaget was inclined to attribute the process to the early Islamic period with the assumed breakdown of municipal controls. However, there is no archaeological confirmation of this pattern except at one site, Palmyra. At other centres, some scholars are more inclined to see this breaking up of the streetscape not as a response to a collapse of authority but as reflecting a new approach by authorities, beginning in the Byzantine period, faced with a deterioration of the Roman-era structures and the need to introduce a new legal framework governing the exploitation of the surviving public spaces.

The Roman-era enthusiasm for colonnaded streets and protected market structures had reflected an era, particularly from the mid-second century AD, when industrial quantities of stone and pre-fashioned pieces such as columns and capitals were available in standardised forms throughout the Eastern Empire. As structures later succumbed to earthquake or fire, it became difficult to replace them as the imperial quarries in Egypt, Greece and Asia Minor closed down beginning with the empire-wide crises of the third century. In some cases it was possible to reuse surviving columns from abandoned buildings, particularly with the closure of temples from the fourth century. It is thus likely that the central avenues were allowed to deteriorate not by choice (several new colonnading projects were in fact initiated in Byzantine and Umayyad times) but for practical reasons related to the scarcity of materials. Both Byzantine and early Islamic administrations thus faced the need to regulate the spaces as best they could. Roman legal frameworks had emphasised the protection of public space for public use; in the Byzantine and Islamic periods, the emphasis shifted to making do with what was available.

If Aleppo now suffered an uncertain fate for several centuries, at least it can be said that it survived. Other cities in the area were less fortunate. Even a major urban centre such as Apamea with its 1.8 kilometre main colonnaded street rapidly declined to the point where the medieval town would abandon the great circuit of city walls and huddle within its near-miniature extra-mural citadel. Cyrrhus to the north quickly lapsed to the point where it was hardly more than a place name in the medieval period with a small Crusader fort to guard the route from Antioch to Edessa. Qinnisrin, though initially favoured under Early Islam, also later shrank to a small village by the nineteenth century.

By contrast, during the Umayyad period, Damascus had housed an Islamic dynasty that emulated some of the splendours of the Byzantine court as the seat of a great empire stretching from Spain to Khurasan. Halab was simply the seat of a local district governor once the headquarters had been transferred from Qinnisrin. These were difficult centuries in this part of Syria and Halab/Aleppo needed all the tenacity it could muster to survive.

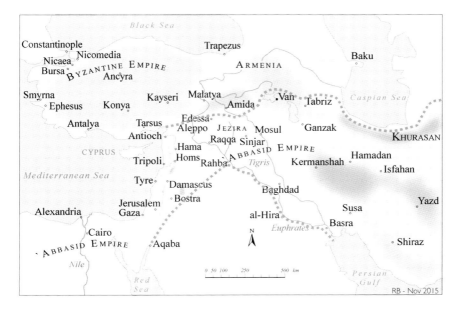

Figure 4.8 Rise of the 'Abassids (to 800)

The 'Abbasids, rule from Iraq

If Halab lay on the perimeter in Umayyad times, this remoteness was further emphasised after 750 when the Umayyads, much criticised for their laxness in morals and matters religious, were overthrown by a new regime that drew its support from the warriors of remote Khurasan. They would soon found a new capital, Baghdad, where the flood plains of the Tigris and Euphrates rivers almost converged. The city would become a flourishing centre of Arab and Islamic culture. Baghdad's direct influence spread up-river to a new sub-capital at Raqqa on the mid-Euphrates some 200 kilometres southeast of Halab on the edge of the ancient city of Callinicum. In Arabic, the name originally given to the Islamic new foundation was al-Rafiqa ('the companion') founded in 771–2 by the 'Abbasid Caliph al-Mansur to house a garrison of Khurasani soldiers to assure the new regime's tenure on the long middle stretch of the Euphrates and thus protect communications between Iraq and major centres in Syria.

The Umayyads had often been criticised for their preference for a Mediterranean-influenced Islamic culture with a style of architecture and art heavily borrowing from the past. The 'Abassids reversed the trend. Raqqa adopted a horseshoe-shaped layout with the straight side bordering the river, an idea unprecedented in Roman or Byzantine planning. Even the materials of the 'Abassids' new art eschewed the mosaics and richly decorated stone embellishments of the Umayyads.

Figure 4.9 Baghdad Gate, Raqqa

A more Mesopotamian- and Persian-influenced vocabulary now prevailed with structures in mud brick and decoration in stucco in strictly vegetal forms. Raqqa was on the western limit of the architectural ideas that from Baghdad spread east as far as the limits of Central Asia. Perhaps the best indicator of this vocabulary would be the Baghdad Gate still standing at the southeast corner of the mud brick city walls of Raqqa. The dating of the gate, however, has been much debated – a tribute to the persistence of the ʿAbbasid style over several centuries. Initial estimates that the gate was part of the city of Caliph Harun al-Rashid (r.786–809) who briefly adopted Raqqa as the regime's capital from 796 are now doubted.

Outside Raqqa, 8 kilometres to the west, the ʿAbassids erected a strange victory monument to celebrate their taking in 806 of the Byzantine city of Herakleion near Constantinople.[14] Dubbed Heraqla, it took the form of a terraced structure over 100 metres square, faced with stone but with a largely solid core of mud brick including corner towers. Its outer shape resembled a Roman fort or *castrum* but largely filled in with earth and gravel except for four long apse-like rooms entering from the outside but giving no further access to the interior, all carefully oriented to the compass points. There are no clues as to whether the terrace was intended to carry a commemorative structure that would have given some point to this enormous folly. The abandonment of Raqqa as the imperial capital shortly afterwards presumably brought work to a premature end. The Syrian investigator of the ruins, Ghassan Toueir, associated the monument

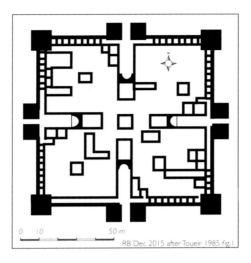

0   10   50 m

RB Dec 2015 after Toueir 1985 fig.1

Figure 4.10 Harun al-Rashid's victory monument at Heraqla (after Toueir 1983: fig. 1)

with Harun al-Rashid's wish to make his mark as widely as possible. Why the taking of such a small city, Herakleion, in distant Asia Minor was elevated to a matter of such significance remains a mystery unless as a signal to the wider world that his campaign against the Byzantines had reached the environs of their capital. Harun al-Rashid had already corresponded with the Holy Roman emperor Charlemagne (r.800–14), whom he regarded as his only peer in terms of aspirations to world empire.[15]

The 'Abbasid sub-capital so far to the west at Raqqa was probably also meant to facilitate renewed campaigns against the Byzantines who still entertained hopes of a return to their Syrian domains. In the sixty years from 782, several campaigns were mounted by Constantinople, again adding uncertainty to Aleppo's position near the frontline. During these centuries we have no physical evidence from Aleppo. Even the towns of the Limestone Massif are largely quiet. We can assume that the population drastically fell as agricultural markets declined. Those communities that stayed on largely did no more building until just before the arrival of the Crusaders at the end of the twelfth century.[16]

'Abbasid decline

The reign of Caliph Harun al-Rashid (r.786–809) is said to mark the apogee of the 'Abbasids; certainly it marked the limit of their aspirations to world empire. Hugh Kennedy has found the Caliph's reputation and aspirations somewhat overstated. As Caliph he probably failed his own ambitions, displaying what Kennedy describes as a 'curiously nondescript character' flitting from scheme to scheme.

He eventually perished in a campaign to regain the 'Abbasid position in Khurasan, a region neglected in the years he had pursued his dreams of matching his rivals to the west. [17]

Notes

1 Kaegi 1992: 146.
2 Kaegi 1992: 149.
3 The sequence of the campaigns is clarified in Howard-Johnston (2010: 464–70).
4 Michael the Syrian 1899: II, 424; Kaegi 1992: 146–8; Kennedy 2007: 88.
5 Few identifiable remains survive at the site of Qinnisrin just outside the village of Nabi 'Iss, named after the tomb of an Islamic holy man topping the nearby hill.
6 Ibn ach-Chihna 1933: 56.
7 Gonnella 2006: 169.
8 Sauvaget 1941: 76.
9 The tensions between Islam and the Byzantines in the region north of Aleppo became the stuff of legends in later centuries. In 715 Suleiman Ibn 'Abd al-Malik succeeded his brother, Walid II, as Caliph but ruled for only two years. In 717, he died suddenly at Dabiq, 35 kilometres north of Aleppo, as he was preparing to lead his forces on campaign against the Byzantines with Constantinople being the ultimate objective. The unfinished business brought to a premature end at Dabiq became the stuff of legends with prophecies describing Dabiq as the expected location of the final encounter between the forces of Islam and the unbelievers. In 2014, a simple structure commemorating Suleiman's death at Dabiq was destroyed by the forces of self-styled Islamic State as one of their first objectives in entering the environs of Aleppo.

Dabiq also provided the scene for the great battle in 1516 in which the Ottoman forces took Syria from the Mamluks (Chapter 9). Ironically, another Muslim leader, the penultimate Mamluk Sultan Qansuh al-Ghauri, perished in 1516 from a massive stroke on the battlefield.

Dabiq was celebrated in the name of the monthly magazine of 'Islamic State' which called for Muslims to rally there for the final battle ushering in the Day of Judgement. IS were expelled from the area in October 2016 by another rebel group, with Turkish backing. For recent insights into the Dabiq legend, see McCants (2015: 102–5).
10 Allen 1983: 7–12. There are two exceptions: the minaret outside the north entrance to the mosque is Seljuk work of the late eleventh century as we will see later and the ablutions fountain in the centre of the courtyard is at least based on Hamdanid work of the 960s (see page 92).
11 The inscription on the structure dates from the period of the Hamdanid ruler Sayf al-Dawla (969), but it is possible that he is claiming credit for a rebuilding or improvement.
12 It has been argued that the decline in wheeled traffic after the Roman centuries contributed to the piecemeal breaking up of the axes (Kennedy 1985: 26). Whereas the wide central street might have accommodated carts and wagons as a means of carrying goods, the decline in their use from the fourth century on removed one reason for keeping the central roadway clear. There may also have been good practical reasons for the decline in wheeled traffic. Bulliet has rightly pointed out that 'wheeled vehicles . . . are inflexible in the restraints they put on city life' (Bulliet 1990: 226). Consequently many Roman-era cities had already banned wheeled traffic. Donkeys or humans were a more practical means of delivering broken-down loads from depots outside a city.
13 Sauvaget 1935: 99–102; Sauvaget 1941: I, 104.

14 Modern Ereğli in western Turkey – on the Asian side, north coast of the Propontis.
15 Toueir 1983: 303.
16 One small exception relates to the monastic presence on the southern slopes of Jebel Sheikh Barakat, an original 'high place'. At two monastic ruins near Tell ʿAdeh, inscriptions in Syriac (significantly not in Arabic and giving dates in the Greek calendar) record rebuilding in the years 858, 907 and 941 (Littmann 1934: #16, 17). Butler (1912: 245) notes that these 'are the only dates among all the inscriptions of Northern Syria which indicate that inscriptions were being carved upon buildings in the region after the Mohammedan conquest'.
17 Kennedy 1990: 146.

5

A DELICATE BALANCE –
BETWEEN TURKIC AND ARAB
WORLDS (947–1097)

Hamdanids 947–1004 /
Byzantines 968–76
Mirdasids 1024–80 /
Fatimids 1038–41, 1057–60
Seljuks 1078–1117

Enter the Turks . . .

After Harun al-Rashid, ʿAbbasid decline was well underway. The empire failed
to hold. In anticipation of factional disputes, it was Harun al-Rashid's younger
son, al-Muʿtasim (r.833–47) who even before his appointment as Caliph began
the practice of buying Turkish slaves on the Baghdad market to serve in his private security force. Later he extended his recruitment programme to bring Turks
directly from Central Asia. When he became Caliph, al-Muʿtasim formed the
Turkish units into a 'model army' to strengthen his close protection. As a warrior
elite, 'tough, disciplined and devoted to their master', selected from infancy and
separated from the general population, they were trained to perfect their skills as
horsemen and archers.[1] The group that had been brought in to form a praetorian
guard for the Caliphs increasingly stepped into the power vacuum in Baghdad and
gradually determined the regime's priorities.

This elite group (*ghulām*) was the first manifestation of the growth of Turkic[2]
influence in Iran, Mesopotamia and Syria. Turkic speakers had gradually been
inducted into Islam following the incorporation of Khurasan during the Umayyad
and ʿAbbasid periods. 'Unfortunately for the ʿAbbasids, their slave-soldiers took
only a few decades to move through the ranks – from palace guard to regimen-
tal commander, unruly provincial governor, founder of a petty local dynasty and
even king maker in Baghdad.'[3] By the end of the ninth century, units raised in the
eastern borderlands formed a significant element of the ʿAbbasid power structure,
though many were converted to Islam only on recruitment. In the tenth century,
however, Islamisation was complete and Turkic-speaking commanders began to

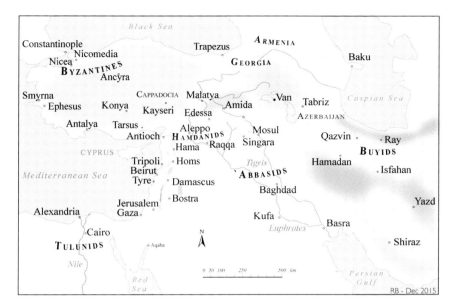

Figure 5.1 Central Islamic lands in the tenth century

lead the ʿAbbasid army. As an ethnic group, later split into several major streams, they were to dominate the affairs of the region for at least the next four centuries. Later they would vie with the Kurds as the dominant military caste within Islamic societies and would return to a prime role in the region with the Ottoman conquest in the sixteenth century.

... via Egypt

At times, direct ʿAbbasid authority was confined to the Mesopotamian heartland and remote areas such as the Aleppo region were claimed by a succession of rival groups. These rivalries reflected growing Turkic power in the borderlands of Iran in today's eastern Turkey but tensions arose even further afield, in Egypt. The first Turkish offshoots were the Tulunids who came to power in Egypt via the appointment of Ahmad Ibn Tulun as ʿAbbasid governor (r.868–84). Ibn Tulun's quest for status was demonstrated by his project for the extension of the Egyptian capital from the first Arab base at Fustat to the new quarter to the north at al-Qataʾi.

The Turkic interest in northern Syria was first manifest in the Tulunids from their base in Cairo. Ahmad Ibn Tulun was one of the rising Turkic generals in the ʿAbbasid system. Though nominally assigned Egypt and Syria in return for an annual tribute to Baghdad, he signalled the exercise of power in his own right after refusing to acknowledge the ʿAbbasid Caliph at Friday prayers in Cairo. Under his descendants, Tulunid reach soon extended north to Damascus and shortly after as far as the Euphrates via Aleppo. The ʿAbbasid claim to empire via the Caliphate was now largely a symbolic one until direct rule from Baghdad was restored from 905.

Ibn Tulun left his mark on Cairo in the form of the magnificent mosque, the centrepiece of al-Qata'i. It brought the architecture of Samarra and Baghdad to Egypt and still carries his name but nothing of this strikingly Mesopotamian architecture survives in Aleppo. Nor did the next Turkic dynasty – again arising from an ʿAbbasid appointee as governor of Cairo – the Ikhshidids (r.935–69) have enough time to leave their mark in northern Syria as Aleppo was now entering the orbit of another ethnic group expanding into the nominal imperial realm of the ʿAbbasids.

Hamdanids (in Aleppo 947–1004)

In 890 at Mardin on the southern flanks of the Anti-Taurus, another ʿAbbasid governor had aspired to rule in his own right, Hamdan Ibn Hamdun. In the coming decades, his descendants gained office in Mosul and even Baghdad. What was remarkable about this group was that they were actually locals but followed the Shiʿa branch of Islam.[4] By the second half of the tenth century, as the power of the ʿAbbasids collapsed from Trans-Oxiana to Tunisia, Hamdanids controlled most of the major centres of the belt stretching from Aleppo to Mosul, often ruling the area as a dual emirate based on the two cities. This was the region in

Figure 5.2 Mosque of Ibn Tulun in Cairo

which Aleppo was now to be immersed for the next three centuries. 'Abbasid power in Baghdad had declined, now focusing largely on its religious claim to the Caliphate, while Cairo after 969 would come under the control of the Fatimids, a Shi'i dynasty who had moved in from North Africa and whose aspirations for wider empire were usually halted in southern Syria at Damascus.

In Aleppo, which had gradually taken back from Qinnisrin the claim to supremacy as the major political centre of northwest Syria, the Hamdanid leader Sayf al-Dawla (r.944–67) came to full power after three years of confrontation with the Cairo-based Ikshidids. This confrontation had introduced a geographical north–south partitioning of Syria (in this case between the Hamdanids and the Ikshidid-influenced south) that would largely influence the affairs of Syria for the next two hundred years with brief interruptions.

The Hamdanids were to have a short but intellectually glorious reign. We have a body of written evidence of their court, long praised for its celebration of the Arabic language in poetry. Perhaps the reason the memory of their court survived among later generations of Arab writers was that it was one of the few instances for many centuries of a ruling dynasty using Arabic as their first language and thus with a real understanding of its rhythms and sonority. Sayf al-Dawla, intent on

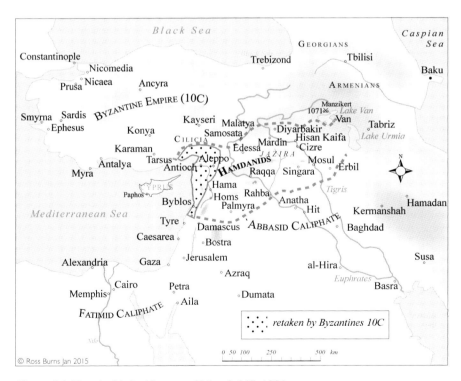

Figure 5.3 Hamdanids in Aleppo and Mosul, 947–1004

projecting an image of a warrior-poet-king if only to hide his extortionist-warlord side, invited to his court a range of the major intellectual figures from Iraq and the Jazira – philosophers, musicians, poets and theologians. Poets of the calibre of al-Mutannabi and al-Farabi graced the court. In surveying this period in the *Encyclopaedia of Islam*, Thierry Bianquis notes, however, that there was a degree of parasitism in the relationship between ruler and court intellectuals, a relation-ship 'justified by the propaganda which their works disseminated to the advantage of the local prince'.[5]

Sayf al-Dawla is known to have strengthened the Aleppo Citadel walls.[6] The scene of the dynasty's splendid court, however, has disappeared. It was located not on the Citadel, which had housed several rulers since Umayyad times, but formed a sprawling array of pavilions and gardens on the banks of the Quweiq west of the city walls in the area marked today by the Aziziye Gardens, through which the sad trickle of the river now barely flows. One small remnant of the Hamdanid era survives in the courtyard of the Great Mosque. The central ablu-tions fountain carries an inscription recording that it was built by Qarghaweh, a servant of Sayf al-Dawla, in 965 as part of the Hamdanid ruler's repairs to the mosque after the destructive Byzantine occupation (discussed below).

'The platform'

One other gesture of Sayf al-Dawla, which should be noted as it will recur in our narrative at several points below, is the shrine known as the Mashhad al-Muhassin. Commenced at the peak of Shi'i influence in Aleppo (Sayf al-Dawla invited a number of Shia clerics from Qum in Iran in 962), the complex today reflects a rebuilding a century later when attempts were made to persuade the remaining Shi'a in Aleppo to return to the Sunni tradition. The building overlooks the city from the southeast (Jebel Jawshan) at exactly the spot that would later attract the sketchbook or camera of countless European visitors seeking the perfect angle for the view of the Citadel towering over the town. It thus often goes under its nickname, al-Dikka ('the platform').[7] The shrine was associated with a stillborn child conceived by Fatima, one of the wives of Hussein who fled to Syria after the battle of Kerbala, reaching Aleppo only to lose the child at this place. It is possi-bly no coincidence that the shrine (and the nearby Mashhad al-Hussein discussed later) were located near the site of the Byzantine monastery of Mar Marutha. Nothing remains of the Hamdanid phase and the building was greatly expanded in Ayyubid times to encourage both Sh'i and Sunni devotees as part of a programme to play down the tensions that had built up between the two communities.

Byzantines return (962–1084)

The dream of an Arab ruled Islamic realm was soon interrupted. The Byzantine general Nicephorus Phocas took Aleppo in 962. It was an opportunistic raid as he was accompanied by only a small force. In any event he was called away by the

Figure 5.4 Aleppo from the shrine of Sheikh al-Muhassin (Mashhad al-Dikka) on Jebel Jawshan

news of his proclamation as emperor in Constantinople. The Muslim visitor Ibn Hawkal described Aleppo under Byzantine occupation as a once-prosperous city that now faced 'captivity in the hands of the Infidels'. The city's walls had not been maintained and proved useless in discouraging even Phocas' small force. Ibn Hawkal continues:

> The Greeks took the city and its stone wall was of no avail to it. They ruined the Mosque, and took away captive all its women and children, and burnt the houses. Halab had a castle, but it was not a strong place and was in no way well built. All the population had fled up to it (to take refuge from the Greeks) and here most of them perished with all their goods and chattels.[8]

Phocas, now emperor, returned to Aleppo in 968 as part of a more serious effort to regain much of coastal Syria and parts of the northern interior. The Byzantine dream of recovering the Syria that Heraclius had so despondently abandoned almost three hundred years before had, it seems, never entirely gone away. This time perhaps it had been reawakened in the Byzantine mind by Sayf al-Dawla's aggressive push into Cilicia three years earlier, a move that had provoked the vigorous counter-offensive by Emperor Phocas.

What motivated the Byzantines' impossible dream of restoring Christian rule to Syria, beyond giving Sayf al-Dawla a bloody nose in response to his attempt

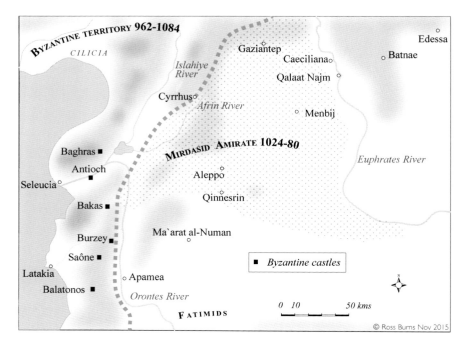

Figure 5.5 Byzantine reconquest and Mirdasids, to 1080

to be an Islamic warrior prince? It was unlikely to have been the prospect for the Byzantines of rescuing a significant Chalcedonian presence, namely the followers of the Orthodox persuasion in northern Syria. Most likely their numbers in a city like Aleppo would by now have been much reduced for reasons whose background will now be examined.

A religious mosaic

Not many of Aleppo's citizens, even its Christians, could have been expected to cheer the Byzantines' return. The first two centuries of Islam had not seen a major push for converts. Islam was still considered to be an elite faith; though conversion was possible, proselytising would only gradually become the norm. Only after the ninth century would the Christian population gradually succumb to a rising wave of conversions to Islam, though Syria remained a land of numerous minorities including some affiliated to the official Byzantine church. Those Christians not of the orthodox persuasion included, in rural areas particularly, numerous pockets of the old 'Monophysite' strain – today's Syrian Orthodox Church. Over to the northeast in the area dubbed by the Arabs 'the island' (al-Jazira) between the Tigris and the Euphrates river systems was a significant presence of the 'Church of the East' – the legacy of an even earlier group who from the fifth century had resisted centralised orthodoxy in the church, sometimes labelled the 'Nestorians'. Both these 'non-Orthodox' communities were simply the western-most presence of churches whose followers had gravitated eastwards to modern Iraq, Iran and even India. Not many would necessarily have had fond memories of Byzantine Orthodox rule.

This Christian mosaic was matched by a diverse collection of religious trends on the Muslim side. The main division remained between the followers of the Prophet Muhammad's son-in-law ʿAli (dubbed Shiʿa after the Arabic 'followers') and the more numerous communities who adhered to the *sunna* or a strict interpretation of Islam as recorded in the actions and words of the Prophet Muhammad – the Sunnis. The line between the two traditions essentially rested on the historical events relating to the removal of ʿAli as Caliph and his replacement by the first of the Umayyad line, al-Muʿawiya. The distinction in doctrinal terms was for a long time difficult to define and the variations in practice minimal but that did not stop rulers at times favouring one interpretation, often as a means of raising the fervour of their communities against a rival.

In the centuries after Muʿawiya's Caliphate, begun in 661, differences emerged. These centred on debate not only over the legitimacy of the line of Caliphs but also over the role of imams in interpreting matters of faith under divine guidance. These differences led to further divisions from which sprang heterodox traditions later identified as:

- The Ismaelis, a missionary movement of obscure Iraqi origin, who adopted as their Syrian base the town of Salamiye 130 kilometres south of Aleppo on the edge of the Syrian steppe, originally settled by descendants of the early ʿAbbasid rulers. A branch spread to North Africa and took power in Egypt from 969. After the collapse of the Fatimids, by the twelfth century, the Ismaelis survived in pockets including Salamiye and in the coastal mountains where the Nusairis (today's ʿAlawis, see below) had also fled to escape persecution.
- The Druze, an offshoot from the Ismaelis of eleventh-century Egypt. Their first leader, Muhammad al-Darazi (d.1020), supported the claim of the Fatimid Caliph, al-Hakim (r.996–1021), to be an embodiment of the One (i.e., God), a belief unacceptable to mainstream Islam. Most Druze today live in southern Syria (around Suweida in the Hauran) or in southern Lebanon but there are a few Druze villages in the region west of Aleppo.
- Alawites (to use the modern term) or followers of Muhammad Ibn Nusair al-Namiri, a supporter of the tenth Shiʿi imam (d.868) who were first organised as a distinct sect in tenth-century Aleppo. By the eleventh century, the then Nusairi leader, al-Tabarani, had moved the community to Latakia on the coast from where they later retreated to their nearby mountain refuge.

Aleppo was a staging post for members of these groups, attracted by the rule of the Hamdanids as an Arab Shiʿi dynasty. Tenth-century Aleppo was thus a melting pot of faiths and diverse tendencies with the Hamdanid court providing a refuge for many persecuted elsewhere. Though a high proportion of the population was still Christian, it would have been a challenge to rule for an 'orthodox' Christian empire with its roots much further west in Byzantium, still alienated from their largely anti-Chalcedonian counterparts in northern Syria. Perhaps this explains why the Byzantines were happy to accept a pact with the Hamdanids who nominally recognised Byzantine sovereignty over the region around Aleppo.

Playing off Byzantines vs Fatimids

To detail the confused history of the next few decades would baffle the reader more than it would enlighten. Basically, the events from the Byzantine occupation of Aleppo in 968, two years after the death of Sayf al-Dawla, until the end of the Hamdanids forty years later was a three-way contest between Byzantine and Fatimids with the Hamdanids caught in the middle. Saʻd al-Dawla (r.967–91), Sayf al-Dawla's successor, was less famous than his father, whose reputation had rested on his artistic patronage. For several years after his nominal accession, he was kept out of Aleppo due to Fatimid attempts to take the city and to the machinations of his chamberlain, Kharguyah, who had done a deal with the Byzantines. In 975, however, the Byzantines decided to change horses when it was clear that the Kharguyah faction was also attempting to reach an understanding with the Fatimids. Restored to power in Aleppo with the help of a Byzantine army, Saʻd al-Dawla was obliged to sign a treaty with the Byzantine emperor in 981–2. This did not prevent the Hamdanid ruler, until his death ten years later, from continuing his attempts to play off Byzantines vs Fatimids, though in the end the result was simply that he undermined the basis of his legitimacy within his own domains.

These games continued under his successor Saʻid al-Dawla (r.991–1002). The Byzantines now pushed further into Syria to stem Fatimid advances. In 994–5, the Byzantine emperor Basil II had to rescue the Hamdanid ruler from a Fatimid siege of Aleppo and went on to take most of the Orontes Valley. This advance was later reversed when the Fatimids defeated a Byzantine army near Apamea in 998. Three years later, a peace treaty was signed between the Fatimid ruler al-Hakim and the Byzantine emperor, which included a side agreement between al-Hakim and Saʻid al-Dawla of Aleppo.

A self-serving court; a glorious failure?

The Hamdanids 'died from within' to adapt the phrase of their recent chronicler, Ramzi Bikhazi.[9] From their Aleppo base they lacked the access to resources in manpower and treasure which would enable them to sustain a commanding role in northern Syria and the Jazira. A power base stretching well to the east should have given them access to greater resources. In the first half of the tenth century, however, Aleppo's agricultural environment had been devastated by the looting of crops and consequent desertion of villages.[10] Under the Hamdanids the situation had temporarily improved but possibly largely because of the growth of transit trade. The Byzantines allowed Aleppo to be used as a customs station for trade to and from the east. The Hamdanid lords became the wealthiest *amirs* in the Islamic world but spent much of the earnings to 'acquire lasting glory by showering with precious gifts their kinsmen and the poets who eulogised them'. Agriculture remained stagnant to the point where the city had to import foodstuffs from Byzantine Antioch. Having squandered their income, the Hamdanids lacked the necessary treasure to meet the costs of campaigning.[11]

Curtain-raiser to the Crusades?

Looking back on the period from 968 to 1055, it is clear that Byzantium's main aim was to ensure that no other external power took direct control in northern Syria. A relative state of equilibrium prevailed with Constantinople, Baghdad and Cairo striving to avoid any direct clashes with each other. Baghdad's role was restricted to serving as a springboard for the rise of Turkic ambitions under the auspices of the 'Abbasid Caliphate. In the context of Egyptian vs Anatolian rivalry in northern Syria, it is perhaps remarkable the extent to which Aleppo repeated the pivotal role it had played between these same entities two millennia earlier. This time the Hamdanids were merely the playthings of two regional powers, Byzantines and Fatimids, who were happy enough to tolerate a weak local princely presence which kept northern Syria as a nominally neutral zone between empires. When it came to contests with the real interests of the quasi-imperial powers in Constantinople and in Egypt, Aleppo could do little more than try to play one off against the other. This provided a rare opportunity for local regimes to emerge in northern Syria. In the process, however, the region was exposed to multiple internal causes of instability.

The Hamdanid handling of the Byzantine presence in northern Syria provided a curtain-raiser to the region's response to the more sustained Christian threat to the Islamic domains in Syria/Palestine in the next century. The Byzantines stayed long enough, especially along the coast, to construct a series of fortifications to remind Syrians that Greek territorial ambitions had not been forgotten. Many of these forts in fact provided the cores around which later Crusader castles were built. While this Byzantine occupation might be expected to have alerted the Islamic rulers of Syria to the existence of a concerted Christian threat, in fact it seems to have had the opposite effect of encouraging complacency. Byzantine ambitions had been contained, deals could be done, it was not the end of the earth to bide one's time.

A recent study of the Byzantine/Hamdanid contest of this period has underlined another factor that might explain the complacency of the Islamic powers in northern Syria. While northern Syria was clearly involved in another of the 'great power' rivalries partly reflecting its geographic position at the intersection of three worlds, it is possible that the Byzantines' ambitions were a little more parochial and focused essentially on their interests in eastern Anatolia. The immediate objective for the Byzantines was to secure Cilicia and thus prevent

Figure 5.6 Byzantine fortified tower around which the later Crusader castle of Saône was built (today's Saladin Castle)

unexpected surprises emerging onto the Anatolian plateau via the Cilician Gates just as Heraclius in the 630s was prepared to sacrifice Aleppo and its region to provide Anatolia with a *cordon sanitaire*.[12]

There was, however, undoubtedly also a religious dimension to the *realpolitik* confrontation in the area. Thierry Bianquis has noted that Sayf al-Dawla 'was motivated throughout his life by the desire to be a *ghazi*, a knight of the *jihad*'. The cause of the confrontation with the Byzantines attracted volunteers from throughout the central Muslim lands as far as Iraq.[13] Aleppo, however, even with the Jazira and Mosul, lacked the resources to pursue a strategy reaching beyond its own region and take on a power (Byzantium) able to deploy a massive standing army, protected by a formidable defence in depth and with hundreds of years of military lessons to draw on.

This enforced complacency would change in the second half of the eleventh century with the arrival of a third force from the east. A more significant power would emerge with a new phase of the Turkic ascendancy – their first formed ethnically based state. The Seljuks had stemmed from an Oghuz Turkish group who had migrated into central Iran and converted to Sunni Islam en masse in 985. We noted earlier the gradual rise to influence in the 'Abbasid court of the Turkic mercenaries raised from infancy as an elite praetorian guard, later assuming a dominant position in the armed forces and as power brokers further afield including Egypt (Tulunids, Ikhshidids). One other manifestation of Turkic ascendancy in the region was in Iran where Turkic members of the Seljuk clan had adopted Persian culture after taking the province of Khurasan in 1040. Their first leader was Tughrul Bey (r.1016–63) who had added Baghdad to the Seljuk domains in 1055 (as noted below, page 100). While the enfeebled ʿAbbasids had no alternative but to accept Turkic 'protection', the Byzantines viewed the threat as more than a localised opportunistic takeover. If the Turks with their remarkable dedication and military skills were to gain a foothold in eastern Anatolia, they would prove to be a more formidable threat than anything that weakened and divided Syria could have offered.

Mirdasids (1024–80)

Before picking up again this still 'over the horizon' Turkish dimension, there is one more phase in Aleppo's eleventh-century experience that continued the Hamdanids' balancing act between Byzantines and the Islamic powers of Iraq and Egypt. The Mirdasids were an Arab tribal group based on the Bedouin Banu Kilab who held the territory south and east of Aleppo and had often intruded into the settled country around Maʿarat al-Numan (see Figure 5.3). They had largely been kept in check under the Hamdanids but with the breakdown of authority, especially under pressure from the Byzantines and the Fatimids, they made themselves useful to the competing power centres in Baghdad, Cairo and Constantinople for opportunistic gain.

By 1017, the Fatimids had a precarious hold on Aleppo but were opposed by the Banu Kilab under Salih Ibn Mirdas (r.1024–9), the figure who gave his name to the new regime which in 1024 was invited by the citizens of Aleppo to take the city from its Fatimid governor. The Fatimid garrison which held out in the Aleppo Citadel finally succumbed, providing Mirdas temporarily with a new realm stretching from Aleppo to Sidon in modern Lebanon. This Mirdasid kingdom soon attracted the hostility of the Byzantines, whose hold on Antioch had endured. At ʿAzaz, north of Aleppo, the Mirdasids defeated a large Byzantine army in 1030. Byzantine strength in the area remained, however, and a peace treaty with the Byzantines the next year required the Mirdasids to pay a yearly tribute, a gesture which provoked an outburst from the youths of Aleppo. The treaty was renewed in 1038–9 following an international conference in Constantinople involving Fatimids, Byzantines and the statelets of northern Syria, largely confirming Aleppo's de facto status as a Byzantine protectorate.

The Mirdasids were even more entrammelled by the confrontations with the Byzantines and the Fatimids than the Hamdanids had been. In the confused world of eleventh-century northern Syria, the Mirdasids' claim to be a second authentic Arab regime of stature never quite convinced given their background as the marauding Bedouin of the region. Though they were in fact more attuned to urban Islamic institutions than most Bedouin tribal groups, they still had difficulty in escaping the reputation of the steppe nomads who preferred pillage to administration.

To the south, in Damascus, the Fatimids had a more secure hold but constantly sought to assert sovereignty as far as Aleppo. They succeeded several times between 1038 and 1060 with the contest between Byzantines and Fatimids again adding a dizzying element to the interplay of northern Syrian Bedouin politics. In 1042, Thimal Ibn Salih, son of Salih Ibn Mirdas, was invited by the Aleppines into the city, though it took another six months to dislodge the Fatimid garrison from the Citadel.

Under Thimal (r.1042–62) the city came to enjoy periods of stability and predictable administration. He confirmed Aleppo's protectorate status each year by sending envoys to both the Byzantine and the Fatimid courts with an annual tribute, an arrangement in the end troubled by renewed challenges to Mirdasid rule fostered by the Fatimids.[14]

The Turcoman factor

One small incident in 1063 picks up the Turkic narrative again and signals a new dimension to the confusion of north Syrian/Jazira politics. As background, it should be noted that among the first Turkic speakers to exercise power as a distinct ethnic group in the Islamic lands were the Seljuks, who as noted above had reached Baghdad by 1055. In Baghdad, their leader Tughrul became protector of the ʿAbbasid Caliph, a role given a new title 'sultan' affirming his temporal as opposed to religious authority. Exploiting this new status, Seljuk Turks were later to play a significant role in the affairs of Egypt, Syria and Iraq as our narrative unfolds.

The first case was soon to emerge. In expectation that family rivalries would be touched off by Thimal's death, in 1063 a group of one thousand freelance Turcoman[15] archers originally from Diyarbakir were hired in eastern Syria by ʿAtiyya (Thimal's brother) towards the end of Thimal's rule. The Turkmen were employed to seize control of Aleppo in a contest which would be won in 1065 by Mahmud Ibn Nasr, who banished his uncle ʿAtiyya to Rahba down the Euphrates. There was a price for the Turkmen's services as mercenaries. The first instalment came with the realisation that the arrival of the Turcoman military contingent would open Syria to other waves of Turkic groups including the Great Seljuks themselves, then based at Isfahan in Iran.[16]

The fact that the Seljuks now had a foothold so far west sounded an alarm with the Byzantines, who had still managed to hold on in Antioch. During their rapid rise to international power, the Seljuks 'had preserved intact their ethnic and tribal identity, and with it their military strength'.[17] The Turkmen were deadly raiders. Byzantine operations against them in the Aleppo area underlined the cost to Mirdasid Aleppo of this exposure. Mahmud was convinced that something had to be done to extract the city from the Turcoman-Byzantine confrontation. As he put it to the citizens at a rally in Aleppo in 1070, 'if he did not yield to the Seljuks, he would be smashed by them'.[18] His answer was twofold: open the gates of the city to the only Muslim power capable of both controlling their Turcoman followers while fending off constant Byzantine raids; and renounce the city's attachment to Shi'i Islam by accepting the Sunni 'Abbasid Caliph (thus dropping the Fatimid *khutba*).

Seljuk foothold in Aleppo 1071

The background to the new reality facing Aleppo was that Baghdad itself had since 1055 been under the direct control of the Seljuk Turks (after 1063 led by Alp Arslan). Alp Arslan, assuming the new title of sultan – nominally subject to the Baghdad Caliph but in all things secular the 'Abbasid supreme commander – demanded as the price for Aleppo's protection that the Mirdasids stay on under Seljuk sovereignty. When the Mirdasid Mahmud Ibn Nasr hesitated and the people of Aleppo mounted their own resistance to the Seljuk siege, Alp Arslan appeared before the city in 1071. Resistance quickly crumbled and Aleppo became the first victory in the Seljuks' campaign to restore Sunni orthodoxy in Syria. Within fifteen years, the Seljuks controlled Damascus and shortly after a Seljuk general prised even Antioch from the Byzantines.

The era of the Turkic forces, rightly assessed as 'an event of immense significance for the Islamic world', was to have consequences even more momentous beyond the Crusades yet it is little remarked in most general histories of the area.[19] It was, however, to lead to centuries of domination by branches of the Turkic people up to 1918. Perhaps this lack of emphasis is due not only to the Western fascination with the prevalent narrative of the Christian perspective on the Crusades but also to the lack of physical remains of that era, at least in Syria.

The Mirdasids had remarkably managed to move from a local steppe-based society (their pedigree in the region was even better established than the Hamdanids) to an urban-based structure, albeit one often forced to accept subordinate status from the competing empires whose perimeters touched on the region. The settled lands of northern Syria and the Jazira were abundant enough to assure them of enough revenue to fund a state structure. In the end, however, the juggling act failed. Bringing the Turkmen into the equation made the balance unsustainable. Their appetites could not be tamed; their raids depleted the resources of the countryside and disrupted trade. Aleppo had no choice but to bow to the inevitable.

Manzikert 1071

If there is one event which brought to a climax (but not a resolution) the confused power play that had welled up since the tenth century, it was the battle between Byzantine and Seljuk forces at Manzikert in eastern Anatolia in 1071. The Byzantine comprehensive defeat at Manzikert became the event that sounded the alarm which was to ring out in the sermon launching the First Crusade at Vézelay in France twenty years later. Yet the battle was an event almost totally unrelated to the context it was soon to acquire. It may seem odd that an event that happened well to the northeast of the Crusading arena of the next two centuries gave rise to the new mentality that lay behind the Crusades.

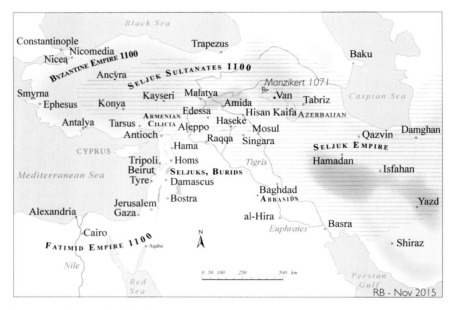

Figure 5.7 Rise of the Seljuks, to 1100

We have already signalled, however, the rising dread that shook Byzantine complacency. This went beyond the long-standing fear of being overrun by the forces of Islam from the steppe lands and deserts of Syria and Arabia. The Byzantines had had five centuries to accustom themselves to competition from these quarters. The fear now was of a new enemy arriving more directly from the East and the limitless spaces of Central Asia. The fact that the newly converted Seljuks had embraced a more sharply defined brand of Sunni Islam (contrasted with the endemic divisions that prevailed among and within the different faiths of Syria) gave further emphasis to the threat.

There were two fateful outcomes that condemned the old balance of power. First, Manzikert 'completed the ruins of Byzantine military strength' in eastern Anatolia;[20] instead of retiring eastwards after each raid, the Turkic forces could now wander at will. Second, the remaining Christian populations of Armenia and Cappadocia were now abandoned by the Byzantines to do their own separate deals with the newcomers.

Seljuks take direct power in Aleppo (1086)

We noted above that the Seljuks had besieged Aleppo in 1071 under Alp Arslan. Though victorious, the Seljuks retired to leave the city again under Mirdasid control. They watched from afar as the Mirdasids once more dissolved into chaos. In 1086, Malik Shah, Alp Arslan's son and successor as Seljuk sultan in Baghdad (r.1072–92), was virtually invited in by the Aleppines to end the anarchy which had found them at the mercy of two empires (Seljuk and Byzantine) and of the local Arab confederations. On Malik Shah's death in 1092, his three sons and their uncle would divide up the domains now ruled by the Seljuk Turks including further new gains in western Anatolia. Aleppo had become a small centre in a Seljuk world which had suddenly burst out of tenth-century Persia. In this Turkic world post-1092, power was parcelled out to minor family members – in Aleppo's case Aqsunqur al-Hajib (r.1086–94) and Tutush (r.1094–95), brother of Malik Shah, and his son Ridwan (r.1095–1113). Seljuk intra-family rivalry, however, was often an obstacle to cooperation, as we will see in the case of Ridwan and his brother Duqaq in Damascus (r.1095–1104).

The development of Seljuk architectural and decorative style is best studied in Iran where their experience was greatly influenced by Persian traditions. The evidence is complicated by the complete change in materials employed – brick and plaster in Iran/Mesopotamia; stone in Syria where easily worked limestone was in plentiful supply near most centres. The evolution of the architectural vocabulary adopted by the Great Seljuks during their thirty-year ascendancy in Syria is thus difficult to trace. Many of their ideas, however, came from their capacities to reflect influences absorbed during their passage through Persian and Arab cultures to the east. It was not a case of one culture obliterating another. While in the present state of our knowledge, this era (1080–1160) is sometimes assumed to be a 'dark age', the reality seems to have been more complicated. Arab, Persian and Turkic cultures inter-acted with each other in a creative way in spite of the fragmented political and religious worlds across which ideas migrated.[21]

The testament of the Great Mosque minaret 1090–4

The Aleppo minaret should provide a superb example of this ability to synthesise various traditions but it was tragically toppled by shellfire during the Syrian conflict in April 2013 and is at the time of writing a pile of fragmented stones scattered around a corner of the mosque courtyard alongside the north entrance that it once flanked. Its rich decoration had covered five levels separated by inscription bands. Though some details possibly owed their origins to repair work after an earthquake the next century, the minaret provided the impression of a rich interplay between Classical ideas, Seljuk forms introduced from their Central Asian and Persian experiences as well as convoluted decoration inspired by the plastic arts (usually in stucco) of ʿAbbasid Samarra and Baghdad. However, a search for direct comparisons of its style has been a frustrating exercise for experts. Yasser Tabbaa has rightly concluded that searching for paths of transmission of ideas directly from other areas has to be balanced against the overwhelming likelihood that the Aleppo minaret is also a product of the local environment.[22]

The minaret was commissioned by the Islamic judge or *qadi* of Aleppo, Abu'l Hasan Muhammad Ibn al-Khashshab, perhaps to serve as a beacon of Islam in troubled times. The influence of the Banu (family) al-Khashshab ran through

Figure 5.8 Minaret of the Great Mosque in Aleppo

many decades of Aleppo's history (and will be examined further in Chapter 6). The minaret was the first intervention by the qadi signaling the dynamic role he would play, effectively saving the city from anarchy over much of the period 1085–1125. He engaged an architect, Hasan Ibn Mukri al-Sarmini, whose name indicates his origins in the small town of Sarmin 50 kilometres to the south of Aleppo that seems to have played a consistent role in supplying architectural and stone-cutting skills in the region. The architect used his own native sense of taste and proportion to produce what was a masterpiece of Islamic architecture – 'the principal monument of medieval Syria', 'of unique significance', reflecting in Herzfeld's view the architect's awareness of the models he saw about him in the hundreds of 'Dead Cities' that dotted the plains and hill country around Aleppo.[23] To the myriad of 'classicising' features (engaged pilasters and capitals, moulded and dentil bands), al-Sarmini added Seljuk and Islamic elements (inscription bands, *muqarnas* friezes) without the slightest trace of assertive self-confidence. What could have been a mess on the scale of a Las Vegas casino facade was instead a brilliant amalgam of taste and proportion.

For a brief moment just before 1100, the world of near-anarchy, at the centre of which stood Aleppo, was ended. The interplay of three faith-based super-powers (Christian Byzantium, Sunni Baghdad, Shi'i Cairo) appeared resolved in favour of the new Turkic element which through its ruthlessness, military skills and religious single mindedness might have aspired to end the anarchic interplay further fuelled by local Bedouin aspirations. Moreover, the Turkic rulers encouraged a new flourishing of the arts (including poetry, this was the era of Omar Khayyam in Iran). Education was allowed to flourish too in the strictly Islamic form of the first *madrasas* or the *khanqahs*, monasteries devoted to the Sufi trend, with the intention of drawing Syrians back from their dalliance with Shi'ism.

This golden age, however, was to be brief. The Seljuk model ended one period of anarchy but brought another in the form of rivalry between the various family members enfranchised through the segmented world of the Turkic political sphere. Into this calm interlude before a new collapse came the Crusaders – fresh, naïve and ruthless; not interested in the complexities of the region; and inspired by one doctrine of faith unifying cross and sword.

Notes

1 Kennedy 2004: 214.
2 Turkic is the generic term used to embrace all the Turkic-language population groups that spread westwards from Central Asia. For present purposes, they are also referred to as Turks. Turkey and Turkish are used to refer to the inhabitants and language primarily of modern Anatolia and of the lands of the Ottoman Empire. For a better definition, see Findley (2004: ebook loc 211). See also note 15 below on 'Turcoman'.
3 Findley 2004: e-book loc 1400.
4 Bianquis, however, notes that the family was possibly of Kurdish origin or at least maintained close links with the Kurds – 'Sayf a-Dawla' *EI*2.
5 Bianquis 'Sayf al-Dawla' *EI*2.
6 Sauvaget believed there might also be evidence of Hamdanid rebuilding in the Antioch Gate of the city walls.
7 'Sheikh' Muhassin appears to be a reference to the stillborn infant cited by later historians, giving his lineage from Hussein (through his wife, Fatima), 'Ali and the latter's father, Abi Talib. (Mulder 2014: 73) This is based on a reference in the founding inscription of Sayf al-Dawla, which disappeared in later rebuilding.
8 Quoted in le Strange (1890: 360).
9 Bikhazi 1981: 979.
10 Ibn al-'Adim (quoted in Bianquis 1991: 53) reports that Aleppo in the 940s was merely 'a town amidst villages' whose products included olives, pistachios, sumac and figs. In the situation of constant unrest, these orchards were often ravaged by competing

armies, giving little opportunity to process and market what product they could salvage. Most of its exports to Iraq, for instance, were sent to Raqqa, which provided the main entrepôt to process the trade.

11 Bianquis 'Sayf al-Dawla' *EI2*. See also Bianquis (1991: 54).
12 Garrood 2008.
13 Bianquis 'Sayf al-Dawla' *EI2*.
14 Thimal's reign was interrupted by four years of direct Fatimid rule 1057–61.
15 To simplify a clearly confusing issue, I have used Turcoman as a singular noun and an adjective to indicate Turkic speakers originating in Turkestan (modern Turkmenistan) but who had migrated to form communities further west. Turkmen is used to indicate the plural of same.
16 Paul Cobb sees the implications of the Seljuk takeover going much further: 'the road to [the Crusader taking of] Jerusalem in 1099 begins in Aleppo in 1064' (Cobb 2014: 78).
17 'Saljuq' in Bloom and Blair 2009: III, 166.
18 Bianquis 'Mirdasids' *EI2*.
19 El-Azhari 2005: 111.
20 Cahen 1969: 149.
21 'This brilliant era . . . had been successful in meeting both internal and external challenges because it managed to make new and meaningful syntheses from the many features which made up the contemporary Islamic world.' (Ettinghausen et al. 2001: 135).
22 Tabbaa 1993: 33–4.
23 Herzfeld 1943: 35; Herzfeld 1955: I/1 164.

6

FORTRESS OF ISLAM – ALEPPO AND THE FIRST CRUSADE (1098–1127)

Seljuks 1078–1117
Artuqids 1117–27
Zengids 1127–70

A Christian *jihad*?

One lesson is conveyed by Aleppo's experiences during the century preceding the First Crusade's arrival at Antioch in 1098: the phenomenon of the Crusades cannot be explained solely in terms of a single-track Western religious motivation – a 'holy war' for Christianity.[1] Pope Urban II's sermon at Clermont in France in 1095 is usually seen as the 'starting point' of the movement which took as its rallying call 'God wills it!' However, the original Western response was touched off by the call from the Orthodox Church in Constantinople for help against the Turks, who in 1071, as we have just noted, had trumped a Byzantine army at Manzikert in eastern Turkey.

In fact it took the Crusading movement some time to focus on the recovery of Jerusalem as its prime objective. That city had been taken by a Seljuk general on behalf of Alp Arslan in 1073 but had since returned to Fatimid hands. Nevertheless, Pope Urban is quoted as putting the challenge in the following terms:

> Under Jesus Christ, our Leader, may you struggle for your Jerusalem . . .
> even more successfully than did the sons of Jacob of old – struggle, that
> you may assail and drive out the Turks, more execrable than the Jebusites
> (Canaanites) who are in this land.[2]

The simple call to faith in 'God wills it' provided the sound bite in 1095 but how had the objective of reversing Manzikert shifted focus to Jerusalem? The fact is that virtually all players in the Crusading period over the next two centuries had quite different strategic preoccupations, not least the Crusaders and the Byzantines. It was not the Christian inhabitants of Syria/Palestine who appealed for Western help against the Turks but the Byzantines seeking allies to hold back Turkic inroads in Asia Minor. Byzantine attempts to restore direct rule in northern Syria beyond Antioch had petered out with Basil II's peace of 1001 signed with the Fatimid ruler al-Hakim (see page 96). We have seen that the Byzantine tenth-century misadventure in northern Syria probably related more to retaining Byzantium's hold on Anatolia than to any ambitions favouring the Christians of Syria.

There is a confusion of war aims here that did not help to focus the eventual military campaign. Not one Syrian-Christian leader, for example, had appealed to the Pontiff to ask that the Western church intervene. In the words of Runciman:

> The lot of the Christians in Palestine had seldom been so pleasant. The Muslim authorities were lenient; the (Byzantine) Emperor was watchful of their interests. Trade was prospering and increasing with the Christian countries overseas. And never before had Jerusalem enjoyed so plentifully the sympathy and wealth that were brought to it by pilgrims from the West.[3]

The Crusades should be seen, then, as part of a much larger picture manipulated by outside players such as the Byzantine emperor and with numerous local groups pursuing their own ends but only partially under a religious banner.

We have seen in the previous chapter that Aleppo, a city that had survived against the odds, continued to play a role well above the level its population might warrant. It balanced precariously on the interface between Constantinople, Cairo and Baghdad, often shifting adroitly to play off one empire against another. Even assessed only at the regional level, it had proved to be a significant foil against Antioch, a city that had remained under the Byzantines until taken by Turcoman forces shortly before the Crusades.

Alone, however, Aleppo could not offer sustained resistance to the huge forces of the Crusaders. Like most of the Muslim East, it had been slow to appreciate the Crusade's ideological dimension. At first, too, the scale of the Crusader presence was not appreciated in the region: 'In the literatures of Iraq and Egypt (the wars against the Franks) were hardly mentioned, in that of Iran not at all' and it was only the 'length and nature of the Frankish occupation which would gradually provoke a reaction'.[4] Carole Hillenbrand drew the same conclusion from the Arabic sources: 'There is no sense that the Crusaders are an unusual kind of enemy, with a fundamentally new agenda.'[5] She has rightly noted that had the Crusaders arrived ten years earlier, it would have been met with a 'strong, unified resistance' under Malik Shah, the last of the three Great Seljuk sultans. In 1098, however, the Muslim world lacked effective leadership, fragmented into small principalities under only nominal Seljuk command. 'The timing of the First Crusade could not have been more propitious' – for the Crusader cause.[6] The lack of focus on the Muslim side was intensified by the ideological battle between Sunni Baghdad and Shi'i Cairo. Seljuk suspicion of Fatimid designs in the Levant and Baghdad's distraction with family feuds further east meant that no Seljuk sultan identified the strategic threat let alone took to the field to emulate Alp Arslan's response at Manzikert thirty years previously. It should be no surprise that initial Muslim attempts to break the Crusader siege of Turkic-held Antioch were so half-hearted.

Investing Antioch (1097–8)

The First Crusade had arrived at the walls of Antioch in October 1097. The challenge faced by the tens of thousands of Crusaders camped around the city's formidable walls was immense. The city had been held since 1084 by a Seljuk governor, Yaghi-Siyan, on behalf of the Baghdad dynasty – one of the last great cities of the central Arab lands to fall into their hands. The garrison was relatively small but it was a further eight months before the Crusaders could take the city.

Enough remains today of the upper reaches of the 5 kilometres of Byzantine city walls to give an impression of the sheer scale of the defences. The city lay between the banks of the Orontes and the twin heights of Mounts Silpius and Staurin to the northeast guarding the narrow river plain (see Figure 3.10 on page 67). The walls embraced not only the town but also the heights behind with a formidable citadel running along the ridge. The Crusaders could not storm such a daunting enclosure by direct attack and even a prolonged siege was compromised by the length of the walls, the difficult terrain and the impossibility of monitoring all the possible points of entry and exit. The Crusaders also lacked a reliable supply chain to feed their men, camp followers and mounts – though this was also a problem shared with the Antiochean defenders.

Figure 6.1 Remains of the Byzantine walls of Antioch as seen in 1780s by French artist François-Louis Cassas (*Voyage pittoresque de la Syrie*, Paris 1798)

During the eight-month siege, the first Muslim force deployed against the Crusaders encircling the city was sent not by Ridwan in nearby Aleppo but by his detested brother, Duqaq of Damascus. In December 1097, the Damascus army was heading north to take the pressure off the Seljuk garrison in Antioch. The Damascus force encountered by happenstance a contingent under the command of Bohemond of Taranto (later to become Prince of Antioch) foraging in the region near al-Bara in the Jebel al-Summaq. Both armies were badly mauled in the fighting and there was no clear winner, though Duqaq's force retreated to Damascus abandoning further operations in the area.

Aleppo, only one of a constellation of Seljuk states, in itself lacked the size to sustain forces in the field against the Crusaders, tired but battle-hardened after their eventful march across Asia Minor. Among the local Seljuk states, the intense rivalry between Duqaq in Damascus and Ridwan in Aleppo prevented coordination of their plans. It was five months into the siege before Ridwan of Aleppo, at Yaghi-Siyan's request, reluctantly agreed to make his first attempt to break the Crusader siege. Ridwan might only have decided to support the garrison now

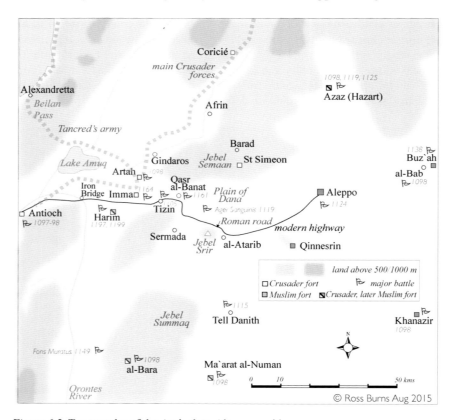

Figure 6.2 Topography of the Antioch to Aleppo corridor

besieging Crusader Antioch as he had come to fear that the Crusaders were close to threatening Aleppo itself. However, Ridwan's 12,000-strong expeditionary force was routed outside the walls of Antioch in February 1098 through a brilliant cavalry charge led by Bohemond.

Antioch vs Aleppo (1098–1119)

On 3 June 1098, Crusader forces prised their way into Antioch's defences and managed to take over the city during the night, though the upper Citadel remained in Muslim hands. The resulting massacre of many of the town's Muslim population (and not a few of its Christians) did much to spread fear of the Crusaders' prowess and determination to stop at nothing. Ironically, it was only four days later that a joint Seljuk force commanded by the Baghdad sultan Kerbogha arrived at Antioch. The Turkish forces camped south of the city and waited. Again it was Bohemond's adept generalship that managed to reverse the advantages in numbers and horses enjoyed by the Muslim forces. He led a Crusader contingent out of the city and tackled the Seljuks attempting to invest Antioch on 28 June. Bohemond's forces scattered the first wave of attackers causing them to fall back amongst their own units. In the chaos, the Crusaders' victory was so decisive that the Muslim army fled. This battle could easily have resulted in the near annihilation of the Crusaders' precarious hold on Antioch; instead, the weaknesses of the Seljuk command throughout the campaign had meant that the city, and soon its Citadel, were confirmed in Crusader hands.

Even during the course of the struggle for Antioch, the effects of the contest began to be more widely felt in the neighbouring region. Feeding the Crusader armies had been a major distraction that required foraging expeditions into the rich plains both east of Antioch and to the southeast in the direction of Ma'arat al-Numan. Few of these initial engagements with Muslim forces resulted in Crusader attempts to garrison inland positions. The crucial advantages of holding the western end of the old Roman route leading from Antioch east to Aleppo began to be clear, however, when the post of Artah (outside modern Reyhanli) was taken in the course of the siege campaign. The town of Ma'arat al-Numan was for a time taken by a Crusader force under Raymond Pilet in November 1098. Challenged by a contingent of Aleppines, the Crusaders were forced to retreat in January 1099 during a harsh winter marked by serious losses, starvation and a desperate resort to cannibalism. After the taking of Antioch, Crusader leaders looked to the possibility of setting up more permanent footholds in the region around Antioch and we will see in the following pages the critical role played by the fortifications in this area over the next twenty-five years.

War aims

The campaign for Antioch and the feeble role played by Aleppo in countering the Crusader invasion raises the following question: did the Crusaders have ambitions to complete the securing of the region by taking Seljuk Aleppo? Put another way: why was Antioch the major objective and not Aleppo? One possible explanation is that it was an improvised decision. Antioch, it is often assumed by historians, was on the Crusaders' path, was once the great metropolis of the East, still enjoyed some Christian associations and was an objective readily endorsed by the expedition 'partners', the Byzantines, who had themselves repossessed the city earlier in the century before it was taken by the Seljuks, and had designs to get it back.

In response, it can be argued in strictly strategic terms that Aleppo might have been a better first objective. It had a weak government and was imperfectly integrated into the 'Abbasid Caliphate through Seljuk 'protectors' who were perpetually squabbling and had initially shown little interest in blocking the Crusaders' advance. In the 1190s, Aleppo would still have had a sizeable Christian population and its capture would have eased the integration of the Crusader outpost at Edessa (see below) into the wider Christian realm. Moreover, in terms of the Christians' path, Aleppo was also a reasonable stopping point. The fact that both Aleppo and Antioch had formidable citadels, requiring immense effort if they were to be overcome, was a neutral factor. Perhaps a clinching argument was that Antioch enjoyed easy access to the port at St Simeon (ancient Seleucia). The Crusaders could not afford to be too remote from the most immediate lifeline available to them, the Mediterranean. Taking Aleppo would still leave the need to move against Antioch to secure the Orontes route to the coast. A second massive siege campaign might indeed have sapped Crusader resources to the limit.

For the moment, Aleppo was bypassed but the idea of taking it did not disappear from Crusader minds. It would be twenty years after taking Antioch, however, before the Crusaders put sustained pressure on this major Muslim strongpoint in the region. In the meantime they gave priority to securing their access through Asia Minor (via Cilicia), to safeguarding their sea communications and to forging their onwards path to Jerusalem. To take one of the formidable inland strongholds of Islamic civilisation in Syria (Jerusalem apart) was something the Crusaders would never achieve. This failure would ultimately lead to the rolling back of the Christian presence along the coastal plains. We will assess later in this chapter the Crusaders' first feint at Aleppo itself but it seems unlikely that they could have seriously contemplated such a problematic strategic move before they had consolidated the Principality of Antioch.

We lack any first-hand accounts of how the news of the taking of Antioch was received in Aleppo. We have seen that there was still little appreciation of the extent to which the Crusader army was a strategic challenge, as distinct from another of those seasonal incursions along the lines of the Byzantines' recent exploratory probes. The possibility that the massive Crusader army would stay or would not confine its operations to its stated objective of Jerusalem may have been far from the minds of the Seljuk leadership.

If the extent of the Crusader threat to the inland Muslim states was still to become apparent, Aleppo must surely have slowly begun to appreciate that it now faced a new, strange, hostile and unpredictable enemy on three sides. This near

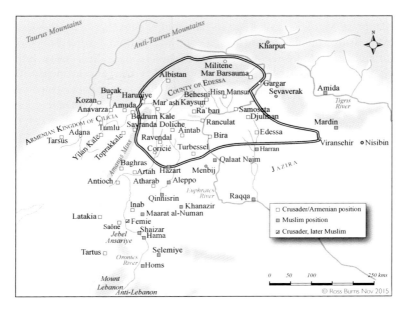

Figure 6.3 County of Edessa (double line) and the Kingdom of Armenian Cilicia

encirclement had come about through an eccentric move by Baldwin of Boulogne who had split off from the main Crusader army as it crossed Asia Minor in 1098 and proceeded to Edessa, well to the east. Baldwin, attracted by the offer of a marriage alliance with a local Armenian family, accepted an invitation to visit Edessa even before the taking of Antioch. Baldwin's quixotic initiative was one of the first examples of the tension among the Crusader leaders between the demands of faith and the desire for territory.

This deflection away from the main Crusading effort gave the Crusaders a new preoccupation: how to secure lines of communication from Antioch to Edessa, circumventing Aleppo. If the Edessa move had any justification beyond a spirit of adventurism on the part of Baldwin, it would certainly present a major concern for Aleppo. Though the life of the Edessa county was to be less than fifty years, it meant that for the first critical period of the Crusader presence in northern Syria, Aleppo had to contend with conflict on two fronts – the battle for the terrain between Aleppo and the principality founded at Antioch; and the threat from the Crusader-Armenian alliance to the north where Edessa could readily interdict Aleppo's main supply lines to its resources base in the Jazira and further east.

On to Jerusalem

After Antioch fell, the Crusader leaders held a council of war to decide on their future strategy in November 1098 at Rugia, south in the Orontes Valley. This resulted in a more concerted attempt to fortify the outer reaches of the new Principality of Antioch particularly in the Jebel al-Summaq, a challenge seized by Raymond of Toulouse, who at that stage was still contesting Bohemond of Taranto's claim to the principality of Antioch. The Crusaders' other priorities were the consolidation of their positions in Cilicia to the north (in uneasy alliance with the Christian Armenian presence implanted there in the previous century by the Byzantines) and securing the sea ports south of Antioch including Latakia. Antioch's eastern front stretching to Aleppo was left to the forces assigned to garrison Antioch (with some support from the neighbouring County of Edessa).

The main army proceeded to Jerusalem, Raymond having decided that his career path lay with the Jerusalem force. The earlier bloody occupation of Maʿarat al-Numan perhaps intentionally had already signalled to a Muslim audience the darker side of the Crusaders' methods that awaited any Muslim town that resisted their path: 'single-minded greed and cold-blooded brutality', in Asbridge's words.[7]

As a result, only a few of the most advantageous fortifications, those better positioned to guard the eastern perimeter of Antioch, were taken and garrisoned by the Jerusalem-bound Crusaders in these early days. Many Crusader leaders were to be torn between their stated religious mission and a desire to use the Crusades as an excuse to gain new fiefdoms in the East. Edessa had provided the template but the Afrin Valley and the 'Dead Cities' zone west of Aleppo were also tempting targets. The Jerusalem force, meanwhile, took a route skirting around Aleppo well to the southeast, through the territory already taken by Raymond. Maʿarat al-Numan had to be reoccupied (accompanied by more massacres). The main force continued down the Orontes Valley keeping the other major inland Muslim urban centres to their left, in some cases securing agreements on safe passage from their Muslim rulers.

The Antioch/Aleppo Front 1098–1120

We will leave the fate of the main Crusader army now and concentrate the rest of this chapter on events in the Antioch to Aleppo sector. An appreciation of the importance of this 85 kilometre route warrants a quick survey of its terrain. The road leaves the outskirts of Antioch heading northeast across the plain around Lake Amuq, today a lush irrigated area. The route crosses the Orontes River, which flows north from the central depression of western Syria before turning sharply west at a point known for many centuries as the Iron Bridge – today rather an exaggeration as the old stone bridge which was the last defence for Antioch over many centuries is now a sketchy ruin north of the modern highway. The historic bridge had fallen to the Crusaders in October 1097, even before Antioch. After the road crosses the Amuq Plain it passes the prosperous town of Reyhanli, the site of the fortress of Artah. Artah's castle (now gone) was long recognised as the strongpoint of Antioch's eastern defences before the highway takes a gradually rising path through rocky terrain (the site of the Battle of Tizin, to be described later on page 116).

After the modern border customs posts, you enter today's Syria glimpsing on the left the ruins of a Byzantine monastery, one of several given the popular title 'Women's Monastery' (Qasr al-Banat), before reaching another alluvial area, the Plain of Dana. The southern side of this plain was to be the scene of the important 1119 battle dubbed the 'Field of Blood' (to be discussed later). To the north is the striking symmetry of Jebel Sheikh Barakat, one of the 'high places' dotting the region noted earlier. Behind the mountain lies the great Church of St Simeon but we continue straight east to skirt another 'high place' (Jebel Srir), passing a remarkably intact stretch of paved Roman road built on a beautifully laid stone bench to carry it over the rocky terrain.

The road rises to the level of the Syrian steppe at al-Atarib, used by the Crusaders as a forward base for their campaigns against Aleppo. From there it is a straight run into Aleppo dodging numerous stone quarries exploiting the rich limestone deposits of the 'Dead Cities' zone. Until recently, the challenge of housing the flourishing economy of Aleppo was also eating into the countryside to the southeast so the last 10 kilometres before descending into the bowl that shelters the historic city of Aleppo is through densely arrayed high-rise apartments.

Through history, many armies have trodden this path but few experienced such a prolonged tussle for its control as in the events that marked the first twenty-five years of the Crusader presence. While this corridor was one of the most active theatres of conflict during the First Crusade, the focus of most Crusader historians

Figure 6.4 Surviving section of the Roman road from Antioch to Aleppo near the village of Tell Atarib

has been further south in the Kingdom of Jerusalem. The two northern Crusader entities, the County of Edessa and the Antioch Principality, are often only discussed when events in their territories had an impact to the south. Yet the northern corridor between the Muslim lands of the interior and the Crusader-held coast had a dynamic of its own. Aleppo served as the corridor's eastern-most pivot as the battle lines moved back and forth in the relatively open country. Figure 6.5 illustrates the intensity of this conflict.

At any point, the resources in men and weapons available on either side were insufficient to produce a decisive campaign. The notable victories were largely determined by good luck rather than sustained campaigning. The stakes were high. Both Crusaders and Muslims came close to taking each other's capital – in the case of Antioch, an outcome that would have proven disastrous to the whole Crusader enterprise before it had a chance to consolidate its presence in both Jerusalem and Edessa.

Recently, Thomas Asbridge has thrown more light on this example of a sustained tussle between two key cities of the Crusader period and examined the dynamics, particularly on the Crusader side.[8] As summarised by Asbridge, the struggle related to the difficulties of establishing a clear demarcation between the territories of the Muslim and Crusader states in the absence of any commanding topographic barrier. The battles moved back and forward like a chess game across the wide stretch of territory contested, nudging against the capitals on each side. It would require a long diversion to summarise the battles here but the essential aim on the Crusader side was to hold a line of defence as close to Aleppo as possible and east of the main line of hills (the 'Dead Cities' zone outlined earlier). The Crusaders' line ran south and southwest of Aleppo through the key positions at al-Atarib and Sardone and was vital in maintaining a lifeline to Edessa, swinging around Aleppo to the northeast via Hazart (modern 'Azaz). The Muslims sought to push the line as far as possible to the west, reaching for a time Artah and 'Imma on the eastern edge of the Plain of Amuq from where it would be easy to harass Antioch. If either power could hold their line, they could easily disrupt life in the other's capital and possibly even take the opponent's city if the defenders could be surprised.[9]

The first critical battle took place in 1105 in the relatively narrow and rocky pass that marks the eastern end of the rising ground east of Artah, after which the battle is sometimes named. (We noted this pass earlier on page 114.) More accurately the battle site was in the rocky no-man's land near the spring of Tizin, today still marked by Byzantine ruins south of the highway. Tancred, regent of Antioch, had assembled a sizeable army to retake Artah, which had initially been handed over by its Armenian citizens in 1098 but later briefly recaptured by the Seljuks. The Aleppan cavalry sought to adapt their traditional skills of archery and horsemanship (inherited by the Turks from their Sasanian predecessors), which involved initially ceding ground while relying on the 'parting shot' as they sped away – a hail of arrows released while swivelling 180 degrees in the saddle. Having then tired out the heavily armoured Crusader horses, Muslim forces

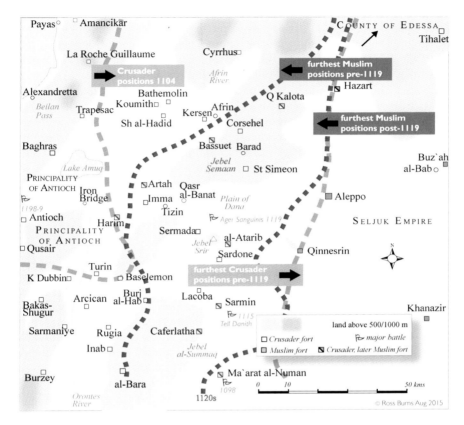

Figure 6.5 Fortifications of the Antioch to Aleppo corridor following the First Crusade

turned and sought to pick them off in a pitched battle. This time, however, the Seljuks were lured onto rocky ground that dispersed their formation, giving the Franks the upper hand and facilitating a Crusader victory.

Tancred's forces pursued the fleeing remnants of Ridwan's army as far as Aleppo, where they harassed and slaughtered many civilians seeking to flee before a truce was called. Tizin was the closest point to Antioch reached by the Muslim forces post-1098. Emboldened by their victory, the Crusaders then sought to sustain a front line as close as possible to Aleppo, virtually encircling the city by taking Hazart ('Azaz), al-Bab and the former Byzantine fortified site at Khanazir on the edge of the steppe to the southeast.

The second major engagement came in September 1115 at Tell Danith just south of Sarmin, a crucial Muslim position southwest of Aleppo protecting the route leading south, eventually to Damascus. The initiative this time came from the Seljuk sultan in Baghdad who sought a role in expelling the

Crusaders from Antioch and Edessa. After various skirmishes with Crusader forces from Antioch, Edessa and Jerusalem, the Baghdad army commanded by Bursuq of Hamadan sought to block future Frankish inroads constricting the main Aleppo–Damascus route. Bursuq's forces were camped near Tell Danith when they were surprised by a Crusader contingent which had combined in a temporary alliance with local Muslim forces from Aleppo and Damascus. The forces of Roger of Antioch (regent 1112–19) were particularly effective, forcing Bursuq's troops to withdraw and ending the intense jockeying for positions in the Jebel al-Summaq area southeast of Aleppo. This temporary alliance of local Muslim leaders with the Crusaders was the result of a common concern to prevent the Baghdad sultan assuming direct rule in Syria but was also to become part of a pattern of Muslim and Crusader leaders combining against a common foe.

Rising discontent in Aleppo

In the first twenty years after the Crusader taking of Antioch, the rather porous front line fluctuated wildly. Aleppo's position, however, changed as the threat on average moved closer and took on a permanent aspect. The consolidation of the Crusader corridor to Edessa via the Afrin Valley, Cyrrhus and Aintab meant that the frontier remained close to Aleppo to the north and northwest. It was only when Aleppo had organised its own internal affairs and was able to draw on the strength of the only hinterland available to it, the territory spreading east towards upper Mesopotamia and the Jazira, that it could adopt a more aggressive stance. Given that the Crusaders were by then often less than 10 kilometres from the walls of Aleppo, its rulers would inevitably see their role as one of the two major inland bastions, along with Damascus, against the Crusader armies. In the end, Aleppo's bastion would be even more steadfast than that of Damascus, partly under the sway of rising Sunni influence in the northern city now providing a renewal of Islamic fervour after years of Shi'i heterodoxy.

Before Aleppo could reach such a plateau of steady governance, however, it had to struggle through another period of prolonged internecine conflict.

> The main thread in the history of Moslem Syria during the next decade was the conflict which raged around Aleppo, as it oscillated between its more powerful neighbours, now appealing for their help and now playing them off against each other.[10]

Ridwan of Aleppo's excessive reliance internally on support from the most extreme faction among the Ismaelis (later to acquire the popular title of 'Assassins') aroused popular resentment. Feelings, particularly in response to the cynical pacts with Christian Antioch against other Muslim powers, registered particular resentment among the people. The figure who emerged to focus this feeling was Qadi Abu'l-Hasan Ibn al-Khashshab, a forthright preacher ('small of stature but loud of voice'). Ibn al-Khashshab was from a wealthy Shiʻi family and was noted earlier as the sponsor of the minaret of the Aleppo Great Mosque.[11]

In 1111, Qadi Ibn al-Khashshab led a large delegation to Baghdad, comprising theologians, descendants of the Prophet (*ashraf*) and Sufis as well as merchants seeking the intervention of the Caliph and sultan. After they burst into the sultan's mosque:

> They drove the preacher from his pulpit which they smashed. They then began to cry out, bewailing the evils that the Franks had inflicted on the Muslims by the massacre of men and the enslavement of women and children.[12]

Their dramatic intervention was repeated the next day at the Caliph's mosque but was initially received with indifference. Later, however, the Seljuk sultan, on hearing news of the fall of Sidon to the Crusaders, suddenly reached an appreciation of the great risk posed by the Franks and ordered the governor of Mosul to march to Aleppo's defence. When Ibn al-Khashshab returned to Aleppo, Ridwan was more alarmed at the imminent arrival of the force from Mosul than he was by the threat from Tancred. He had Ibn al-Khashshab imprisoned, denied the Mosul relief army supplies and sent them packing but not before the Mosul force took the opportunity to plunder the city's outskirts.

Popular dissatisfaction at the humiliation handed out by Tancred of Antioch, humiliation to which no Syrian leader seemed to have an answer, was now at a peak.[13] After Ridwan died (1113) his sixteen-year-old son, Alp Arslan, initially tried to appease the Aleppines by turning on the Ismaelis. He extended the bloodbath to include his brothers, advisers and officers. In the process, he lost his protective shield and was himself slain by his eunuch who was terrified that he might be next. There followed a brief reign of another son of Ridwan, six-year-old Sultan Shah (r.1114–17) but the Seljuk interlude was over.

> Under the leadership of the Qadi al-Khashshab, the citizens of Aleppo decided to take their fate into their own hands. . . . From this point on, a ground swell would slowly rise, beginning in the streets of Aleppo. Little by little it would inundate the streets of the Arab East.[14]

For the moment, however, Aleppo was a broken city – its economy shattered; its treasury empty. Constantly the prey of various Seljuk or Turcoman adventurers interested only in booty and not in protecting the city from the Franks, Aleppo needed a military figure to release it from of its slump. Such a leader might provide a way forward reflecting the qadi's belief that the city's position on Islam's front line required an end to survival dependent on precarious and humiliating deals with the Franks. The strongman who emerged was Ghazi Ibn Artuq, Artuqid ruler of Mardin and Diyarbakir, who was reluctantly endorsed by Ibn al-Khashshab and brought in to garrison the city for a fee in 1117/18.

The Field of Blood 1119

Ghazi's arrival could not have been better timed nor met with greater success. The third, and perhaps most critical, engagement on the Antioch–Aleppo corridor took place in 1119 northeast of Sermada. The consequences of this battle were so dire for the Crusaders that the site passed into history as the 'Field of Blood' (*Ager Sanguinis*).

The Franks had been closing in on Aleppo by retaking 'Azaz which had earlier been recovered by the Muslims some time before 1114. Baghdad had proved only sporadically interested in the fate of Muslim centres so far west. After failing to attract a Muslim relief force, the townspeople of 'Azaz had surrendered to the Crusaders who followed up by again encircling the city of Aleppo from the east, taking Buza'ah on the eastern outskirts of al-Bab. The environs of Aleppo were so unsafe that the annual caravan of pilgrims to Mecca was forced to pay tax to the Franks to ensure their passage.

By 1118, Ghazi had succeeded in forming a pact with Tughtagin, the Burid (Seljuk) ruler of Damascus. The armies of Aleppo and Damascus were to have assembled at Qinnisrin in June 1119 but Ghazi decided to take the fight to the Franks even before the Damascus troops arrived. Ghazi's first objective was al-Atarib, the customary rallying point for Crusader forces closing in on Aleppo. The decisive battle took place on ground near the town of Sermada, half way between al-Atarib and the Crusaders' last strongpoint before Antioch, Artah. Again, Roger

Figure 6.6 Town of Sermada with the scene of the 'Field of Blood' on the plain to the left

was commanding the Crusader forces. This time, the Crusaders suffered a crushing defeat. Not only was a large proportion of their 30,000-strong force killed (Roger was among the fatalities) but many of the survivors were led into Aleppo in captivity. The territory between Artah and Aleppo was now largely in Muslim hands.

The Artuqid forces of Ghazi, however, failed to follow through on their stunning victory. Earlier cries heard in Aleppo urging its citizens to join in *jihad* were not sustained. There was no attempt to move on Antioch. Part of the problem was Ghazi's personality, described as 'flamboyantly barbaric' in some sources.[15] He is reported to have celebrated his victory in prolonged feasting and drinking and neglected strategic follow through: 'The fruits of the Field of Blood were thus thrown away by the Moslems.'[16] It needs to be borne in mind, however, that the Artuqid connection had given Aleppo a very weak and temporary shield from the Crusaders. Their victory on the Field of Blood was a fortuitous one and any strategy to enable the Muslim forces to take a city of the importance of Antioch would have required a costly and sustained campaign. The intervention of an army under Baldwin II, King of Jerusalem (and previously the second count of Crusader Edessa), soon returned much of the Antioch–Aleppo corridor to Christian hands.

Ghazi proved not to be the saviour Aleppo needed. He apparently preferred to spend most of his short tenure in his other capital, Mardin, the base for his unruly band of Turkmen followers whose main stimulus came from plunder. For his Turkmen, Aleppo had no riches to offer. Ghazi's attempt to provide an alternative incentive by promoting the idea of jihad had made some impact on his followers particularly when Ghazi invited the redoubtable Qadi Ibn al-Khashshab to address the troops before the battle. However, the effect of his stirring words soon faded. Often, Aleppo's forces were fully engaged in the Jazira and in northern Iraq, even western Iran. The Crusaders were still not the biggest preoccupation when fortunes were to be made in the world of near anarchy in the lands stretching further to the east.

The fragility of the political situation in Aleppo, particularly after the death of Ghazi in 1122, made it difficult enough to hold the rest of the Muslim gains east of Antioch in the coming years. To expect weakened Aleppo to pursue any ambitious plans for the recovery of territory now studded with forts and vantage points was a big ask. In spite of Qadi Ibn al-Khashshab's rabble rousing, a preoccupation with the Crusaders was still not necessarily dominant on Aleppo's agenda.

Ghazi's nephew and successor in Aleppo, Balak, however, managed to consolidate the Muslim hold on some of the towns east of Aleppo. In 1124, it was al-Bab, which was again held by the Crusaders, that presented the raw nerve. Baldwin II's successor in Edessa, Joscelin I, had fortuitously fallen into the hands of Balak in 1123 but was ransomed the following year and celebrated his release by returning to the campaign field. Balak re-joined the fray by investing al-Bab but was fatally hit by a random arrow shot.

Nominally Timurtash, Ghazi's son, took command but his heart was not in the job and he longed to escape the constant demands of the campaigns against the Crusaders and return to his native Mardin. His first gesture was to release a prisoner as valuable as King Baldwin II of Jerusalem in exchange for a cash ransom. He compounded this impetuous gesture by presenting the king on his release with 'robes of honour, a gold helmet, and ornamented ankle boots, and even gave him back the horse he had been riding on the day of his capture'.[17] Baldwin repaid the prince's naivety by turning up a few weeks later before the walls of Aleppo with an invasion force. As the Crusaders pressed their attacks right up to the walls, the young Timurtash simply walked out on Aleppo, retired to Mesopotamia and left the citizens to defend themselves.

Aleppo besieged 1124–5

Baldwin's forces invested Aleppo from 19 October 1124. The citizens were on their own with Qadi Ibn al-Khashshab again seeking to rally the city to the cause of jihad. The citizenry's appeals to other Muslim states were unanswered for three months until envoys were sent to Mosul to plead for the protection of a power whose dominance Aleppo had so tenaciously resisted.

Thomas Asbridge has noted that the Crusader attack on Aleppo was 'the first concerted effort by a Latin Christian power to seize control of the major Muslim city in northern Syria' possibly with the intention of installing a puppet Muslim ruler.[18] Arab sources indicate that Baldwin (and possibly Joscelin of Edessa) were acting in concert with Arab forces, including the Bedouin leader Dubays Ibn Sadaqa and the Seljuk former puppet-princeling Sultanshah, deposed ten years earlier by Ghazi. This collusion with Muslim forces, an uncomfortable detail omitted in Crusader sources, facilitated a sustained and serious siege.[19]

With the arrival of a relief force from Mosul under Aqsunqur al-Bursuqi on 29 January 1125, however, Aleppo was saved and Aqsunqur went on to push back the Crusader lines. His counter-offensive failed to dislodge the Franks from 'Azaz but a subsequent treaty recognised a wider belt of Muslim control. The three-month siege of Aleppo had been a bitter experience for its citizens. Hostility towards the Crusaders had aroused Muslim–Christian animosity within the city. The Crusaders controlled ground so close to the walls that they were able to desecrate important shrines on the outskirts of the city. One of the shrines (the Hamdanid Mashhad al-Muhassin) had Shi'i associations said to date from the early years of Islam (see page 92). In retaliation, Qadi Ibn al-Khashshab again played a dynamic role in stiffening resistance. He ordered that four of Aleppo's churches be seized and transformed into mosques (later madrasas). One of these buildings was the remains of the Cathedral of St Helena examined earlier (pages 60–64); two of the other three still function as mosques or madrasas in the centre of Aleppo.[20]

The same year (1125) in a new sign of the chaos to which Aleppo had descended, Ibn al-Khashshab was stabbed as he left the Great Mosque in Aleppo, probably by a disgruntled Ismaeli in retaliation for the qadi's opposition to the sect's growing influence and their willingness to collude with the Crusaders. A few months later, Aqsunqur himself fell victim to an assassin's knife in the Great

Mosque in Mosul. Between them, Ibn al-Khashshab and Aqsunqur had begun the formidable task of restoring order to Aleppo, repairing its defenses and calming the disputes between rival factions; but much remained to be done.

Notes

1 A recent work which looks at the issues in a wider (Mediterranean) context and from both Crusader and Islamic perspectives is Cobb (2014).
2 Balderic of Drol's account (quoted in Krey 2012: 19).
3 Runciman 1965: I, 37.
4 Cahen 1969: 167.
5 C. Hillenbrand 1997: 136.
6 C. Hillenbrand 1997: 132.
7 Asbridge 2005: 267.
8 Asbridge's work, notably Asbridge (2000), also drew on the account of northern Syria during the Crusader period by Cahen (1940). Asbridge and Edgington (1999) have also provided a useful translation of the Crusader sources on the campaign. Asbridge has further highlighted the importance of the efforts to take Aleppo in the 1120s in a recent article (Asbridge 2013). The work of Eddé on the slightly later Ayyubid period in Aleppo is fundamental for insights from the Muslim side (Eddé 1999).
9 Köhler (2013: 64) suggests that the rhythm of clashes was also broken by occasional treaties between Antioch and Aleppo.
10 Gibb 1969b: 449–50.
11 Maalouf 1984: 81. Originally a family of wood sellers (hence the tribal name, 'al-Khashshab'), the al-Khashshabs had become one of the most prosperous sponsors of architectural projects in the late eleventh/early twelfth centuries.
12 Ibn al-Qalanisi, trans. in le Tourneau 1952: 104.
13 Maalouf (1984: 85) reports that Tancred even demanded that a cross be erected on the Great Mosque in Aleppo. Ibn al-Khashshab arranged a riot which saw the cross removed and stored in the former Byzantine cathedral, later appropriated for Islam at the qadi's urging.
14 Maalouf 1984: 90.
15 C. Hillenbrand 1981: 252.
16 Runciman 1952: II, 152.
17 Maalouf 1984: 97.
18 Asbridge 2013: 82.
19 Ibn al-Athir reported that Dubays encouraged the Crusaders to believe that Aleppo's Shi'a would favour his rule for sectarian reasons (Asbridge 2013: 79–80).
20 Besides the Madrasa Halawiye (former cathedral), the two surviving buildings are the Mosque al-Mawazini and the Madrasa Muqaddamiye. The fourth example, the Madrasa al-Hadadin, once lay southeast of the Great Mosque but was overbuilt by later Ottoman projects.

7

ZENGID ALEPPO (1127–74)

Zengids 1127–74

Zengids (1127–74)

A saviour – 'Imad al-Din Zengi

Just as the city seemed to have descended to the worst depths of chaos with the Crusader assault of 1124–5, relief was in sight. The Mosul forces had lifted the immediate threat to the city in 1125 but the Crusaders made further attempts to harass the city until 1127. The years of weakness, privation and factional disputes among the Muslim parties had seen Aleppo forced to pay tribute to Antioch to protect itself from attack. That changed in 1127. Onto the scene came 'Imad al-Din Zengi, the son of a former Seljuk governor of Aleppo. His father had been beheaded for treason in 1094 and Zengi was brought up in Mosul in the Turkish court. In 1126, after a notable record as military leader in Iraq, he took power as *atabeg* in Mosul and the next year in Aleppo. Once again, the citizens of Aleppo had been desperate enough to end the decades of near anarchy and stop–start leadership by inviting in a ruler from the Jazira.

During his reign of almost twenty years, Zengi met the definition of 'tyrant' in every respect. No paragon of religious probity or decency, at least he got things done.

> Zengi was tyrannical and he would strike with indiscriminate reckless-ness. He was like a leopard in character, like a lion in fury, not renounc-ing any severity, not knowing any kindness.[1]

He kept a firm hand on Aleppo and the Jazira but his real ambition was to take Damascus where the Burid atabeg, Unur, would even be prepared to engage Jerusalem's support in fending off Zengi's campaign to take the city in 1138. Damascus was an objective Zengi would never achieve but he succeeded in one thing – the implantation of a strong state across northern Syria and the Jazira, ending the mosaic of rival principalities that had divided the region. He was brutal;

but effectively so when it came to the integrity of his realm. In Aleppo, he held together a city that had spent decades worn out by internal fighting, by a restive population and by the Shi'a versus Sunni rivalries that still prevailed. The policies of capitulation which had partly served a leader's personal interests were gone. For all his faults, he turned Aleppo around after more than a century of chaos and his taking of Edessa from the Crusaders in 1144, two years before his death, was to provide the first strategic reversal for the Christian cause.

Holy and war

Above all, Zengi perfected an existing practice of making the struggle against the Crusades a joint religious and military operation. The Artuqid Ghazi had exploited the encouragement of piety to foster military zeal but lacked the commitment to carry it through, seeking solace in the bottle. His nephew and successor, Nur al-Dawla Balak, had sought to develop the tradition further during his brief reign. His tomb is one of the first monuments associated with a historic figure in Aleppo that has come down to us.[2] The tomb inscription, in which he is addressed as *shahid* or martyr, is entirely devoted to his religious zeal: 'Those who die in God's cause are not dead; they live in the presence of their God through whom they are sustained.'[3]

Zengi developed this interpretation of *jihad* in the strict sense of the term – the promotion of personal religious piety as a means of preparing for military struggle to advance the faith. Zengi was building on the role played by the influential Qadi al-Khashshab. This alliance between religious figures and the political-military establishment was now embedded as a central element in the city's evolution for the rest of the century, making Aleppo the test case for the development of the new political/religious model. The new programme relied not just on vague and fitful manifestations of piety but also on a structure of education focused on strict observance of religious precepts and the study of Koranic and other texts.

Byzantine designs on Aleppo 1137

The Byzantines had not given up their dream of retaking the city. In 1137, to add to the challenge Aleppo faced, a Byzantine army under the emperor John II Comnenos stood before the walls of Crusader Antioch. Antioch had always been the Byzantine emperor's expected reward for allowing the Crusader armies to cross his territory. In the Crusaders' view, the claim had been voided by the failure of the Byzantines to join in the siege of Antioch in 1097–8. Relations were constantly an issue, especially in the context of the control of Cilicia where the Byzantines had installed an Armenian presence, partly to serve as a buffer.

In the end, a confrontation was avoided in 1137 but the Byzantine price was that Raymond II, Prince of Antioch (r.1136–49), swore allegiance to the emperor and pledged to hand over Antioch to Byzantium if the Crusaders were able to gain Aleppo and three other inland Muslim towns. This was a big 'if' and Ralph-Johannes Lilie sees the negotiation of the treaty as a masterly manoeuvre by Raymond, pledging a notional form of fealty to the Byzantines which could only involve an actual transfer of sovereignty over Antioch in the unlikely event that the Crusaders could conquer the major towns of the interior.[4] It was never to happen and a joint Crusader/Byzantine operation to encircle Aleppo via al-Bab in 1138 failed. Within seven years, the first of the four Crusader entities, the County of Edessa, vanished. The episode underlines, however, the extent to which the taking of Aleppo (like Damascus) remained on the Crusaders' agenda.

The first madrasas

The new emphasis on faith as a focused and abstemious path to God would eventually require the suppression of the last manifestations of Shi'i and more heterodox religious traditions (Ismaelis, 'Alawi, Druze) which had implanted themselves over the years. We have seen earlier (pages 90–91, 95–96) that Shi'ism had been introduced to the city with the Hamdanids from northern Iraq, with some additional stimulus from the occasional waves of Fatimid influence. Now the Zengids sought more aggressively to advance the initial moves the Seljuks had taken to restore the city's attachment to the Sunni tradition. It was the introduction of a new form of educational institution, the *madrasa*, which embedded the process in the community. The first madrasa (Madrasa al-Zajjajiye) intended to implant a more strictly Koranic approach to piety and education was started in 1116 under the Seljuks but work was halted following the violent objections of the Shi'i community.[5] This cleansing of religious practice was to take much of the twelfth century.[6]

Zengi's new agenda (1128–46)

The Sunni tradition pursued under Zengi now sought to downplay the elaborate pietism associated with saintly figures, including those martyred in the cause of 'Ali in the seventh century. The emphasis was now on text, on the essential one-ness of God, on religious experience stripped of intermediaries. After 1128, Aleppo became a changed city. Its experience of the focus on faith and power by the end of the century would be reflected in its architecture, which borrowed much from Seljuk Iran with its arresting simplicity, symmetry and massing of basic shapes such as arches, domes, niches and the use of water channelled to draw the viewer into a world of austere harmony.

What had been an impoverished city, desperate to find protectors against the Crusader incursions and rarely able to take an army into the field, became over these decades a new centre of steadfastness. Under Zengi's rule, much of the focus of his military activities shifted south. The creation of the County of Tripoli in 1109 had partly moved the centre of gravity away from the Aleppo–Antioch corridor towards the more central gap in the coastal range leading directly from the coast to Homs and the Orontes and Beqaʻa Valleys. Though Zengi was more intent on taking the fight to the Crusaders, he failed to rally firm support on the Muslim side. Few were inclined to join him as he was feared not just for his ruthlessness against the Franks: 'Zengi's lack of scruples and inability to keep his word to the Syrian amirs ensured that virtually throughout his reign, there could be no common front against the Crusaders.'[7]

Still in his prime, Zengi took Edessa from the Crusaders in 1144, the first of the four Crusader political entities to be toppled in a campaign that rallied the Muslim forces of the region in an anti-Crusader jihad. Two years later, Zengi died on the Euphrates while besieging the castle of Qalaat Jaʻabr, then held by a recalcitrant Arab amir. Zengi (apparently in a state of total inebriation) was killed by a Frankish slave whom Zengi had accused of helping himself to the contents of a wine jug. Zengi had given Aleppo something it had not enjoyed for centuries: stable albeit ruthless rule and a capacity to take the fight to his opponents through both spiritual and military renewal. Perhaps his melodramatic end detracted from that message; it certainly ensured that his body was simply buried at the neighbouring battlefield at Siffin (scene of the confrontation between ʻAli and Muʻawiya in 657) and no funeral monument was erected in any of the cities that he had ruled.

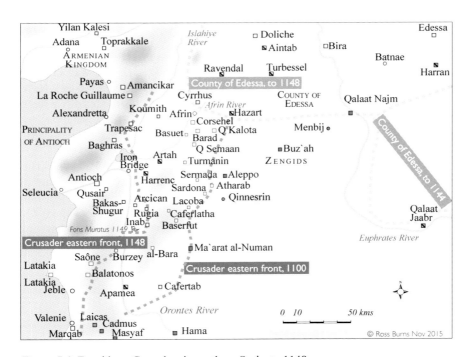

Figure 7.1 Zengids vs Crusaders in northern Syria, to 1148

The ascent of Nur al-Din Zengi (r.1146–74)

It was Zengi's second son, Nur al-Din ('Light of Faith') Mahmud Ibn Zengi, who claimed the succession at Qalaat Ja'abr by taking the ring from his dead father's still-warm hand. Having accompanied his father on several campaigns, Nur al-Din had already displayed many of Zengi's martial qualities but tempered them with a greater ability to lead through honour and personal example: 'Although Zengi's son had inherited his father's qualities of austerity, courage and states-manship, he had none of the defects that made the atabeg so odious to some of his contemporaries.'[8]

Nur al-Din's first challenge was to unite the emirates that had resisted his father's suzerainty and to prevent northern Syria from descending again into a mosaic of small principalities squabbling over booty. Mosul and the Jazira were the first to join his cause. Aleppo formally came under his control without difficulty when the Zengid governor Sawar recognised Nur al-Din as Zengi's suc-cessor. Nominally, the 'Abbasid Caliphate still held supreme authority, a situation respected by the pious Nur al-Din. Neither the residual Shi'i community nor the Ismaelis, who still had a presence in the city, offered any resistance. Aleppo pro-vided him with a base for extending his rule over the rest of Syria and his stocks rose considerably when he fended off an attempt by the last Count of Edessa, Joscelin II, to retake Edessa for the Crusaders in 1146.

The Second Crusade 1148

Looming over the Arab states, however, was the growing realisation that a second Crusader army had assembled in Europe and was now making its way through Asia Minor. The western Christians had reacted with alarm to the fall of Edessa and the Second Crusade reached the East four years later in 1148. This might have been a good opportunity for the Crusaders to move against Aleppo, as urged by Raymond II of Antioch, and continue on to recover Edessa. At that point, Nur al-Din had not imposed his rule securely over Muslim Syria.

In July 1148, the three Crusader armies assembled at Acre in Palestine. The three kings (France, Germany and Jerusalem) faced a strategic choice: which city should they take first? Edessa, which had been the ostensible reason for the new crusade? Aleppo, whose forces had snatched Edessa from Christian hands? Or Damascus, a city much cited in Holy Writ 'whose rescue from the infidel would resound to the glory of God'?[9] The fact that Damascus was also the largest of the inland Muslim cities was attractive but should have cautioned against a rushed campaign to assault it head on with an army largely of freshly arrived foreigners. Moreover, Damascus' ruler, Unur, had in the past settled into a happy compro-mise with his neighbour in Jerusalem.

The subsequent decision to target Damascus might therefore seem surprising. It brought a humiliating defeat before the very walls of the city, underlining how intemperate the decision had been and how little it reflected the experience of the local Crusader barons. On gaining a better appreciation of the difficulties of an assault and learning of the Zengid armies active not far to the north, the three Crusader forces found themselves scattered across the orchards and water channels of the Damascus oasis, and were forced to retrace their steps to Jerusalem. As in Aleppo in 1124, the Crusaders faced the humiliation of a failed assault on the walls of a major inland Muslim city.

Nur al-Din wins Damascus 1154

Damascus, which had wavered in its enthusiasm for the counter-Crusade, now repeated what Aleppo had done after 1124 – it saw the need for an outsider to end the decades of weak indecisive leadership which had frequently resorted to serial pacts with Crusader Jerusalem. Nur al-Din had been taking advantage of the weakened position of Crusader Antioch to move into the country southwest of Aleppo. In the Jebel Zawiya, he took the town of al-Bara (September 1148) which had for decades been under Crusader control and even had a Latin bishop. In temporary alliance with the Kurdish amir of Masyaf on the eastern side of the Orontes Valley, he campaigned north along the valley towards Antioch. He joined battle with Raymond's army and its temporary allies, the Ismaelis ('Assassins') of the coastal mountains, at a site known after its springs as Fons Muratus (near the town of Inab) in June 1149. Nur al-Din won a crushing victory that resulted in the death of Raymond of Antioch and took that city out of the game for decades. Aleppo's outer defences on the west now once again enveloped the Limestone Massif up to Artah and extended to the south to Apamea. For the moment, the Muslims could survey Antioch's approaches from the Rouj area of the Orontes Valley as well as the fortress of Harim (Harrenc), which today still peers across the Amuq Plain immediately east of Antioch (see Figure 7.2).

The threatened arrival of Nur al-Din's forces had been a major factor behind the Crusaders' panicked retreat from Damascus in 1148. Nur al-Din, however, did not move intemperately to secure Damascus for his cause. For the next five years he resorted to psy-ops directed at the population of Damascus to prepare the ground for a peaceful takeover. Not only did he not wish to cause injury to fellow Muslims, but also he was conscious that a head-on move against Damascus could again trigger a bid by its ruler, Mujir al-Din Abaq (Unur's successor), to call on Jerusalem to help maintain his rule. Instead Nur al-Din co-opted the Damascus street in a campaign signalling that he was available.

In 1153, Nur al-Din, following his victory over the Crusaders in the north, was free to reap the rewards of his mind games and move south. His forces arrived outside the Damascus city walls in April 1154 and imposed a blockade to make it clear that the citizens now had to choose between Aleppo and Jerusalem as their protector. The people of Damascus invited him to take power (1154). The *khutba* was read out at Friday prayers, signalling the restoration of the Sunni Caliphate. Abaq and the last Burids were quietly allowed to flee. Syria was now peacefully

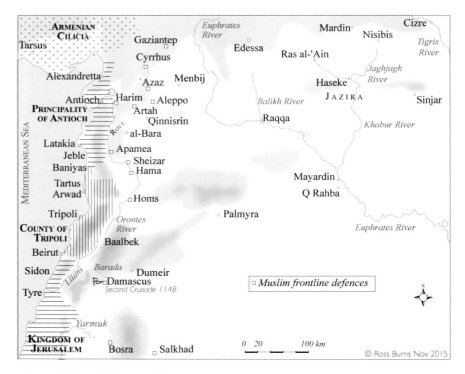

Figure 7.2 Zengid Syria and Crusader states

united under the banner of jihad. Damascus, which now replaced Aleppo as the forward-most point on the frontline against the Crusaders, became the pre-eminent capital of the Islamic cause.

Nur al-Din, however, still needed to consolidate his control further to the north-east, securing now a firm hold in the Jazira and the wider country between Aleppo and Mosul. Aleppo's encirclement had not been ended by the taking of Edessa as several remnants of the old Crusader county remained. However, Joscelin II was snatched while travelling north of ʿAzaz in 1150 and taken to Aleppo. Nur al-Din returned to Aleppo the next year and had the count's eyes gouged out. He remained in captivity in Aleppo for a further seven years until his death. In 1160, his son and successor, Joscelin III, was captured during another pillaging operation north of Aleppo and was held for sixteen years in the Aleppo Citadel.

Building on message

We are now reaching a point in the narrative where we can call on the help of a reasonable range of buildings to illuminate the life of an era. Nur al-Din was an enthusiastic builder. A more considered man than his father had been, he saw

130

the advantages of underlining his agenda in physical form. The religious teaching institutions built under his rule totalled fifty-six, of which twenty were his personal projects. In the latter category, Aleppo received almost as many new projects as Damascus – five and six respectively.[10]

Though Nur al-Din ruled from Damascus after 1154, Aleppo was to play a more central role in the development of new architectural ideas and as a base for the development of Sunni thought. Perhaps symbolic of his pre-occupations was the wooden preacher's stand or *minbar* which Nur al-Din ordered built in Aleppo for eventual transfer to the al-Aqsa Mosque once Jerusalem fell to the forces of Islamic renewal. On completion, the minbar was installed in a temporary home in the Aleppo Great Mosque. Nur al-Din did not live to see the event that would trigger its transfer to Jerusalem but his successor, Saladin, was careful to observe his wishes in 1188. Nur al-Din's choice of Aleppo as the place where the minbar should be crafted was a means of underlining the city's role as a centre of creativity both at a spiritual level and through the skill and proficiency of its craftsmen.[11]

Much needed to be done to restore the city physically after a major earthquake in 1157 caused extensive damage in many parts of Syria including both Damascus and Aleppo. Three of Nur al-Din's projects in Aleppo (dating from the first years of his rule) clearly established some of his major preoccupations – piety, the restoration of Sunnism and victory over the Crusaders. The Frankish intruders were still pressing close to Aleppo even if Zengi's elimination of the County of Edessa had given some relief.

Nur al-Din's projects in Aleppo all conveyed these messages. Though Nur al-Din contributed to the rebuilding of Aleppo's Great Mosque after a serious fire in 1168, much of that work did not survive later conflagrations and we will return to the building in the context of the Ayyubids. The first surviving example of his projects is an odd building – a small, elongated mosque lying between two converging streets on the axis of the ancient colonnaded spine. It lies just inside the Antioch Gate and replaced the original mosque built on the small square to mark the point where the Muslim forces under 'Umar Ibn al-Khattab first offered prayer on receiving the city's surrender in 637 under the terms noted in Chapter 4 (pages 74–5). It has the popular name 'Mosque of the Mulberry Tree' (al-Tuteh, see Figure 4.3 on page 75), though the tree has long since vanished. For decades last century it provided one of those architectural historical puzzles which draws the observer's attention to the rich carved relief which define the architrave in a seemingly Classical form. The mosque was thus assumed to be possibly rebuilt from remains of a Roman archway marking the western end of the main axis.

Today the small mosque is more prosaically known as the Mosque al-Shu'aybiye after its dedicatee, the jurist Shu'aybi Ibn 'Ali-Hasan much favoured by Nur al-Din. More careful study of the richly decorated cornice has also shown the mosque was not assembled from recycled Roman stones (its vine scroll relief was thought to have been over-carved with a Koranic inscription) but from new material dating from the early years of Nur al-Din. And what was its message? The front facing the square comprises merely a small porch and a fountain framed by an arch (both now filled in with added masonry).

The elaborate classicising frieze on the entablature illustrated in Figure 7.3 marks out this building from other Islamic architecture of its era, which had moved on from the Classical and Byzantine canon to explore ideas emanating from Iraq and Persia, many introduced via the Seljuks. This virtuoso display of a Classical idiom has been seen as a triumphalist gesture: the new order of Islam is in no way inferior to the Mediterranean world. The Koranic text thus sends a new message, choosing a consciously Classical base to illustrate that Islam trumped the era of the temples and their multiple deities. It urges Muslims to shun false gods. The mosque is the place where:

> men who wish to be pure gather. Allah favours those who seek purity. Do not invoke any name but Allah's whose mosques should only be visited by those who believe in Him and in the Last Day, who observe prayer and alms and who fear none other than Him.[12]

The Shu'aybiye Mosque was a billboard for Nur al-Din's campaign against the Shi'a, a cause which dated back to Seljuk times. The preacher referred to in the building's name was a reliable Shafe'i jurist, originally from Andalusia, and Nur al-Din had just passed a series of measures designed to stamp out Shi'i practices in worship.

Figure 7.3 Entablature and cornice of the Shu'aybiye Madrasa with its classicising references

To a great extent the medium or the materials also influenced the choice of repertoire. Aleppo was still the centre of a world of wonderful Classical and Byzantine remains, all of which showed a mastery of stone. On this little mosque the decoration certainly picked up those Classical references with enthusiasm, as had the minaret of the Great Mosque fifty years before. It returned to a style that would have been impossible to execute in plaster or brick, the usual Mesopotamian materials. A closer examination of the extraordinarily rich decoration of the entablature shows a virtuoso display of intricate shapes, scrolls and vegetation in five registers, interwoven with a beautiful Arabic script and with such Corinthian touches as the modillions supporting the jutting cornice. This is not the work of a novice but of a workman steeped in his materials, his craft and his environment, perhaps even following intricate pattern books now lost to us.[13] It is more evidence that the influence of the monuments of Aleppo's environs had never gone away.

At all centres under his control, Nur al-Din sought energetically to advance the cause of Sunnism. Public displays of Shi'i devotion, particularly those linked to the 'saints' of early Islam, were outlawed. Instead, madrasas or *dar al-Hadith*s (institutions devoted to the study of approved texts commenting on tradition) proliferated, beginning with Aleppo. As part of Nur al-Din's discouraging of Shi'i institutions, the extra-mural Mashhad al-Dikka (a Hamdanid project, see earlier on page 92) was adopted by the Zengids. The Shi'a later riposted by funding through public subscription the nearby Shrine to Hussein, which remains to this day a major centre of Shi'i pilgrimage.[14]

Nur al-Din's next two projects in the city related to two of the four buildings seized from the Christians in reprisal for the Crusaders' demolition of extra-mural Islamic shrines during their 1124 siege, including the Mashhad al-Dikka. The churches had been converted to mosques but Nur al-Din now had them rebuilt as madrasas. The Madrasa Halawiye, originally seized by order of the firebrand Shi'i cleric Ibn al-Khashshab, now became a bastion of Sunni orthodoxy. The madrasa still stands alongside the western wall of the Great Mosque in Aleppo, with columns of the centralised Byzantine church framing the alcoves of the prayer hall. (The madrasa's predecessor, the sixth-century Cathedral of St Helena, built adjacent to the ancient forum area, is discussed in Chapter 3 and can be seen in Figure 3.5.) Nur al-Din's second converted mosque (1169) was the building known today as the Madrasa Muqaddamiye to the south in the central suqs area. In this case, nothing remains of the original church and the prayer hall has been rebuilt as a cross-vaulted room south of the courtyard. This time the style is sober with the only pioneering architectural idea confined to the crossed barrel-vaults over the doorway.

Our last example of Nur al-Din's message is a rather sad affair. The Maristan (hospital) of Nur al-Din (also 1169) is found just south of the main suqs area in a state of advanced decay. The only identifiable part is the doorway, hidden behind a closely barred grille and permanently locked. Most of the structure behind remains, though parts have been cannibalised over the centuries for other purposes.

The decoration surrounding the door is more spartan than our previous example but shows a style that was to become characteristic of Zengid-era projects in other centres including Damascus. The decoration is less consciously Classical and borrows from the Seljuk style found in Asia Minor. The institution of public hospitals was a novelty encouraged under Nur al-Din, illustrating the emphasis he put on the welfare of Aleppo's citizens. The rather better preserved counterpart in Damascus provides a mixture of Mesopotamian and Seljuk elements while the use of *muqarnas* or small triangular segments of a sphere to mark the transition from a curved to a square form still provides a striking canopy over the entrance.

Aleppo was now to play a further role in developing numerous ideas stemming from Zengid contacts with the provinces to the east. Some projects developed further the form of the four-iwan plan where high open-sided rooms on each side face onto a central courtyard. The idea was essentially a development of Sasanian structures first noted in palatial buildings as a way of sheltering activities around the courtyard throughout the year, moving around with the sun. By the twelfth century, the idea had arrived in Aleppo via Iraq and became a second option for the design of mosques, in Syria a form so far dominated by the ground plan established by the Great Mosque of the Umayyads in Damascus. In this classic plan (said to have been partly modelled on the Prophet's house in Medina), a prayer hall was set on the south side of a courtyard, around which ran porticos on three sides. The four iwan plan now became the second option which could be applied not just to mosques but to other institutions.

On Abraham's path

As the military challenges from the Crusaders rose, Nur al-Din increasingly resorted to these themes of piety, to the promotion of the interests of the poor and to the canonical texts, stripping Islam of the embellishments added by the heterodox Shiʿa and returning it to the essential obligations of the faith through education. His residential capital, Damascus, was now more exposed to the Crusader threat than Aleppo and thus received greater attention in terms of its defences. To underline the message that Islam was about the oneness of God, Nur al-Din encouraged the cultivation of places deemed to be associated with Abraham, seen as the original monotheist. This neatly provided the public with alternatives to the Aleppan sites associated with the followers of ʿAli.

As an Old Testament Prophet, Abraham was, of course, equally respected in the Muslim as in the Christian or Jewish traditions. The legends of his journey from Ur in Mesopotamia to Jerusalem were now embellished by promoting places in or around Aleppo said to enjoy this pious association. The sites are still revered today though the buildings that stand were largely rebuilt in later centuries and do not necessarily represent the Zengid style. We will look first at the Maqam Ibrahim ('shrine of Abraham') in the Maqamat Cemetery south of the walled city of Aleppo.

As an introduction, however, we should note the importance of this area out-side the city's southern walls known as the Salihin and Maqamat quarters, both names conveying sanctity (see Map A.3). The land lies outside the gate known today as Bab al-Maqam 'Shrine Gate' but also termed historically the Damascus Gate. This was not the first extra-mural extension of Aleppo. Written records indicate that an area southeast of the walls carrying the generic designation al-Hadir was settled by Arab followers with the Islamic conquest after 637. Another zone directly to the east of the later Bab al-Maqam, Qalaʻat al-Sha-rif, had been fortified in the eleventh century during one of the many struggles between rival factions for control of the city. (When the walls in this area were later extended south, Qalaʻat al-Sharif was incorporated into the walled city.) More importantly the route south from the Bab al-Maqam followed the path taken by the annual Hajj pilgrimage, fortifying the area's holy status. The pil-grims assembled on the open *maidan* outside the Citadel's south walls and departed in procession through the gate, heading south towards Damascus and the Hijaz. The full extent of the route from the Citadel would later be further developed as a ceremonial axis (described in Chapter 8).

This extra-mural area would later host several other major religious projects as well as prestige tombs. The small complex dedicated to Abraham was located in a cemetery area east of this path. The legend associated with the site is that Abraham paused here on leaving the city, the remains of the rock on which he rested being preserved in a cavern under the prayer hall. The shrine must have suffered in its exposed position during countless invasions. We know, though, from literary sources that it existed as early as the Seljuk period as it was one of the first places honoured when the first Seljuk ruler, Malik Shah, arrived in 1086. A *mihrab* survives commemorating his gesture in today's rather jumbled complex.

The other two Abrahamic sites are marked by mosques on the Aleppo Citadel. Both the Mosque of the Citadel at the highest point on the rise and the Mosque of Abraham are recorded as part of Abraham's itinerary in medieval sources (includ-ing Jewish and Christian itineraries). The former marks the site of a medieval Christian church, of which nothing remains, said to mark an 'altar of Abraham'; the second to have contained a stone on which he sat while milking his goat. The surviving structures of both mosques belong more correctly to our next chapter but the significance given to the legends linking Aleppo to Abraham are worth noting as initiatives of Nur al-Din. By reminding the faithful of the Abrahamic tradition, Nur al-Din is underlining the purity of the message of Islam. This rep-resented a return to simple monotheism before it was obscured by the teachings and stories of Christianity, which superimposed the concept of the Trinity not to mention the interminable debates over the 'dual' nature of Christ's personal-ity that obsessed early Christianity. The Abraham story countered the numerous saintly devotions encouraged in Christianity and heterodox Islam. The message was: keep it simple.[15]

Figure 7.4 Two projects initiated by Nur al-Din on the Aleppo Citadel: the Mosque of
Abraham (half way up on the left) and the Great Mosque of the citadel at the
top, with minaret

Into Egypt

Nur al-Din's strategic vision took account of the fact that if the Muslims were to
mount a sustained campaign against Jerusalem, they needed appropriate resources.
While he dealt with this situation, Nur al-Din, who now controlled all the inland of
modern-day Syria and south into Jordan, was resigned to signing yearly truces with
Jerusalem, paying tribute while he bided his time.

The Seljuks would be kept well to the north in Asia Minor, an objective aided
by a pact with the Byzantines to confine their common enemy. However, to take

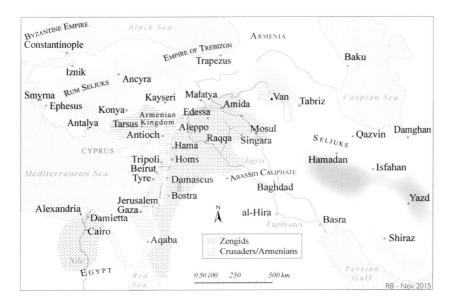

Figure 7.5 Zengid lands in 1172

on the Crusaders, the manpower and resources the Syrian lands yielded were not enough. Only Egypt (still Fatimid and thus nominally Shi'i and hostile to the Baghdad Caliphate) could provide the strategic depth against the Crusaders, now replenished after their humiliating defeat outside Damascus in 1148. Much of the focus of Nur al-Din's rule was thus on the Egyptian front, which the Crusaders had been quick to assail through operations in the eastern Nile Delta. Now that the Antioch front was pushed well to the west and with Syria under Zengid control, Nur al-Din could switch his campaigning to the south.

Nur al-Din accordingly preferred to leave the Antioch enclave safely confined by its inland counterpart, Aleppo, conscious that successfully removing the Crusader principality would only have the effect of inviting the Byzantines back into the confrontation. This sort of *realpolitik* was not shared by Reynald of Châtillon, a pugnacious minor noble who arrived in the East shortly before the Second Crusade. He had catapulted himself into the top tier by marrying the widow of Raymond of Antioch in 1154. Reynald saw no need to accept the live-and-let-live situation in the region often favoured by the native Crusader barons and almost succeeded in picking a fight with the Byzantine emperor, Manuel. When Reynald realised the risk that he might well come off second best, he offered a craven apology.

Nur al-Din was relieved of the prospect of Reynald provoking further trouble on the northern front, however, when in 1160 the feisty prince was fortuitously taken prisoner. The prince was pursuing his favourite sport of pillaging when caught in an ambush northwest of Aleppo in the Afrin Valley. Reynald's refusal to abandon his booty brought his capture and imprisonment in Aleppo. He shared the fate of Joscelin III taken the same year (see page 130) and was put in the Aleppo Citadel where he languished for sixteen years, a fate apparently determined by the fact that 'none of his fellow Crusaders could bring themselves to pay the funds to ransom this turbulent prince'.[16]

After 1163, as Crusader forces entered the Nile Delta, the southern focus of Nur al-Din's strategic vision came fully into play. In Cairo, a renegade Fatimid vizier, Shawar, invited Nur al-Din to campaign against the Crusaders using the rising Crusader threat as a pretext to circumvent the Fatimids' refusal to accept Zengid dominance. Nur al-Din spent the next ten years consolidating the Egyptian front while the weak last remnants of the line of Fatimid Caliphs in Cairo continued their blocking role, even seeking to encourage Crusader efforts to outflank Muslim Syria.

In 1164, Nur al-Din commissioned a fellow Kurdish amir Asad al-Din to lead the expeditionary force to Egypt. Shirkuh was accompanied by his nephew, the son of his brother, Najm al-Din Ayyub. The apparently reluctant participant was the seventeen-year-old Salah al-Din Yusuf Ibn Ayyub, later to pass into history as Saladin. In Cairo, the Zengid force found itself caught in a web of intrigue with Shawar now seeking to play off Crusaders and Zengids against each other. Issues came to a head in a battle outside Cairo in 1167. Both Crusaders and Zengids agreed to leave Egypt while Shawar managed to regain his status as a client of the Jerusalem king. This state of subservience irritated the Cairo crowd. When Crusader forces again entered the Delta to enforce their expectations of Shawar's compliance, the vizier had had enough of being the Crusaders' plaything and called on the Zengids again to rescue him. In 1169, Crusader and Zengid armies again drew up in battle lines outside Cairo. The Crusaders withdrew once it was apparent that the Zengids had recovered their control over Shawar and now held the upper hand. Shawar, however, had played his last card and was beheaded by his Zengid rescuers.

With the protector of the Fatimid Caliphs gone, everything was now in place for the confirmation of Sunni supremacy on all the frontiers of the Crusader states. A Zengid administration took over in Cairo and the Fatimid Caliph stayed on as little more than a discredited cypher. Saladin was appointed as vizier, a selection which appealed to the Caliph who entertained the delusion that the thirty-two-year-old would be a pliable appointee.

Switching Caliphs

As vizier in Cairo following the Zengid coup in 1169, part of Saladin's remit, transmitted via his father, Ayyub, was to manipulate the final transfer of Egypt's loyalty from the Fatimid token Caliph in Cairo to the Sunni ʿAbbasid Caliph in Baghdad. Nur al-Din appeared to think Saladin was slow in forcing the change but it seems likely that the younger man was simply being cautious, waiting for an opportune moment and distracted by yet another Crusader expedition against Egypt, this time targeting Damietta. Saladin had laid the groundwork in Cairo by founding a series of madrasas attuned to the Sunni agenda and replaced many of the Fatimid-appointed *qadi*s. Ismaeli schools were closed down. By 1171, Saladin felt he could openly have the khutba proclaimed in favour of the Baghdad Caliphate, a move accompanied by the fortuitous death of the last Fatimid Caliph three days later.

The Islamic world was now united across the core Islamic lands after centuries of division. The transition, though, had come at the cost of considerable tension between Saladin and Nur al-Din. By this time, the two had fallen out over a second issue: the emphasis to be given to the Egyptian campaign against the Crusaders. Nur al-Din wanted to return the focus from Egypt to the struggle against Jerusalem from the Zengids' Syrian base. Saladin's father tried to mediate with a stern warning to his son: 'Nur al-Din leads this land. If he asked your father or me to cut off your head, we would. If he wanted just to depose you, he could summon you home in an instant.'[17] By now Nur al-din was ailing after numerous health problems over the previous decade. Still sensing Saladin's resistance, he stubbornly planned to set out for Cairo to impose his authority directly on the young vizier but before plans for the journey could be implemented he died on 15 May 1174, a victim of angina.

Nur al-Din was buried in a building that is perhaps the most remarkable tribute to his single-minded faith. Amid the narrow lanes of the Damascus markets, his tomb chamber lies in a long-neglected madrasa (recently under reconstruction). Above the sepulchre, an extraordinary dome paid tribute to the flood of new architectural idea stemming from the Islamic societies to the east – a muqarnas dome that carries its zone of transition from round to cube with a cascade of tiny segments of a sphere, a brilliant metaphor of the creativity that flowed from the forces that the Zengid leader had brought together.

The mantle of the great leader was a difficult garment to don. The unity of his realm, its focus on a few essential and largely noble aims, was a new phenomenon in the region. Who would be big enough to take on such a weighty responsibility without risking disintegration of the inheritance; or squandering the spirit of moral integrity that had held it together?

The answer today seems obvious: Saladin. Problematic though his relations had been with Nur al-Din in his final years, Saladin was a figure who followed his predecessor's path of faith and had the capacity for military leadership. But his climb to the post of sultan was not straightforward and the qualities seen in his subsequent career (and much admired in later generations, including in the West) were not yet obvious. His years absent in Cairo, the fact that Nur al-Din's infant son was designated as heir and the jealousy of generals well senior to Saladin complicated matters.

A mixed city

Before looking further at Saladin's path to succession, we return to Aleppo. In a moment, we will be plunging into one of the most dynamic phases of its built history. But first, what sort of society had it become after the Zengid restoration of stable government? The narrative above has emphasised the role Zengi and Nur al-Din saw for Islam as the fabric that bound society and defined its struggle against the Crusaders.

We have no precise figures but it is clear from travellers' accounts, including by the Jewish visitor Benjamin of Tudela, that Aleppo still harboured a mixed population in both ethnic and religious terms. The peak phase of conversion of Christians to Islam had long since passed, though their numbers continued to fall at a slower rate. The Christian proportion of the population had probably slipped below 50 per cent by Seljuk times and Anne-Marie Eddé has noted that the number of rural monasteries still functioning declined noticeably between the eleventh and the thirteenth centuries.[18] Citizens who had accepted *dhimmi* status and paid the poll tax in lieu of military service were left to regulate their personal lives within an over-arching and predictable framework of law. The pressures on Christians in the early twelfth century had largely been reprisals prompted by the Crusaders' hostility towards Muslim shrines not actions prompted by the behaviour of the native Christians themselves. There was now no concerted push for further conversions and Christian shrines were again respected. Many Christians and Jews specialised in medical, trading and financial fields. Muslim heterodox populations (Shi'a, Ismaelis and 'Alawis in particular) were encouraged to discover the error of their attachment to non-approved practices. While the main thrust emphasised persuasion rather than compulsion, sanctions against the Ismaelis were more deliberately harsh.

Aleppo was clearly a mixed city where ethnic origin was not a major distraction. The Zengid leadership was Kurdish but there was a significant Turkic admixture and, particularly on the religious side, a prominent role for Arabs. The latter were drawn from many parts of the Islamic world. Leading Islamic figures travelled widely to spread the learning generated in such centres as Baghdad, Cairo or the cities of Andalusia. Alongside the military leaders in Zengid society, an aristocracy of learning was also consolidating – a 'turbanned elite'.[19] Aleppo was, in short, now a society that had much more ballast in terms of social stability and tolerance than had been possible in the previous three centuries. Even when the affairs of the military elite became less stable in the period we are about to embark on – the years of Saladin and the successors drawn from his family enterprise, the Ayyubids – the city's social fabric largely held.

The Zengid years had restored prosperity to Aleppo and with it the city's infrastructure. It took on an increasingly important role not just as a trading hub for the region but also as a centre of religious scholarship whose fame gave the city a new profile in the Islamic world. Under Nur al-Din, 'Aleppo had become a capital of an empire which was well governed and powerful. Security, justice, economic prosperity, civic order were all restored.' Nur al-Din earned the praise of one of the city's Arab historians for having deserved the citizens' calls for divine merit to be bestowed on him across the ages. It was some centuries since anyone had earned such spontaneous accolades.[20]

Notes

1 ʿImad al-Din al-Isfahani, quoted in C. Hillenbrand (1999: 113).
2 Found in the Salihin Cemetery in Aleppo and transferred to the National Museum in Damascus in the 1930s.
3 Sauvaget 1938: 208.
4 Lilie 1993: 121.
5 Work on the Madrasa al-Zajjajiye was later resumed and the building finished in 1123. The building was replaced by an Ottoman *khan*, the Khan Ahmad Pasha. Medieval chronicles (notably Ibn Khallikan) report that Ghazi had the body of his father, Aqsunqur, transported from Mosul and buried in this madrasa (Herzfeld 1955: I, 184).
6 No example of an early madrasa has survived in Aleppo. We therefore have few clues as to how the building style later became so characteristic of the Ayyubids and Mamluks came into being and the extent to which it drew on a repertoire of forms already found to the east in Iran and Iraq.
7 Elisséeff 1967: II, 343.
8 Maalouf 1984: 143.
9 Runciman 1965: II, 181.
10 Sauvaget (1941: 123) counts only three for men and another (unnamed) for women; Elisséeff gives six (1967: III, 914–18). My count includes the following projects, all for males – Halawiye, Mawazini, Shuʿaybiye, Muqaddamiye and Hadadiye (*intra muros*). This excludes the earlier Zajjajiye Madrasa which was an Artuqid project (1116) but whose controversial beginning was interrupted for reasons explained earlier (page 126).
11 The minbar survived in Jerusalem until 1969 when it was incinerated during the blaze in the al-Aqsa Mosque started by a deranged Australian tourist.
12 Herzfeld (1955: I, 223) provides a French translation from which this has been adapted. The issue is examined fully in Raby (2004).
13 The detail is best appreciated on the website of the Smithsonian Institution in Washington which has followed an enlightened policy of displaying high-resolution images of the drawings prepared by Herzfeld before the First World War.
14 The two shrines are examined further in the Postscript below.
15 Another reason for honouring the Shrine of Abraham on the Citadel was its association as a repository for the head of John the Baptist's father, Zachariah. The skull was said to have been discovered in Baalbek in 1043 and transferred to Aleppo's downtown Great Mosque after 1260 under Baybars.
16 Elisséeff 1967: II, 553.
17 Elisséeff 1967: II, 673 – present author's edited translation from the French.
18 Eddé 2006: 158, 176.
19 Sauvaget 1941: 138.
20 Sauvaget (1941a: 127–8) partly referring to Ibn al-ʿAzimi.

8

SALADIN AND THE
AYYUBIDS (1174–1260)

Saladin extends his rule

We enter now on the period which Sauvaget nominated as 'the most illustrious in the city's medieval history'.[1] Its opening phase, however, was uncertain. Nur al-Din had in principle designated his young son, al-Salih Ismael, as his successor before his death in 1174. In October 1174, Saladin rushed back to Damascus from Cairo to take control of events. To switch the succession from al-Salih Ismael, the boy would have to be neutralised as a rallying point for the Zengid local leaders resistant to Saladin's rise. Saladin's claim on the succession was advanced when the Baghdad Caliphate formally recognised him as sultan from 1175, though his mandate extended only as far north as Hama. Saladin's cause was further

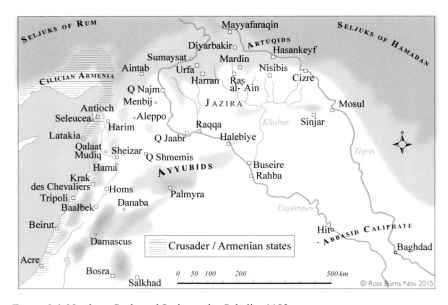

Figure 8.1 Northern Syria and Jazira under Saladin, 1183

142

advanced when the official guardian in Damascus of young al-Salih Ismail, Ibn al-Muqaddam, signed a peace treaty with the Jerusalem Crusaders, a move that brought the population of Damascus out in open support of Saladin.

Damascus was a city with which Saladin had clear ties. His father Najm al-Din Ayyub had served there as Nur al-Din's city governor. Ayyub had owned a house in the city of which Saladin enjoyed happy memories of his youth.[2] Saladin made a point of treating its people magnanimously and professed to be acting simply as protector of Ismael. Aleppo was more problematic. It remained 'an object coveted by all', held by Zengid followers opposed to Saladin.[3] The clique that held Aleppo under the atabeg Gumushtakin refused to recognise Saladin's supremacy throughout Syria and had spirited away al-Salih Ismael to the northern capital as their mascot. A eunuch previously serving Nur al-Din, Jamal al-Din Shadhbakht, plus one of the Zengid *amirs* effectively seized the Citadel.

Saladin took his forces north to Aleppo in December 1174, signalling to the recalcitrant amirs that 'I did not come here out of greed or desire for the world here below. What I have in Egypt is sufficient for me. I come only to save that child from the clutches of those of your ilk.'[4] The twelve-year-old boy-king's protectors responded by arranging his appearance before the crowd on the city's main square (the *maidan* outside the great gate of the Citadel), urging the citizens of Aleppo to save him from Saladin. The crowd's favourable response ended Saladin's hopes of a diplomatic outcome. Having failed to enter the city as ruler, he resorted to siege but broke it off after two months when it became obvious that the Zengid amirs' campaign to get aid from the Crusaders and Mosul had brought new threats Saladin would be forced to address.

It took almost a decade for Saladin finally to wrench Aleppo and northern Syria from Zengid hands, even after his marriage to Nur al-Din's widow, 'Ismat al-Din, in 1176. The difficulty remained Saladin's need to extend his control as far as Mosul to gain the upper hand in northern Syria. When combined, Aleppo and Mosul were simply too formidable a combination. The Iraqi city, however, was not to fall to him until 1185. In 1175, Saladin's name was proclaimed in the *khutba* across most of Syria and Egypt. Aleppo had nominally accepted Saladin's supremacy in May of that year, shortly after a Zengid force had been beaten by Saladin's army at the Horns of Hama. Saladin offered the Aleppo forces an armistice. (The alternative would have been to insist on a full victory which could only be achieved by siege.) Zengid amirs were allowed to stay on at some centres, now clearly appointed under Saladin's authority.

However, it took another decade to consolidate all Saladin's gains in northern Syria east to Mosul and replace the Zengid local princes with his own appointees. From 1175, Aleppo only grudgingly accepted Saladin's authority with al-Salih Ismael's protectors still conniving to undermine Saladin from their base at the Aleppo court until the young Zengid prince himself died in 1181. In between northern campaigns, Saladin was still required to attend to the Crusader threat in the south, preventing him from bringing the affairs of northern Syria to a resolution.

It is thus not surprising that Saladin had less time and inclination to leave his mark on Aleppo compared to Damascus. As if Saladin had not enough on his plate, he had to attend to another threat in northern Syria – the residual presence of the Ismaelis (or Assassins). Increasingly isolated as the dominance of Sunni Islam prevailed across northern Syria, these heterodox Shi'a had carved out an enclave on the eastern side of the Syrian coastal mountains. Their cluster of small forts gave them a dominant position looking over the central Orontes Valley and a capacity to wreak havoc both inland or against the Crusaders on the coast. By the 1170s, they chose to make their major targets the main Sunni inland cities, requiring Saladin to campaign against them.

Finally, Saladin could not neglect Egypt. He spent much of 1181–2 strengthening the physical defences of the Cairo Citadel, which was to bristle with all the new ideas in military architecture developed during the campaigns against the Crusaders. We will see the same ideas exploited in Syria in the decades to follow but meanwhile the restive internal affairs of the Muslim north still had to be dealt with. After al-Salih's death, the pro-Zengid northern amirs made a final lunge for power to prevent Saladin removing them from their Aleppo power base. They again sought Mosul's aid and could count on residual support from the people of Aleppo. Saladin campaigned across the Jazira in 1182. He took the northern city of Amida (Diyarbakir) and brought the previously pro-Zengid Artuqid amirs of Mardin and Mayyafaraqin into his fold (1183). Having achieved a firmer grip on the northeast, he decided the time was ripe for a concerted move against recalcitrant Aleppo. A show of force was enough to persuade the amir, 'Imad al-Din to surrender Aleppo on 22 June 1183 in exchange for distant Sinjar: 'All Muslim Syria belonged now to Saladin.'[5]

A question of authority

Saladin might now be expected to concentrate on the struggle against the Crusaders free of distractions. His brother, al-'Adil, was sent to take charge of Aleppo but the obsession with gaining Mosul remained unfulfilled. A campaign to capture it in 1185 was called off when Saladin retired ill to winter in Harran. Saladin was now openly criticised in chronicles as lacking the stamina and commitment to confront Jerusalem. The momentum that Zengi and Nur al-Din had built up seemed to be slipping away. In 1186, however, Mosul finally reached an agreement with Saladin to recognise his sovereignty in northern Iraq and to put Mosul's army at the disposal of Saladin. The issues that distracted him from the pursuit of the religious struggle against Jerusalem were now overcome.

The next year, 1187, Saladin resumed the campaigning season in Palestine and carried off a brilliant victory over the Crusader forces under King Guy at Hattin in Galilee. The capture of much of the Crusader army along with their king gave new momentum to the Muslim campaign, which went on to take Jerusalem and in the next year to roll back the Crusader presence at numerous centres near the coast, stopping only on the outskirts of Antioch. Saladin's son al-Zahir Ghazi (see next section) brought his forces from Aleppo to participate in the siege of the formidable Crusader castle at Saône, his bombardment of the elongated ridge site from the northeast providing the key that opened the castle to assault. Of the coastal fortresses, only Tyre remained in Crusader hands. In 1188, allowing time for Tyre to be replenished while moving first against Jerusalem then campaigning up the coast, seemed symbolically the right decision but proved to be a fatal weakness in Saladin's strategy. By retaining this major Crusader coastal city, the Franks were able to retake Acre (1191), which became the new capital of the Jerusalem Kingdom and a base from which to extend their residual coastal enclave.

In 1193 Saladin died. He, like Nur al-Din, was buried in Damascus in a tomb on the edge of the Great Mosque. Given the quite different images Nur al-Din and Saladin enjoy among Western audiences, it might seem strange to argue that the authority and relatively enlightened rule that prevailed in Syria in Nur al-Din's time did not necessarily endure in Saladin's. The contrast is perhaps seen as particularly strong in Aleppo. Nur al-Din is sometimes viewed in contemporary Western images as the tougher figure, more fanatical in his religious motivation. Saladin is envisaged in Western eyes from Crusader times onwards as a man inspired by a sense of chivalry and generosity, based partly on his commanding authority on his own side. In fact, seen from Aleppo, Saladin was a less consistent leader and had a greater challenge in establishing his control over the city. Though accommodating and generous at times to his Zengid enemies, Saladin never enjoyed at home the stature that Nur al-Din had been able to achieve.

Moreover, by failing to consolidate a unified system of rule – taking so long to impose authority over the local amirs and commissioning relatives to assume local power under what would eventually become a fragmented dynastic arrangement – Saladin's reign was marked by the 'absence of any cohesive principle, of a higher moral or ideological order, (and) constituted a serious weakness in the nascent Ayyubid state'.[6] In the post-Crusades Western romanticised picture, Saladin became a towering figure. Saladin, though, should not just be judged from the optic of the Crusaders. There was a lot more to his achievements; and his failures.

We should therefore not be surprised, given the short period when he controlled the city, that Saladin endowed no building projects in Aleppo. (Perhaps less surprised given that there are virtually none in Damascus, either. Even his own mausoleum was an existing madrasa reappropriated by his family after his death.) His descendants were to make up for that record and the label 'Ayyubid' applied to many illustrious religious buildings refers largely to the following decades.

Al-Zahir Ghazi (r.1186–1216)

The succession to Saladin in Aleppo was the least controversial amid the difficult transitions that beset the division of Saladin's inheritance further south. The weak point of Saladin's plan to divide up his kingdom among various members of the family was that it represented a return to the more unstable practices of the Turkic system, a 'semi-feudal family federation'.[7] There were few reasons why family members were any more likely to avoid squabbles than outsiders. While it took almost twenty-five years finally to resolve these disputes further south, the succession to Saladin in Aleppo was more successful. Saladin's third son, al-Zahir Ghazi, was only fourteen when appointed as governor of the city by his father in 1186; thus twenty when his father died. In 1197, he consolidated his sultanate by taking the port of Latakia that had been briefly reoccupied by Bohemond II, Prince of Antioch, after falling to Saladin in 1188.

Ghazi had time enough to gain a good grasp on the handles of power in the north and his line was to rule Aleppo for the rest of the Ayyubid period. The city thus enjoyed a greater stability than any of the Ayyubid capitals. Al-Zahir Ghazi learned largely to stay away from the fractious disputes between his uncle (al-ʿAdil) and brothers (al-ʿAfdal, al-ʿAziz) that destabilised the south. Ghazi briefly joined with the dissident princes in 1199 in besieging Damascus but lost interest and withdrew. Al-ʿAdil resented his nephew's feeble contribution to the cause and attacked Aleppo's territory, forcing al-Zahir Ghazi to recognise his sovereignty in Syria. In 1200, al-ʿAdil was proclaimed Sultan in Cairo while Ghazi was formally recognised as Prince in Aleppo. In 1212, Ghazi restored his relations with his uncle by marrying al-ʿAdil's daughter, Dayfa Khatun, one of a number of remarkably influential women who assumed powerful roles in Ayyubid courts and was a great builder, as we will see below.

In 1184, the city of Aleppo, particularly its Zengid monuments, impressed the Andalusian visitor Ibn Jubayr, who provided our first expansive account. This visitor was almost overpowered by the beauty of the city and the scale of its major buildings:

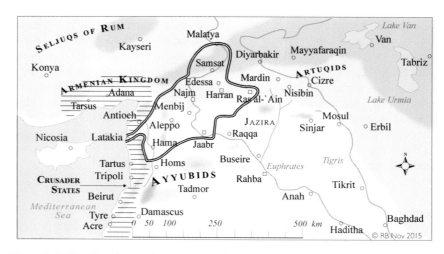

Figure 8.2 Ghazi's sultanate in northern Syria, 1198

[The Great Mosque] is one of the finest and most beautiful of mosques. . . .
At its west side stands a Hanafite college which resembles the mosque in its
beauty and perfection of work. . . . Besides this college the city has four or
five others, and a hospital. Its state of splendour is superb, and it is a city fit
to be [the seat of] the Caliph.[8]

Surviving the transition

One curious building may be worth noting as we review the transition from the
Zengid to the Ayyubid city of Aleppo. Near the eastern (Citadel) end of the axis
that stretches between the Citadel and the Antioch Gate, the busy commercial
street does not allow much time for the visitor to savour the history of this most
crowded of Aleppo's thoroughfares (at this point known as the Suq al-Zarb). Let
us just pause in front of one building that can be lost in the chaos but which gives a
snapshot of different currents at the end of the twelfth century. The small madrasa
known as al-Shadhbakhtiye (or the Mosque of Sheikh Ma'ruf) is approached from
street level by a short steep flight of stairs. The descent amounts to almost a third
of the height of the doorway, indicating how the ground level has risen over the
past eight centuries. Today the suq in the front of the madrasa is covered in elegant
stone arcading in cross-vaulted style. We will look further at the evolution of the
covered suqs later but when Ibn Jubayr passed this way just before the madrasa
was built the roofs were in wood.

Figure 8.3 Courtyard of the Great Mosque in Aleppo looking east with its striking
eighteenth-century paving

The patron of this small religious school had a career which illuminates some of the complex history of the transition to Ayyubid rule in the face of Aleppo's attachment to the Zengid princes in the region. Jamal al-Din Shadhbakht, as noted earlier, took control of the Citadel after Nur al-Din's death. Apparently of Indian origin, he had started as a personal slave of Nur al-Din, rising through freedman status to a major role in the Aleppo court. Twenty years after Nur al-Din's death, he built this madrasa for followers of the Hanafi school of Islamic jurisprudence, a clear sign of his reconciliation with the Ayyubid regime (Figure 8.4). The architecture, the first surviving Ayyubid madrasa in Aleppo, has many echoes of the strict Zengid style including the oldest example of the *muqarnas* half-dome over the sunken entrance and a wide *iwan*-hall off the courtyard. Terry Allen has speculated that Shadhbakht employed an architect who had earlier worked on Zengid projects and whose style he favoured. But the beautiful *mihrab* is thoroughly in accord with the more assured style of the Ayyubids which we will see at its peak fifty years later in the superb strapwork-decorated mihrab of the Paradise Madrasa.

The northern front after 1188, trade

After his great victory at Hattin in 1187, Saladin had not pressed his sweep north from Palestine to risk an assault on Antioch in 1188. Nevertheless, the Crusader principality was reduced to a small enclave with much of its agricultural

Figure 8.4 Iwan of the Madrasa Shadhbakhtiye

hinterland now in Muslim hands. The pressure on Aleppo was relieved and an easier atmosphere prevailed with the Armenian Kingdom in Cilicia, disinterested in moving southeast into Ayyubid lands even after their victory over an Ayyubid army in the Amuq Valley in 1206. Byzantium, which had quietly allowed passage across Anatolia for the three European kings' contributions to the Second Crusade (1148), now seemed content to recognise Ayyubid supremacy in northern Syria.

This was, then, a period of relative calm and prosperity for Aleppo, echoed in the Arab chroniclers' appreciation of Ghazi:

> The character of the prince procured him general respect; he was reso-
> lute, vigilant, studious of the welfare of his subjects, well acquainted
> with the proceedings of (contemporary) princes, animated with a lofty
> spirit, skilful in administration and government of the empire, diffusing
> justice throughout the land, fond of the learned, and generous to poets.[9]

Warfare was a more sporadic preoccupation. Ghazi began a policy of extending his alliances northeast into the Kurdish-dominated areas around Mardin and Diyarbakir, partly to consolidate the dynasty's ethnic links but also to discourage a revival of Seljuk designs on northern Syria. The Ayyubid principality of Aleppo, however, should not be seen as a manifestation of 'Kurdism': 'It does not seem that the presence of Turks beside Kurds in the Ayyubid regime differed profoundly from that of the Kurds besides the Turks in the Zengid regime.'[10] The crude racial or religious sense of 'identity' dominant in the Middle East or elsewhere today should not colour our picture of societies eight centuries ago. Moreover, all ethnic groups lived under a mantle of Arab culture. For the moment, Syria was the heartland of Arab scientific and religious thought. That culture eventually became more extensively implanted in Cairo, especially given the battering Syrian society was soon to suffer in the face of the Mongol invasions. Now, basking in the Ayyubid moment, Aleppo's turbanned elite played a role elevating the city to a status it had not enjoyed for centuries.

This was certainly an era where fewer military confrontations and domestic stability brought continued economic prosperity partly based on international trade. After the tensions of the early Crusading period, religious minorities enjoyed a more relaxed environment. Sunnism was largely unchallenged as the dominant Islamic trend, though a Shi'i element survived in the mix. Leaders such as Saladin and al-Zahir Ghazi issued decrees reiterating that Christians could not be subject to arbitrary harassment or seizure of their goods. There were fewer reasons to see outsiders as a threat and even Western Christian clerics were allowed to operate within the local Christian communities as long as they did not seek to convert Muslims. Italian trading houses (Genoa and Trieste) were using not just the Crusader ports but now also Latakia and from there visiting the Muslim cities of the interior, notably Aleppo. Moreover, Aleppo's links with the East were more fully developed than with other cities of the Muslim interior and its caravan connections reached as far as Tabriz.

Ayyubid building program – the 'Chosen Pearls'

The decades of relative peace and rising prosperity, as well as the stability of leadership in Aleppo, brought an unprecedented wave of construction activity. It was under Ghazi that the walls today seen encircling the Citadel were substantially constructed. Ghazi also took this opportunity to acknowledge the city's growing need for space. Whereas previously the line of city walls had gripped the Citadel like a pincer, he considered it time to begin a process of pushing out the circuit to the east, thus enclosing the Citadel on all sides within civilian areas.

The new line of eastern walls (not completed for many decades) followed the course of an outer defensive ditch which had been built under Nicephorus Phocas during the Byzantine tenth-century reoccupation of the city to slow down any assault on the Citadel from the east. This expansion allowed the city's living space to grow by around 30 per cent but also meant that the Citadel was now stranded, thus less free to play a role in the city's defence (see Figure 8.5).

The new walls required the reconstruction of the city's gates. Not only was a new set needed along the eastern city walls but also some of the other gates were substantially rebuilt on their original locations. The gate which exhibits the most complex construction history is the Antioch Gate (Bab Antaki – see Figure 4.2 on page 74) on the city's west side. Practically the whole history of post-Classical

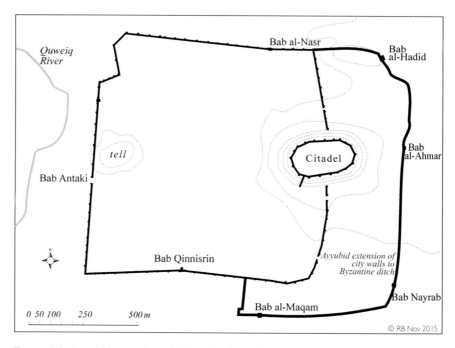

Figure 8.5 Ayyubid extension of Aleppo's city walls

Aleppo can be read in the various types of masonry in this gate. It was through a gate at this point that the Islamic victors entered the city in 637 (see pages 74–5). In the surviving version, two enormous bastions were constructed in the Arab manner with an eccentric entrance passage through the right-hand tower. Inscriptions on the gate go back as far as the Fatimid period but most of the present configuration dates from 1245.

The city retained the imprint of the ancient grid plan for most of the length of the main axis between Bab Antaki and the Citadel. Most of the new prestige projects were inserted into this ancient street pattern. Outside the walled city, however, the city had already spread beyond its new bounds to accommodate a rising population, particularly of Turkmen recruited since Zengid times and who now underpinned the Ayyubids' hold on territories to the east. Much of our information about the city at this time comes from chroniclers who give detailed lists of the city's buildings, their founders and affiliations, particularly Ibn Shaddad whose work is preserved and expanded in Ibn al-Shihna's *The Chosen Pearls* – the title underlining the pride the inhabitants felt in the beauty of their city and its monuments.

Aleppo had again become a princely capital determined to advertise its prestige. In the years from 1192 to 1260, thirty-six major projects were either initiated or involved significant rebuilding of existing institutions. Two-thirds of these projects were religious in nature, reflecting the continuing concern to display Islamic piety and promote the triumph of Sunnism through Koranic learning. The style of building, taking over the plain style of Nur al-Din's time, remained severely uniform; now even more beautiful in its proportions and consciously limiting extravagant decorative flourishes. By contrast, the contemporary architecture of the Ayyubids' Seljuk and Artuqid neighbours to the northeast had lapsed into an eclectic melange of all stylistic trends over the previous millennium. For the Ayyubids, the message was simple: plain, proportionate, evoking a sense of harmony and balance. The occasional decorative flourish came around a column capital, an alcove or mihrab with the use of muqarnas bands as zones of transition. Cross-vaulting and domes added height to prayer halls or tombs. In most cases, though, the perspective drew the visitor towards the point of greatest significance – the *mihrab*, indicating the direction of prayer with nothing else to distract the attention except the preacher's *minbar* or stepped platform.

Sixteen of the major buildings that date from the Ayyubid years after 1192 have survived into modern times, perhaps stamping the Ayyubid style in Aleppo more thoroughly than in any other Middle Eastern city. So great was the city's reputation as a test-bench for architectural ideas that its style spread to Damascus and from there as far as Egypt. Eight of the sixteen intra-mural projects were important Islamic foundations, all of them educational institutions apart from the rebuilt Great Mosque itself. The mosque was comprehensively gutted by fire in 1168. Nur al-Din had straight away initiated a major rebuilding, expanding the mosque's ground plan (see Figure 9.6 on page 181). His new version was in turn partly destroyed by later fires and an earthquake which made further reconstruction necessary. The mosque as seen today in fact straddles in style the Zengid to Mamluk periods: most of the fabric of the prayer hall (except its courtyard wall) are Ayyubid with major reconstruction after the Mongol invasions notably that of 1260.

From this late twelfth-/thirteenth-century resurgent and prosperous city we gain the initial first-hand descriptions from visitors. The Andalusian Muslim Ibn Jubayr provided richly florid impressions following his four-day visit in 1184. Scarcely any superlatives are neglected in praising Aleppo: 'massively built, wonderfully disposed, of rare beauty . . . fit for a Caliph'. Even before Ghazi's rebuilding of the Citadel circuit of defences, he wondered at its 'strength and grandeur, beyond description'. Aleppo's markets won particular attention, rated as 'paradisal': 'large markets arranged in long adjacent rows so that you pass from a row of shops of one craft into that of another until you have gone through all the urban industries. These markets are all roofed in wood so that the occupants enjoy an ample shade and all hold the gaze from their beauty.' Ibn Jubayr also noted, however, that Aleppo's setting did it no favours. Its magnificence was 'all within; it has nought without save a small river'. It was the Great Mosque which inspired his highest praise: 'one of the finest and most beautiful of mosques'.[11]

A princely Citadel

The centrepiece of the city's new princely presence was the Citadel. We have noted earlier that under al-Zahir Ghazi, the Citadel fortifications were replanned to take more or less the form in which we see them today. Some modifications and rebuilding had already taken place under Nur al-Din but the crowning ring of walls atop the flanks of the encircling *glacis* (a smooth sloping stone surface which made scrambling up almost impossible) was commenced under Ghazi – a classic display of Arab fortification techniques. So extensive was the Ayyubid ruler's work on the fortifications that we have difficulty identifying any remains that preceded him though it is still possible to find small sections incorporated in the Ayyubid masonry.

While the Crusaders' Krak des Chevaliers on the edge of the Orontes Valley east of Homs is everyone's ideal fairytale castle, Aleppo's great Citadel tends to receive a lower billing. Perhaps this is partly due to the fact that its interior was badly knocked around in later centuries, though the outside is largely intact. Only the two massive out-towers and the upper part of the entrance gateway are later (Mamluk) additions, the rest of the fabric giving us a textbook illustration of Arab medieval fortification techniques, which we will examine now.

The Citadel is essentially a ring of curtain walls and towers set on a partly artificial hill, the sides of which have been shaped to provide the formidable glacis – the classic 'truncated cone'. It is encircled below by a deep ditch or *fosse*. The ditch, like the glacis, was originally paved with carefully laid limestone slabs,

Figure 8.6 Entrance gates and bridge of the Aleppo Citadel

Figure 8.7 Aleppo Citadel taken in the 1930s (Michel Ecochard, courtesy Archnet)

today much reduced by erosion and stone robbing but conveying enough of the formidable defences that daunted any potential enemy. The enhanced mound incorporates the natural rock formation at its core. The rest of the cut-off cone is artificially formed using natural earth and the detritus of centuries.

This massive cone shaped to support a ring of walls is common to most Islamic fortified sites of the Syrian interior.[12] What they also have in common (apart from a tightly deployed pattern of gate defences, examined below) is a central corridor joining all the main facilities within the citadel, the passage usually partly roofed for protection (see Figure 7.4 on page 136). Along the corridor of the Aleppo Citadel lie the two main Islamic sanctuaries serving the Ayyubid court – the Great Mosque and the Mosque of Abraham (both noted in Chapter 7 in relation to the Abrahamic tradition). The Citadel Great Mosque was rebuilt by Ghazi in 1214, its minaret intended to dominate the city. Its architecture is one of the most striking tributes to the restrained beauty of Ayyubid architecture at its best. The Abraham Mosque was also restored under Ghazi but shows less of the Ayyubid stamp.

Prototype of Islamic fortifications

The Aleppo Citadel became the prototype for a series of Islamic fortifications in the wider region. All shared the truncated cone profile and the same layout – a single entrance gate, a central corridor, steeply sloped glacis. Not only was the

Figure 8.8 Prayer hall of the Great Mosque of the Aleppo Citadel, as rebuilt by Ghazi

form quite different from the Crusader style of castle but the way its components were deployed reflected quite different strategic aims.

The Ayyubid redevelopment of the Citadel involved the rebuilding of a fortified entrance gateway. This new gateway followed the Arab design of a tightly defended entrance passage set between two towers with the doorway positioned to break the momentum of any assault. Al-Zahir Ghazi's towers were set with the entrance to the Citadel proper offset in the right tower, thus exposing any attackers to a withering range of fire from three sides, including from five sets of machicolation boxes able to rain down heated oil or bolts onto this confined space.

After the great bronze-clad door, the path twisted along a circuitous route through the twin-tower structure, further slowing down invaders and subjecting them to another range of murderous devices – more apertures for dropping hot metal and oil; firing slits embedded in the internal walls; and paving intended to baffle the hooves of horses. Psychological warfare was not forgotten with the outer and inner doorways embellished with talismanic figures of entwined snakes or dragons and lion heads, devices commonly found in Seljuk imagery.

This extraordinary gate complex still impresses with its massive bulk rearing above the fortress ditch. In fact, the structure above the Ayyubid gate was a little less elevated than it appears today as the Mamluks three hundred years later would add another set of staterooms on top, probably replacing an earlier superstructure.

The Third Crusade (1191) had signalled that three European monarchs were anxious to redress the disaster at Hattin and restore the Kingdom of Jerusalem, now confined to Tyre and a coastal strip. The implications for Aleppo were rather remote.[13] While Saladin had sought unsuccessfully to bolster the increasingly precarious Muslim hold on Acre (reclaimed by the Crusader contingents of the Third Crusade from England and France in 1191), Ghazi's main preoccupation was to protect his own domains from the already endemic pattern of inter-Ayyubid rivalries. He rejected the idea of fragmented princely enclaves only loosely affiliated through the family. He preferred a centralised model and his domain in Aleppo was the only one which earned the ruler the title of sultan, previously reserved for Cairo. Given the difficult nature of the politics of northern Syria with the pressures from Turks, Byzantines and the fractious family entities (not only in southern Syria but also in the Jazira and northern Iraq), Ghazi opted for a wide belt to protect his capital defended by his own constellation of castles whose designs followed the Aleppo model.

The prototype is most clearly reflected in the castle 100 kilometres to the east on the Upper Euphrates at Qalaat Najm (Figure 8.11), recently restored by the Syrian authorities.[14] This outer ring of Ayyubid fortifications would eventually stretch as far as Ras al-ʿAyn well to the east, reflecting Ghazi's belief that Aleppo's security could only be assured through supremacy over the Jazira from where most of the city's foes had stemmed. It was also the route by which the city's economy could siphon the trade flows that had always ensured its prosperity.

Figure 8.9 Inner gateway of the Aleppo Citadel with the original Ayyubid twin towers in the lower half

Ayyubid stability

Events to the south rarely involved northern Syria at this time. The Third Crusade extended the Jerusalem Kingdom's precarious toehold on the coast at Tyre to form a more viable enclave. Both Crusader Tripoli and Antioch managed to retain their own enclaves but had little capacity to threaten the inland.

Al-Zahir Ghazi died relatively young in 1216 but his legacy did not perish. In 1212, his marriage to Dayfa Khatun, the daughter of Saladin's brother, al-'Adil, had been a move aimed at the time at forming an alliance to fend off further Ayyubid

Figure 8.10 Talismanic lion heads guarding the last doorway of the Aleppo Citadel
entrance complex

succession tensions but which proved a lasting and fruitful union. On Ghazi's
death in 1216, his three-year-old son by Dayfa Khatun, al-ʿAziz Muhammad
(r.1216–36) succeeded under a tutelage arrangement supervised by the Turkic atabeg Tughrul. The child's mother was appointed to the regency council and would
become the formidable matron of the Ayyubid court. Challenges were warded off
by political alliances with the Ayyubid leaders of Upper Mesopotamia and the
Seljuks of Konya, thus preventing the predatory instability that plagued the rest
of Ayyubid Syria.

Another major new Ayyubid project was now undertaken just south of the
Weather God temple location on the Citadel. Nur al-Din had built here the palace
known as the Dar al-Dhahad ('Golden House'). We know little of this phase as it
was largely destroyed in a serious fire in 1212 during Ghazi's reign – in fact on
the night of his wedding to Dayfa Khatun. The present-day gateway to the palace
(Figure 8.12), however, would appear to date from Ghazi's rebuilding as the Dar
al-ʿIzz ('House of Honour') but the remains behind it probably represent a further
rebuilding in 1230 under al-ʿAziz Muhammad.

The Ayyubid palace of the Citadel is another notable achievement, providing us
with a rare glimpse of the architecture of an Ayyubid court.[15] The Aleppo complex
preserves a range of spaces devoted both to ceremonial and living arrangements
with a bath complex to the east. (The palace was restored as far as surviving material would allow in the 1980s.) The building is relatively small and is based on the

Figure 8.11 Sloping *glacis* of the Ayyubid fortress at Qalaat Najm on the Euphrates

four-iwan layout with a beautiful central courtyard with flowing water providing relief to the otherwise static and symmetrical perspectives.

Fostering piety

The later Ayyubids did not just concern themselves with grand civic and regime-sponsored teaching and religious institutions. The thirteenth century was also marked by a growing trend towards individual piety. This became particularly evident in the cemetery zone, the Maqamat, which stretched around the southern outskirts of the city's walls extending to the west to the Salihin area already marked by the Shrine of Abraham (see pages 134–6). This increasingly became an area favoured for interment given its associations not just with Abraham but with the annual Hajj pilgrims who streamed out of the city through these burial grounds.

One of the most interesting figures associated with this holy space was Abu al-Hasan ʿAli Ibn Abu Bakr al-Harawi, a wandering ascetic born to a Persian family in Mosul and who died in Aleppo in 1215. Al-Harawi was drawn to Aleppo (probably as early as Saladin's rule) partly due to its enlightened court environment. Most famous for his *Guide to Places of Pilgrimage* across the Middle East, his curiosity was not confined to Islamic pilgrimage centres but included those which also attracted Christian and Jewish patrons. He spent some years compiling his study of the pilgrimage trails but may also have served his political masters in conveying intelligence on religious practices in other centres.

Figure 8.12 Entrance to Sultan al-Zahir Ghazi's palace on the Aleppo Citadel

Al-Harawi's fascination with pilgrimage was probably inspired by lingering Shi'i sympathies. Saladin and his son, al-Zahir Ghazi, may also have appreciated his claimed insights into the occult, reflecting the considerably wider scope of Islamic inquiry in the late twelfth century. He was also known for his skills as a conjuror and magician. His burial place on the southwestern outskirts of Aleppo is honoured by visiting pilgrims.

Al-Zahir Ghazi's interest in less orthodox traditions in Islam may also be reflected in the welcome he gave as a young man to the Persian Sufi mystic Shihab al-Din al-Suhrawardi, known as 'Sheikh al-Ishraq' (Master of Illumination). Suhrawardi's writings sought to revive ancient Persian fascination with the spiritual force of light, borrowing elements from Zoroastrianism and Neo-Platonism. He took up teaching at the Madrasa Halawiye and was welcome at al-Zahir Ghazi's court. However, his brash self-assurance appears to have increasingly offended the city's religious and political cadres. He was executed in 1192 on the orders of Ghazi, led on by his political advisers who were ostensibly offended by Suhrawardi's spreading his 'illuminationist' philosophy to other leaders in the wider region. Suhrawardi was simply too strong a personality to be allowed free rein in the still-fragile power relationship in northern Syria between Ayyubids and the surviving Zengid and Artuqid elements – a situation often exacerbated by residual Ismaeli activism. Members of the 'turbanned elite', who united the religious and mercantile establishments and funded the new array of Aleppo madrasas, were able to overcome Ghazi's intellectual fascination with the Persian philosopher and to demand his elimination.

Anticipating paradise

In more conventional terms, three major madrasas in the Maqamat area not only contributed to the reinforcement of the orthodox schools of Islamic jurisprudence but were also built as statements of faith by major figures of the ruling Ayyubid family in Aleppo. They remain to this day supreme expressions of the balance of simplicity and restraint of the thirteenth-century Aleppo 'simple' style.[16]

The greatest of these buildings is the institution often called the Madrasa al-Fardous or 'School of Paradise'. This madrasa is a tribute to the great vision of Ghazi's wife, Dayfa Khatun, who survived until 1242, a quarter century after the

Figure 8.13 Madrasa al-Fardous ('School of Paradise'), courtyard and portico of the prayer hall

death of her husband. One of a series of powerful women in thirteenth-century Syrian courts, she played a role which stretched across generations of leaders. ('Ismat al-Din Khatun, an earlier example, had wed successively Nur al-Din and Saladin – dynastic marriages that developed into real partnerships of souls.) As the widow of al-Zahir Ghazi, she survived the decades spanning not only al-'Aziz Muhammad's reign (r.1216–36) but the first years of that of her grandson, al-Nasir Yusuf II (r.1237–60). She thus provided an element of stability, keeping Aleppo apart from the rivalries that marked the long period of decline that beset most other Ayyubid principalities.

Why 'School of Paradise'? Many attempts to give buildings a 'message' fail the hubris test. In this case, the name may well be warranted. The Sufi madrasa was originally surrounded by orchards suggesting a paradisal setting but the attribution in this case has more specific grounds. One of the extraordinary additions to the building are two long inscription bands running around the outside and inner walls. They total over 70 metres, one of the longest Arabic inscriptions ever recorded. The external band starts to the right of the entrance with verses from the Koran rarely employed in Islamic architecture – Sura 43, 68–72:

> Enter Paradise . . . in all delight. You shall be served with golden dishes and golden cups . . . you shall find all that your souls desire and all that your eyes rejoice in.[17]

Not only an adroit political counsellor, Dayfa Khatun was also a great patron of religious architecture especially of institutions to explore the deeper recesses of spiritual thought. The inscription is one of the first to honour a woman as a building's

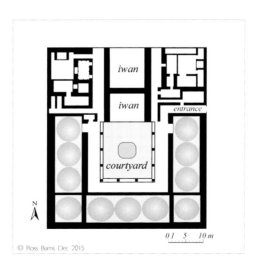

Figure 8.14 Madrasa al-Fardous or School of Paradise

founder and provide her honorifics and titles. Her influence on the city was profound: she 'taps the collective spiritual power of the Sufis to cross the divide between this and the other world, between mystic practice and paradise'.[18] Perhaps the legacy of al-Sahrawardi had not expired forty years before when Dayfa Khatun's husband, then a young man, yielded to his more hide-bound advisers and agreed to the mystic's execution.[19]

The Paradise Madrasa, located in the holy grounds flanking the path to Mecca, is one of the greatest accomplishments of Ayyubid architecture. Its purity of line, its uncompromising proportions and symmetry, the restraint of its largely monochrome decoration are remarkable. Yet it reserves flashes of virtuoso display for the important zones that require the faithful's eye, particularly the mihrab (Figure 8.15), whose niche is framed by colonnettes (a reference to classical style?) and above which swirls a tangle of multi-coloured bands in stone. The person who single-handedly awakened Europe's interest in the mastery of form achieved by the builders of the Islamic Middle Ages, Gertrude Bell, put it succinctly after a visit to Aleppo in 1909:

> They were great builders (the Ayyubids and Mamluks) . . . and in nothing greater than their mastery of structural difficulties. The problem of the dome, its thrust and its setting over a square sub-structure, received from them every possible solution; they bent the solid stone into airy forms of infinite variety. Their splendid masonry satisfied the eye as does the wall of a Greek temple, and none knew better than they the value of discreet decoration.[20]

Dayfa Khatun's second major project was a school for Sufi students within the old city, though it would appear that as a state-funded institution its treatment was more mundane. The Khanqah al-Farafra lies just north of the main cross-city axis in the walled city. Two earlier Ayyubid madrasas in the Maqamat area south of the walls follow the doctrine of restraint more closely. The first of the major new schools, the al-Zahiriye Madrasa (c.1215) preceded the Paradise Madrasa and was the first to carry an elaborate muqarnas canopy over the doorway (Figure 8.16).

The Madrasa Zahiriye was initially intended as the funerary college for al-Zahir Ghazi until it was decided to install his sarcophagus in the Sultaniye Madrasa (1224) at the foot of the Citadel, just to the east of the axis leading to the Bab al-Maqam (Figure 8.17). This unfinished building was hurriedly pressed into service to house the sultan's tomb in a domed chamber east of the prayer hall. The austere building, probably never completed as originally intended, reserves its only flash of exuberance for the prayer hall mihrab, again in interlaced three-colour stone. The second new project south of the city walls was the Madrasa al-Kamiliye. This was the third marker of Dayfa Khatun's period of influence in the 1230s. The plan reflects the popularity of the four-iwan layout introduced decades earlier from Mesopotamia, though it was possibly the work of the same architect as the contemporary Paradise Madrasa.

Figure 8.15 Mihrab of the Madrasa al-Fardous

A new axis

The use of the space immediately south of the grand Citadel entrance complex has already been mentioned in the context of its development under Nur al-Din as a venue for processional display, partly linked to his ceremonial arrival in the city as well as to his appearances at the courts of justice.

As redeveloped in al-Zahir Ghazi's time, the Citadel gateway served to define further the perspective along the north–south axis just described. Near the foot of the Citadel gateway lay the Dar al-'Adl where the sultan followed his predecessors' practice of descending to supervise the dispensing of justice twice a week, another essential foundation of Ghazi's reign. After passing an important group

163

Figure 8.16 Muqarnas half-dome over the doorway to the Madrasa Zahiriye

Figure 8.17 Madrasa Sultaniye, burial place of Sultan al-Ghazi was left of the prayer hall

of major madrasas and mosques, the route would realise its key religious role each year during the Hajj, taking the faithful out of the city into the cemetery area (noted earlier page 158), dotted with pious structures between the tombs of the Salihin and Maqamat areas. From there, pilgrims would join the flow of faithful heading south for Damascus where they formed an organised caravan for the difficult and long trip on to Mecca. From the Ayyubid period on, the ceremony and the safe delivery of the Hajj became the defining tasks of the regime, underlining not only its temporal power but its ability to channel the religious life of the city and its place within the Ayyubid realms. Using the city's architecture to raise the status of Aleppo as a way-station on the annual pilgrimage became an important element in al-Zahir Ghazi's consolidation of the city's life, one that endured even in the face of the disruption that elsewhere marked the closing decades of the Ayyubids.

The message of the Ayyubid rulers of Aleppo, however, was not solely spiritual. Piety helped buttress power. The axis as it left the Citadel served as 'a conduit between the secular and religious domains of the Ayyubids'.[21] The message of power and control was underlined as the route departed through the city walls at the Bab al-Maqam ('Shrine Gate', built 1230 under al-Zahir Ghazi's son, al-'Aziz Muhammad). Defence was not its prime purpose. Unlike all other city gates of the Ayyubid period with their evasive passages, here one walked straight through. It was the equivalent of the typical Roman 'triumphal arch' found throughout the empire, often outside a city entrance and with triple openings. Though its defensive role was preserved with the openings placed tightly between deep flanking towers, its main purpose was to emphasise prestige and stability.

This brief survey of the Ayyubids' contributions to the fostering of piety through architecture and its decoration would not be complete without noting

Figure 8.18 Bab al-Maqam seen from the south

a final tribute to the era by the last Ayyubid Sultan and grandson of al-Ghazi, al-Nasir II Yusuf Ibn al-'Aziz Muhammad. (The spectacularly unsuccessful denouement of Al-Nasir Yusuf's career (r.1236–60) will be picked up in the next chapter.) Housed in an annexe to the Madrasa Halawiye is a wooden mihrab whose marquetry is of an extraordinary grace and complexity. Originally commissioned under Nur al-Din, the mihrab as we see it today was refurbished in 1245 by al-Nasir Yusuf as recorded by the inscription that wraps around the outer frame, itself a thing of great beauty. Remarkably, it would survive fifteen years later the first Mongol sack when the city itself was abandoned by this last Ayyubid, bringing to an end what had otherwise been a period of extraordinary achievement for Aleppo.

Figure 8.19 Mihrab in the Madrasa Halawiye commissioned under Nur al-Din and restored by the last Ayyubid Sultan of Aleppo, al-Nasir II Yusuf Ibn al-'Aziz Muhammad, in 1245

Notes

1 Sauvaget 1941: 129.
2 Parts of the house still stand, incorporated into two buildings – the bath known today as Hammam al-Sultan and the neighbouring madrasa housing the tomb of the Mamluk ruler Baybars (Burns 2005: 199).
3 Eddé 2011: 68.
4 Quoted in Eddé 2011: 71.
5 Ehrenkreutz 1972: 182.
6 Ehrenkreutz 1972: 191–6 (quote on page 191).
7 Cahen 'Ayyubids' *EI2*.
8 Ibn Jubayr 2003: 260.
9 Ibn Khallikan 1843: III, 443.
10 Cahen 'Ayyubids' *EI2*.
11 Ibn Jubayr 2003: 260–4.
12 The best examples can be seen at Homs, Qalaat Mudiq (Apamea), Gaziantep (Aintab, Turkey), Qalaat Shmemis (east of Hama) and Qalaat Rahba on the lower Euphrates.
13 The leader was Emperor Frederick Barbarossa of Germany with separate forces under Richard the Lionheart of England and Philip Augustus of France. Barbarossa died in 1190, probably of a stroke, while crossing a freezing stream in eastern Cilicia, en route to Syria.
14 Tabbaa (2006: 179) notes an outer ring of defences within a circle 150 kilometres around Aleppo – Harim, Saône, ʿAzaz (formerly Crusader Hazart), Najm, Tell Bashir to the northeast (Turbessel, also seized from the Crusaders) and Trapesac and Latakia towards the coast. His acquisitions to the south pressed firmly against Hama's territory including Saône.
15 We have some insights into the rather grander ceremonial Ayyubid staterooms in Damascus, preserved inside the Citadel. Its four massive central columns, almost certainly recycled from the city's Jupiter Temple, once supported a domed roof over a central pool – a sumptuous space strikingly frozen in time even while the complex remained in service as a barracks and later a prison until the 1980s. By contrast, there is little that gives us a clue as to the Ayyubid palace arrangements on the Cairo Citadel as most of the fabric has disappeared in landslides.
16 The term is used in Allen's study of the Ayyubid architecture of Syria.
17 The Koran 1983.
18 Tabbaa 1997: 182.
19 Dayfa Khatun did not arrive in Aleppo until probably twenty years after al-Sahrawardi's death but his ideas would still have circulated in the city.
20 Bell 1911: 13.
21 Tabbaa 1997: 67.

9

A WIDER WORLD OPENS – ALEPPO UNDER THE MAMLUKS (1260–1516)

Our focus in the previous chapter was on Aleppo's horizons to the east, reflecting the fact that its political and economic fortunes were usually played out in the lands stretching eastwards towards the Tigris and modern-day northern Iraq. Both the ethnic composition of the leadership under the Zengids and Ayyubids (often with strong Kurdish links) and the struggles between the ruling principalities that marked the Ayyubid system post-Saladin focused on this zone. Even in the last decades of the struggle against the Crusaders, Aleppo somewhat kept its distance. In the next phase of the city's history, however, a stronger north–south orientation developed, knitting Aleppo more closely to an Islamic world whose main centres lay in Damascus and Cairo to the south.

Mongols (1258–60)

The first shock came with another wave of invaders from the east, this time from as far as Central Asia. The Mongols first emerged as a definable ethnic group during the sixth to the twelfth centuries in what is today northwest China and Mongolia. They began to push west in the first half of the twelfth century, raiding the cities of Khurasan and establishing their reputation for massacres and disruption on a huge scale – 'employing terror as a strategic weapon'.[1] Their sacking of Baghdad in 1258 with fatalities estimated in the hundreds of thousands rang the first alarm bells in the central Islamic lands. The Mongols, traditionally predominately Shamanists, were yet to go over to Islam. Before their conversion the Mongols had no religious inhibitions which might temper the savagery and disorder of their campaigns in Islamic lands. (Admittedly, their later reputation for massacres indicated that they rarely let such inhibitions spoil their game.[2])

The Mongol army was an entirely cavalry force and thus could deploy with astonishing speed. The numbers of their ranks have probably been exaggerated. Given their emphasis on mobility, campaigning with armed hordes in the hundreds of thousands would have crippled their logistic tail. They spent little time on administration in the lands they moved through, preferring to rely on existing bureaucratic machinery and draining the local tax base.

The Great and lesser Khans

The first widely recognised leader of the Mongols had been Genghiz Khan (an Anglicised form of Čingiz-Khān) who rose to power around 1198 in Mongolia and gradually was drawn into rivalries with the Khwarazmians, a Turkic group in Khurasan on the northeastern edge of Iran. The empire he set up known as the Great Khanate (the prime entity that had emerged from the westward spread of the Mongol empire) extended at his death in 1227 as far as modern Uzbekistan. Thirty years later in 1257, Mongke, the leader of the Great Khans, appointed his younger brother, Hulegu (both grandsons of Genghiz Khan) to cross the Oxus River and move into Iran and Iraq. (The western expedition resulted in the establishment of the Ilkhan dynasty in Iran and was matched by an eastwards thrust under Kublai Khan which took China.)

In Baghdad, Caliph al-Musta'sim responded to the Mongol threat with a mixture of bravado and indecision. Initially hesitating, he surrendered unconditionally after his army had spent six days trying to fend off the Mongol assault. His concession was too late, either to spare the city or to save himself from execution. To avoid direct responsibility for spilling royal blood, the Mongols killed the Caliph by wrapping him in a carpet and trampling him with their horses.[3] The city was not spared the massacres or wilful destruction at a level of ferocity that tested even the Arab chroniclers' powers of description.

The 1258 fall of Baghdad is one of those epoch-defining events that is supposed to tell us that 'nothing will ever be the same again'. A recent historian of Baghdad has commented: 'It was, by far, the most shattering blow the Muslim world had ever received and imperiled the very future of Islam.'[4] We should remember, though, that the 'Abbasid Caliphate had long been a hollow shell and Cairo had already wrested from it the mantle of the greatest city of Islam.

Aleppo falls to the Mongols 1260

As the Mongols moved further west into the central Islamic lands, their progress sent on ahead waves of fear and floods of refugees, amplifying the sense of dread. In response, there was little common purpose among the Ayyubids. The last Ayyubid ruler of Aleppo, al-Nasir Yusuf II (r.1236–60), had taken advantage of the weakness of other Ayyubid rulers in Syria to take over Damascus in 1250. By 1259, the Syrian *amir*s were consequently in disarray and one (Homs) even sought the early intervention of the Ayyubid praetorian guards or *mamluks* from Cairo on the news of the advance of Hulegu's army from the northeast. The option of forming a unified Ayyubid force to block the Mongol advance just did not happen. By 1260 the Mongol army would be joined by Christian forces from Cilician Armenia under King Hethum. Their alliance was an indication of a belief by some Christians that the Mongols could be useful allies in ending Muslim dominance in the Middle East.

Al-Nasir Yusuf's regime was 'dissolving from within' as Hulegu's horde approached from al-Bira (Birecik on the Euphrates), reaching Aleppo in December

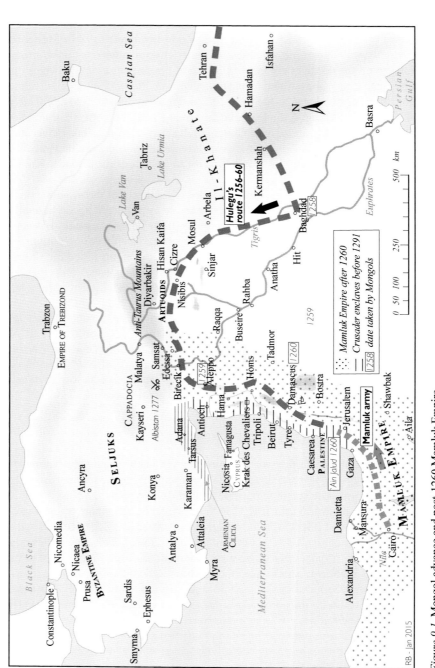

Figure 9.1 Mongol advance and post-1260 Mamluk Empire

1259.[5] Sultan Yusuf himself had fled south weeks beforehand. From southern Syria, he sent gifts and greetings to Hulegu in Baghdad, symptoms of a pattern of defiance mixed with craven submission that continued to mark his responses to the Mongols' approach. It was left to his great-uncle, the commander of the Aleppo Citadel, al-Muʿazzam Turanshah, to try to interrupt the Mongols' advance.

Though the Mongols offered reasonable terms for surrender, Turanshah, as a product of a more honourable generation, was convinced that if Aleppo gave up without a fight, Hulegu's forces would have an easy passage through the rest of Syria. The aged and last surviving son of Saladin believed the only honourable course was to refuse the terms, confident that Ghazi's stout walls would hold while boasting: 'The only thing that will stand between me and the Mongols is a sword'.[6] The Mongols brought up more than twenty mangonels, their bombardment continuing day and night, concentrating particularly on the east and south walls.

The fact that the city held out for less than a week encourages suspicions that one of the gates was opened by forces inside. Once admitted, Mongol forces unleashed a systematic programme of pillage and fire that endured another seven days. In a pattern to be repeated over the next 140 years, the Mongols indiscriminately slaughtered the citizens of Aleppo, sparing only craftsmen who might have a future use.[7] Eighty-year-old Turanshah had to witness this carnage from the Citadel, which managed to resist for another week. Impressed by Turanshah's courage and dignity, Hulegu offered to receive the garrison's surrender on a guarantee of safe passage. For once, the Mongol leader's undertaking was respected and Turanshah's troops marched out of the still-smoking city – an experience too much for the veteran Ayyubid, who died a few days later.

The door to the rest of Syria had indeed been flung open. Hama, strangely, was spared destruction by simply accepting a Mongol viceroy. Homs had already made overtures and signalled it would accept Mongol rule. Damascus surrendered without resistance, its Ayyubid army having scattered at the mere thought of Hulegu's tidal wave. Al-Nasir Yusuf panicked at the news received from Aleppo and was on his way via Palestine to Egypt having oscillated between flight and foolish schemes for resistance that never quite worked out. The Mongols' strategic but selective use of terror was paying off.

However massive the disruption that the Mongols brought with them, the invasion did not turn into an enduring occupation, even though the crisis post-Baghdad had brought the collapse of the virtually defunct Ayyubid leadership in Cairo and of its Syrian princes. Shortly after the taking of Aleppo, news had arrived of the death of Hulegu's elder brother, Mongke. Hulegu felt obliged to return to Karakoram to claim the succession, abandoning whatever plans he might have had for Syria and in due course setting up the Mongol dynasty known as the Ilkhans.

Fortunately, the army Hulegu had left behind in Syria under the Mongol general Kitbugha was to put up a poor show when it faced its first blocking force. In the face of Ayyubid collapse, an army of mamluks assembled in Cairo from the

Figure 9.2 South walls, *glacis* and ditch of the Aleppo Citadel with later outer bastion (Mamluk)

remnants of the Ayyubid administration's praetorian guard moved northwards into Palestine. The issues were to be quickly resolved. In the battle at 'Ain Jalud ('Springs of Gilead') in northern Palestine (1260), the scratch mamluk force assembled under a general by the name of Qutuz and managed a brilliant victory. This mercenary force might have saved Syria but they had no intention of saving the Ayyubids. They took Syria, Egypt and everything in between for themselves.

Al-Nasir Yusuf II, still lurking in southern Jordan in a paralysis of indecision, was intercepted by Kitbugha and taken prisoner. He was sent to the Mongol headquarters at Tabriz, ostensibly as the Mongol general's guest in case he might prove useful in asserting Mongol authority in Syria. Kitbugha, on learning that al-Nasir's residual Ayyubid force had fought on the mamluks' side at 'Ain Jalud, impetuously decided the last Ayyubid sultan of Aleppo was of no further use. He dispatched al-Nasir with his own sword.

Though further incursions occurred in the coming decades, Hulegu and the Ilkhans would never realise any ambition they might have had of governing Syria, confining future interventions to quests for plunder. The first of these new incursions was at the end of 1260 when a Mongol force, still determined to avenge 'Ain Jalud, returned to Aleppo. They held the city for another four months, this time concentrating their campaign of slaughter on refugees who had flooded into the city from neighbouring regions. They withdrew when a combined army assembled by Mamluk-appointed generals decisively defeated a larger Mongol force. Terror in numbers, the Mongols' strategic weapon, had begun to lose its efficacy – for the moment.

The Bahri Mamluks (1260–1382)

We divert for a moment to look at the origins of the new Turkic phenomenon that had struck like lightening to seize the central Islamic Lands. The mamluk forces that had served the dying remnants of the Ayyubid dynasty in Cairo had largely been recruited from Kipchak Turkic villages in modern-day Kazakhstan. Purchased or seized from their families as young boys, they were on-sold into the Cairo market and raised as a military caste owing prime loyalty to their Ayyubid masters. After 1250, however, the mamluks formed one of the only assets holding the Ayyubid regime in Cairo together and the idea naturally came into their minds to turn their military skills to serve their own political ambitions. In Cairo in 1250, the mamluks previously owned by the Ayyubid sultan al-Salih Ayyub (r.1240–9) turned against his son and nominated successor. Instead they accepted a compromise whereby the succession to al-Salih passed via his widow, Shajar al-Durr, though in effect the army commander in chief (Aybak, married off to the new *sultana*) became the effective boss of the mamluk forces. After Aybak sought to extend his influence into Syria and the Jazira in 1257 by arranging another marriage alliance – this time with the daughter of the ruler of Mosul – Shajar al-Durr felt aggrieved and arranged Aybak's assassination. Her involvement in Aybak's death, however, was discovered and she in turn was executed.

Shajar al-Durr had sought to conceal Aybak's death in order to buy time to establish new succession arrangements but she could not manipulate how the succession would be managed among the various factions. The victors rallied around Qutuz, who had distinguished himself at ʿAin Jalud. The mamluks had emerged from their role behind the throne and the first Mamluk 'dynasty', the Bahris, was to arise from their stunning victory over the Mongols in 1260. The coined description, Bahri, simply denotes that the original barracks of the Turkic mamluks were on the island of Rhoda on the Nile (Bahr al-Nil).

Baybars (r.1260–77)

Already distinguished for leading the mamluks to victory against the Franks under Louis IX at Mansura in the Egyptian Delta, Baybars had served in the vanguard of the mamluk army that fought under Qutuz at ʿAin Jalud. When Qutuz was assassinated (with Baybars' help)[8] shortly after the battle, Baybars was elected to replace him. The new Mamluk sultan then abruptly brought to an end decades of rivalry and weak leadership with an outburst of well-directed energy, rebuilding the structure of a unified state that had been allowed to fragment after Saladin.

Figure 9.3 Tomb of Shajar al-Durr in Cairo

Reversing Ayyubid indifference to the campaign against the Crusaders, he made it his mission to strengthen the Muslim defences and take the fight to the Franks as well as to build the administrative and communications infrastructure of his empire.

Over the next two decades, the huge army Baybars collected darted across the Middle East, threatening the Crusaders in their fortresses from Antioch to Shawbak (southern Jordan). His forces conducted thirty-eight separate campaigns in less than half that time; fifteen he led personally. One by one, the rebuilt Crusader strongpoints were picked off. By 1271, even the great Templar fortress, the Krak des Chevaliers, fell after a two-month siege. He divided his non-fighting time between Cairo and Damascus and took on that long-standing mission of Sunni Muslim leaders – to wipe out the Ismaeli presence in the Syrian coastal mountains. Aleppo, for the first time in over 200 years, faced no credible threat in its region with Crusader Antioch in Baybars' hands by 1268 (see below).

Baybars in one decade had turned the Middle East's strategic picture on its head. The old pattern of convenient truces between Muslim and Crusader forces was over. The momentum Saladin had let slacken had been restored. By 1272, Baybars was ready to extend his control into Asia Minor and the Armenian Kingdom of Cilicia, reaching as far as Kayseri in Cappadocia. His aim was partly to prevent further Mongol inroads via their Seljuk or Christian allies but by 1277 he had had to concede that the natural borderline between the two great empires, Ilkhanid and Mamluk, probably lay in eastern Turkey.

Cairo remained Baybars' power base and he strengthened its authority in religious terms too by reinstalling in 1261 a nominal ʿAbbasid Caliph in Baghdad – Abu'l Qasim al-Mustansir, a nonentity but with the convenient claim that he was an ʿAbbasid family refugee from the Mongols' slaughter in 1258 Baghdad. Having legitimised al-Mustansir, Baybars completed the arrangement by securing his own legitimacy when the Caliph declared recognition of Baybars as the universal sultan of the Islamic lands from the Euphrates to the Nile. Even more than under Nur al-Din or Saladin, the whole Middle East formed a unitary state with an effective structure of administration.

Baybars, a Turk, had laid the foundations for a new flowering of Arab culture of which Aleppo was to be a major beneficiary. The Mamluk sultanate would become an entity of international stature, commanding the sinews of commercial exchanges between Europe and the lands to the east for two and a half centuries. Aleppo was to seize its part in these exchanges with enthusiasm. The city the Mamluks took possession of in 1260 was virtually a smoking ruin – 'its walls knocked down, its *suqs*, its Great Mosque and all its monuments pillaged and burnt, whole quarters consumed by fire, its streets piled up with the bodies of those who could not escape in time – no more than a deserted ruin'.[9] The city's fortunes were so low they could only get better; but that would take time.

Securing Aleppo

Aleppo was one of numerous mid-sized cities in the extensive Mamluk world but it was politically an important one, lying on the interface between the Mamluk interest in securing their hold in central Syria and in backing the frontline campaign in the Anti-Taurus Mountains to the north where relations between the Ayyubids and the Turkic states had long been fluid. Whatever plans the Ilkhanids might have had to rule central Syria died out, along with the dynasty itself, by the middle of the fourteenth century. However, border wars or occasionally more extensive raids still occurred for the next eighty years, motivated largely by plunder.[10]

Control of Aleppo had been one of the first preoccupations Baybars had to address. The Mamluk-appointed ruler of Damascus, ʿAlam al-Din Sanjar al-Halabi, refused to accept Baybars' supremacy over the empire, preferring to reserve Syria as his own fiefdom. The Syrian Ayyubids had resisted the Cairo mamluks' manipulation behind the scenes that had installed the Mamluk regime and had particularly resisted the appointment of a woman to head the sultanate. After ʿAin Jalud, to secure the new regime's supremacy over Syria, Mamluk governors were appointed in Damascus and Aleppo, charged with expelling the Mongol forces and dislodging the Ayyubids still in control. Before his assassination, Qutuz had undertaken to appoint Baybars to Aleppo, seeing advantage in keeping his rival as far as possible from Cairo.

Baybars had to respond not only to al-Halabi's revolt but also to the residual presence of Mongol forces in the Aleppo region. After the Mongols reoccupied Aleppo for four months (noted earlier pages 172–3), they scattered on hearing that

Baybars had sent a force to retake the city in April 1261. Unfortunately, when he arrived in Aleppo the commander of the Mamluk relief force, Shams al-Din al-Barli, took the opportunity to plunder the city himself, though he in turn fled when a new force approached the city commanded by three of Baybars' appointees, including the disgraced Sanjar al-Halabi, who had somehow survived his recent revolt in Damascus and was reassigned to Aleppo. It was another year, though, before Baybars was able to restore order in Aleppo. Al-Halabi had found the challenge too much for him and Baybars had to take to the field to restore control. Baybars appointed a range of new amirs and took al-Barli back to Egypt, no doubt to keep him under close surveillance. Al-Halabi went on to serve the cause of the Mamluks for another twenty years.

Clearly these experiences persuaded Baybars that with subordinates constantly on the lookout to turn events to their own advantage, his empire could only be kept together through rapid communications and short response times. He put considerable effort into setting up a communications relay system for both postal items (a twice weekly service supported by fixed staging posts where horses and couriers could be exchanged) and, in some sectors, transmission of higher value intelligence by carrier pigeons or optical signals. In theory, a routine message could be sent from Cairo to Damascus in four days. Aleppo presumably would require another two days but that was a significant advance and in a real emergency some stages could be jumped by resorting to optical signals.

It was not just speed but reliability of communications which was at stake. Responses had to be turned around quickly:

> for thereby he could organise the affairs of Syria, the fortresses and most of his possessions once or twice a week. . . . he could grant and withdraw assignments, make and unmake appointments in the whole of the [provinces of] Damascus and Aleppo and intelligence . . . was not concealed from him.[11]

In this way, after the chaos of the Mongol intervention, Baybars moved quickly to abolish the old Ayyubid system of decentralisation to local family appointees and switched to hands-on administration of a centralised empire, resolved on letting nothing escape his intention. It was a remarkable turnaround.

Taking Antioch 1264–8

Access to fast intelligence soon showed its benefits when the king of Armenian Cilicia, Hethum, intruded on Aleppo's territory with the support of Prince Bohemond of Antioch. It was a long time since Christians and Muslims had confronted each other in northern Syria but Hethum again felt emboldened, having made a cynical pact with the Rum Seljuks in Asia Minor. On this occasion, Baybars left it to his local amirs to handle the threat, which they soon despatched. Baybars set out for Aleppo three years later but a broken foot required him to return to

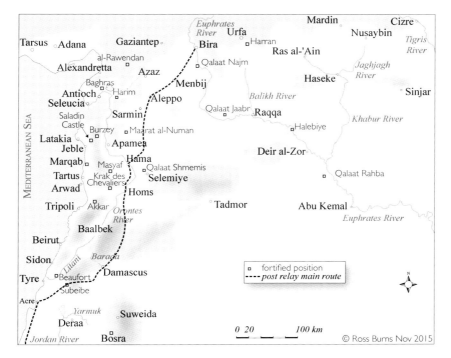

Figure 9.4 Mamluk Syria with major fortified positions

Cairo. In 1268, he took up his Syrian plan again, initially to campaign against the Crusader County of Tripoli but then deciding to continue on to Antioch. It was payback time for the Prince of Antioch who had spurned all the tacit understandings between Aleppo and Cilicia to indulge in a pact with the Mongols.

In fact by now Antioch was barely a palimpsest of its former prestige – a small enclave city with virtually no contiguous territory and a falling population.[12] Envoys from the city came out to negotiate terms for surrender but talks failed when they refused to consider an annual tribute (though they had been happy to pay one to the Mongols). The citizens of Antioch, however, proved to have no enthusiasm for a fight and the city fell to Baybars on the second day of siege (18 May 1268). Baybars sent his troops into the city and closed the gates after them. They were let loose to kill and loot at will. Baybars later wrote a gloating letter to Bohemond, absent in Tripoli, helpfully describing the scene which the Crusader prince had been unable to witness:

> You would have seen your knights prostrate beneath the horses' hooves, your houses stormed by pillagers and ransacked by looters, your wealth weighed by the quintal, your women sold four at a time and bought for a dinar of your own money! You would have seen your Muslim enemy

177

trampling on the place where you celebrate the mass, cutting the throats of monks, priests and deacons upon the altars, bringing sudden death to the patriarchs and slavery to the royal princes. You would have seen fire running through your palaces, your dead burned in this world before going down to the fires of the next.[13]

After 170 years of manoeuvres, rivalry and conflict, it was over: Antioch, the great metropolis of the Roman East, was now destined to spend the next seven centuries as little more than a small rural town. Aleppo, by contrast, had won local supremacy, and would go on to use its status in the wider Islamic world to become a major trading and political centre. The 7 kilometres of Antioch's walls, its Citadel looming from the heights and the constellation of castles, towers and cave-citadels that had dotted the countryside between the two long-standing rivals, began a long career as picturesque ruins. The most forlorn ruin of all was Bohemond's dream of an alliance of Armenian kings, Mongol khans and Frankish barons against the new empire controlling the Islamic lands.

A city on its knees? Aleppo in the 1260s

Northern Syria, however, was not necessarily a peaceful haven which could immediately reap the rewards of victory. After two bouts of Mongol vengeance, Aleppo was exhausted and largely in ruins. It had suffered much more intensely than other Syrian cities which had avoided reprisals by offering early surrender. Its population had been decimated. Anne-Marie Eddé, the foremost modern historian of Ayyubid Aleppo, estimates that Aleppo may have had a maximum population of 85,000 on the eve of the Mongol invasion of 1260.[14] While some 50,000 probably survived, this still left total deaths (or losses through enslavement) at 30,000 or more.

Any mid-sized city would find this level of casualties hard to absorb. The economy of much of the surrounding countryside had not escaped the ferocity of the Mongols either. Even without the Mongols and the Crusaders pounding at the walls, other enemies lay in wait. The Armenian kingdom in Cilicia lived on until 1335 and the lackeys who still offered loyalty to the Iraq-based Ilkhans sought to exploit opportunities to intrude into Mamluk territory. The Seljuks of Anatolia were keen for a tactical alliance but they were an impulsive potential ally and Baybars was not usually tempted to take his forces to areas so remote from Egypt. In 1277, however, he returned to Aleppo and agreed to the Seljuks' request to campaign jointly against a sizeable Mongol force which had arrived in Asia Minor. In a decisive victory on the plain of Albistan on the western side of the Cilician Gates (Figure 9.1), Baybars' forces left some 7,000 Mongols dead on the battlefield.

Six weeks later, Baybars died in Damascus before he could take a final decision on resuming his campaign in the north. The cause was ostensibly a bad draught of fermented mare's milk (*koumiss*) but even shortly after his death speculation

178

surfaced that he had been poisoned. Other possibilities included dysentery or a poisoning scenario directed against another that had gone wrong. He was buried in Damascus, his sudden death having made it difficult to contemplate other interment options. His tomb (examined below) remains a remarkable monument to the inventive early decades of Mamluk architecture.

In seventeen years, Baybars made a good start in providing the central Islamic lands with stable and reasonably predictable governance. He could be ruthless to those who stood in his way but he was also determined to deliver good administration and economic progress. He has missed out on the highest rating from history programmes that would see Saladin at the pinnacle of Islamic leaders but he should perhaps be ranked higher. He produced a remarkable turnaround in the wider Syrian/Egyptian region wracked by invaders and he gave it a semblance of peace it had not known for centuries.

The Mongol threat in the form of the Ilkhanate still existed over the horizon in Iraq but for the moment it was reduced to a capacity to raid and plunder rather than overturn established rulers further west. In 1280, the Mongols again briefly took Aleppo, staying only long enough to sack the city. The Mongols, however, returned to western Syria the next year. Aleppan forces joined southern Syrian and an Egyptian expeditionary force under Sultan Qalawun in defeating the Mongols in a subsequent battle at Homs (1281). In these conflicts, it is notable that the Aleppan army was always careful not to engage the Mongol forces immediately. Its strategy was to move south and combine with the forces of Hama before seeking engagement.

Building the Mamluk world

The Mamluk 'image makers' were already seeking to find ways of departing from the austere style which had suited the Ayyubids' less flashy temperament. In those early decades, Aleppo gives us little evidence of the new building programme but the just-mentioned tomb chamber of Baybars' mausoleum in Damascus provides a wonderful insight into where they were seeking ideas. The externals of this infrequently visited tomb chamber are less revealing (still largely following the Ayyubid style) but the interior shows a flamboyant inventiveness drawing on a range of ideas, including from the Classical and Byzantine eras. Whereas the *mihrab* of the Ayyubid Madrasa of Paradise in Aleppo sits in a frame weaving bold straps of interlaced marble decoration, Baybars' mihrab shows a whole new vocabulary mixing geometric and vegetal forms. Even more remarkable is the band of mosaic that runs around the room above the top of the mihrab. It is clearly inspired by the mosaic decoration that then covered much of the wall surfaces of the prayer hall of the Great Mosque of the Umayyads nearby, the work of early eighth-century Byzantine experts brought in to decorate the great project of Caliph Walid.[15]

Impoverished and under-populated, Aleppo could show nothing to rival Baybars' mausoleum as a masterpiece of early Mamluk art but the ideas seen in the

Figure 9.5 Baybars' tomb chamber in the Madrasa al-Zahiriye in Damascus

tomb chamber came to be reflected piecemeal as the decades unfolded. One small gesture to Aleppo was Baybars' decision to transfer the remains of Zachariah, the father of John the Baptist from the Mosque of Abraham on the Citadel to the downtown Great Mosque. The Aleppo congregational mosque was rebuilt to provide a more accessible location for this drawcard, though one not quite on the scale of the much older claim by the Damascus Umayyad Mosque to have the head of John the Baptist himself in its shrine. The Great Mosque of downtown Aleppo now perhaps reached more or less its twentieth-century form though unravelling the various phases of the patchwork of reconstructions and repairs during the Zengid through to the Mamluk periods is a challenge imperfectly addressed. The beautiful cross-vaulting of the prayer hall and the *riwaqs* on the eastern and northern sides of the courtyard would appear to be the work of the Mamluk reconstruction.

For at least the next half-decade, Aleppo's past as a poor broken city was still evident in its hesitant building programme. Aleppo's Citadel had taken a severe hit during the 1260–61 Mongol invasions and there was work to be done to restore the nearly 6 kilometres of city walls and gates that had been initiated by al-Zahir Ghazi fifty years before. Their repair and the rebuilding of the Great Mosque perhaps absorbed most of the budget for building works in the first Mamluk half-century. Most of the handful of new projects undertaken in Aleppo in these years were small in scale and few involved sponsors of official rank.

It is not until 1302 that we find the first project undertaken by a senior official, rather oddly the governor's food-taster. This relatively small Mehmendar Mosque

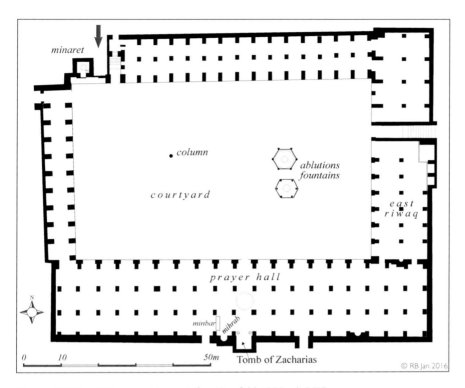

Figure 9.6 Great Mosque, Aleppo (after Herzfeld 1955: pl. LIII)

Figure 9.7 Mamluk eastern portico or *riwaq* of the Great Mosque of Aleppo

lies north of the Great Mosque on the widened axis of today's al-Mutannabi Street. Most remarkable is its minaret, which would not be out of place in contemporary (Mongol) Iran or in the Artuqid city of Mardin to the north of modern Syria. It is a beautiful adaptation of the Seljuk- and Mongol-influenced style of zigzag

Figure 9.8 Minaret of the Mehmendar Mosque with its Seljuk-influenced ribbed decoration

stonework in fine detailing, with a lower octagonal band of interlaced niches (not unlike the form found two centuries earlier on the Seljuk-era minaret of the Great Mosque). Moreover, it is round, a distinct departure from the Ayyubid love of square minarets of stolid construction.

The difficulties in discerning the steps in the process of transition from Ayyubid to Mamluk styles of building decoration are illustrated by another small mosque of this period. The Dabbagha Mosque today stands on the edge of a busy central city roundabout, Sabaa Bahrat Square. Its tiny prayer room is probably new but its minaret is earlier and the original mosque was later extended to take in a tomb added to the east. So gradual was the movement from one era to another that experts have had trouble deciding whether the minaret is Ayyubid or Mamluk. The use of a peculiar form of decoration around the window frame on the Dabbagha minaret may be a clue.

This design (a mixture of chevrons and cusps) has even earlier (pre-Zengid) origins. It was found on the doorway to Nur al-Din's Maristan and was also used even earlier under Ghazi in the frame around his inscription on the minaret of the Shrine of Abraham. The other details used to define the different zones of the Dabbagha minaret are familiar from both Ayyubid and Mamluk styles but either the architect of the Dabbagha Mosque minaret is consciously using an 'archaising' reference to decorate the window frames or the minaret is indeed from the pre-Mamluk period. Its square-plan design would certainly make that possible.[16]

The first buildings commissioned by Mamluk city governors were tombs, all dating from the first two decades of the fourteenth century – the Tomb of Qarasunqur built outside the Bab al-Maqam (in the zone already marked by the

Figure 9.9 Window of the Dabbagha Mosque with its frame of chevrons and cusps

major Ayyubid madrasas) and the nearby Tombs of Saudi al-Mansuri and Musa Ibn ʿAbdullah al-Nasiri (see Appendix, Figure A.3). By 1318, governors were beginning to think on a grander scale and to demand sites in the central monumental area just south of the Citadel entrance gate.

Several of the new Mamluk projects filled in the space liberated when the city's eastern walls were rebuilt further east, thus allowing an extension of the princely zone south of the Citadel. The mosque of the Circassian governor of Aleppo, ʿAla al-Din Altunbugha al-Nasiri, was built in this area in 1318 and a monastery for Sufis added five years later. Except for the rather elaborate frame of the *muqarnas* portal, the lower structure could be Ayyubid, though a towering

Figure 9.10 Courtyard of the Maristan Arghun al-Kamil

184

octagonal minaret seeks to express a more elaborate bid for attention. It repeats the cusp and chevron frame around the panels of the upper register, again a reference to the form of decoration dating back two centuries. Later in the fourteenth century, this zone was further embellished with the Sakakini Mosque built by the Mamluk governor Sayf al-Din Ashaqtimur during his mandate (1379–81).

Perhaps the most notable construction of the mid-fourteenth century is the 1354 hospital for the mentally ill endowed by Sayf al-Din al-Taija, a senior official of the Mamluk governor Arghun al-Kamil (Figure 9.10). By far the largest in scale of the projects of the Mamluks so far, it spreads across three courtyards with rooms designed for different types of treatment. The doorway is in fact recycled from an Ayyubid building on the site and the conscious tributes to the old style are shown in the fact that there are few non-Ayyubid elements in the beautifully harmonious proportions of the rooms and courtyards.

First impressions

Aleppo at this time certainly impressed the Andalusian traveller Ibn Battuta on his two visits in the course of his global travels (1325–54). Ibn Battuta offered few of his own impressions in a rather prosaic account of an itinerary seeking the widest possible exchanges with Islamic scholars. For descriptions, he quoted the earlier work of his Andalusian predecessor, Ibn Jubayr (earlier page 147) as well as a number of highly poetic works from Arabic poets. Thus, for example, Ibn Battuta recycles the flavour of the Hamdanid-era poet al-Khalidiye's description (perhaps not improved by a rather flowery translation):

> Lo! On her grim and mossy rock
> That holds to scorn the foeman's shock
> With lofty tower and perilous steep,
> Majestic stands Aleppo's keep.
> The bosom of the windswept clouds
> Her topmost pinnacle enshrouds;
> The spangled stars of heaven rest,
> A glittering circlet, on her breast.[17]

By 1350, the rate of building was clearly accelerating. Governors now regularly endowed the city with mosques or madrasas. The capital cost would have been a charge on the founder who would also be required to set up a separate revenue-generating project (a *waqf*) which would assure the annual upkeep of the religious building, and in the case of madrasas, the expenses of its students and teachers. Sometimes the building might convey a specific political message as well. The minaret of the Mosque of Mankalibugha al-Shamsi was tall enough in a crowded part of the city to draw attention to its purpose, namely to flag the great Mamluk victory over the combined forces of Armenia, Cyprus and Rhodes at Ayas in nearby Cilicia in 1367. The minaret is cylindrical. Each of its four registers is plain, the decoration confined to thin muqarnas bands and to a wider ring of muqarnas supporting the top balcony.

Between 1350 and 1400, over twenty surviving buildings were constructed, not only by governors and senior officials but also by leading figures in the city's commercial or religious life. They were still fairly limited in scale but began to strive for a more ambitious impact along the street front. The Mosque al-Bayada (1378) in the quarter of that name inside the northeast city gate (Bab al-Hadid) sprawls along a sizeable façade. The decorative treatment has become more eye-catching. Windows are framed with recessed panels decorated with a muqarnas frieze along the top. Two-coloured stone (*ablaq* or contrasting basalt and limestone) was now becoming popular and arched doorways are demarcated or decorated by panels of intricate joggled shapes. All these ideas are repeated in another long façade, the Mosque al-Daraj (1399), built just outside the eastern walls.

Elaborate muqarnas-decorated half-domes over entrance doorways were now the rule. Whereas Ayyubid muqarnas designs had been assembled from undecorated segments of a sphere, now more fanciful ideas had evolved. The segments themselves carried carved palmettos and often cascaded down to end in stalactite-like pendants. This display of flashy stonecutting showed how skilfully the local masons had developed their craft and projects began to outbid each other in effect. An often-noted example is the Tawashi Mosque (1372) south of the Citadel on the way to the Bab al-Maqam. To the repertoire already mentioned, it adds colonnettes to frame the window recessed panels. Imitating an idea that went back to the wind-blown acanthus capitals of the great Church of St Simeon,

Figure 9.11 Façade of the Mosque al-Bayada

Figure 9.12 A windswept acanthus capital from the Mosque al-Tawashi façade

the colonnette capitals carry small versions of this Byzantine device. Clearly a good deal of artistic license was now being given to builders in the search for flamboyant effects.

Another sign of the increasing prosperity of the city by the late fourteenth century was the opening of lavish baths. The largest bath-house in Syria was built in the regime heartland just southeast of the Citadel entrance. This was restored in the 1980s and the outcome provided a spectacular insight into the standard of urban comfort in Mamluk times. Each section of the baths – dressing room, warm room, hot room – repeated the four-*iwan* theme with a dome covering the central space. The baths had a complicated construction history. The original baths on

187

this site were rebuilt by the Mamluk governor Yalbugha al-Nasiri in 1389 but were reconstructed in the next century. It is not known from which version is dated the use of ablaq stone in contrasting colours which now spreads across the whole of the façade with spectacular effect.

Tamerlane 1400

Central Asian leaders anxious to recreate the empire of Genghis Khan had not quite finished with Aleppo. Timur (or Tamerlane) was a Turco-Mongolian ruler, born at Shahrisabz near Samarkand, who had since 1370 pursued territorial expansion from modern-day Uzbekistan. For thirty years he campaigned to the west and established an empire destined to be as short-lived as it was brutal. The Mongols by now had fully adopted Islam (of the Shi'i variety), though Timur seemed indifferent towards any notion of favourable treatment for fellow Muslims. He took Iran by the 1380s and campaigned into the Caucasus and even India, reaching Delhi in 1398. After Delhi he quickly turned west again and arrived in Syria via Armenia and Georgia in 1400.

Arriving from the north, Aleppo was first on Timur's list for Syria. The Syrian reaction to this looming new threat managed to combine arrogance with panic. When an envoy from Timur arrived in Damascus to explain the mission of the approaching Timurid forces (ostensibly to investigate the murder of Timur's previous ambassador), the amir of Damascus had this second envoy slaughtered too, this time by cutting him in half. The account of the events leading up to the invasion by the Egyptian historian al-Taghribirdi gives a vivid account of the frenzied chaos in Mamluk ranks with each high-ranking mamluk only eager to see how the situation could be used to his best advantage as both sides outbid each other in horror. The aggressive instincts of Timur's forces could only have been further provoked when four of their vanguard were taken prisoner and were themselves severed at the waist.[18] This savagery was stage-managed in front of the Syrian amirs who had assembled in Aleppo to discuss how to counter Timur's approaching storm. Though they had assembled a sizeable strike force, the amirs' sense of commitment might have been enhanced if the Mamluk sultan himself had turned up to rally their still-squabbling ranks.

Timur initially professed a 'let's talk about . . .' approach to the looming confrontation, sending an envoy in to Aleppo initially to demand again that the Damascus amir who had murdered Timur's envoy be produced. The discussions inevitably broke down and led to a new confrontation. The Syrian amirs prepared for battle. On 28 October 1400, Timur's troops invested Aleppo. Two days later the townspeople themselves exited the city and sought to stiffen the resolve of the amirs' forces by joining the battle formation. Timur attacked, his army 'filling the landscape'. Their fearsome advance was spearheaded by a troupe of war elephants brought in from an Indian campaign. It was not long before the motley Syrian contingents disintegrated, many fleeing into the city while Timur's forces overwhelmed the rest of the Mamluk army 'like locusts over a green crop'.[19]

The accounts we have from Arab chronicles describe a new peak in brutality when Aleppo fell to Timur. His entry into the city, according to Arabshah, was facilitated by the Mamluk garrison commander, Timurtash. Coming immediately after the slaughter of the Timurid envoys, the taking of Aleppo in the face of the aid the city's civilian population had given to the Syrian amirs was excuse enough for prolific violence. While the Syrian amirs locked themselves in the Citadel, the ferocious slaughter in the lower town continued.

> The women and children fled to the great mosque of Aleppo . . . but Tamerlane's men turned to follow them, bound the women with ropes as prisoners, and put the children to the sword, killing everyone of them. They committed the shameful deeds to which they were accustomed; virgins were violated without concealment; gentlewomen were outraged without any restraints of modesty; a Tatar would seize a woman and ravage her in the Great Mosque or one of the smaller mosques in sight of the vast multitude of his companions and the people of the city; her father and brother and husband would see her plight and be unable to defend her because of their lack of means to do so and because they were distracted by the torture and torments which they themselves were suffering; the Tatar would then leave the woman and another go to her, her body still uncovered. They then put the populace of Aleppo and its troops to the sword, until the mosques and streets were filled with dead, and Aleppo stank with corpses.[20]

The amirs in the Citadel sued for amnesty but Timur had them brought out in chains.

Timur remained on in Aleppo for a month. The vengeance he had meted out to the citizens gave the city's surviving religious leaders little choice but to accept Timur's invitation to philosophical mind games. In Ahmad Ibn Arabshah's account, the *qadi*s were terrified at Timur's familiar practice of using mercurial humour to mask grim menace. His main ploy was to set riddles to trap them into acknowledging 'Ali as the last true Caliph.

Timur stayed in Aleppo for a month before he went on to Damascus, where his prolonged siege of the city again provided opportunities for black humour. Timur's long philosophical debates with local or visiting religious figures provided a grim diversion from the mass carnage carried on by the Timurid troops in the rest of the city. The famed Egyptian cleric Ibn Khaldun even journeyed from Cairo to engage in several prolonged discussions. Ibn Khaldun's stated intention was to test his belief that Timur was a figure who could lead a great new world empire.

Two years later Timur returned eastwards via Aleppo and again unleashed his forces on the city before he continued his campaign against the nascent empire of the Ottoman Turks, at this point confined to the central regions of Asia Minor. Like many of his other plans, Timur's aim to restore Seljuk authority in

Asia Minor foundered with his early death in 1405 while the lack of a credible heir brought the collapse of his unwieldy empire.

Recovery

The last of the great incursions from Central Asia had been marked by the deportation of many Syrian craftsmen to embellish Timur's capital at Samarkand. The effect on Aleppo's rebuilding programme was noticeable though perhaps not as marked as had been the case after 1260 when the devastation had been more prolonged and the city more deeply impoverished by the Mongols' laying waste the countryside in addition to the city itself. One project was initiated immediately after the 1400 invasion, although its completion took longer than average (almost a decade). This was the al-Otrush Mosque, the penultimate project to occupy the prestige zone below the Citadel gateway, the maidan which for many generations had partly served as a cavalry parade ground and horse market.

This sizeable mosque, begun in 1401 by Mamluk governor Aqbugha al-Jamali al-Otrush, now became a showcase for the full repertoire of Mamluk

Figure 9.13 Al-Otrush Mosque with its richly decorated window and door frames

decoration – recessed window panels all along the two street façades, a minaret reaching upwards to include two galleries, high and deep doorway with rich geometric decoration. Though on a lesser scale than the magnificent funerary madrasas built by the Mamluk sultans in contemporary Cairo, it nevertheless expressed a boldness of concept which Aleppo had not seen to date. Perhaps it helped that al-Otrush had started as a slave of the Mamluk Sultan Barquq and would have seen the sultan's tomb-madrasa in Cairo (1384–6). Al-Otrush's complex followed the Cairene examples by including near the entrance the founder's tomb, a tall domed structure. It was now possible for a former slave-boy to signal that being governor in Aleppo was something to be proud of.[21]

Perhaps the most extravagant initiative taken in this period of recovery was the new banqueting hall erected above the Ayyubid gatehouse of the Citadel. A city which had just lost a sizeable proportion of its citizens might have had other priorities but Aleppo picked up where it had left off before 1400 in its quest for prestige and status. The hall was built over the two towers of the Ayyubid entrance gate. The fact that the extension was given windows indicates an assumption that the Citadel had lost most of its defensive value.

All we have of the hall, presumably part of a new palatial complex to replace the thoroughly ruined palace of the Ayyubids just to the north, is the reconstructed reception room substantially rebuilt in the 1970s. Until then, the hall lay in ruins, only three of its nine domes surviving, the rest of the interior open to the elements. The reconstructed hall was pressed back into service but no attempt was made to

Figure 9.14 Façade of the Mamluk banqueting hall added above the towers framing the entrance to the Aleppo Citadel

recreate its domes. Instead a flat concrete roof was installed and the ceiling decorated in a 'Damascus' style of painted wooden decoration, resembling mansions of the eighteenth century and later but on the scale of a basketball court.

A trading city, the suqs

It is time to delve into one of the features of Aleppo which have brought the city so much fame in recent centuries, namely its suqs or central market area (the Medina). Over 2 linear kilometres of covered markets spread either side of the line of the original Roman axis of the city covering some 50 hectares. As described earlier, this maze of narrow alleys winds along the path of the original colonnaded main street, the wide central vehicle passage now segmented into three or more parallel paths each lined with booths or with doorways leading to large caravanserais or *khans*.[22] (See Figure. 4.7 on page 211.) The area had served as the historic heart of the city's commercial life going back to Roman times (a detailed plan of the central suqs is given in Figure 10.4). Often described until recently in extravagant terms as the most impressive of the Middle East's traditional bazars, the suqs warranted every word of such descriptions if only because they formed not just a romanticised tourist drawcard but a living market area where much of the small-scale commerce of the city still congregated. The khans, however, no longer serve as accommodation and bulk storage facility for long distance traders but house local distribution agencies. The Medina comprised a mixture of suqs (small shops lining narrow paths), some twenty larger khans (warehouses), *qaisariye* (sections of suq that can be independently locked to protect precious goods), mosques and latrines.

In this chapter, we trace the information we have on the earliest structures that survive in the Medina and then look at the commercial life which was drawn here in the early centuries of Aleppo's opening to international trade under the Mamluks. The greater part of the story will be pursued in the next chapter looking at the flourishing role of the suqs in the Ottoman period, from which most of the surviving buildings date and when so many Western traders and visitors formed a community that gained through Aleppo an insight into an Arab world that most Europeans still found perplexing.

The conversion of the Roman broad avenue into smaller passages was traced earlier in Chapters 2 and 4 (see Figures 2.13 (page 42) and 4.7 (page 81)). The process probably began in the Byzantine period, perhaps encouraged by the collapse of the widely spaced column rows in earthquakes or invasions but also probably reflecting a disinclination to run the city along the strictly controlled lines the Roman rulers had introduced. The process of breakdown has been documented at other centres, notably in excavations in Palmyra, with informal shops springing up using stone rescued from the previous column rows and the shops behind. As the spaces filled with ad hoc booths, the pedestrian paths, once confined to the flanks of the central roadway, weaved between shops. The process at Aleppo actually appears to have been relatively orderly with the new

Figure 9.15 Aleppo Suq al-ʿAtarin

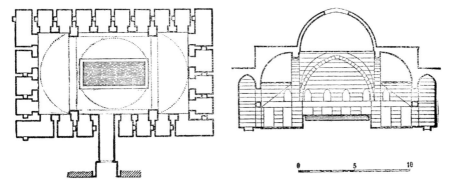

Figure 9.16 Plan and elevation of the Latrines of Amir Taz (Sauvaget 1941: fig. 43)

pedestrian paths still retaining a grid-like layout though sub-divided into three or four alignments.

There is no evidence that the alleyways were covered as part of this process. Ibn Jubayr's description (1180s), noted earlier, is the first to relate that the suqs were roofed in wood. The first evidence we have that official measures were taken to improve the informal booths, divide them into regularly spaced shops and provide cross-vaulting in stone dates from the Mamluk period. This period also saw the first of the khans which survive. The oldest is the Khan al-Qadi, located south

193

of the main suqs on the street leading to the Qinnisrin Gate on the south walls. This Mamluk construction (1441) was originally intended as a school but was soon converted for commercial purposes. It shows none of the flamboyance of the later commercial buildings.

The emphasis given as early as Ayyubid times to the comfort of shoppers is best illustrated in the grand latrines built close to the Great Mosque, the Latrines of Amir Taz al-Nasiri. An earlier Ayyubid structure on this site required rebuilding in 1357, the Amir Taz then taking all the credit. Taz, cup-bearer to Sultan Qalawun (d.1341), had been a rising star in Cairo in the days of the endemic power struggles between rival mamluks when 'the qualification to rule was the ability to snatch the sceptre'.[23] In Cairo Taz had constructed his huge (and still surviving) palace complex in 1352. After involving himself in an attempted coup in Cairo Sultan al-Hasan had assigned him in 1354 to Aleppo where he again aroused suspicions by raising a huge army. His appointment in Aleppo did not allow much opportunity for anything more grand than the rebuilding of the Ayyubid latrines. Summoned back to Egypt, Sultan Hasan took no chances this time. Taz was blinded and assigned to exile in Mecca (d.1361).

Burji Mamluks (1382–1516)

Two decades later the squabbles of the first line of mamluks, whose numbers had proliferated to reach perhaps twelve thousand, provoked an implosion which brought the need to raise a new core of mainly Circassian amirs. The origins of this group began with an elite contingent formed by whittling mamluk numbers down to perhaps three thousand. The nickname Burji (from the Arabic *al-burj*, tower) originated in their being assigned protected housing in the Cairo Citadel. The Mamluk Empire now faced dangers more difficult to predict than the occasional Mongol incursion or the presence of Christian Crusaders along a sliver of the coast. Two ambitious regional powers would emerge in the course of the fifteenth century – Safavid Persia and the Ottomans of Asia Minor – while the Portuguese began to threaten Cairo's monopoly of the spices trade through their presence in the Indian Ocean. The old structures introduced by Baybars, now eroded by the intense rivalries among mamluks, were not sufficient to face the challenges of new empires.

The Venetian presence

International trade had become increasingly important to the Mamluk state. Venice had been active in building economic links with northern Syria for several centuries. Formal permission allowing Venetian traders to operate in the Levant had been granted by the Ayyubids in 1207/8. The Crusades had kept the Italian trading cities out of the Levant for a time but the Venetians gradually were able to circumvent the restrictions that had been imposed by the Pope and the major contributors to the Crusades. From the thirteenth century, Venice's commercial representative in Aleppo lived outside the city in the al-Hadir quarter. Trade in the first century and a half of the Venetian presence had been disrupted by the chaos of successive Mongol invasions and trade flows had drifted to the northern-most route via the Black Sea where Genoa had the upper hand.

In anticipation of the campaign by Tamerlane in 1400, European representatives had fled Aleppo via the south. However, after the collapse of Timur's imperial ambitions with his death in 1405, the rest of the fifteenth century brought conditions that encouraged a new flourishing of commerce in spite of the uncertain political environment. Venice established its first resident consular representation in Aleppo (subordinate to the Venetian consul in Damascus) in 1422. The full consulate was transferred to Aleppo in 1548.

A move to the old city enabled the Venetian traders to escape the security uncertainties inherent in their old location outside the walls. Acceptance of the first European trade representatives inside the old city indicated a concession to encourage greater European trade as well as the Europeans' appreciation that al-Hadir had taken the brunt of Timur's vengeance. It seems likely that Venetian consuls and merchants used the khan not only as a warehouse and base for trade deals but also as living quarters in the galleried rooms above the courtyard. We have no evidence of the presence in the walled city of other European residents before Ottoman times.

Venetian consuls and merchants, usually sent out by patrician families, faced a rigorous life in their gated warehouse/residences where later chaplains and doctors were to serve the needs of the small communities of no more than ten merchants. Dealing with local officials was a lot tougher than the Venetians had found in Egypt where local Mamluk representatives were more under the eye of the Mamluk sultanate. The Europeans' aim was to make as much money as possible in a few years and return home to retire on the proceeds.

Most European trade in this era shipped via Latakia or Tripoli, a demanding six to nine days away by donkey or camel train. The composition of the Venetian trade was varied. Raw cotton seems to have been an important export to Europe and for some time additional Venetian representation was maintained outside Aleppo at Sarmin in the major cotton-growing area to the south. No doubt, however, some of the products passed on to Europe included goods or spices traded from India, the Gulf and Central Asia including Persian silk, pearls and precious stones. Venetian exports had traditionally included tin, an important element in making copper, copper itself and a range of speciality fabrics (produced in Bergamo, Brescia, Florence, Padua). As early as the fifteenth century, the range of fabrics extended to fine English woollen cloth which by mid-century would provide a dominant proportion of goods exported to Syria through Venetian intermediaries.

Aleppo was the point at which several important trade routes from the East converged (see Figure 10.2 on page 207). The most important were the routes via the Gulf and Iraq as well as several strands from Central Asia and Persia which joined to follow the old 'Royal Road' beneath the Anti-Taurus Mountains. Just as

Venice's trade, however, had built to a sustainable level, it began to encounter the competition from the Portuguese opening of a sea route to India at the end of the fifteenth century. Nevertheless there remained many sources of commodities that could more easily be tapped via existing land routes through Aleppo, particularly once the Mongol threat had receded. The effects of the Portuguese dominance of the Indian Ocean was mainly felt in trade with India and China.

The improvement in the economic environment is reflected in Turkish population figures. In 1519, just after the Ottoman conquest, Ottoman records give figures of 60,000–70,000 inhabitants for both Aleppo and Damascus.[24] Aleppo was again a sizeable city and the main trade entrepôt linking the Fertile Crescent with western Europe, a position it would retain until overtaken by Beirut in the nineteenth century. Though Cairo and Alexandria were still the giants in population terms, Aleppo excelled in other indicators of economic activity.

Mamluk rule by the mid-fifteenth century was not quite the tautly run enterprise of Baybars' time. Though the governors, senior officials and the religious caste could still tap the arteries of prosperity, a rising level of popular resentment towards their masters was discernable among the people of Aleppo, who rose in revolt in 1413, 1448, 1456, 1480, 1484 and 1491, the highest indicator of discontent in the empire. The causes were the level of corruption and taxation imposed as well as arbitrary treatment by officials and by the soldiery still operating as an external warrior caste. The instigators were often the unemployed who had little stake in the economy, less often Bedouin from outside the town.

Khans and palaces

A new flourish of construction in the second half of the fifteenth century reflected this new prosperity and brought five new khans to Aleppo's commercial centre. The plain style of the earlier examples was now replaced by showy display intended to impress clients with the prestige of the owner whose spaces were rented out to individual merchants. Four of the new khans were the work of Mamluk governors. The Khan al-Sabun (1479), intended for the soap trade, was a sizeable khan just to the west of the Great Mosque. Above its entrance, the Mamluk love for elaborate window surrounds reached a new peak of exuberance.

The recessed panel around the window (Figure 9.17) was defined by colonnettes with plaited fluting surrounded by an intricate tracery of fine stone-carving and topped by delicate stalactites falling from a muqarnas band – a masterpiece of Mamluk decoration. It is a perfect justification of Gertrude Bell's commendation of the 'grace and ordered symmetry' of Aleppo's medieval architecture.[25] Inside the courtyard is more restrained but a broken-arched gallery ran around the central space providing a pleasant environment for merchants' accommodation.

Aleppo with its new prosperity was now bursting beyond its walled enclosure. The first khan erected outside the walls, Utch Khan, of which only an elaborately decorated gate remains, was built outside the Bab al-Nasr on the north walls.

Figure 9.17 Decorated window frame of the Khan al-Sabun

Other extensions of the city began beyond the Bab al-Hadid to swallow the village of Banqusa. The suburb long famed for its charming streets and buildings is the 'New Quarter' (Jdeide) outside the northwest corner of the walls. The suburb grew up around a small cluster of churches (possibly once attached to extra-urban monasteries) of the late fifteenth or sixteenth century, the oldest of which appear to be those belonging to the Maronite, Armenian and Greek Orthodox churches. The term 'new' (*jdeide*) was first ascribed to the area in a written source of 1421 (Ibn al-Shihna). As resident European merchants increased in number, this became the quarter where their Syrian facilitators settled after the post-Mongol security conditions allowed settlement again outside the walls. Usually Christian, they acted as intermediaries with officials, provided translation services and themselves engaged in trade.

Aleppo provides only a couple of glimpses of the life of a wealthy Mamluk amir. The khan known today as Qurtbey's began as a project for a family palace by the governor, Aztimur al-Ashrafi, in 1493. The building was never completed as a residence but the scale of its courtyard iwan and decoration rival those of the houses of contemporary Cairo. It was taken over and completed as a khan by the son of one of the early Ottoman governors and will be examined in the next chapter (page 229).

Another Mamluk palace building in service during the Mamluk period had an eventful subsequent life. The Matbakh al-'Ajami (Figure 9.18) began as a Zengid palace in a prime position near the Great Mosque. It was remodelled under the Mamluks when it came into the possession of the large landholding family, the Banu al-'Ajami, serving for a while as a madrasa. The building was cruelly compromised when the street was widened in 1950. The building's façade was dismantled and the street line pushed back, preserving a doorway which is so much a product of several eras that it is impossible to assign its origins between the Ayyubid, Mamluk or Ottoman periods. The façade itself is actually a transplant from an eighteenth-century palace of the Ottoman governor 'Uthman Pasha, rescued when that building collapsed in the 1960s. The dome which can be seen just behind the street façade is a recent addition to provide protection over the courtyard when the building was repurposed as a civic reception room.

A lost cause, 1516 (Marj Dabiq)

One of the possible contributors to this last-mentioned building's complex history is Khayrbey Ibn Malbay, the last Mamluk governor of Aleppo (r.1504–16) who served long enough to make his mark on the city's building record. Khayrbey had the Matbakh al-'Ajami restored. The last Mamluk khan also carries Khayrbey's name. It lies a little east of the Great Mosque and was finished in the months leading to the regime's downfall.

Khayrbey's lasting claim to fame, though, was his spectacular display of disloyalty to the Mamluk regime which had appointed him. Even before the decisive military battle that saw the victory of the Ottoman Sultan Selim, Khayrbey had been in touch with the Ottomans and had planned his defection.

Khayrbey's cynical betrayal was a gesture worthy of the ego-driven politics of the late Mamluks. His sultan, Qansuh al-Ghauri – famed for his greed but admired for his military prowess – had led a combined force of Mamluk amirs to northern Syria to meet the Ottoman threat. Al-Ghauri took advantage of Aleppo's formidable defences to leave in the Citadel a prodigious pile of treasure which he had taken the precaution of transporting from Cairo to prevent its falling into the hands of his rivals. Perhaps conscious that so much of his acquired wealth was at stake, the sultan fought on at Marj Dabiq against impossible odds, even when it was clear that governor Khayrbey had changed sides. Finally conscious that defeat was imminent, al-Ghauri died of a massive stroke just as he attempted to wheel his horse around to escape: 'No sultan of Egypt had ever been subject to

Figure 9.18 Façade of the Matbakh al-'Ajami as reconstructed after street widening

a disaster like this, dying under his own standard on the day of battle.'[26] The fact that most of the Mamluk amirs had already fled the field of Dabiq indicated the extent to which the Mamluk cause had simply spontaneously collapsed.

An accidental conquest?

When the victorious Ottoman sultan Selim I entered Aleppo to be greeted by a crowd only too happy to be rid of the Mamluks, he was astonished by the treasure the Mamluk ruler had deposited in the Citadel. The Ottoman victory, though, was more than a treasure hunt. It was part of the flow of events which had been changing the course of the Middle East for centuries. The late Mamluks had been simply marking time for decades, more intent on their games against each other than on securing their place in a world that was undergoing mammoth changes. The decision of Ottoman Sultan Selim in 1516 to push into Syria was really planned as a precautionary diversion intended to protect his flank during a campaign intended to fend off Safavid Iran's push into Asia Minor. It was only at the last minute that the sultan turned south, intending later to return to the campaign against the Safavids. The Ottomans, moreover, had perfected a device that gave them a strategic advantage – gunpowder. Though gunpowder was known to the Mamluks, they had been too fixated on their centuries-old style of Central Asian-inspired mobile warfare to change their military doctrine to reflect this new dimension in weaponry.

199

It was, however, disunity among the mamluks and failure to find common cause which were the compelling factors in the Mamluk sultan's pathetic demise. Khayrbey was a typical manifestation of a late Mamluk sclerosis. The accumulation of riches and display had become the overwhelming purpose of life – even better if a leader's fame (whether for good or ill) could live on in death as demonstrated in the magnificent tomb-madrasas they built to out-do each other in Cairo.

Having successfully segued to the Ottomans on the field of battle, thus opening the path of the Ottomans to all of Syria and Egypt, Khayrbey's reward was his appointment as Ottoman governor in Cairo, dying there six years later. Khayrbey had already decided to upgrade from his modest chamber tomb in Aleppo. He built a much more lavish second tomb in the Egyptian capital. Few, either in Aleppo or Cairo, had a good word to say for the rapacious and opportunistic Khayrbey who had made a singular contribution to condemning both cities to provincial status under the Ottoman Turks for hundreds of years.[27]

Notes

1 Marozzi 2014: 138.
2 Their first leader of any stature to adopt Islam, Ilkhan Ghazan Khan (r.1295–1304), converted on assuming power, at which point his Mongol cohorts in Persia followed his lead (Morgan 1986: 160).
3 Other gruesome variations are cited in Marozzi (2014: 147).
4 Marozzi 2014: 149.
5 Humphreys 1977: 348.
6 Quoted in Eddé 1999: 177.
7 'Aleppo would not recover from the carnage for another century' (Humphreys 1977: 349). The carnage is also assessed in Eddé 1987–8: 171 and Jackson 2017: 172.
8 One explanation for Baybars' hostility to Qutuz is that the latter had reneged on a promise to appoint Baybars as governor in Aleppo once the Mongols had been defeated (Little 'Qutuz' EI2).
9 Sauvaget 1941: 159 citing Ibn Shaddad.
10 For the Syrian Ilkhanid wars of the 1260–70s, see Amitai-Preiss (1995: 106–38).
11 Ibn ʿAbd al-Zahir quoted in Thorau 1992: 106.
12 Antioch's non-contiguous coastal enclaves would be merged with the County of Tripoli in 1275.
13 Gabrieli 1977: 311.
14 Eddé 2000: 159–61.
15 It would appear that the same team went on to Cairo to decorate the new audience hall built by Sultan Qalawun in the Cairo Citadel (Rabbat 1997–8: 237).
16 The lack of minarets of the Zengid period inhibits comparisons. There is another surviving example preserved in a mini-taxis station outside the Antioch Gate – the minaret of the Hajjarin Mosque. The rest of the mosque was removed but the square-plan minaret survives isolated in a patch of park south of a market building. I am indebted to Youssef Khanjou of the Aleppo Museum for a photo of the minaret.
17 Ibn Battuta 1956: 95.
18 Taghribirdi, trans. Popper 1954: 36.
19 Arabshah 1936: 124.
20 Taghribirdi, trans. Popper 1954: 38.

21 The disrupted first decade of the fifteenth century probably accounts for the fact that the mosque took ten years to complete and after al-Otrush's death in 1404 was finished by his successor Damurdâsh al-Muhammadi.

22 The terms are virtually interchangeable but caravanserai more often refers to buildings outside a major city while khan can cover both urban and rural establishments.

23 Irwin 1986: 156.

24 Though tax and other records give us considerable insights into the number of households in the city at various points in the Ottoman centuries, it is not always easy to reconcile these with other data to reach consistent criteria for population figures. It is also not clear whether the counts are made within the walled city or include the suburbs to the east and north. The best analyses are in the works of Raymond, Riis and Masters listed in the Bibliography. I have aimed at a consensus guesstimate based on the trends they have identified.

25 Bell 1911: 13.

26 Ibn Iyas quoted in Petry 1994: 228. On the significance of Dabiq see page 86 (and note 9).

27 Good use was later made of the abandoned Aleppo tomb when a second chamber was used for the burial of a local sheikh ʿAli (Behrens-Abouseif 2007: 67–8).

10

THE FIRST OTTOMAN CENTURIES (1516–1750)

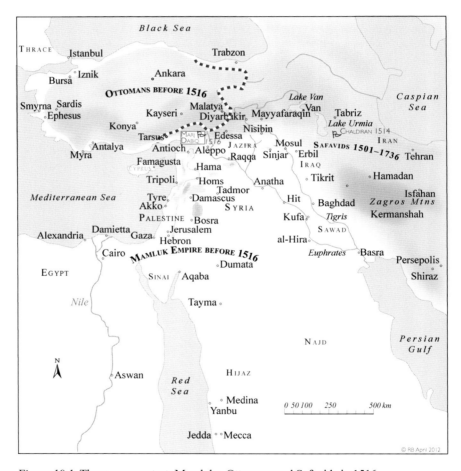

Figure 10.1 Three-way contest: Mamluks, Ottomans and Safavids in 1516

The enthusiastic welcome the townspeople of Aleppo conferred on the victorious Ottoman sultan was perhaps partly concocted and more a reflection of the unpopularity of the Mamluks in the last tyrannical phase of their rule. The fact was there was no inherent enthusiasm for the new masters. Turkish supremacy in the Middle East had been many years in gestation. It had taken seven centuries for them to emerge from a small contingent of bodyguards for the Baghdad Caliphs to become now a power in their own right in the central Islamic lands. Now firmly Sunni Muslims, the Ottomans needed something to boost their status as outsiders. Their Islamic credentials necessarily became the touchstone of their authority.

The Ottomans had simply been one among many small Turkic states scattered across Asia Minor in the wake of the collapse of the Seljuk, Ayyubid and Ilkhanid aspirations to empire. In 1326, Orkhan (r.1324–60), the ruler of one of the smallest statelets pressing up against the remaining Byzantine enclave from the east, took the major city of Bursa. Orkhan was the son of the dynasty's reputed founder, Othman, described by Ibn Battuta as 'the greatest of the kings of the Turkmen and the richest in wealth, lands, and military forces'.[1] Orkhan went on to take other cities in the region and manipulated the Byzantine court into offering Theodora, the daughter of a senior Byzantine court official, in marriage. The Ottomans maintained a cynical alliance with both the Byzantines and the Genoese while slowly tightening their grip on the Dardanelles, securing their first foothold on European soil at Gelibolu (Gallipoli) in 1354. By the time the Byzantines 'had come to the realization that calling in the Turks had not been such a good idea' it was too late.[2] When the Ottoman ruler Murad took Edirne (in European Thrace) in the 1360s, the base for a firm Ottoman push into the Balkans and eventually Constantinople was effectively laid.

By the opening of the fifteenth century, the Ottoman army had become a formidable fighting force, able almost to take territory at will. The Ottomans could also use their religious cadre, the dervishes, as advocates of their more spiritual version of Islam, less formidably doctrinal than conventional Sunnism and thus more appealing to a still largely non-Muslim population. The Ottoman agenda, however, was still heavily oriented towards spreading the broad message of Islam though this did not prevent further opportunistic pacts with the beleaguered Byzantines, including against the threat of Timur's invasions in 1400.

By the 1420s, the Ottomans were again pressing against the Christian enclave in Constantinople while making further gains in northern Greece (Thessaloniki) and Serbia. The final fall of Constantinople (thereafter, Istanbul) in 1453 brought the end of the Byzantine prolongation of Rome's millennial empire and handed the Ottoman rulers a capital of world ranking.

Planting the Ottoman imperium

When the Ottomans arrived in Syria fifty years later through their victory at Marj Dabiq, their rule put Aleppo at a crossroads. While it was just one of numerous provincial cities of the empire, Aleppo found itself in a position more significant than at any point in its already long record. For a time it would become the third city of the Ottoman Empire, after Istanbul and Cairo, in terms of economic activity – a position it was to lose in later centuries to Izmir as international routes switched away from those favouring Venice's role as intermediary.

Trade with Iran and India were about to become major factors in Aleppo's fortunes just as the arteries of this commerce were coming under new strains from the wider environment of events in the region. The circumstances in which the Ottomans had taken Aleppo were a turning point in the broader struggle between the Shi'i and Sunni streams of Islam over the centuries. As mentioned, the Ottoman campaign in Syria was essentially a by-product of the Ottoman efforts to assert Sunni orthodoxy in the face of the inroads of Safavid Iran. The Safavids had rallied Iran firmly behind the banner of Shi'ism in the face of the Ottoman campaign to push them back in eastern Anatolia. This resulted in a Turkish victory at the Battle of Chaldiran near Tabriz in northwestern Iran (1514). It was this victory which had given Sultan Selim I the opportunity to deflect his attention south towards Aleppo, essentially in order to prevent the Safavids co-opting the Mamluks as their allies against Ottoman supremacy.

Aleppo had already proven its capacity for survival. It had outlasted the Crusaders and stayed on as a minor capital of a Mamluk province near the Anatolian borderlands. As the Mamluk Empire declined into 'an aging exhausted, decadent and degenerate state', the Ottomans came upon the scene as a thrusting outward-looking regime, already two hundred years in existence but still vigorous, and which now identified Aleppo as central to its interests.[3] The takeover of a swathe of new Eastern territory through the conquest of Syria and Egypt (1516–17) and Ottoman penetration into modern-day Iraq and the Arabian peninsula brought enormous new distractions from the previously Anatolian/Balkans focus of the Ottomans. Safavid Persia, the sole power capable of resisting the Ottoman push into Mesopotamia and Eastern Anatolia, had been contained.

The Ottomans thus faced no challenge on their eastern frontiers comparable to the dimensions of the threat from the European powers which would over the next two centuries begin to reclaim Turkish-ruled lands in the Balkans and southern Europe. The challenges in Syria and Egypt were more matters of implanting the authority of a Turkish power in lands which were largely Arabic-speaking, though long accustomed to embracing a mix of ethnic and religious communities. It was a long time since Aleppo had been ruled by fellow Arabs. The Turkish/Arab divide – soon to be emphasised by linguistic difficulties under the Ottomans with few officials out-posted to Aleppo in a position to master Arabic – was a phenomenon more marked than the language divide under the Mamluk and Ayyubid rulers who had been inclined to absorb much of the cultural instincts of the local milieu including the Arabic language.

Nevertheless, the three-way struggle for northern Syria, lying at the interface of the rivalries between Ottomans, Mamluks and Safavids, now settled into a more manageable balance – Sunni Turks or Arabs versus Shi'i Persians. Aleppo was now positioned back from this front at the heart of a swathe of imperial territory embraced by a 'Pax Ottomana'.[4] It could get on with making money and exploit its position where the trade routes down the Euphrates or across to the fringes of Persia divided from the north–south link to Cairo. The city no longer saw its relations with the imperial power filtered via Damascus. Aleppo now focused in economic terms on its neighbouring urban centres in Anatolia to counterbalance the ties with the cities of southern Syria.

Aleppo in the Ottoman world

If Aleppo lay at a point critical for the management of the religious and economic affairs of the Ottoman realm, it was not necessarily a major preoccupation in Istanbul when weighed against the affairs of more troubled Ottoman provinces. The Ottoman realm stretched from central Europe and the borders of Russia, through the Levant and across North Africa with diversions sweeping along the frontiers of Iran and into the Holy Places of Arabia. It was an enormous enterprise. On the security front, much of a sultan's time was necessarily spent campaigning in Europe rather than in the core provinces of the Islamic lands. The Turkish system was extremely decentralised for the first two centuries of their presence in the Levant, with governors and tax farmers responsible for much of the raking in of funds to support the system and to keep essential services such as the army running.

Aleppo was initially, under Selim's arrangements for Syria, made subordinate to the Ottoman governor in Damascus. The first appointee in Damascus was a former Mamluk official who had not initially defected to the Ottoman cause, Janbardi al-Ghazali. Janbardi refused to accept the authority of the new sultan, Suleiman, who replaced Selim on the latter's death in 1520 and who would pass into history with the title 'Suleiman the Magnificent' (r. 1520–66). Janbardi's rebellion was put down and Aleppo's resistance to his takeover was rewarded with its own governorate or *vilaya* controlling nine districts or *sanjak*s. The rest of Syria and modern Lebanon were allocated between Damascus and Tripoli. (Later, in 1660, Sidon and Raqqa became separate *vilayat*.)

Having resumed the Mamluk provincial divisions, Mamluk *amirs* were simply replaced with Turkish appointees as *vali* or *beyerbegli* (governor) usually carrying the honorific title of *pasha*. For the first two hundred years, most governors were 'professional' Ottomans, unable to speak Arabic and with few ties to the local communities. They were products of the *devşirme* system, the practice of snatching Christian (less often, Muslim) youths from frontier areas (usually in the Balkans) and training them to form a military and administrative elite bonded to the sultan. It remained a highly centralised administrative system but the sheer distances involved in centre–periphery transmission meant that local initiatives often lay with the governors. The latter had at their disposal army units headed by a commander or *agha*. These units initially comprised troops from two sources:

- *janissaries* or forces raised through the *devşirme* system;
- locally raised and garrisoned forces.

These forces could intervene to impose imperial authority in the face of frequent local rebellions, tribal disputes or banditry. However, the governors were only appointed for a year (sometimes renewable), giving little encouragement to identifying imaginative solutions to intractable problems and often giving rise to tensions between the governor and the elite military units inclined to become a law unto themselves. Moreover, the governors spent their limited time in a post amassing funds to buy their next assignment, most often tapping the wealth of the local merchants or the religious minorities.

The second key appointee sent by the Ottoman administration in Istanbul (the Porte)[5] was the *qadi*, or judge, appointed under the Ottomans. He was not subject to the governor's command but was separately answerable to Istanbul, thus preserving a degree of separation between the legal/religious and executive streams. The qadi, often fluent in Arabic, administered a dual system of law reflecting both Ottoman legislation from the Hanafi tradition as well as *Sharia*.

The Ottoman system was also necessarily a political entity that bound together peoples of many faiths and ethnic backgrounds though with a Turkish core. Too long our picture of the empire has been stuck with the tired slogan crafted in the nineteenth century, the 'sick man of Europe'. Now that we have had more time in the past hundred years to savour the results of the empire's messy break-up, it is perhaps dawning on a wider audience that the label does little justice to a structure that held together an enormously diverse range of provinces as complex as anything faced since the Roman Empire. At the time of writing, it looks a whole lot better than the picture a hundred years after the dissolution of the Ottoman system.

Faith and trade

In 1516 when the victorious Selim I entered Aleppo shortly after the battle of Marj Dabiq, the Friday prayers in Aleppo's Great Mosque were offered in his name, for the first time recognising him as the supreme authority in the central Islamic lands. When Selim went on to take Egypt from the Mamluks, in Cairo in 1517 he received a delegation from Mecca which offered to put the holy places of Islam under Ottoman protection. 'Caliph' was then listed among the sultan's attributes and reinforced as an Ottoman title when Suleiman the Magnificent captured Baghdad, the old seat of the Sunni ʿAbbasid Caliphate, in 1534.[6]

This effectively confirmed that the religious leadership now saw the mantle of the Caliphate as transferred to the Ottoman sultan though his formal recognition was played down with the preferred emphasis resting on his role as protector of the Islamic Holy Places. The symbolic revival of the Caliphate, however, helped soften the acceptance of Ottoman rule in a largely Arab environment and recognised the reality that the Ottomans were now the sole Sunni Muslim political power. The Ottomans also for the first time ruled over a population which was majority Muslim. The need to gain respect for the regime's Islamic credentials became a major priority.[7]

The 'Silk Route'

For Aleppo, however, it was its importance as a centre for economic activity which boosted its status for the Ottomans and drew European interest in a city previously seen abroad only as a remote and obscure corner of the narrative of the Crusades. Aleppo could now not only access a hinterland which stretched north to Diyarbakir and east to Mosul, but it was also absorbed into a political entity which provided a 'common market' from the Balkans to the Gulf. Identifying the sinews and nervous system of this burgeoning trade role for the city are essential to an

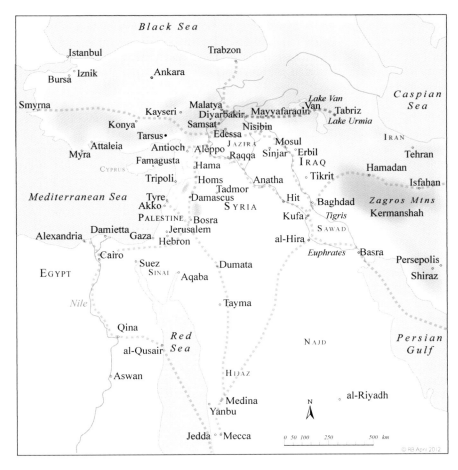

Figure 10.2 Ottoman trade routes

207

appreciation of Aleppo's extraordinary rise to prominence in the next two centuries. Yet our understanding of the picture is at risk of stumbling over a simplified picture of a 'Silk Route' used in romanticised Western commentary isolating only a few factors out of the many which prevailed in a hemisphere as broad as that from Europe to India.

By its nature, caravan trade involves factors more unpredictable than even modern trade flows. Accounts which seek to find a single explanation for the fluctuations in trade that Aleppo had to master in the coming centuries are thus hazardous where every input is a variable. It is too easy, for example, to identify the Vasco da Gama's discovery of the sea route from Europe to India in 1498 as bringing doom to the caravan traffic. The caravans continued largely undiminished for another 250 years; in fact, fifty years later it was the Portuguese who were out of the game in the Persian Gulf. The frequent hostilities between Safavid Persia and the Ottoman Empire barely impacted on merchants and their caravans, which continued to pass in each direction. The Ottoman interpretation of Islamic law regulating the trade should have favoured Muslim traders (or even Sunni or Shi'i participants at the expense of each other) but in fact over the centuries a dramatic growth in Christian participation was the most notable phenomenon, particularly in Aleppo.

As much of the trade was necessarily opportunistic and dependent on numerous variables, the lack of steady demand for products is understandable. Besides wars, other factors such as plague or the loss of goods through shipwreck or banditry could bring massive setbacks for at least a season. Exchanges were also often inhibited by the lack of European product able to attract steady demand in the East before the Industrial Revolution in Europe brought competitive advantages to European producers. The fact that buying patterns were later dependent on specie to finance purchases from European sources inhibited steady growth in a situation where access to foreign currencies was limited. The changing picture of world trade by the nineteenth century with the rise of a mercantile economy was the final factor which brought the suppression of local production in Syria and high dependence on imports.

A full reality check would thus require a rather detailed account of the factors affecting the trade flows in the Ottoman years, beyond the scope of this general work. The careful examination, particularly of the Ottoman records and the proceedings of the Aleppo Islamic courts by Bruce Masters, however, avoids the need to repeat his detailed picture relating this material to the wider economic and political scene. However, this is a question we will need to return to in the course of this and the following chapter.

For now, it should be borne in mind that while the Ottoman authorities faced challenges in extending their rule to an environment quite different from their traditional realm in Anatolia, they sought to apply much the same structure of administration. This was based on broad Islamic principles but with variations in Syria that took into account the system the Mamluks had left in place. Sensibly applied, as it largely was in the first two Ottoman centuries, this provided the right framework for Aleppo to seize the opportunities of its new environment and to earn its place as the third most important city of the empire. The challenge of Vasco da Gama caused barely a blip.

An Ottoman 'image'

It did not take long for the Ottomans, particularly under Suleiman the Magnificent, to appreciate how crucial Aleppo's position was in three respects: for the successful absorption of the Arab provinces; for the promotion of a wider trade picture; and for the success of Ottoman religious credentials. We can turn to the city's architecture to see how the Turkish rulers used the physical presentation of the city to convey a picture of their rule to a non-Turkish audience.

For the first three decades of Ottoman rule, little effort was made to mark the new Ottoman presence. An inscription band around the second tower to the west of the Citadel entrance gateway took the opportunity of repairs to the walls in the first years of the reign of Suleiman to convey a relatively muted sign of the Ottomans' arrival. By mid-century, however, the need was felt for a more concerted assertion of the Ottoman presence. The fact that Suleiman was the second Ottoman sovereign to visit Aleppo (during the course of his first campaigns against the Safavids in Iraq, 1534–6) perhaps accounts for his reaching an appreciation of how architecture could shape the city's perception of the benefits of Ottoman rule. The Turks initially borrowed some aspects of the Mamluk architectural vocabulary that had drawn on ideas originating from Iran to Cairo. The Ottomans' own experience of Anatolian traditions (including the rich Byzantine cannon stemming from the great churches of Istanbul mimicking Ayia Sofia) had resulted in a more closely defined Ottoman 'look'. Once this new architectural canon was fixed, however, Ottoman rulers were less interested in the sort of experimentation that had been the practice among rulers of the Arab lands across the centuries.

The first buildings undertaken in Aleppo by Ottoman governors thus defined a more distinct break compared to the mixing of experiences that marked the transitions from Zengid to Ayyubid rule or from Ayyubid to Mamluk. More of the ideas now came from outside in a series of package deals. This was partly the result of the sixteenth-century Ottoman system that employed a court architect directing a busy and productive workshop with responsibility for numerous projects throughout the empire. As the execution of projects was the work of military engineers, an official from the workshop would be assigned to see the job carried through on the ground along with the organisation of labour and the coordination of materials.

Under Suleiman the Magnificent, the brilliant and prolonged role of Sinan, as court architect (*mimar*), moulded the way in which the empire expressed its aspirations in physical form. Sinan was given this role in 1539 after an earlier spell in military service. During his military years, Sinan was possibly in the sultan's entourage during his visits to Aleppo (1535–6) perhaps explaining the subsequent close harmony between political and architectural agendas. Sinan was also sufficiently

Figure 10.3 Modern statue of Mimar Sinan in Kayseri, Turkey

inventive and interested in the use of other idioms to incorporate some of the elements of the Mamluk style from the environment in which his projects were realised over a span of nearly half a century.

A monumental axis

Just as the more ambitious late Mamluk rulers had availed themselves of the space released from the exercise ground south of the Citadel gateway, the Ottomans planted their first signature buildings in the western sector of the zone. From here, a remarkable set of buildings spread along the spine of the ancient city's axis, punctuating the skyline with a series of domes and thin pencil minarets which hailed the new era.

Sinan's (and Suleiman's) acquaintance with Aleppo may have been a factor in the determined way in which Ottoman plans for the city now unfolded. The first of the projects was the Khusrofiye Madrasa positioned where the exercise grounds met the buildings on the eastern edge of the central core of the Medina. Here was found the essential religious and commercial life of the city going back to Hellenistic times. The major Ottoman buildings now introduced into this already densely packed area required demolition and rebuilding on a colossal scale. The next three projects were:

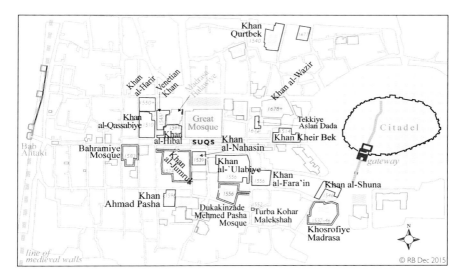

Figure 10.4 Remaking of the Ottoman medina in the first two Ottoman centuries

- the mosque known today as the 'Adeliye built on land partly unencumbered by buildings. The mosque's location near the old Ayyubid/Mamluk palace of justice (Dar al-'Adl) to the east is still reflected in the popular name, al-'Adeliye;[8]
- the grandest of the city's *khan*s, known as the Customs Khan or Khan al-Jumruk (the Arabic reworking of the Turkish designation). This complex of warehouses, travellers' accommodation and retail shops lies in the heart of the Medina (1574);
- the Bahramiye Mosque built ten years later (1583) by the governor Bahram Pasha who, along with his brother, is buried in the complex.

The consciously interventionist nature of these exercises in town replanning emphasised a further factor which appears to have been consciously exploited in marking out a new monumental axis in an already densely packed city. This was a return to the emphasis on the old Hellenistic-Roman spine linking the original settlement near the Quweiq River with the temple of the Weather God on the Citadel hill. Some 1800 years later, this planning axis was given a new purpose.

At the western end of the axis, outside the Antioch Gate on the far side of the Quweiq, lay vacant river flats. Here an Ottoman palace was built on Gök Maydan to accommodate Suleiman the Magnificent's passage through Aleppo on his way to campaign in Iraq in the 1530s. The Ottoman artist Natrakçi Nasuh depicted the relationship between palace and town shown in Figure 10.5, a manuscript recording his experiences when he (like Sinan) was part of Sultan Suleiman's military

Figure 10.5 Natrakçi Nasuh's depiction of Aleppo, probably sketched during his visit in 1535–6

campaigns. Though the style is admittedly somewhat 'expressionist', Natrakçi Nasuh's miniature is our first surviving pictorial depiction of Aleppo clearly underlining the relationship between palace and town.[9]

It was three decades into the Ottoman era before the first projects along this spine emerged.[10] The sequence of major buildings then spread west in a conveniently chronological pattern along the central *suq*s, forming a 'monumental corridor' obviously inspired by a coordinated vision.[11]

One of the first modern writers to highlight the importance of this corridor, André Raymond, downplayed the possibility of a concerted *plan global* behind the development.[12] While there was no urban planning in the modern sense, it seems correct to see the projects as inspired by a vision realised over forty years for a new central spine building upon the ancient Hellenistic axis and even respecting its component blocks. We will look now in some detail at how this building programme unfolded as it gives much insight into the priorities the empire sought to observe in this key city of the empire's extra-European footprint.

al-Khusrofiye (Mosque-Madrasa of Khusrof Pasha)

The complex of the Madrasa Khusrofiye brought the Ottoman style to Aleppo with a flourish and was one of the first projects that bore the stamp of Sinan's

212

Figure 10.6 Aleppo's monumental axis as sketched by Grélot for Bembo's memoirs (1674) (courtesy Minnesota University Library)

workshop. A project of the Ottoman senior official Khusrof Pasha it was probably completed in 1546. Khusrof Pasha was a good example of the new generation of upwardly mobile officials. He had served in Aleppo in 1531–4 and visited again later in the decade while on his way to the campaign against the Safavids. His Aleppo complex was the fruit, however, of his years as the fourth-ranking Istanbul court vizier, an appointment culminating a career spent in the provinces as an 'unscrupulous and highly mendacious official, but also a remarkably efficient one'.[13] His appointment to high office was brought to an early end in 1545 when he fell out with the sultan. In a rare instance of suicide at the Ottoman court, he starved himself to death in protest at his detention. He had had the foresight to engage Sinan to build his tomb in Istanbul where he was interred. Khusrof's demise did not prevent the completion of the Aleppo *madrasa* complex, though it may have slowed it.

The mosque's flat dome was supported by flying buttresses with a multi-domed porch wider than the prayer hall behind. Its pencil minaret with candle-snuffer top immediately signalled the Ottoman world. Subtle tributes were paid to the local style – use of contrasting stone to define the arches of the porch, a simplified form of muqarnas that almost abandoned the spherical segments in favour of flat triangles. Inside, however, the treatment of space was entirely novel with the long-standing local preference for column-supported prayer halls replaced by an uninterrupted centralised space. The use of external buttresses allowed a spacious prayer hall under the dome unprecedented in local terms with its diameter of 18 metres. To carry the transition to the octagon supporting the dome above,

Figure 10.7 Madrasa Khusrofiye, completed in 1546 under supervision of the Ottoman architect Sinan

the corners were spanned by arches serving as huge squinches maximising the internal space.

To maintain such a huge new enterprise with its student rooms and charitable dependences, several ancillary buildings were built as income-generating projects. In the immediate area, the Khan al-Shuna across the street from the entrance provided a spacious new covered bazar while other enterprises located outside Aleppo from Hama to Aintab produced income assigned to Khusrof's project.

al-ʿAdeliye (Mosque of Dukakinzade Mehmet Pasha)

The second of the signature buildings along the axis was the initiative of the Ottoman official Dukakinzade Mehmet Pasha. He was briefly governor in Aleppo in the period 1551–3 before his transfer to Cairo, returning later to see the completion of his project. A notable quality of the Khusrofiye had been that it was intended to make its impact as a stand-alone complex, without the clutter of commercial streets and competing façades. This was less achievable in the case of the ʿAdeliye complex given its position on the edge of the suqs area and built on rising ground that had been used for javelin training. The southern wall of the mosque was thus too high to give a view of the building as a whole, unless glimpsed in the distance from the east, while the street view on the remaining three sides was hemmed in by dependent commercial buildings.

214

This was again the work of Sinan and followed his signature plan with a domed prayer hall preceded by a wide portico roofed with five domes. The portico introduced to Aleppo the Ottoman taste for faience ceramic panels. The complex was completed through the creation of the neighbouring Khan al-ʿUlaybiye as an income-generating component of the terms of the waqf were also intended to encourage Dukakinzade's family to reside in Aleppo if they were to share in the fruits of its endowed buildings.

Khan al-Jumruk

The next project in chronological and geographic sequence was the grandest of all the Aleppo khans, the Customs Khan (Khan al-Jumruk), though it ceased that official role in the late eighteenth century. Like the later Khan Asaʿad Pasha in Damascus, it represents an extraordinary attempt to combine the commercial with the spectacular. Centuries of service to trade have been less than kind to the Khan al-Jumruk, its courtyard busy with later additions and obscured by goods – not to mention predatory wiring, signage and machinery. It is, however, simply one of the boldest achievements of Ottoman architecture in Aleppo.[14] The khan was again commissioned by a senior Ottoman official, Sokolu Mehmed Pasha (though the waqf document carried the name of his son, Ibrahim Khanzade Mehmed Pasha). Sokolu Pasha clearly had a taste for commissioning on a grand and inventive scale. (The khan spreads over 6200 square metres, the largest of the Aleppo khans). Sokolu Pasha was responsible for a network of large commercial facilities in the eastern empire including in Sidon and Payas (Cilicia).[15]

The Aleppo khan, however, needed to strive for the spectacular as it competed with the crowds along the main artery of the suqs. The project commandeered two passages of the main suq to form *suwayqat* running along the northern periphery of the khan but crossed by the axis of the khan's entrance. As you approach heading west along the suqs suddenly you realise that the confined booths and crowded passage of the Suq al-ʿAtarin are relieved by a soaring cross-vaulted corridor climaxed by a domed space bringing light and air into the gloom (Figure 10.8). This heralds the entrance to the khan off to the left. Once you step aside to take in the scene, the great central dome linking the two suwayqats heralds a space that transports the visitor into a transformed world.

A massive iron-clad door leads along a passage to the khan's internal court. Off this open space, galleries around three sides give access to a warren of rooms (52 warehouses on the ground floor and 77 rooms above) spread over 0.6 hectare. In the centre of the courtyard lies an octagonal pavilion, a mosque built atop a fountain house. A glance back towards the entrance reveals a pair of beautifully decorated window recesses with banded stone and muqarnas decoration in an exuberant style (Figure 10.9).

Gülru Necipoğlu notes that the Khan al-Jumruk is listed among Sinan's projects, consistent with his guiding hand in the other major works along the monumental corridor.[16] The master's influence is certainly clear through the formidable control of spaces and light along the series of domed or cross-vaulted sections of suq that precede the entrance (Figure 10.8).

al-Bahramiye (Mosque of Bahram Pasha)

Bahram Pasha was governor of Aleppo when he commissioned the last of the sign-post projects along the city's east–west axis in 1583. Suleiman the Magnificent was dead and Sinan had already retired after a long and productive career but this last project brought the sequence to a fitting end. This third major mosque again followed a typically Ottoman inverted 'T' plan marked by a wide domed portico but the realisation shows many compromises with the Ottoman norm. Jean-Claude

Figure 10.8 Entrance to the Khan al-Jumruk from the outer *qaisariye*

216

David labels it a 'bastard' achievement – 'a composite building both ambitious and awkward'.[17] A flattened dome over the prayer hall is internally supported on four piers, a significant departure from Sinan's use of uncluttered prayer spaces. The ambitious dome spanning 18 metres succumbed early to an earthquake and had to be rebuilt. The insertion on the southern side of a deep pentagonal apse with the *mihrab* embedded at the end was an element that also jars with Sinan's preference for sweeping internal views. Significantly, the use of strap decoration in variegated stone around the mihrab is a conscious reversion to Mamluk themes but in a busy and over-burdened attempt at the style. Some parts of the mosque had to be reconstructed after an earthquake in 1699 and the minaret and much of the portico colonnade are replacements.

Figure 10.9 Decorated window frames over the entrance to the Khan al-Jumruk

While these four remarkable buildings were a conscious attempt to Ottomanise the city's central corridor, other sixteenth-century buildings (some also planned on an ambitious scale) represented a reversion to local Mamluk traditions in architecture with little acknowledgement of the styles favoured by the new masters. North of the Great Mosque, even a son of Khusrof Pasha, Qurt Bey, continued the Mamluk idiom in taking over an incomplete palace in the Mamluk style, later to be transformed into an extensive khan in 1546 but retaining the courtyard iwan.

City within a city – al-Medina

The new projects ensured that the Medina of the city remained the heartland where commerce and religion rubbed along in consensual co-existence. The suqs of the central city were now largely roofed not with fire-prone wooden structures but in vaulted masonry, shielding the shopper from the extremes of the city's climate. In the 1660s, the Turkish traveller Evliya Çelebi marvelled both at the scale of the bazar (he estimated 5700 shops or booths) and at the range of goods on sale: 'Except for the elixir of life all other sorts of rare and precious merchandise can be found.'[18]

Scattered between the retail spaces (suqs or suwayqat) were the larger khans which provided warehousing space at the wholesale level along with accommodation for visiting merchants. The Khan al-Jumruk, just mentioned, has introduced us to the world of the trading houses established by European interests, to be examined further in the next section. The sixteenth century saw a range of other new

Figure 10.10 Courtyard of the Khan al-Harir or Silk Khan

218

khans built in the central Medina area to facilitate the expansion of trade under the Ottomans and to generate income for the mosques. Those clustering around the Khan al-Jumruk included the Khan al-Nahasin (1541), the Khan al-Fara'in (1550), the Khan al-Hibal (later to be known as the French Khan, 1594) and the Khan al-Taf (1596). By the seventeenth century, the area around the Great Mosque had become the centre of the wholesale sector, the engine driving the city's prosperity through its command of the trade in fabrics, raw silk, coffee, spices, drugs and saltpetre which were exchanged for a rising quantity of imported fabrics.

Most of the khans followed a common pattern in the layout of their facilities. A single entrance with a high door allowing the passage of loaded beasts was followed by a short passage flanked by staircases giving access to a second storey. The courtyard was surrounded by large rooms for the housing of bulk goods. Above, a gallery ran around the open space and gave access to rooms used by traders for accommodation and as offices. The courtyard also usually provided a small mosque and a fountain. Some khans might offer larger suites of rooms to one side with a small central corridor or more prestigious apartments above the entrance gatehouse.

It is also worth remembering that the area around these major projects was being redeveloped at the same time, completing the transformation of the maze of the suqs to the form seen today. We have little idea what other buildings had occupied the main spaces in the Medina before the sixteenth century as only a few fragments of earlier projects survive. The major mosques were financially sustained by a range of commercial projects including the building of new suqs with regular series of booths with uniform frontages lining the old passages. Thus the whole span of the central Medina, upgraded with well-regulated selling spaces, reflected the new prosperity which Ottoman control brought through the absorption of Aleppo into the wider trade activities of the empire. The Medina was also transformed by the displacement of noxious industries that had once been carried on within the walled city (tanneries, dye works, coppersmiths, soap factories) but were now moved outside to create a less confined environment.

City administrative structures

The shaping of the city's growth depended less on decisions by local administrative structures than on individuals who took the initiative perhaps in conjunction with officials of the Ottoman administration back in Istanbul. Usually this involved the energetic follow-through of a local administrator (mostly the governor) and required supportive interventions from time to time by the city's religious leader (qadi) and the commander (agha) of the armed forces contingent (janissaries). André Raymond has emphasised, however, that the element which ensured that these efforts in the long term would contribute to the smooth running of the city after their completion was the system of *waqf*s or religious endowments.[19]

Waqfs were not only a means of ensuring continued income streams for the mosques. By stipulating how the income was earned and distributed, they played a directly interventionist role in ongoing administration and their supervision by the religious authorities to a large extent ensured their terms were respected. The fact that they have lasted many hundreds of years underlines the pervasive good sense behind the system, reinforced by modern legislative frameworks. Certainly the success of the waqf system was an important factor in the maintenance of the traditional environment in Syria's historic city centres.

Among the innovations which marked the arrival of Ottoman rule was the introduction of a land survey to which was tied a specific set of laws relating to the taxation returns expected. This also entailed the official counting of the number of urban households for taxation purposes, the first being undertaken in 1537. While the data on quarters and households is not necessarily easy to interpret in terms of net population figures, Raymond estimates that Aleppo's population in 1537 was around 80,000. This increased to 115,000 in 1683, that is, a 40 per cent rise in 140 years. Much of this increase was absorbed by extra-mural quarters of the city with the walled city's population probably remaining fairly constant at around 40,000.[20]

Strangers in the city

Over the three centuries of Ottoman rule, the city's economy was at times buffeted by the fluctuations in trade flows due to events such as the interruption to silk production in Iran with the end of the Safavids (effectively in 1722) or the opening of the Suez Canal in the 1850s. Aleppo managed to hold its position as the main channel for goods arriving from the East for the European market. The framework for Aleppo's rise to dominance in the Eastern trade lay partly in the sequence of treaty agreements which the European trading centres signed initially with the Mamluks and later with the Ottoman central authorities in Istanbul. With the extension of Ottoman rule to the Levant, European states gave even more weight to treaty arrangements, referred to as 'Capitulations', to protect trading interests and bolster the role of their agencies ('factories') as well as consular representatives in the East. The treaties stipulated where Europeans could reside, exempted representatives from the *jizya* tax on non-Muslims and quarantined them from the provisions of Islamic law in their personal life. The French took the initiative among nation states and were accorded the first Capitulation treaty with the Ottoman Porte in 1535.

The Venetian presence, however, had long preceded the first Capitulation treaty. The base for the Venetian presence in the early Ottoman period is still appropriately known as the Khan al-Banadiqa (1548), an Arabised version of the Italian Venezia. This centrally located building lies just behind the Halawiye Madrasa in the block adjacent to the Great Mosque on the west. Most of the interior of the khan has been extensively rebuilt over the centuries though the gateway remains impressive. Its Venetian contingent was still substantial in 1605 when the Portuguese traveller Pedro Teixeira spent two months in the city. The Venetians could still boast a presence comprising fourteen merchants, exporting wool cloth, silks and brocades as well as silver coin. In return they bought raw silk, indigo,

Figure 10.11 Entrance to the Venetian Khan (Khan al-Banadiqa), used by the Venetians
from the late sixteenth century

cotton and spices. Their presence was sizeable enough to require a physician,
apothecary, a barber and several chaplains (Franciscan friars).

Representatives of two other powers were soon installed in the Medina –
England (a vice-consul 1583, raised to consul three years later) and Dutch
(1613). In 1605, the English presence was strengthened by a permanent 'factory' or agency of the Levant Company (established by royal charter in 1581 to
handle English commercial relations) comprising three merchants and a consul
(in fact a merchant himself). It grew in the course of the seventeenth century,
reaching a community of forty in 1697. The French followed the same path in

1666 when Louis XIV's finance minister, Colbert, granted a French trading company a monopoly of the French trade. Combining the role of company representative and consul greatly amplified the strength of commercial pressures that could be applied in the local market and in the courts. The Capitulations – and the subsequent treaties which allowed merchant houses to nominate translators (dragomans) who enjoyed the same rights as their employers – thus created a 'fire wall' protecting European interests and the interests of local Christians, notably Catholics. These privileges would later foster great resentment from the Muslims of Aleppo until the dissolution of the Ottoman Empire.

By the opening of the eighteenth century, well-organised networks of European trading interests spread along the Levantine coast. Most ports served one or two inland cities with Tripoli initially servicing Aleppo (by 1612 replaced by Alexandretta). So closely were the port towns associated with their principal inland market that Shakespeare mistakenly referred to Aleppo as a port, though it was at the time working in tandem with the port of Alexandretta three days' trek away:

> Her husband's to Aleppo gone, master o'th' Tiger.
> But in a sieve I'll thither sail,
> And like a rat without a tale
> I'll do, I'll do, and I'll do.
> (*Macbeth* Act I, scene 3)[21]

Our image of Ottoman Aleppo is informed by a wonderful range of written and visual material stemming from the presence of European trading houses from the sixteenth to the eighteenth century and by the consulates established to protect the merchants' interests. There are few cities of the Middle East from where we can gain comparable insight into the relationship between Europeans and the world of the Eastern bazar. Yet it is important to remember that though these sources give us a picture of a brilliantly colourful and exotic experience for the small European population of the city (which we will dip into later in this chapter), they controlled only a small fraction of the city's economic life which carried on as it had for centuries handling a range of local and regional products going well beyond the fabrics and spices demanded by the European luxury market or the later local taste for English worsteds.

For this sizeable European community within the depths of the Medina it cannot have been a comfortable environment which attracted Europeans to this zone. The account by the Russell brothers of life in the eighteenth-century English 'factory' located in the Khan al-Jumruk is hardly a picture of ease and luxury. Instead they found a life confined to living 'above the shop'. While their activities during the day focused on making money to fund an early retirement back in Europe, it was at night that the restrictions of their life were more keenly felt. To protect the traders and their goods, the khan's single gate was locked after dark and their confinement to small suites of rooms in one corner of the khan caused Russell to reflect on the

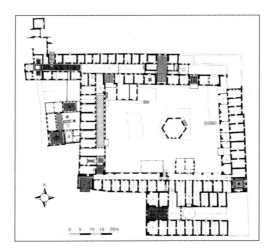

Figure 10.12 Khan al-Jumruk (after Hadjar 2006: 138)

disadvantages of their accommodation. In comparison, he noted the Syrians could enjoy their more spacious houses with open-sided *iwan*s facing a refreshing court-yard with its flowing fountains and usually a comfortable winter salon or *qaʿa*.

It was not, however, a situation of total confinement and the accounts of life among Europeans in Aleppo is a roster of social calls, day trips into the coun-tryside and the protocols of the community itself, including constant diversions to entertain other European visitors. If there was a sense of 'otherness' in their existence, it was not always a negative experience. Many accounts, including of Europeans not previously familiar with the East, evoke their curiosity rather than hostility towards the local community. The curiosity is often superficial but not necessarily driven by animosity towards Islam. The greatest negative is towards the Turkish officials rather than the locals.

It is also important to remember, as Jean-Claude David has recently reminded us, that Aleppo under the first three centuries of Ottoman rule operated under a system remote from the sense of national identity which marked both monarchi-cal and later republican systems in Europe. While the Ottoman political system sought to buttress an imperial structure across a vast geographical spread, it did so by embracing a diversity of identities:

Ottoman centralization was fundamentally different from French monar-chical and subsequent Jacobin centralism. Diversity of identities was a constituent element of the Empire: co-existence was on an organ-ized basis, and inclination to openness and to exchange were generally favoured. . . . National identity or identities did not exist, even in embry-onic form, before the nineteenth century.[22]

223

David goes on to point out that it was this sense that 'Aleppo was characterized by diversity, by tolerance and by a cross-fertilization of cultures' even more so than other cities of the empire which attracted sizeable numbers of European visitors and residents – Damascus and Cairo for instance. However, even the more intelligent foreign residents who were sufficiently open-minded about the society they were living in to make contacts across confessional lines, do not talk in terms of real friendships between Europeans and Arabs. Russell, for instance, did not see the blame as necessarily lying on the European side: 'An aversion to the Franks, as enemies of the true believers, is certainly not imaginary.'[23]

'An Epitome of the Whole World'[24]

It is time to be more specific about the impressions Aleppo conveyed to visitors from other worlds. To most visitors it was an exotic city but also one in which they could feel reasonably at home. Before 1600, when Aleppo had become a code word for the exotic in Shakespeare, most visitors from other regions had left fairly prosaic descriptions of the city in their accounts of their travels. The Muslim writers in particular concentrated on cramming factual information into their chronicles. With the establishment of the European 'factories' in the late sixteenth century, the trickle of occasional visitors from Europe turned into a fairly steady stream of merchants who often spent periods of five years or more in the city.

From 1600 to 1800 we thus find a stream of descriptions of the city which begin to relay more colourful and often insightful accounts of life in the city as the Europeans saw it. From the second half of the seventeenth century alone, we have sixteen sources on life in the city by visitors from France, Italy, Spain, Turkey, Germany and England ranging from chapters in longer travel accounts to the Russells' two-volume study of the city's 'natural history'. The physicians and chaplains it would seem had most time at their disposal to pursue their curiosity about the local society. While some accounts stand out for their ability to comment dispassionately, the clergy initially were more inclined to want to expound on the evils of Islam and the misguided beliefs of the 'Infidels' in attempts to rival the thunderous prose of the Old Testament.

> They are a base, beggerly, and rogish people; wandering up and downe, and living by spoile, which they account no sinne, because they are Mahomets Countrimen, and he allowed them liberty to live by theft.[25]

The three accounts which give the most insight into the city at the time are:

- the description of his passage through Aleppo in 1671 by the young Venetian nobleman Ambrosio Bembo, only recently edited from his manuscript memoirs;[26]
- the memoirs, published posthumously, of the years spent in Aleppo by the French consul Laurent d'Arvieux (consul 1679–86);

- the extraordinarily detailed and dispassionate account of Aleppo during the period 1740–54 by Alexander Russell, physician to the English factory – *The Natural History of Aleppo,* later expanded into a two-volume edition by his brother, Patrick (1794).

European life in the Medina

By the time Bembo arrived in Aleppo, the Venetian community which had pioneered the European trading presence, was limited to one, the consul (in fact, Bembo's uncle). Nevertheless, his welcome from the other trading and consular representatives was prodigious. After calling on the qadi where he was received with sober ceremony, Bembo found the hospitality extended by the European consuls somewhat overwhelming:

> After the visit with the Qadi we received [the visits] of the consuls. The first was that of the consul of France, who came on the appointed day at the 24th hour. He wore shoes and robe all in red (except for his hat), which is the way other consuls also dress. He was accompanied by all his countrymen, dragomen and janissaries. . . . All the nationals remained in the portico where, as was the custom, a great, long table was spread with a breakfast that can well be called a dinner, even if it was made up of cold foods, cakes, pastry, sweetmeats and similar things. Much glass was broken without regard during the meal [in toasts] to the health of the rulers and officials. In the gaiety full bottles of wine were thrown to the ground and, without exaggeration, a lake of wine was formed in the entire portico.

Figure 10.13 Bembo's depiction of the ceremonial arrival of a foreign consul in Aleppo, 1671 (courtesy of the Minnesota University Library)

But that wasn't all. The 50 metre walk to accompany the French consul to his home (then the Khan al-Jumruk) turned into a further feast.

> When we arrived at the house of the French consul, we found set in the portico another breakfast, this time rather modest, and the same revelries and toasts were repeated with infinite destruction of goblets and bottles. In the heat of the drinking, they overturned the table with all the food almost on top of their consul.[27]

The emphasis on taking meals together is explained by Bembo as follows:

> Since the Turks are not easy to deal with or to converse with, the Franks have little familiarity with them outside of business matters. The entertainment of the Europeans thus consists of exchanging frequent meal invitations by day and night.[28]

The Russells' two-volume account of their long stay in Aleppo provided a greater opportunity for the Enlightenment mind to lead us into numerous by-ways of the city's life, its environment and the animal and vegetal curiosities of Syria. Not only does *The Natural History of Aleppo* provide the antidote to the religious phobias of the earlier clerical descriptions of the city, its informed narrative would counteract even the sort of travel writing that cranks out 'life style' babble these days.

The Russells' commentary on the three dignitaries in Figure 10.14, for example, reveals an intense curiosity for detail leading to a close understanding of their style of dress and posture as related to their functions – from left, the qadi, the agha or janissary commander and (right of the servant waiting to remove the coffee cup) a pasha or high official.

In summarising the insights these strangers took away, it is worth remembering that their world was largely confined to the centre of the city, deeply embedded in both its commercial and religious life yet allowing exchanges with the local population that were heavily structured in their scope. In another urban centre far from Europe, however, outsiders might have been placed on the periphery or in their own ghettoes; in Aleppo they worked in a world no more than 100 metres from the Great Mosque amid the major khans, suqs and madrasas. Excursions outside the Medina for recreational rides, hunts or simply to accompany arriving or departing visitors were part of the routine. Security was a marginal concern with the usual precautions to secure their warehouses at night and discouragement from walking in the city after ten in the evening. Precautions also needed to be taken in areas well outside the city limits against Bedouin inclined to prey upon unescorted and conspicuously prosperous travellers.

Life in this inward-looking community that offered limited release from routine was reinforced by the bonds of protocol which required elaborate rounds of calls, processions to pay tribute to officials or to colleagues and the provision of

Figure 10.14 Depiction of a group of Aleppo dignitaries, from Russell *Natural History of Aleppo*, 1794 edition vol. 1, plate II

entertainment within the 'factory' environment for European visitors. To savour just a few pages of the diaries, letters or memoirs of the Europeans is to enter a dizzying round of calls, meals and toasts, not to mention masses. D'Arvieux's memoirs are a whirligig of entertainment on an extravagant scale, though perhaps a little more restrained than Bembo's. Honouring a group of visiting Dutch sea captains in 1681, d'Arvieux describes:

> On 7 June, I provided the most magnificent supper I could manage – a table for 24 with two side tables, each of twelve. All of the Dutch and the heads of the French communities were invited. The meal was served in an orderly, correct way in abundant quantities and with delicacy. The presentation was in the Turkish style. Music was provided by oboes, flutes, cymbals, violins, psalteries and accordions. The Jews entertained us with dances and games. In the Greek style we drank excellent wines and liquor. The company was gay and most content, delaying their departure until after midnight. They were escorted back to their quarters by my janissaries, footmen and officers.[29]

D'Arvieux generally found the Aleppines 'the gentlest, least malevolent and most accommodating of all the people of this vast empire' a claim he had some grounds to make given his wide experience in the service of France among the Ottoman provinces of North Africa, the Levant and in Istanbul.[30]

Nevertheless, there are occasional rumblings at the rigours of their life in an environment far from a comfortable world back home. Melancholia was clearly a problem among some. The Venetian consulate was staffed with at least one doctor to address symptoms of alienation and the sixteenth-century Venetian resident Barbarigo complained of an intense sense of dislocation and isolation. Mostly, however, the heavy routines seem to be accepted, along with the ups and downs of a commercial system that must necessarily operate in a world of hazards and unpredictability.

The confined world of the Medina offered few of the comforts available in the outer reaches of the city. Take the Khan al-Jumruk examined earlier, which though sizeable (0.6 hectare) (see Figure 10.12) now had to accommodate at least three of the European factories at any one time, as well as housing the Ottoman customs house. We lack information on exactly how the khan was divided but it seems that the English had rented the annexed wing on the southeast whose upstairs apartments included a large domed central hallway. This would have provided a space some 30 by 40 metres or 1200 square metres which had to accommodate 'thirty or forty firms, comprising perhaps fifty traders and partners, as well as numbers of European clerks and officials', not to mention their bales of silk or worsteds.[31]

Allowing for these considerations, however, Aleppo offered an environment remarkably free of tensions between races or faiths. Outsiders frequently commented on the Aleppines as 'the most civilised' in all the Turkish empire and the European merchants as 'enjoying in no other place the same liberty or respect'.[32] People were aware of (and curious about) differences while the protocols of life were normally enough to regulate exchanges. Ottoman administrative and legal structures built upon a relatively tolerant application of Islamic law.

Aleppo, it should be remembered too, was still a city of minorities whichever way you looked at it. One might be a Muslim but of which stream; following which code of Islamic law; adhering to which Shi'i or heterodox variation? Christians might be Maronite, Orthodox (Greek, Armenian or Syrian), other Eastern Christian streams or even (once many saw advantage in turning to the Uniate branches of the Christian sects) Catholics of the Roman, Greek, Syrian or Armenian varieties. The Jewish community had been assessed by the Jewish visitor Benjamin of Tudela in the thirteenth century at 5000 – perhaps an exaggeration but now in any event swollen by accepting many who fled persecution in Europe, requiring the Bandara Synagogue to open a second prayer hall for the Sephardic community on the eastern side of the courtyard.[33] In the face of this diversity, issues of race hardly got a look-in – Arab (town or Bedouin), Kurd, Turk, not to mention the communities of Persian or Indian traders stationed in or visiting the city – were all part of a complex mix.

There were some attempts to enforce distinctive dress codes (specifying types of hats and shoes, for instance). Language would often readily give outsiders away but Aleppo also became a centre in which Europeans could chose to learn Arabic at a serious scholarly level. The first Professor of Arabic at Oxford Edward

Pococke, had applied for the post of chaplain to the English Company in order to school himself at the highest standard before returning in 1635 to England to take up the inaugural Laudian chair in the language.

If there was one motivation, however, which seemed to apply to most of the Europeans who stuck it out for up to ten years before retiring home with their fortune, it was curiosity, usually of the healthy variety. With the Enlightenment gathering pace in Europe, Aleppo offered many opportunities to satisfy curiosity in a relatively congenial environment. Much of their preoccupation with status, protocols, profits and feasting may seem to us wearying but it helped grease the mechanism of this complex society and aid them in feeling 'at home', for a while. Most did want to learn and within the confines of a fairly religious framework (Catholic or Protestant), avoided an absolutely 'us *vs* them' approach to the Aleppo environment. Nevertheless, life among the largely young unmarried traders of the factories must have been little different from the isolation of the 'bachelors' quarters' of later colonial situations. While some Catholic traders married local Christian women, Protestants infrequently mixed socially outside their ranks.

To sum up, the absorption of this European community into the city's life is not simply important as an illustration of the European mind in an exotic environment. It also gave something to the city: 'The inhabitants of Aleppo, alone among the fabled caravan cities of the Fertile Crescent, had prolonged experience of Europeans living among them . . . (giving) the city both opportunities and challenges which gave the city's Christian inhabitants a historical trajectory unique among cities until the nineteenth century when European influences became pervasive everywhere.'[34] The cultural renaissance among Christian minorities previously impoverished and marginalised helped give the city the basis for its later economic success.

Elite housing

By contrast with the cramped life of the European community, elite houses could rise to a level of extravagance that could only be marvelled. A project for a palatial building was started in the late Mamluk period around 1493 by Aztimur al-Ashrafi. The uncompleted building (initially mentioned earlier on page 198) was converted into a khan in the sixteenth century by Qurt Bey, the son of Khusrof Pasha, responsible for the first Ottoman mosque complex described above (pages 212–14). This building marked the transition to the style of symmetrical courtyard houses which would now become standard – oriented strictly north–south with an extensive central pool and a deep iwan positioned on the south side as its dominant feature.

By the early seventeenth century, two remarkable houses were constructed in the city. A Kurdish amir, Junbalat Ibn Qassem al-Kurdi, who had served as Ottoman district head at Kilis, north of Aleppo, rose to be leader of his community in Aleppo.[35] He transformed an allotment in the northern Bandara Quarter and its existing buildings into a palace on a magnificent scale. The tall iwan looking onto the south side of the main courtyard rose 15 metres. Constructed in 1550 it

Figure 10.15 Iwan on the southern side of the courtyard of the Junblatt house

was never to be challenged as the largest in the city. Although the architecture is basically Aleppan in inspiration, the rear wall of the iwan carries ceramic panels with a diagonally repeated decoration which closely resembles some of the tiles that Suleiman the Magnificent provided to decorate the outer walls of the Dome of the Rock in Jerusalem.

When Junbalat's son, Hussein, was elevated to the governorship of Aleppo in 1604 the palace remained his residence. His elevation was short-lived as he was executed the next year in Van for refusing to join an Ottoman expedition against the Safavids. The Junbalat family name passed into history as a result of the career of a nephew, ʿAli Pasha, who after taking over the governorship in 1606 later fled to Lebanon. He converted to the Druze faith but was executed in 1610 having acquired ambitions for a principality of his own. The building was seized by the Ottoman state and passed through several hands in later centuries. Largely in ruins in the 1950s, the southern courtyard area was restored for the Kuwait royal family in the 1990s but the northern courtyard still awaits a new use and refurbishment.

The form of the Aleppo house now followed a layout that remained stable for centuries. Life revolved around a central courtyard with, in the case of wealthy patrons, perhaps one or two such outdoor areas to differentiate family from visitors' spaces. On the south side of the courtyard a large open room or iwan provided protection from the summer sun while the qaʿa or sitting room on the north could be heated in other seasons. Central fountains and sometimes trees provided a relaxing environment throughout the year. Until the second half of the nineteenth century, external windows were rare, unless an opening protected from view by a protruding wood-screened box was provided.

The second house which gives us a rare insight into the life of an early seventeenth-century family lies in the Jdeide Quarter, by now a haven for the Christian community. The Beit Wakil (named for a later family who held the house immediately before the First World War) was built possibly as early as the late Mamluk period. In 1601–3 its wealthy Christian owner, 'Issa Ibn Butros, employed a Persian craftsman to paint the wooden wall panels of the main sitting room with a rich tapestry of scenes of animal, vegetal and geometric ornamentation. In 1911, the family sold the panels to a European resident who arranged via the German scholar Friedrich Sarre to sell them to the Museum for Islamic Art in Berlin. There the panels remain, comprising part of the Pergamon Museum complex. The skeleton of the house was converted in the 1990s to serve as one of Aleppo's first boutique hotels and restaurant. Though largely only the qaʿa survives of the original Mamluk house, stripped of its panelling, its splendid proportions (if not the modern replacements for the wall panelling) give some idea of a luxurious early seventeenth-century domestic environment (see Figure. 12.4 on page 289).

Beyond the walls

The trade which sustained Aleppo depended on the regular and safe arrival of caravans, often from distant sources. While the journey within the immediate region of Aleppo could be carried through much of the year on donkeys (except when snow closed the pass to Alexandretta across the Amanus Range), the long distance caravans from Persia via Mosul and down the Tigris to Baghdad and Basra were largely camel-borne. Caravans between Aleppo and Baghdad took forty-five days. They were often consolidated into large convoys of up to 2000 camels for security reasons and scheduled during the cooler months when forage was plentiful. On the long stretch of the central Euphrates where there were few settlements, security was highly dependent on the protection of the Bedouin sheikhs who were paid to keep unruly desert followers in check. The arrival of a Baghdad caravan at Aleppo would spark a peak of intense activity as beasts were unloaded at designated points outside the walls and the goods carried into the khans by man or donkey for assessment at the customs post (Khan al-Jumruk) and distribution to the specialised khans for sale.

A 'new' quarter (Jdeide)

A range of locally engaged staff assisted the foreign traders and consuls. Some were local Christians usually described by the term 'dragoman' but with other specialisations covered by Jews or Muslims. Many of the Christians congregated in the Jdeide Quarter, introduced in the last chapter (page 197), which already had Christian associations given its origins in a small collection of monastic churches outside the walls. New Christian settlement in the quarter was encouraged as early as the Ottoman conquest under Sultan Selim when the sultan released further parcels of land to settle forty Christian families. A century later Sultan Murad IV, passing through Aleppo, authorised extensions to the Armenian cathedral in the Jdeide Quarter. The Ottoman encouragement of the Christian community partly stemmed from the need to find staff who could support the activities of European merchants as interpreters. It did not reflect any desire to establish an isolated community. It also reflected the influx of Christians from the Armenian and non-Orthodox ('Jacobite') communities of eastern Anatolia as well as Greek Orthodox from the towns of central Syria. After 1600, the growing silk trade from Iran also brought new infusions of Armenians from the New Julfa (Isfahan) through whose agency the export trade in silks was tacitly encouraged by the Safavid rulers of the country.[36] There was already a mosque in the Jdeide quarter and by the seventeenth century a Muslim waqf saw the foundation of the Ibshir Pasha Complex comprising mosque, hammam, *qaisariye*, khan and coffee house, thus covering needs across communities (discussed below).

Other extra-mural offshoots

By the end of the first century of the Ottoman presence, Aleppo had spread well beyond its walled limits, increasing its footprint by as much as 50 per cent. The usual pattern for the establishment of new quarters outside the walls was the relocation of industrial facilities previously found within the city or for facilities supporting the caravan trade. To the north, outside the Bab al-Nasr, the first offshoots accommodated coppersmiths and dyers.

In the Banqusa Quarter outside Bab al-Hadid, at the northeast corner of the newly expanded city wall, small new mosques, khans and baths are noted from the fourteenth century. On the western edge, outside the Antioch Gate and within reach of an eastward bend of the Quweiq River, the tanneries displaced from the northwest corner of the walled city[37] found a new home in a complex whose income formed part of the massive waqf embracing the Khan al-Jumruk. The new location, close to where Suleiman the Magnificent's temporary palace had stood (see page 211), was picturesquely known as the 'Bridge of Tortoises' and must have managed to retain enough of its charm to provide a favoured spot for riverbank leisure as noted by Ambrosio Bembo in 1671:

> Near the bridge there is a waterwheel and around it are many houses that look onto the water, and for pleasure the Great Turks often go to eat and enjoy themselves. . . . Not far from the bridge . . . there is a great stretch of very beautiful sandy plain that they call the maydan, where every Friday the pasha and his people go to play the game of jerida on horseback after dinner.[38]

The *Hajj*

We noted above that a major touchstone in affirming the legitimacy of Ottoman rule had been its religious credentials. There was no more central duty for the Caliph and Guardian of the Holy Places than to ensure that the annual pilgrimage to Mecca got through and returned safely. While the Hajj had been operating for many centuries as a regime-sponsored enterprise, from Ottoman times most of the pilgrims were drawn from the territories of the empire itself so extensive was its reach into the Balkans, Anatolia, the Caucasus and northern Mesopotamia. Aleppo was the point at which several of these routes converged. Here pilgrims first began to form into an organised caravan. From Damascus, it was afforded official protection and provisioned for the last stages across the long and arid stretch of the Hajj route to the Holy Places, the governor of Damascus

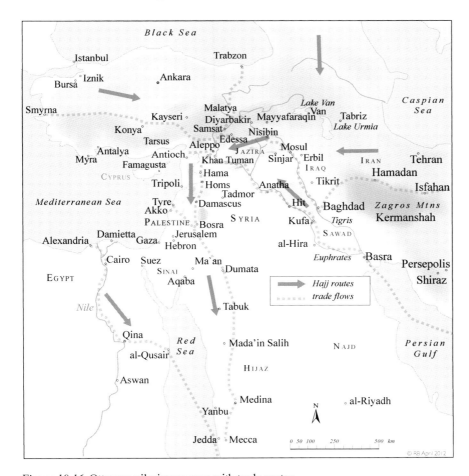

Figure 10.16 Ottoman pilgrimage map with trade routes

233

usually seeing off the caravan amid great ceremony and charged with assuring its security.

We have noted earlier the growing association of the extramural reaches south of the city walls as a burial place of holy men or those seeking sanctified ground. Its cluster of Islamic schools, tombs and shrines associated with legendary figures were partly attracted by the fact that the area lay on the pilgrims' first steps towards the Hijaz and its Holy Places. As the Hajj assembled, the thousands of pilgrims camped outside the walled enclosure of Aleppo would visit sites such as the Shrine of Abraham or the tomb of the fabled holy man, al-Harawi and stock up on provisions. The route south still largely followed the stages that had been marked by the series of caravan stops or khans associated with the Ayyubid or Mamluk years.

The first halt on the way south from Aleppo was the Khan al-Tuman, about 12 kilometres south of Aleppo's walls. Khan al-Tuman was also the point to which European travellers would head or at which they would be greeted on their arrival from the coast. The khan, first constructed in 1189, survives though part of its crumbling southern annexe was carried away during the construction of a new railway line to Aleppo in the 1970s. From there south, a regular series of stone-built enclosures, still mimicking the style of ancient Roman forts, followed the interface between fertile land and steppe. This was the lifeline of Ottoman control joining along the way such other major towns as Hama or Homs. The caravan halts operated all year and provided basic rest and watering facilities for all travellers, including the Hajj pilgrims. It could only offer accommodation and stabling to some tens of travellers but it provided an official presence and secure base to discourage attacks on wayfarers. The line can still be traced along the north–south road and rail corridor through Syria and Jordan.

Aleppo's decline

Population displacement

The energy released during the early years of Ottoman rule did not last; but nor did it suddenly splutter out. As eastern cities went, Aleppo had achieved a level of fame enjoyed by few other Eastern cities, apart from the mega-centres such as Istanbul or Cairo. It was famed for its ability to attract the greatest minds. Its scholars achieved fame throughout the Muslim world: 'This was the natural habitat of powerful, wealthy and learned men, the sort of place where luxury and pretension thrived. People from lands as distant as England and India came there to trade, study, visit and settle.'[39] Yet is was a city that often lived only on the margins of assured prosperity. Its rainfall was unreliable and could bring massive crop failures in the barren regions to the east and southeast. Not far beyond the settled zone, the steppe sheltered tribes hostile to central authority and ready to prey on passing sources of wealth.

By the late seventeenth century, Aleppo's economy largely needed to be sustained by its immediate region rather than through the wider trade routes. Though the English factory remained in operation, the number of its factors fell and it kept going by tapping a growing demand for English broadcloth, with exports to England playing a more minor role. A number of written sources indicate that the region was increasingly unable to play a sustaining role as it had in the past. The population of the countryside around Aleppo had already begun a serious decline in the second half of the seventeenth century. Yet the city population exploded as many had taken refuge in Aleppo's peri-urban suburbs to the east and north, fleeing from disease and poor agricultural productivity (often exacerbated by harsh taxation measures by rapacious tax farmers). Aleppo's population climbed (as noted earlier, page 220) to around 120,000 in the space of a few decades. Efforts by the Ottoman authorities to force peasants back to their villages ran into resistance from the jurists who could find no Islamic precedent to authorise such use of compulsion.

The effect of population fluctuation can be seen in this description of the depopulated countryside between Alexandretta and Aleppo which startled the French visitor abbot Bartholémy in 1672:

> A very old man, who was nearly a hundred years old, told me that this country used to be one of the richest, most fertile, and well-populated parts of all Syria, and that, when he was young, he could count 50 towns and 400 villages, which now lay in ruins for a stretch of fifteen or twenty leagues around. This was due to the bad government of the Ottoman empire, whose policy was to destroy the country for fear of strangers mastering it. . . . They seem by this means to contribute to their own ruin, for they have now nothing left but their chief towns, and even these could not subsist without the help of foreign nations, who by their trade, merchandise, caravans, and travellers contribute the principal revenue of those places.[40]

The non-Muslim population of Aleppo also rose due to heavy-handed official treatment of the Christian communities of neighbouring Anatolia as well as to Armenian traders moving from Iran.[41] Many Christian arrivals, however, were fleeing their own communities, seeking a more tolerant environment in the face of Orthodox hostility towards former members who had begun to flock to the 'Uniate' churches, which from the fifteenth century had started to break away from orthodoxy and sought union with Rome.

The seventeenth century, therefore, saw a considerable intensification of settlement in the largely Christian suburb of Jdeide. One governor of the city, Ibshir Mustafa Pasha, took a remarkably enlightened approach to the city's needs for new commercial space. When Ibshir Pasha became governor in 1651, he sought to give the city's commercial life new space in which to grow given that the

Figure 10.17 South façade of the Ibshir Mustafa Pasha complex

Medina of the old city had been crowded with buildings since the early Ottoman expansion of the khans. He turned his attention to the Jdeide area where the growing Christian community lacked facilities for commercial activities. He turned to what might be called today 'mall development' – the provision of a range of shops, khans, qaisariyes for precious goods and, most revolutionary of all, a coffee shop. This complex gave a new stimulus to growth in both the Christian and the Muslim quarters north of the city as well as providing a small mosque.

Ibshir Pasha's palatial coffee shop might suggest a frivolous modern preoccupation with relaxing over a cup of coffee but the tradition goes way back before our time. Coffee does not seem to have had an easy introduction to the Ottoman world, coming in from Yemen (and presumably sourced in the Horn of Africa) in the late sixteenth century. It immediately attracted the disapproving scrutiny of the Islamic authorities but efforts to ban it were thankfully largely allowed to fall quickly into disuse given that most of the commodity was being traded by pilgrims returning from the Hajj. The first mention of coffee in Aleppo dates from 1586 but it was already known to have been adopted as a recreational drink in Damascus earlier in the century. The efforts to ban it had largely expired by the mid-seventeenth century when Ibshir Pasha's spacious hall was opened in 1653. The popularity of coffee was clear from Evliya Çelebi's visit to Aleppo in 1671–2 when he marvelled at the range of houses serving coffee (105 in his estimate). Ibshir Pasha's coffee house remains one of the largest public spaces in traditional Aleppo[42] though sadly not used for its original purpose.

Khan al-Wazir

A final attempt to gain more space in the inner city for large-scale commercial exchanges was the Khan al-Wazir (or 'Governor's Khan') a little to the east of the Great Mosque on the northern edge of the Medina. This ranks with the largest of the Aleppo khans, though part of its northern wing was pushed back as part of a street widening project in the French Mandate period and later reconstructed on a new alignment. The khan was built in 1682 by the Ottoman governor Kara Mustafa Pasha to encourage the growing silk trade from Iran, though it was completed just as the trade was beginning to decline.[43] The Khan al-Wazir's façade and the inner face of the gatehouse outclass even the Khan al-Jumruk with its rich tracery of decoration in a neo-Mamluk style and its bold use of banding.

Heavy hand of centralism

Part of the knot of problems Aleppo now faced was that the Ottoman system required a heavier hand of centralised rule than had been imposed even in Mamluk times. Instead of a series of local Mamluk governors who had held a longer stake in the affairs of their amirates, the Ottoman governors enjoyed only limited terms (before the eighteenth century). Additionally, they were drawn usually from non-Arabic speaking regions of the empire, (and thus from communities that had little experience of the Arab world and its traditions) and were supported by janissary forces who too had few links with the local population, at least initially. Both the chief religious figure and the garrison commander were Ottoman officials. The courts administered only one brand of Islamic law, Hanafi (whereas in preceding centuries, a litigant could choose among the four legal frameworks). Christians or Jews had access to their own courts for settling domestic issues though Christians increasingly preferred to opt for Islamic jurisdiction on issues such as bride price or even divorce. Cases involving both Muslim and Christian parties were necessarily heard in the qadi's courts. Resident foreigners, recognised as 'nations' under the terms of the Capitulation treaties, were supervised by their own consuls, though they could take cases to the qadi's court if internal disputes needed to go

Figure 10.18 Coffee house within the Ibshir Mustafa Pasha Complex (after Jean-Claude David (1982 pl. 7))

Figure 10.19 Courtyard of the Khan al-Wazir

to a higher arbiter. The Portuguese traveller Pedro Teixeira remarked that both Muslims and Christians had respect for the qadi who was judged 'to be not only an accomplished natural philosopher, but a most upright judge'.[44]

Failure to draw on local sources of energy in running the city can be seen in the city's architecture. After the centrally driven push to 'Ottomanise' the main axis of the city, invention petered out in the decades following the death of Sinan (1585), given the lack of a replacement for his driving vision. Until the wave of Europeanisation began to sweep through Ottoman architecture from the late eighteenth century, much of the activity depended on tepid imitation and repetition. Sinan's ability to weave imaginative local ideas into his projects was replaced by a more conformist Ottoman style without the master's ability to amass spaces and shapes in extraordinary combinations within an overall Ottoman vocabulary.

This failure of invention has been well described by Jean-Claude David:

> Imperial architecture, after several prestige projects, was to be confined to parentheses. It was now destined to serve as a foreign idiom – an exogenous style brought in by functionaries that came to assume a role as an imposed expression of power and religion.[45]

The Ottoman model, in other words, was handed over to talentless plagiarists. To be fair, though, there were some exceptions and Ottoman plagiarism could extend

Figure 10.20 Entrance to the Khan al-Wazir

to the inclusion of pre-1516 ideas. This was particularly the case if a project was sponsored by a local notable or sought to appeal to a basically Arab audience.

The religious 'fringe'

The building of monasteries or *tekkiye* for devotions associated with the Sufi interpretation of Islam provide further interesting cases in point. Ottoman rule did not rely on a hard and fast interpretation of Islam. Along with the Sharia and *Hadith* as interpreted by scholars ('outer truth') went popular piety which often overlapped with mysticism ('inner truth'), itself capable of scholarly treatment.[46]

In the context of the second, inner truth, a growing devotion to Sufism marked the early years of the seventeenth century in Aleppo. The sect had spread to Aleppo from Iran as early as the twelfth century. Its sudden growth in the sixteenth century reflected the increasing appeal of Sufism among soldiers in the Ottoman army but also a concern among Ottoman rulers that the appeal of Sufism not be allowed to wander into paths of extreme spirituality where it would remain beyond the reach of traditional Islam amenable to the influence of the state.

There are four such Sufi projects in early Ottoman Aleppo. The dervish lodge now known as the Mosque of Aslan Dada lay in the heart of the Medina, on the eastern edge of the Great Mosque. The unusual choice of a centre-city site probably reflected the fact that when it was built in 1672 it replaced an earlier *khanqah*. It comprised two domed chambers placed on opposite sides of a central courtyard. The domed room on the north served as a meeting room for the dervishes, the southern a prayer hall with a tomb chamber to one side. The style of architecture bore little relationship to contemporary Ottoman taste.

This was not the oldest tekkiye of which we have evidence. The earliest (again indicative of a continuing Mamluk architectural preference) survives outside the walls on the block east of Aleppo's Archaeological Museum. This site was originally just outside the Bab al-Jinan (now largely removed) and near a bend of the Quweiq, close to the area once occupied by the Hamdanid pleasure grounds and the first Ottoman pavilion built for Suleiman's 1530s visits. In the tekkiye, a series of pavilions are arranged around a central open space built to meet the needs of the Mawlawiye order of Sufis who sheltered in Aleppo in the early sixteenth century to escape Safavid discrimination against the order.

The third and most celebrated of the Sufi monasteries lay on an elevated site 3 kilometres outside the northern walls. The urban spread of the last half century has encroached on the cluster of buildings still fragilely isolated in open space. The Tekkiye of Sheikh Abu Bakr al-Wafa' (d.1583) was established in the early seventeenth century to honour the memory of the Sufi holy man who enjoyed great fame for his heroic asceticism. Some of his exploits in the quest for divine

Figure 10.21 View towards the Tekkiye of Sheikh Abu Bakr al-Wafa (from Maundrell 1703 edition, courtesy State Library, Sydney)

favour troubled officials but the decision to further the sheikh's memory two decades after his death provided an alternative to the attraction of the Mawlawiye sect closer to the city. Sheikh Abu Bakr's adoption of extreme forms of privation including nudity and heroic fasting were headed off by the official sponsorship of a new tekkiye or monastery where crowds of pilgrims provided a tempering influence on the Sheikh's followers.[47]

The new tekkiye was crowned with the building of a large audience hall to accommodate visits by the Ottoman governor, underlining the official endorsement of the memory of Sheikh Abu Bakr. The new building assumed an extravagant official style which would have jarred with his preference for the ascetic. The Sufi shrine even became a pleasant diversion for visitors. D'Arvieux describes taking a party of Dutch sea captains to the shrine in 1681 to inspect the pavilions and the tombs. They were received with great ceremony by the resident sheikh and provided with coffee and sherbet.[48]

Taking into account the continuing attraction for more conventional Sunnis of the holy zone south of the city, Aleppo was now ringed by sites providing its population with a wide choice of religious options. It is worth noting that there may have been a cultural distinction between the spread of institutions south of the city which appealed to an Arab clientele and the Turco-Persian influences evident north of the city. In the poorer suburbs to the east, popular with the troublesome janissaries and impoverished immigrants, several more modest shrines had already sprung up since the thirteenth century, particularly to cater to the Kurdish community though many had to be rebuilt following the destructive handiwork of the Mongol invaders.

Two years later, a fourth Sufi place of worship was built in the northeast quarter of the city. In 1634, the Ottoman Grand Vizier himself, Tabani Yassi ('al-Arnavut'), who wintered in Aleppo in 1634 on his way to the sultan's campaigns against the Safavids, founded the tekkiye known as al-Ikhlassiye to honour a holy man still living, Sheikh Ikhlas Khalwati. The continued encouragement of Sufism had long reflected the influence that the sect had built up among Ottoman soldiers and the need recognised at the highest level to channel their devotion in ways not threatening to the regime.

Inquiring minds

By the end of the seventeenth century, the inquiring minds among the European community sought to cast their net wider than the city itself to satisfy curiosity back in Europe about the impact of the Roman Empire in its Eastern provinces. Earlier the previous century, a group of merchants had accompanied the French consul on an excursion of several days to two regions of the Limestone Massif inspecting the Byzantine ruins. An incentive for wider exploration was a particular fascination among scholars in Europe for what might have survived of the great caravan centre at Palmyra in the Syrian steppe southeast of Aleppo. In 1678, a group of English merchants in Palmyra were sufficiently inquisitive to mount a somewhat ill-prepared attempt to reach the caravan city's ruins and to provide an account for a European audience. The mission failed as it had taken insufficient care to prepare its arrival and to persuade the local Bedouin sheikh (whose support was needed to ensure their security) of their good intentions. After a tense confrontation, the group hastened back to Aleppo after less than twenty-four hours in Palmyra, though two of the merchants apparently had time to prepare a wide-format sketch of the ruins' central axis.

A better-prepared expedition was put together by another group of largely English merchants in Aleppo thirteen years later. Led by William Halifax, the chaplain to the English factory, the party reached Palmyra in 1691 after an uneventful six-day journey from Aleppo. They returned to Aleppo via the Euphrates Valley, completing an excursion that lasted eighteen days. Halifax's account heavily relies on recycling legends and incorrectly ascribes to the Turks much of the destruction actually caused over the centuries by earthquakes:

> And had not the Barbarity of the Turks, Enemies to everything that is Splendid and Noble, out of a vain Superstition, purposely beat down those beautiful Columns both here and in other places, we had seen the most exquisite Carvings in Stone which perhaps the World could ever boast of, as here and there a small remainder, which has escap'd their Fury, does abundantly evidence.[49]

Halifax published his account of the journey in the learned journal *Philosophical Transactions*. His description of the ruins, including the Temple of Bel (which at that stage housed the Arab village), passed back to Europe the first 'rude account' of the fabled city, including its 'Noble Piazza of more than half a Mile long', a reference to the city's great colonnaded axis.[50] Halifax's question as to 'whether any City in the World could have challenged Precedence of this in its Glory' only whetted the outside world's appetite for more. His transcription of some of the city's rich store of inscriptions and his account of the funeral towers of the 'Valley of the Tombs' particularly tantalised.[51] In the same journal, a panoramic black and white sketch of the city's ruins was published, further stimulating interest in the extraordinary remains of a classical city in a remote wilderness that had survived so many centuries undisturbed (Figure 10.22).

It was fortuitous that the Dutch traveller and artist Hofstede van Essen was resident in Aleppo in the 1690s and appears to have joined the second expedition as artist. He transformed his panoramic sketch into a sweeping depiction of the lost city in oils.[52] This was the result of an initiative of the European community in Aleppo. The Dutch consul Coenraad Calckberner had been commissioned by a leading figure in Netherlands intellectual and political circles, Gisbert Cuper, to collect and send back whatever material he could gather in the form of coins and texts of inscriptions. At Cuper's request, Calckberner commissioned van Essen's painting following the publication of the Halifax party's account. Van Essen's spectacular depiction of the colonnaded axis of Palmyra was later recycled in numerous versions while the original painting hangs in Amsterdam University's Allard Pierson Archaeological Museum.

A surge of accounts of Palmyra now ensued, including in the course of the century 'improved' versions of van Essen's panorama, three operas on the theme of the city's legendary third-century queen Zenobia and numerous paintings by masters including Tiepolo. It would be more than half a century after the Halifax party's visit before the first careful study of the city's ruins would be published. In 1750, the Englishman Robert Wood and party visited Palmyra. It was Wood's account and the seminal collection of detailed drawings prepared by the expedition's draughtsman Giovanni Battista Borra that touched off even greater interest in the Syrian oasis city.[53] By the mid-eighteenth century, the European audience craved new (previously unpublished) evidence of the Classical traditions that could be incorporated in the pattern books of the Neo-Classical movement in art and architecture. More than any other centre of the Arab world, therefore, Aleppo's small European community fed the European imagination with precise information to inform their curiosity.[54]

End of the silk route

Iranian silk had fuelled the boom years in Aleppo's international trade in the seventeenth century. Raw silk became the dominant single commodity exported to Europe that century: two-thirds of Iran's annual production of one thousand tons reached Europe, almost all via Aleppo. The English in Aleppo had handled most of the flow and in return England's Levant Company had continued to exploit a useful market in English broadcloth. France and the Netherlands had largely moved their representation elsewhere in the face of the English competition.[55] Fifty years later, the Levant Company's Aleppo factors were themselves facing non-viability. The overthrow of the Safavids in Iran by Nadir Shah in 1722 had virtually halted the caravan trade to Iran for the next twenty years and its silk

Figure 10.22 First depiction of the Temple of Bel at Palmyra (from the panoramic sketch published in *Philosophical Transactions* (Halifax 1695)

industry lost most of its output. By the middle of the eighteenth century, the 400 members on the Levant Company's trading register in the 1670s had slumped to forty or less.

Moreover, after centuries in which Aleppo had outperformed trade via Damascus, the southern city was beginning to reap the benefits of stable political leadership just as Aleppo slid into new bouts of rivalry between internal factions. The rise of the al-'Azem family who virtually monopolised the franchise over the Ottoman governorship of Damascus during the period 1725–1807 may have institutionalised corruption on a massive scale but they did serve as a political point of stability which prevented Damascus from experiencing the endemic strife that Aleppo was soon to undergo and which will be examined in the following chapter.

Notes

1 Ibn Battuta quoted in Fleet 2010: 314.
2 Fleet 2010: 316.
3 Ziadeh 1997–8: 337.
4 Eldem et al. 1999: 35.
5 Or 'Sublime Porte', a reference to the elaborate gateway marking the entrance to the palace complex.
6 The authenticity of the claimed transfer of the Caliphate in either 1517 or 1534 is much disputed (Deringil 1998: 46–7).
7 Mamluks had moved the nominal Caliphate from Baghdad to Cairo. It was revived by the Ottomans in the fourteenth century after they had spread westwards beyond their original base at Sögüd in northwest Anatolia. Adopting Bursa for a time as their capital, they later moved further west into European Thrace and took Edirne, the ancient city of Adrianopolis (Sourdel 'Khalifa' *EI*2). In 1369, that city was adopted as their new capital and as a base for fresh conquests for Islam in the Balkans. However, the term 'Caliph' only came into general use a century later, following the final move of the capital to Istanbul.
8 The 'Adeliye runs along relatively open space on its southern side but here the prayer hall lies on a platform that forms a blank wall rising two storeys above the street.
9 The manuscript is held in the library of the University of Istanbul. It is discussed in Watenpaugh (2004: 219–28).
10 Glimpses of other projects during these decades are frustratingly scarce. Besides the renewal of the Citadel walls noted earlier, the Tawashi Mosque was renovated by a local merchant in 1537 and a tomb was constructed for a grand-daughter of the former sultan, Beyazid, who died in Aleppo in 1552 while returning from the Hajj. Both these projects reflect a continuing attachment to the old Mamluk style.
11 The phrase 'monumental corridor' (Watenpaugh 2004: 52).
12 Raymond 1979: 116.
13 Bacqué-Grammont 'Khosrew Pasha' *EI*2.
14 Sauvaget was clearly not initially impressed with the rather battered and improvised look of the much used khan. His initial survey intended to classify Aleppo monuments for preservation suggested that only the central fountain house with mosque above should be given full protection (Sauvaget 1931).
15 A flair for the inventive is evident too in his commissioning from Sinan one of Istanbul's most beautiful smaller mosques, justly described as a 'minor masterpiece' for its massing of shapes across a challenging terrain.

16 Necipoğlu 2005: 471.
17 David 1991: 184.
18 Quoted in Masters 1988: 136.
19 Raymond 1979: 113.
20 Raymond 1984: 458; Raymond 1991: 90, 106.
21 It would seem that in the opening years of the seventeenth century Aleppo's status as code word for the exotic in English minds was stimulated by the opening of the first English consulate in the city (Wood 1935: 15). There is a second reference to Aleppo, in *Othello* (Act V, scene 3, lines 361–5) referring to a fight between a Turk and a Venetian in Aleppo.
22 David 2008: 330.
23 Russell and Russell 1794: I, 216. Summing up the expatriate experience, Masters notes: 'their homesickness, desperation and despair. Alcoholism and disease seem to have been recurring problems, and there is an overwhelming preoccupation with procuring the comforts of England: books, cider, tea, cheese, and ham' (Masters 1988: 79).
24 Letter from the first chaplain of the English factory at Aleppo, dated 1628.
25 Biddulph 1609: 69 (http://name.umdl.umich.edu/A68944.0001.001).
26 Bembo and Welsh 2007.
27 Bembo and Welsh 2007: 59–60. Consul du Pont (Dupont in other sources) used his time in Aleppo to good advantage. He assisted his chaplain, Pere Besson, in acquiring an important collection of Hebrew bibles later presented to the French National Library.
28 Bembo 2007: 71.
29 D'Arvieux 1735: VI, 415, present author's translation.
30 D'Arvieux 1735: VI, 415.
31 Davis 1967: 5.
32 Chassebœuf 1959 [1787]: 275.
33 The Jewish population of Aleppo was assessed at 380 households in 1672 (seventy-three were Sephardi, the rest 'Arab Jews'). At the beginning of the century, however, Teixeira had put it at 'one thousand good houses' (Teizeira 1902: 116).
34 Masters 2001: 71–2.
35 The options for transliterating this name from Arabic/Turkish are almost limitless. Masters (1988: 19–20) opts for Canpulatoğlu from the Turkish version of the Kurdish name; Jumblatt is a more common transliteration of the Arabic version in use in Lebanon today though the origins of the modern Lebanese Druze family of this name are probably unrelated (see Hathaway 2008: 72).
36 Masters has noted the rise in the Christian population as counted in the Ottoman tax records between the sixteenth and eighteenth centuries, of which the Armenians were a significant element.
37 The area vacated by the sixteenth-century tanneries today accommodates an Ayyubid mosque still known as the 'Dabbagha al-'Attiqa' or 'old tannery' mosque – page 183.
38 Bembo and Welch 2007: 68.
39 Marcus 1989: 28.
40 Carré 1947: I, 40–1.
41 Masters (2001: 55) cites Ottoman tax records as indicating the number of Christians in Aleppo rose from 2500 in 1640 to 5391 in 1695.
42 David and Chauffert-Yvart (1982: 35) notes that it is larger than most of the domed mosque prayer halls of Ottoman Aleppo.
43 In 1736, Kara Mustafa's daughter, Abide Hanim, petitioned the Porte that her father's intentions in constructing the khan, namely the facilitation of trade with Persia and Baghdad, be encouraged by enforcing the khan's monopoly in handling the Baghdad/

Iran caravans. The case was upheld but little seems to have been done to enforce it (Masters 1989: 214–15).

44 Teixeira 1902: 116.
45 David 1991: 192, present author's translation.
46 The terms are explained in Masters 2013: 105–6.
47 This, of course, was exactly what the Emperor Xeno did in the fifth century by adopting St Simeon as a symbol of heroic asceticism, building the massive church complex outside Aleppo as a means of heading off Monophysite adoption of the saint's cause – see page 57–8.
48 D'Arvieux 1735: VI, 62–3.
49 Halifax 1695a: 87.
50 Halifax 1695a: 95.
51 Halifax 1695a: 91.
52 Weingarten 2016.
53 Robert Wood was also accompanied by fellow Oxford scholars James Dawkins and John Bouverie, though the latter died early in the expedition.
54 De Bruijn had confined his visit to Aleppo but his travel memoirs give few insights into the city beyond his own distrust of and hostility towards Arabs. However, he has left us a memorable visual record of the city of Aleppo during his stay in 1682–3 – this time his own work and the result of careful observation of the city.
55 The Venetian official presence was closed by the Ottomans in the 1640s in response to the hostilities between Venice and the Ottomans over Crete. It was not reopened until the 1740s.

11

MODERNISING ALEPPO
(1750–2000)

Ottomans 1516–1918
French Mandate 1920–46
Independence 1946–

Waning of authority

After a brilliant opening in the sixteenth century, the next two centuries were to bring a gradual erosion of the 'imperial' model in the Ottomans' administration of such an important economic centre as Aleppo. Two factors are relevant in the case of Aleppo: the erosion of centrally controlled authority at an empire-wide level; and the collapse of a substitute capable of assertive control over events at the local level. Neither factor brought down the Ottoman system. Though shaken at times, it survived. The explanation seems to lie in the fact that there was no better alternative apart from chaos.

After the first two centuries, the tightly held layering of administrative, military and religious authority, once largely in the hands of appointees who were part of the Turkish (or Turkish-speaking) elite, began to collapse.[1] At the centre, by the eighteenth century the sultanate was in the hands of a self-perpetuating court whose members knew no life outside the harem. At the local level, too, the idea of a trained and expert administrative/military cadre began to be abandoned. In Damascus, the old system was replaced by long assignments given to local notables (the *a'yans*). At least the city benefited from the continuity of rule by members of the al-'Azem family over more than a century. Aleppo, however, continued to receive men assigned from the Porte, some of whom never actually survived long enough to make it to their new office.

An additional factor encouraging the break-up of authority was that the provision of janissaries from the centre had died away in Aleppo in favour of local recruitment from the early seventeenth century.[2] As their power grew, the local janissaries even forced the withdrawal of the remaining units assigned from Istanbul. By the next century the troops became increasingly under-motivated, under-paid and required even to find their own weapons and uniforms. They became little better than a rabble whose ranks swelled to some 5000–10,000, up to 12 per cent of the city's population, which had fallen to around 80,000 by the end of the eighteenth century.[3] The janissaries' roots increasingly lay in the migrants (many non-Arabs) who had flooded into the city from the impoverished country-side and assumed the profile of a compacted underclass. The soldiery were seen in 1784 by the French traveller Constantin-François de Chasseboeuf (Count Volney) as 'artisans and peasants as ignorant as any but much less docile'.[4] The janissaries preserved, however, two privileges – the right to collect customs revenues and the right to be judged by their own peers.

The practice of continuing to appoint governors from outsiders selected in Istanbul may have been a recognition of the difficulties any local figure would face in taming these tensions. If so, the logic failed. The only group in Aleppo capable of countering the janissaries' disruptive power comprised those who claimed descent from the family of the Prophet (known collectively as *ashraf*) and who congregated in their own quarter around the south eastern walls of the city. By the end of the eighteenth century, their self-identified membership rose to well over 6000. Both janissaries and Ashraf, however, were motivated less by the aim of alleviating the lot of their fellow citizens against a cruel and indifferent authority than by a determination to preserve their own instruments of oppression as the power of the central government wasted away.

The city's declining fortunes are backed by statistics in the account of Count Volney at the time of his visit. His account is notable for its dispassionate analysis, as befitted a savant of aristocratic background fired by the ideas of the Enlightenment. He noted that the province was in a state of disorder even graver than most in the Ottoman world. Amplifying the impressions of the Abbé Carré a century earlier (see page 235), Volney reported that the governorate which had once embraced 3200 villages now counted only 400. The rest of the countryside was largely depopulated: 'Everywhere the traveller found collapsed houses, cis-terns fallen in and abandoned fields. The farmers had fled to the cities . . . where they were no less exposed to a rapacious despotism that preyed on the popula-tion.' In spite of this decay, Comte de Volney found the city agreeable: 'Aleppo is perhaps the cleanest and best built city in the Empire. Whichever way you approach the city, its clustered minarets and bleached domes flatter the eye long accustomed to the monotonous brown of the plain.'[5]

Rule by consensus?

In spite of these privations, during these decades many local Muslim families had one option to consolidate their position in the ranks of the *a'yan* or local nota-bles, namely gaining contracts to serve as tax farmers for the increasingly frayed Ottoman elite. They now won appointments to serve as deputies to the governor or chief tax collectors, building around such networks of economic power based largely on forcing local farmers to switch to crops which gave greater returns on

Figure 11.1 Bust of the Comte de Volney (Constantin-François Chassebœuf) in the Fine
Arts Museum, Angers (Selbymay, Wikimedia commons)

European markets, especially tobacco and cotton. The a'yan provided the core of
the governor's consultative council (*diwan*). This body's role, however, was at
best nominal, though it was intended to give a voice to all the major factions. The
a'yan found themselves caught between the rival Ashraf and janissary factions
and too divided among themselves to seize the commanding position of power
gained by the al-'Azems in Damascus.

We will return at the end of this chapter to the question of how the Ottoman
system lasted so long given its seemingly endemic disorders, its propensity to
corruption and the fractious behaviour even among its own ranks. We would note
in this context, though, the continued importance of the legitimacy that the role of

the sultan as 'Protector of the Faith' gave, symbolised each year in the progress of the Hajj. This, Masters argues, brought a collaboration between ruler and subjects which excluded any challenge: 'Without that collaboration, the domination by the House of Osman over the political life of the [Arab] region would have become tenuous at best. The empire in the Arab lands did not survive by the threat of force. Rather it endured as the Ottoman dynasty had co-opted the region's elite as its willing collaborators.'[6] Over the squabbling factions of Aleppo, the sword of the Sultan/Caliph still hovered.

Embracing Rome

While the elite who accessed top political positions were totally Muslim, Christians could win prestige and economic influence in other ways. The non-Muslim community whose fortunes bloomed by the end of the eighteenth century were increasingly Christians who had chosen to switch from one of the principal Orthodox-based confessions (Greek Orthodox of the Antioch rite, Syrian Orthodox, Armenian Orthodox) to join one of the 'Uniate' offshoots encouraged by more active proselytising by the Vatican. The Maronite Church, which had declared its loyalty to Rome as early as the Crusades, formed the core of the Catholic rites now actively encouraged by the Franciscan and Jesuit missions established since 1560 and 1627 respectively.[7] Their work was supported by the non-English Western consulates with their sizeable contingents of chaplains. (There were twenty-eight 'chaplains' in the French and Venetian consulates in 1681.)

By the opening of the eighteenth century, Christians affiliated to Rome amounted to 50 per cent of the city's Christian population. This increase benefitted from the flow to the Catholic rites of Christians who wanted to improve their chances of receiving positions in (or the nominal protection of) European consulates. Under a rather loose interpretation of the Ottoman Capitulations, consuls claimed the right to list nominated Syrians as under their protection.[8] Such opportunistic defection to the Uniate churches was resented by the Orthodox bishops who unsuccessfully sought to engage the Ottoman authorities in measures to discourage it. It also reflected the growing involvement of Christians in trade with Europe to the point where Muslim traders had begun to abandon the field to them.

Some among the Christians who profited from the European trade invested in houses which showed their wealth in spectacular fashion. Architecture now reflected a more heterogeneous range of styles than the relatively restrained examples of Muslim houses examined earlier. The house built by the Qara 'Ali family in the 1750s, for example (it was later to carry the family name of its second owners, Beit Ajiqbash), was greatly influenced by the budding Ottoman taste for European Baroque decoration. The house was a triumph of the Baroque style with windows on the courtyard richly decorated with swirling stone tracery. Its plan reflected Syrian domestic architecture with its central courtyard and pond, its northern winter salon or *qa'a*, and a deep southern iwan facing north.

Figure 11.2 Courtyard of the 1757 house later acquired by the Ajiqbash family in the Jdeide Quarter

Return to an 'imperial' style

We have seen that after the initial spate of 'imperial' building projects of the first Ottoman century, the seventeenth century had been marked by a more locally influenced architectural style while emphasis had begun to focus on the endowment of small-scale neighbourhood mosques. The eighteenth century, however, saw a return to a more distinctively Ottoman imperial identity – pencil minarets with candle snuffer tops, flatter domes and arcaded courtyards. The result is seen most clearly in the Madrasa of ʿUthman Pasha al-Duraki (1730–8) which lies just inside the city's northern Victory Gate (Bab al-Nasr). The complex of charitable institutions followed the form of the great *külliye* complexes of Istanbul. Though on a slightly smaller scale than counterparts in Istanbul, it is the largest of such projects in Aleppo. Its footprint, however, had to make many compromises with a confined allotment tucked away south of the gate.

Two hundred years after Sinan, while there was no imperially determined architectural programme, individual governors, particularly those closely connected to the imperial family, were still inclined to borrow heavily from a centralised vocabulary. ʿUthman's family stemmed from imperial appointees who managed to hold the post of governor in Aleppo across three generations (though with nothing like the consistency of the al-ʿAzems of Damascus) thus mixing both local and imperial connections. Though many aspects of the architectural style of the

251

Figure 11.3 Madrasa of 'Uthman Pasha al-Duraki (1730–8)

complex reflected an imperial agenda, there are quite a few subtle departures – the dome is a little too steeply sided compared to the canonical Ottoman profile, the portico does not spread beyond the prayer hall (instead two side iwans face onto the courtyard), pendentives mark the transition from the interior of the dome to the square prayer hall. Nevertheless, the project has a distinctly Ottoman feel to it and Jean-Claude David has commended the building for its successful mixing of 'monumental grandeur and economy of means'.[9]

Disintegration and invasion

After the build-up of tensions described at the beginning of this chapter, the city reached a low point in its long history when in the 1780s it was largely delivered over to anarchy in a series of civic rebellions which saw three governors driven out. Aleppo was controlled by various factions of the janissaries (supposedly the sultan's enforcers on the ground) whose officers effectively ran a series of protection rackets that milked the poor. When central control was finally reimposed after a decade of anarchy, it managed simultaneously to be both weak and brutally arbitrary with governors increasingly reliant on the great families for advice. Things were hardly any more stable by 1799–1805 when a local notable (for only the second time) was appointed as governor and sought to end the power of the janissaries. His plans failed, and in the aftermath, the governor and the Ashraf turned on the janissaries. Their move backfired and the governor himself was expelled.

Thereafter, while the Porte continued to send short-term appointees as governors, it was the janissaries who effectively ruled. Only a decision of the Porte to dissolve the janissaries throughout the empire brought this situation to an end. To signal the reimposition of imperial authority in Aleppo, the governor, Jelal al-Din Pasha, invited the janissaries' leaders to a meeting and had them massacred in 1813. The governor's use of arbitrary terror in this and other instances, including through the summary execution of shopkeepers on frivolous pretexts, caused the English Consul, John Barker, to tremble at the thought of his next audience with Jelal al-Din:

> Can one be charmed by the artificial and perfidious smiles of such a monster on a visit of ceremony? For my part, although I know there is no danger of my being decapitated too, I cannot help feeling a kind of involuntary horror and shudder as long as the audience lasts.[10]

It was not only Aleppo which was suffering the factional divisions which were crippling the cities of the empire. Parts of Anatolia and the Balkans were also plagued by prolonged confrontations or local *coups d'état* against central authorities from the turn of the eighteenth and nineteenth centuries. Lack of effective control brought further insecurity in the countryside and thus famine and flight from the land. Harsh repressive measures failed to work.

Aleppo's unrest, though, was not so much a challenge to the sultan or the empire itself as an attempt to rebalance centres of influence at the local level. In 1818, for example, Aleppo's poor rose in open revolt after decades in which the a'yans had imposed an inordinate series of taxes, both authorised and improvised. The revolt was channelled by a council of notables, largely from the Ashraf, which took over the running of the city for their own ends. In 1819, a contingent of Ashraf entered the eastern quarter of Qarliq that had been heavily populated by the janissaries and carried out a massacre. It required a contingent of central troops despatched from Adana and Kayseri in Anatolia to put down the disturbances. The central authorities followed up not by exploring the Ashraf's willingness to return the city to Ottoman authority but by a brutal armed reoccupation. Two years later a severe earthquake, the worst for many centuries, added to the city's misery.

By 1830, the situation across Aleppo Province was so bad that an unnamed tax official dared to write to the Porte to describe the devastation of the countryside east of Aleppo and down the Euphrates. It was, he reported, only a pale shadow of the lands ruled by the 'Umayyad Princes' 1200 years earlier. He described swathes of countryside, right up to the edge of major towns, pillaged by Bedouin tribes of the steppe and even the fundamentalist Wahhabis raiding from the Najd (modern Saudi Arabia). Villages were deserted, agricultural lands abandoned.[11]

Even in Aleppo, the population was estimated to have fallen from a peak of around 110,000–120,000 at the beginning of the eighteenth century to an estimated 70,000–85,000 by 1840.[12] Much of this decline was undoubtedly also due to the prevalence of endemic diseases and plague, especially in the deprived quarters east of the walled city. The foreign community, too, had already collapsed in numbers. In 1787, while Volney found a French community that still included seven trading 'counters' (representatives of trading houses), the scale of English, Venetian, Dutch and Livorno representation had fallen to one each a half-century later. While trade with Europe had declined, local production of soap and some cotton and cotton/silk fabrics still found a regional market and the caravan trade with Iraq even managed a steady rise. In return for Aleppo's products, the caravans continued to bring Iranian and Indian cloth, spices, and indigo as well as coffee from the Yemen but all on a much-reduced scale.

Revolt in Egypt

In 1831, the Ottomans' eastern empire suffered another major reverse. In Egypt, the Ottoman-appointed governor, Muhammad 'Ali, had risen against imperial authority and proclaimed his personal rule over Egypt. This extended to territorial ambitions across the central Islamic lands, initially prompted by his campaign to recover Mecca and Medina for the Porte but later seeking to take advantage of the Ottoman army's preoccupation with serial problems in the Balkans.

Muhammad Ali's efforts to ingratiate himself further with the Ottomans in order to establish grounds for demanding more territorial concessions in the Levant soon came to grief. He had contributed his fleet to the Porte's campaign to prevent the British from supporting the Greek bid for independence. Following the comprehensive British naval victory near Navarino off the Peloponnese coast in 1827, Muhammad Ali's bid for territorial compensation for the loss of his fleet in the Ottoman cause was refused. He decided to help himself to the required reimbursement by moving into Syria. The invasion in 1831 was led by his son, Ibrahim Pasha, and Syria was placed under Egyptian control.

Egyptian occupation 1831–40

The consequences for Aleppo of Ibrahim Pasha's decade of control in Syria brought further uncertainty into an already difficult environment. Yet the turmoil and its effects on the Ottoman system were not without longer-term benefits. Two measures that were introduced had a lasting effect particularly on the status of minorities. Taxation was extended to all citizens not just the minorities or those covered by land tax; and conscription into a professionally led army was introduced. A third decision gave authority to the members of the local council or *majlis*, including members drawn from the a'yans. The councils' authority now covered matters previously settled via the Islamic courts.

By the time Ibrahim Pasha was forced out of Syria, Lebanon and Palestine in 1840 by a show of force by the European powers (notably Britain), it was clear that restored Ottoman rule could not simply continue as before. Ibrahim Pasha's decade in control had brought a taste of reform. Security and transport infrastructure, which had long been barriers to economic progress, had been improved. The

Ottomans could only match the firepower of the Europeans if they also matched their capacity to field an army which was technologically up to the mark. This required a range of skills and organisational prowess in which the Ottomans were deficient. The Ottoman structure of the eighteenth century, whose energies were drained by internecine squabbles, corruption and failure to address the problems of outlying communities, including impoverished tribals or the minorities, was not a basis for meeting the challenge of the European powers.

The outlook for Syrian minorities during the 1830s Egyptian occupation had benefited from removal of some of the disadvantages they had suffered under the more traditional *millet* system. This took place under the increasingly watchful attention of the European consuls whose capitals had adopted a more intervention-ist approach to religious minorities with whom they claimed a particular affiliation – Catholics in the case of the French; Jews and Protestants for the British; and Orthodox Armenians, Antiochean-rite Greeks for Russia. These links had partly been a product of the employment of members of these communities in the for-eign trading houses or consulates with the additional number registered with the consulates as eligible for protection often rising to thousands, well beyond the ranks of paid employees and their families.

A 'reordering' (Tanzimat)

The empire had effectively suffered huge territorial losses: Egypt was now enfran-chised to Muhammad 'Ali and his descendants; Yemen and Iraq were little more than nominal possessions; North Africa and the Balkans were beginning to slide away. It was time to regenerate the idea of the sultanate in the core territories which would now define its last century – a 'reordering'.

Many of the measures of reform introduced under the Egyptian occupation were carried into the decree issued on 3 November 1839 by Sultan Abdul Mejid (r.1831–61). The replacement of the diwan or advisory council of the governor by the new institution of the majlis introduced a body with supervisory powers over local officials and some role as a court of appeal against decisions of the Sharia courts. These reforms began a process of whittling away the powers of the reli-gious establishment. In another significant reform with long-term consequences, in 1844 Aleppo became the initial base for a new Fifth Army to ensure the security of the governorates of Arabistan, thus replacing the disbanded janissaries with professionally trained troops under central control.

1850 anti-Christian disturbances

Traditionally, Aleppo had comprised a higher proportion of non-Arab and non-Muslim people than most major Syrian cities. As we have seen, it had long found itself on the interface of a world where Arabs, Ottoman Turks, Turkmen, Kurds, Armenians, Ismaelis, Shiʿa, Alawis, Christian Orthodox, Catholics and Jews rubbed along together. Whatever feelings one community might have towards another, they largely did not let them affect their daily lives or ability to pursue their trade or profession. Even when there was a collapse of centralised control in the face of local or imperial political tensions, the protocols of normal life had effectively helped squash any reaction in the form of visceral communal (ethnic or confessional) disturbances.

If there was one issue which ran right through the political developments of nineteenth-century Aleppo, however, it was the rise of a new sense of a sectarian divide. As Aleppo became increasingly drawn into the world economy, we have seen that it was the Christians who could easily slip into roles as the point of contact with outside importers or exporters. The barriers to full Christian participation in society were being torn down by the Ottoman administration itself in the aftermath of the Egyptian occupation and through the Tanzimat reforms. This was confirmed in the Reform Decree of 1856 which gave more explicit rights to non-Muslims – all distinctions based on 'religion, language or race, shall be forever effaced from administrative protocol'.[13] While those were commendable objectives, the reaction on the Christian side often made it difficult for Muslims to absorb quietly their gradual relegation to a secondary status in economic terms.

The formal abolition of the corps of janissaries in 1826 not only brought a loss of pay to a reasonably coherent social class but also ended their access to a percentage of the taxes they had once collected. Meanwhile, Christians, having risen in the social order through the reforms to the Tanzimat era, now wielded a degree of influence in society no longer dependant on alliances with the merchants of the Muslim commercial elite. Amid all these changes over the previous fifty years, the poor Muslims were the biggest losers and the Christians (notably the Catholics) seemed to have suddenly acquired overwhelming influence (and possibly the arrogance which went with that new status): 'a community that had once largely existed outside the public gaze of Muslims had become triumphalist'.[14] Religion which had once been quietly allowed not to dominate social intercourse now became a flashing signal of identity.

A second factor running beneath decades of events over the course of the century was the growing reality that international trade, now seen as a challenge that the empire either had to address or go under, brought a train of other reforms that had to be introduced if the Ottoman world was to compete – better education, reformed administration, infrastructure, even the way people dressed had to be brought in line with European norms. Most telling of all, though, was the fact that the move away from the millet system, whereby each religious community ordered internally its responsibilities to the state, now delegated that relationship to the individual albeit under the protective umbrella of the sultan.

The increasing prosperity of the Christians of Aleppo and their stranglehold over foreign trade is seen as one factor behind the anti-Christian riots that broke out in October 1850. The Christians had been singled out by the major European powers for protection under the Capitulation treaties but this was seen as effectively giving them a head start above other citizens under the Tanzimat reforms which were supposed to give everyone the same status. This anomaly was seen as the background to the events. Was this enough to cause social tensions to snap? Disturbances originated in the city's eastern suburbs (where ex-janissaries and Muslim immigrants congregated). Rioters entered the Christian quarter, Jdeide, looting houses and churches. After a fortnight in which the authorities managed to impose an uneasy calm, protests broke out again in the eastern suburbs. These suburbs were then bombarded by the army with deaths in the thousands, considerably higher than the single-figure casualties in Jdeide.

Although the rioting had been prolonged, property bore the brunt of popular anger. The Armenian and Jewish communities were not targeted (the worst reprisals being directed against the wealthy Uniate communities) and the objective was plunder and arson of Christian property rather than against Christians themselves.

The city, in other words, did not descend into a mindless sectarian frenzy of killing, apart from the army's own actions against fellow-Muslims. The riots have been interpreted as not solely a reflection of communal tensions, Muslims versus Christians. Rather they can be seen as a reflection of the intense economic gulf between the haves (particularly those who benefitted from the trade with the outside world, largely Christians) and those who had become increasingly marginalised (the proletariat of the eastern suburbs, all Muslims). It should also be noted that when Damascus a decade later was engulfed by much more serious events with fatalities in the thousands, Aleppo remained quiet.

These disparities between communities, however, were made worse by the fact that Aleppo's prosperity had fallen, though there were early signs of a recovery by the mid-century. The slow downturn in the long-distance Eastern trade was to some extent compensated by the city's growing commercial exchanges with the regions of the Jazira and Asia Minor to the north. Measures by the Ottoman authorities to allow private title over lands long abandoned by Bedouin groups opened a new field for prominent Aleppines to invest in agriculture. Recovery, however, was slow and the city's population was not to reach its late seventeenth-century level (page 235) until the early twentieth century when the Ottoman census of 1908 gave a figure of nearly 120,000.

Arabs in the late Ottoman world

The last point to note in the context of the watershed of the 1850 events is that they did not represent an attempt to overturn Turkish rule. After three and a half centuries, Turks and Arabs still admittedly lived in largely different worlds. Some among the Arab elite of Aleppo who had the means relished being part of the Ottoman Turkish-speaking milieu, sending their children to be educated in Istanbul or commissioning idyllic scenes of the capital to decorate their drawing rooms walls. Many Islamic scholars, too, included Istanbul among the centres visited in their quest for knowledge. But few really integrated themselves into that environment. They preferred to remain true to an Arab identity in cultural terms.

The Ottomans, however, had left it too late to blend representatives of the Levantine Arab world into their power structure. Even when the first parliament was convened in 1876, only thirty-two of the 232 seats were filled by Arabs, although by then, with the Ottoman losses in the Balkans and Greece, the Arab share of the empire's population was rising significantly.[15] Virtually all top officials were still Muslims of Turkish or Balkan background and even the religious leaders in each governorate were still appointed by the Porte. There was no fundamental challenge to the Ottoman system as it applied in the Arab lands and Arab parliamentary representatives still saw themselves not as representing an Arab bloc but as defending their local constituencies within a larger Ottoman sphere.

As a result, there was no manifestation of nationalism, beyond a boosting of pride in Arab achievements and an increasing interest in education in Arabic with a modern syllabus. That would change, but only marginally, with the rise of more heated anti-Ottoman sentiment immediately before the First World War – the first signs of a sense of a national state. It would still be a long way, however, before Aleppo's sense of its position would challenge the long-standing consensus that there was no better alternative to remaining part of the over-arching domain of the Sultan-Caliph.

Reign of Abdul Hamid (1876–1909)

A troubled 'Golden Age'

The second half of the nineteenth century began by exploring a gradual trend towards further liberalisation, essentially intended to develop through the framing of a redefined 'Ottoman state' the concept of an Islamic polity infused with many of the ideas of a liberal economic and political model as promoted by the European powers. A key step was the adoption of a new but initially short-lived Ottoman constitution at the beginning of the reign of Sultan Abdul Hamid II (r.1876–1909).

Abdul Hamid had been propelled into office in 1876 by the reformers in the Porte and was assisted by the liberal Midhat Pasha as prime minister under the new constitution. The next year, however, Abdul Hamid threw off all previous claims to be a liberalising ruler, effectively freezing the Tanzimat reforms which he now sought to block. Using the war environment resulting from the 1877 conflict with Russia, he turned to subterfuge and repression to tackle the near-impossible task of holding the empire together in the face of fiscal collapse, painful economic reform and rampant corruption. The constitution remained on the books but was not to be revived until a group of young army officers, the 'Young Turks', forced Abdul Hamid to reinstate it in 1908.

'Shadow of God on Earth' – the Sultan-Caliph

Abdul Hamid's three decades in power brought a cynical effort to save the state by linking its fortunes to two foundation narratives – Islam and Ottomanism. Neither concept was new to the public but the ways of signalling them were made increasingly specific. The long line of Ottoman rulers was a useful way to promote the dynasty's origins in a mythic past. The legendary tombs of the first two (thir-teenth/fourteenth century) sultans in Bursa were accordingly reconstructed after an earthquake in 1855 to form part of a 'foundation myth' that embedded Ottoman legitimacy.[16]

A related example of this widespread effort to create a new legitimacy was the identification of a site near Aleppo with the death by drowning of a legend-ary ancestor of the early Ottoman sultans. Suleiman Shah (d.1326) according to early chronicles was said to have drowned in an accident on the Euphrates near the castle at Ja'abr on the mid-Euphrates. Under Abdul Hamid, a site for the legendary incident was identified and a tomb erected. Even after the end of the Ottomans, the almost certainly spurious legend had been so well implanted that the site was recog-nised as a small Turkish enclave in the 1921 Treaty of Ankara, the agreement later endorsed as defining the post-First World War frontier between Republican Turkey and French Syria.[17]

Co-opting 'Arabistan'

The flipside of the emphasis on the sultan's role as a religious figurehead was that he could hardly claim this as a ground for legitimacy if he failed to retain the support of the original Muslims, the Arabs of the old lands of Arabia and Syria now often grouped as 'Arabistan'. Most Arabs, as we have seen, were still not inspired by a sense of Arab nationalism. They saw the empire as perhaps the only option on offer, though there were few who appreciated with enthusiasm the standard of officials deployed to rule them. Some efforts were made to encourage the children of Arab notables to undertake higher education in Istanbul with the hope they would take up posts in the bureaucracy but these efforts to broaden the base of the empire's machinery made only slow progress until the last decades of the Ottomans. These belated efforts to consolidate the empire by reaching beyond its Turkish core were accompanied by an increasingly heavy-handed imposition of Turkish as the means of communication with Arab subjects. Instead of binding the Arabs more closely it alienated them.

While examples of Arab officials who rose to senior ranks in Istanbul remained isolated, a few found short cuts were possible. One case showed how much had to be compromised to achieve such eminence. Sheikh Abu'l-Huda al-Sayyida was born in Khan Shaykun, one of the caravan halting points on the route south from Aleppo, in 1850. The Ottoman sultan's increasing attraction to a conserva-tive brand of Islam to reinforce his claims as Caliph provided an opening for the ambitious Abu'l-Huda, whose career throws light on the openings for career-ism in Abdul Hamid's era. An under-privileged background did not prevent Abu'l-Huda's rapid rise to become the most senior local religious figure (na'ib al-ashraf) in Aleppo at the extraordinarily young age of twenty-four. His path to fame came via his links to the Rifa'iye sect of Sufism but his ascent through the religious hierarchy was aided by the favour he enjoyed in 'reactionary and con-servative circles who were happy to keep the Sultan away from any concessions to the liberals or those who preferred to decentralise the basis of Ottoman power'.[18] He thus became one of the rare examples of a senior Arab figure in the circles of the Porte and used his status as a turbanned celebrity to endorse an extremely conservative reading of Islam.

Abu'l-Huda and the Rifa'iye sect became particularly influential in Iraq where they served as a useful lure to bring followers of the Shi'i persuasion back to a Sunni stream. By the time of his death in 1909, Sheikh al-Sayyida's standing was long past its zenith (as was his Sultan-Caliph's who was forced into exile the same year). The fact that the sheikh quickly became a by-word for the corruption and crass showmanship of the late Ottoman court perhaps accounts for his poor reputation in Aleppo as 'a self-seeking sycophant, a hypocrite with a pious demeanour, currying favour with the sultan'.[19]

Hamidism in architecture

There are few buildings which demonstrate in physical form the priorities of the late Ottoman sultans in relation to Aleppo. Unlike Damascus which saw a wide range of new commercial and civic buildings as well as officially inspired street beautification projects from the late nineteenth century, Aleppo largely survived on its existing urban repertoire. No major new religious projects were built with official sponsorship but four new civic structures flagged the reformist priorities of the late Ottoman period and the importance of Aleppo as a pivot for the exercise of Ottoman control in Syria. In the early 1830s, a massive new complex

Figure 11.4 National Hospital in Aleppo (April 2011)

260

Figure 11.5 Sultan Abdul Hamid's clock tower in Aleppo (1895–9), one of scores
erected around the empire to promote timeliness

had been initiated on the rising ground north of the city, conveniently located a
little southwest of the cemetery area where the Tekkiye of Sheikh Abu Bakr was
located.[20] This reflected efforts during Ibrahim Pasha's occupation of Syria (later
reinforced with the army reforms introduced during the restoration of central
Ottoman authority) to deploy armed forces recruited and trained on a Western-
style model and enjoying conditions which would discourage their tendencies to
be a plague on the civilian community.

It was sixty years before the second major project was undertaken, this time
reflecting Sultan Abdul Hamid's new priorities. While much of his reign saw the

261

treasury depleted by further expansion of military facilities, the major initiative in Aleppo was a National Hospital (1890), the beginnings of a programme to introduce Westernised medical facilities. It was built in the zone traditionally used to signal a regime's priorities at the foot of the Citadel gateway and on the edge of the main eastern entrance to the Medina.

A third project of Abdul Hamid showed a more quirky approach to the modernisation of the empire. The symbolic gesture this time was an oddly designed clock tower built 1895–9 on the intersection once marked by the Bab al-Faraj on the northwest city walls. This was one among scores of such time-related projects, some even more ungainly, scattered around the Sultan's realms. They served not only a practical purpose but as reminders of the regime's modernisation programme through the introduction of centralised time keeping.

Binding Aleppo by rail

The fourth major civic project of the last Ottoman years was the Baghdad Station. The background to this project lay in the loss of the Balkan provinces around the turn of the nineteenth/twentieth century as well as the war with Russia, which resulted in massive casualties among the Armenians in eastern Anatolia in 1895. Troubles on the Balkan and Russian fronts made it increasingly obvious that the Arab world was vital if the empire was to have any future. It was thus no surprise that the main physical reminder of the process of drawing northern Syria more tightly into the Ottoman realm was the building of its first railway connections.

Damascus and Beirut had been linked by rail in 1895. An extension of that line north from Rayak in the Beqa'a Valley in Lebanon reached Aleppo in 1906. A new line branching from Homs to the sea at Tripoli gave Aleppo a direct rail connection to a seaport. More important in terms of Abdul Hamid's priorities was to bind the empire more firmly to the holy cities of the Hijaz. The idea of a Hijaz Railway was vigorously promoted by 'Izzat Pasha al-'Abed, who had risen to the rank of 'second secretary', certainly the most influential Syrian at the Porte. Not only was it sold as an important economic, military and religious asset but it was also promoted by al-'Abed as the lifeline for a new 'Arab policy' locking Arabs into the empire (with the non-incidental purpose of advancing al-'Abed's interests in the Hauran grain trade when it was not carrying pilgrims). The project's religious credentials were underlined by pointedly using only capital raised in the Muslim world and with Muslim engineers and workmen. Though al-'Abed's influence plummeted with the arrival of the Young Turks (see next section), the line to Medina commenced operations in 1908 linked to the existing system from Damascus. It entered into service too late to burnish Abdul Hamid's Islamic credentials by providing a more comfortable option for the annual pilgrimage and the train was barely operational when suspended early in the First World War.

When it was opened in 1912, Aleppo's Baghdad Station was named in recognition of the second purpose of the expansion of rail building into northern Syria. Aleppo was also envisaged as an important junction where the Hijaz line

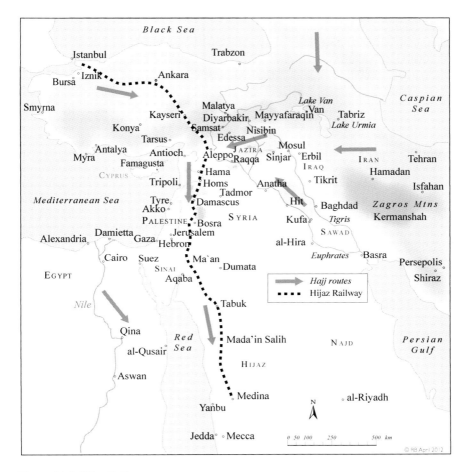

Figure 11.6 Hijaz Railway

would link with the proposed Berlin to Baghdad railway, initiated in 1899 when the first concession for the ambitious line was issued. The project, part of Kaiser Wilhelm's policy of *Drang nach Osten* intended to outflank British influence east of Suez, was contentious from the start, involving not just the usual range of great power rivalries in the Eastern Mediterranean but the specific issue of Anglo-Ottoman-Persian competition in the Persian Gulf, of rising significance due to the discovery of the Iraqi oil fields whose product would be made accessible through a link on to the port of Basra.

The Kaiser's railway was one of several projects increasingly drawing the remains of the Ottoman Empire into a game in which it would become impossible to divorce itself from Germany's war aims. Though Aleppo's Baghdad

263

Station was in operation for the Hijaz link from 1912, the line from Aleppo to Anatolia was only partly in service by 1914. The unfinished tunnels through the Taurus Mountains limited the value of the line for the transport of materiel for the Turkish-German effort to hold Arabistan during the First World War. The main track from Istanbul to Baghdad was not completed until just before the Second World War.

End of the House of Osman 1909–20

However imperfect, the Ottoman Empire had endured on the basis of a broad consensus. It was not a democratic choice but to most people it seemed the obvious one. Left to itself, the empire might well have worked out its path to modernising its institutions, though it would have faced a formidable parallel battle to restore the solvency of the state whose resources the modernising programme had sapped.

The House of Osman, though distinctly not Arab, had managed to retain an authority in Arab lands which endured long after the Balkan and Greek-speaking provinces had defected from a consensus which many non-Muslim communities could not share. It was not a Caliphate in the old sense but it did claim the role of protecting the Holy Places, preserving the supremacy of Sharia and at least nominally offered the prospect of a system of 'well-protected domains'.[21] The fact was that it did not offer an Arab 'identity'; but then no identifiably Arab regime had existed for many centuries.

The 'Young Turks' and Arab nationalism

Until the end of the nineteenth century, the citizens of Aleppo had felt little need for a national identity within a unit of their own in terms that would be recognised today; they felt more a link to Mosul or Urfa, for instance, than they did with Damascus. The Ottoman Empire, however imperfect in its day-to-day operation, continued the framework they had long been accustomed to. Why did it have to change?

Until 1908, Aleppo had not been a major centre for the first signs of a simmering confrontation between Turks and Arabs. A greater sense of Arab identity was evident in Palestine, Beirut and Damascus but it still did not amount to a movement for separation from the empire. The first signs of collaboration among Arab citizens to express their influence as a group went back to the 1860s, the decade before the Hamidian era. It was not, however, a manifestation of solidarity as an ethnic group seeking emancipation via a separate national identity but a movement seeking to redress the corruption and misrule among imperial officials.

The pressures for change were in fact within the imperial structure. In 1909, a group of young Turkish army officers (the 'Young Turks') rose up against Sultan Abdul Hamid. The previous year, Abdul Hamid had made a panicked attempt to fend off the inevitable by restoring the suspended constitution. The gesture was mocked by the Arab historian, George Antonius:

He abolished the censorship, released all political prisoners and disbanded his army of 30,000 spies. Like a carnival queen, Liberty (or at any rate a paper incarnation of her) made her entry from around the corner and bowed, scattering her favours by the armful.[22]

The pantomime, however, came too late and the flow of events over the next year brought Abdul Hamid's deposition and banishment. The young army officers wielded power as the 'Committee for Union and Progress' (CUP). Their vision for Turkey was partly an attempt to head off the sultan's efforts to establish an inclusive state that promoted 'Ottomanism' above all '-isms' and thus theoretically embraced all component ethnicities and faiths of the empire. The Young Turks had a more narrowly defined version of a multi-ethnic future, a Turkey defined by a policy of aggressive 'Turkification' and less by an overarching Islamic identity. Their programme included suppression of the Arabic language in education and it was no surprise to find that Arab critics of the Young Turks and their CUP now began to emerge.

The Young Turks' vision of a revived Turkish realm had awoken the first real signs of a sense of Arab nationalism. By 1908, Arabs outnumbered Turks within the empire by a ratio of three to two yet in the new parliament of 245 elected members there were only sixty Arabs (though the new figure doubled their proportionate representation in the assembly brought in under the 1876 constitution – page 258). It was becoming evident to its supporters that it was no longer enough to be Arab speakers within a multi-faceted empire, occupying notionally an honoured status under the mandate of the sultan as guardian of Islam. In fact some supporters of reform in the Ottoman system (particularly in the army) saw support for a new caliphate under Turkish auspices as a means of introducing an order in which the Arab tradition, once at its core, was consigned to the margins. The fact that education might now be deprived of its Arabic stream became the symbolic cause which threatened the balance that had long existed between the Turkic and Arabic identities within the empire.

In the six years that were left between the new parliament and the outbreak of war in 1914, these tensions were not fully played out. Like many issues relating to the Ottoman world, they were unresolved in the rough and tumble of a new democratic order. Arab representatives, for example, in the new parliament still largely

> had faith in the Ottomanist vision that the 1908 Revolution promised. . . . for most Arabs the new constitution and Parliament dispelled any need for a separate existence.[23]

As 1914 approached, and Turkey became increasingly boxed in by close identification with German ambitions in the wider theatre, the question was even raised as to whether Aleppo might not be a safer base for the empire's capital. This debate was touched off in an article by German Field Marshal von der Goltz in the German press in 1913. Von der Goltz had earlier served in the Ottoman armed forces and argued that the imperial future could best be protected by an extension of the Austro-Hungarian dual national framework to the Middle East. The idea was thoroughly impractical in the circumstances of a looming war but underlined the extent to which ensuring the loyalty of Syria was becoming a major preoccupation.

1915, collapse of Ottomanism by consensus

The decision to shackle the empire's cause to Germany's in the course of the First World War proved a fateful choice. The ascent of the Young Turks in 1909 had already forced the pace on modernism. The residual Ottoman state survived the transition to the Turkish Republic in 1922 and would introduce a new formula for an Islamic polity within a republican model. For Arabistan, however, the transformation the empire had to face came at a helter-skelter pace and once again responded to a Western agenda rather than seeking to address the roots of the issues.

It was not the cities of Syria that would prove the weak point of the Turkish presence in Arabistan but the remote Hijaz where Sharif Husayn leaned towards a decisive break with the Ottomans. Action was taken against small groups of Arab nationalist elements who had sought to profit from Ottoman vulnerability. When the CUP opted to fall in with German plans to mount a thrust towards Egypt to dislodge the British from the Suez Canal, it was more vividly clear to the Levantine Arabs that Turkey was simply being used as a pawn in a German game. The main achievement of the CUP's brutal suppression of the dissidents was to provide the first rallying point for Arab nationalist sentiment that had barely surfaced before the war. The public executions of nationalist supporters in Beirut and Damascus jolted an Arab population previously relatively indifferent to the nationalist cause. Aleppo, though, was not one of the centres where the dissidents faced execution by hanging in August 1915.

A campaign for a 'holy war' against Britain's interests in the Middle East might have been a useful way to whip up Arab sentiment if it had not faced the inconvenient reality that the Germans were hardly credible partners in jihad. The importance of the Arab front grew apace. In late 1914, one of the CUP triumvirate, Jemal Pasha, had been despatched to Damascus as both governor of Syria and commander of the Fourth Army. He stepped up the campaign against Arab nationalists with pitiless efficiency. After Sharif Husayn took the Hijaz into alliance with Britain in 1916, the ersatz holy war fizzled out when the German-engineered invasion of Egypt collapsed in a rout. The task of persuading Arabs that the Holy Places should be taken from Arab hands with heavy German assistance was now unwinnable.

Armenian deportations

Another set of events in 1915 was a further reflection of the 'perfect storm of paranoia' that was overwhelming Turkey.[24] The deportations of Armenians from the eastern provinces of Asia Minor and Cilicia had a profound effect on Aleppo during the First World War. The orders given to local Ottoman officials in eastern Turkey to depopulate Armenian villages and send the inhabitants to supposedly underpopulated regions in Syria placed Aleppo at the crossroads of this grim deployment. The first signs of expulsions began in the district of Marash north of Aleppo in March 1915 but the intensification of the programme when conflict with Russia broke out the next month caused a deterioration of the position of Armenians in the Van region, sending a new stream that would swell to a flood in coming months. Whatever the stated intentions of the programme to disperse the Armenians, it took on ominous new dimensions as tens of thousands, displaced often by local officials interpreting their instructions with deliberate or callous disregard for the deportees' capacity to survive, were driven south. Ostensibly refugees were to be diverted towards 'resettlement' areas along the Euphrates that had no capacity to support new arrivals. Even taken at face value as some form of exercise in rebalancing the Muslim and Christian populations of eastern Turkey, the programme lacked any capacity to reach its ends without massive resort to cruelty and deliberate starvation as the destinations were ill-prepared or unfit for purpose.

Both Jemal Pasha as army commander in the east and the Ottoman governor in Aleppo, Jelal Bey, drew attention to the fact that the programme had not been provided with the resources to meet its stated purpose. Jemal sought to turn the deportations to more efficient ends by diverting part of the stream to urban centres where the local Armenian communities (especially in Aleppo, Damascus and Beirut) could provide support and the influx could be used as forced labour. Even so, many thousands died in the process. Jemal survived the authorities' disapproval but Jelal found himself reassigned to Ankara where he could be kept under closer watch.

Later attempts were made on the Turkish side to explain away the programme as a response to wartime exigencies (prevention of Armenian/Russian collaboration on the eastern front). However, the fact that it began in Marash, an area well back from the front, and spread quickly even to Syrian Orthodox villages in southeastern Turkey with no Russian affiliations, demonstrated how much local initiative and hostility towards Christians in general were allowed to take over the operation.[25] Even where local Turkish authorities might have been inclined to be helpful, they had no resources to provide food or shelter. By July 1915, 13,000 Armenians had taken refuge in Aleppo province from neighbouring Adana province alone with thousands of others driven from points east via Menbij directly down the Euphrates. European and American consuls began reporting evidence of deliberate atrocities with bodies of women and children floating down river or authorities turning a blind eye to massacres committed by local Kurdish or Circassian communities.

Only those survivors who managed to reach Aleppo were handled with any concern for their livelihoods but the numbers were daunting with tens of thousands arriving or dispersed via the city in one month alone (August 1915). The new governor, Bekir Sami Bey Kunduh informed his superiors in Istanbul that there were no signs that the Aleppo Armenians were any threat to Turkey. Though he did not question the overall deportation programme, he saw no reason for the accompanying atrocities. Even those Armenians who found refuge in the city, however, faced a new threat from famine and disease. The continuing programme of 'dispersal' used to justify the grim traffic had assumed a momentum of its own, even with some efforts by the central authorities after August 1915 to address abuses in its execution. By September the flood had assumed unmanageable proportions, with 100,000 Armenians said to be heading south towards Aleppo with half that again expected to follow.

Though only a proportion were able to stay on in the city, by the end of the war the Armenian influx had greatly changed the Christian mix in Aleppo. The formerly Catholic-dominated Christian numbers were now outweighed by the largely Orthodox Armenian refugees (13 per cent of the total city population) whose numbers rivalled those of native Christians. Further rebalancing continued during the French Mandate with an outflow of Armenians to Lebanon and the arrival of Syrian Orthodox refugees from eastern Turkey. By 1944, Aleppo's total population was over 300,000 of whom over a third were Christians, with Armenians comprising half their numbers.

Aleppo at war's end

The war devastated Syria. The Syrians' involvement in the conflict between European powers brought terrible privations through conscription, forced labour, famine, refugee influxes and disease. The commander who took over the battered Turkish forces from Jemal (and who would emerge as the new strongman of Turkey), Mustafa Kemal, quickly appreciated in 1918 that the Arab provinces were lost – not only physically to the Entente forces but also spiritually to any dreams of an Arab-Turkish dominion in what remained of the Ottoman lands.

After a long absence from the war since his triumph on the Dardanelles front in 1915, Kemal had resurfaced in late 1918 as the new supremo charged with stiffening the front in Arabistan against an expected assault by British forces moving north from Jerusalem. He arrived in Aleppo on 5 October, four days after the Australian contingent had first entered Damascus. If he had entertained any hopes of turning back the tide, he quickly abandoned them. Turkish forces were instructed to fall back towards Aleppo, reading the lesson of the fact that many Turkish units had the previous month streamed north into Damascus in disorder thus intensifying the chaos in that city. Aleppo should be spared this fate. Kemal quickly sent a telegram which identified who was to blame:

> The withdrawal could have been carried out in some order if a fool like Enver Pasha had not been director-general of operations, if we did not have here a commander (Jevat Pasha) at the head of a military force of five to ten thousand men, who fled at the first sound of gunfire,

abandoning his army and wandered around like a bewildered chicken, and a commander of the fourth army, Jemal Pasha, ever incapable of appreciating a military situation, and if above them we did not have a group headquarters (under German general, Liman van Sanders) which lost all control from the first day of battle. Now there is nothing left to do but to make peace.[26]

By 25 October, the situation in Aleppo was chaotic with Bedouin and citizens competing to occupy and sack buildings. Kemal rallied his forces, estimated at around 20,000 survivors of combat and disease, but did not pause at the city. He established his headquarters 46 kilometres to the north at Qatma in the Afrin Valley. British and Arab forces closed in on Aleppo on 26 October. A group of Arab units under Allied command reached as far as the Citadel but were forced to make a tactical retreat. Kemal, however, took the precaution of withdrawing his Aleppo garrison to join the retreating Turkish forces and had already distributed arms to pro-Turkish militia to Aleppo's north. He judged a full British attack to be imminent with the likelihood that Aleppo's Arab population would harass any Turkish attempt to defend the city.

Kemal's fear of a large-scale confrontation with British forces was not to happen as an armistice was signed between Turkish and British representatives at Mudros in Greece on 30 October. By planting his flag well to the north of Aleppo, however, he had at least set a marker for the future frontier between the Ottoman and French domains. This was the point at which the dreams of Arabs joining with Turks in a new 'Arabistan' collapsed definitively. Kemal had ensured that Turkish forces would fall back to lines that would sever the last Arab links.

'Liberation' from what?

Relief that it was over diminished any sentimental attachment to further Ottoman rule. Yet there is no evidence that any of the Arab peoples of the empire felt 'liberated' when British Empire and Arab forces occupied the Arab provinces including Aleppo, Damascus and Baghdad by the end of 1918. The war had above all shown that the Ottomans could not protect their citizens from the catastrophe that had overwhelmed the region and which had begun with the fateful decision of the Young Turks to embrace German tutelage.

And nor should the Syrians feel 'liberated'. As we will now see, it would be the coming experience under French Mandate which awakened nationalism to become the main ideology within Syria:

> Arab grievances with the Ottoman imperial government in Istanbul in the last years of the Empire were of sufficient magnitude to add nationalism to the cauldron of effective political ideologies in the Syrian provinces. But it was the Mandate system which ensured that nationalism became the overwhelming flavour of the stew.[27]

Turkey, on the losing side, was still armed and able to negotiate its preferred borders. Syria, by contrast, was liberated by the winners but left to an uncertain fate. It was left without stable government and with insufficient means to tackle the terrible problems of feeding its population, settling the Armenians displaced from eastern Anatolia during the war and handling the scourges of malnutrition and influenza.

Moreover, Syrian Arabs in 1918 at all levels had little appreciation of the deals that had been done in the fog of war to lop off parts of the central Islamic lands in the interests of re-awakened European dreams such as a Jewish homeland in Palestine or a French neo-Crusader domain in Lebanon. Two secret agreements had provided a terrible legacy. The Sykes–Picot Agreement signed between France and Britain in 1916 divided the Levant into French and British spheres of influence (thus sweeping aside the assurances given to Faysal to overcome his initial reluctance to contribute his forces to the Allied side). The Balfour Declaration of 2 November 1917 and published a week later promised part of the concession assigned to British protection to accommodate a 'Jewish homeland' without any safeguards for the existing population of Arabs.

The first agreement was a product of European 'greed at its worst';[28] the second an example of double dealing at its most cynical whose consequences still plague the Middle East. The resulting messy dispositions emerged in treaties from the post-war European peace conferences and took almost no account of Arab wishes. It would seem a good deal more probable that if the Arabs had been left to work out their future within the framework of the 'new Ottomanism' – even the more ethnically defined Young Turks' version of it – they could hardly have been worse off than under the messy compromise that put Arab interests last. It was indeed, the 'Peace to End all Peace'.[29]

New frontiers

When British Empire forces took Aleppo at the end of 1918, they briefly paused to consolidate a light occupation of the city and kept going to seize much of the countryside to the north. The Anatolian frontier took some time to sort out at the tables of the European peace conferences. There was plenty of 'dead ground' between the British/Indian occupation forces and the Turks. The border specified in the Treaty of Sèvres (August 1920) was subsequently moved south to the line of the Baghdad railway, giving a considerable win to the dying Ottoman sultanate. The uncertain situation in the border zone, however, stimulated widespread armed resistance to the French presence. Northern Syria became entangled in an outbreak of direct hostility to French control from 1920, touched off when the Arab population realised that Faysal had yielded to British pressure and settled for the withdrawal of his forces and the handover of his promised 'Arab kingdom' to the French.

These events stimulated widespread unrest particularly in the mountainous areas to the north and west of Aleppo. The 'Hananu revolt', as it became known – seen in later interpretations of the events as nascent Arab nationalism – took the form of guerrilla bands seeking to harass efforts to impose France's presence. Whether they were seeking the return of Turkish rule or had Arab nationalist aspirations was unclear, particularly as the bands roaming the countryside were a mixture of Arab and Kurdish elements as well as Turks. Their figurehead, Ibrahim Hananu (whose name was later used to rebadge the Ottoman barracks complex in Aleppo), served as a symbol of Arab resistance to the annulment of Faysal's kingdom when a French administration of Syria and Lebanon came into formal existence in 1920. At the time, however, the 'revolt' under Hananu (himself a Kurd and a former Ottoman official) embraced a mix of often contradictory demands – the return of Turkish nationalist rule, support for Faysal, nascent Arab nationalism and outright banditry for private profit.

In many ways, the borders of the new entity of Syria which were confirmed in the Treaty of Lausanne in 1923 reflected the customary geographic limits of the Roman, Umayyad and later Mid-Eastern provinces. However, modern nationalism and its emphasis on ethnic identity brought new adjustments at the fringes. Now that Aleppo had lost much of its old hinterland, what had for almost thirteen centuries been provincial divisions within wider imperial domains now became international borders that constricted Aleppo tightly to the north and the northeast. In the scramble to define borders of the Syrian state, much of the city's hinterland as far as Aintab had been lost in France's concessions to Turkey. In the process of this change, a relatively mixed city reflecting the ethnic and confessional complexity of Aleppo's history had to adjust to a different profile determined by a narrower concept of national identity largely new to its inhabitants.

A mandate for confusion (1920–46)

On the wider Middle Eastern canvas, over the next two decades, Aleppo lived in an environment where nothing was ever what it professed to be. As the Turkish empire imploded, a range of disparate issues had collided in an environment that disintegrated beyond anyone's control.

The consequences were at two levels. At the level of the internal processes in the Arab states, the issues included:

- What would succeed the Ottoman state's claim to preserve a version of a Caliphate with guardianship over the central Islamic lands?
- What would replace the multi-ethnic framework of the Ottoman state, already shaken by the Young Turks' ambitions to assert a more distinctly Turkish identity across its domains?
- While Arab nationalism was still a fragile concept in the Syrian provinces, it had taken hold with tenacity in intellectual circles. What new framework did it offer for people who had previously been lulled into a belief that they were all under the sultan's protective mantle?

We will never know how successfully these pressures might have been handled by internal processes if the framework imposed following the Versailles Peace

Conference had not come into play. There is no doubt, however, that the conference decisions greatly increased the degree of difficulty by allowing Britain and France free hand to interpret their Mandatory roles largely in the light of their own interests.

There was a second level of challenges facing the Middle East as a whole. As the deals done between European powers became public, how could this further series of contradictory bids be reconciled?

- The contradiction inherent in the British–French understandings on their spheres of influence in the Middle East (Sykes-Picot).
- The contradictory promise to Faysal of an Arab kingdom.
- The understandings given in response to Zionist demands for a Jewish 'homeland' necessarily to be squeezed into territory which was central to Arab perceptions of their own identity (Balfour Declaration).

The Mandate was supposed to have been awarded in recognition of France's special relationship with Syria when in fact its interests since the Crusades had been marginal and its understanding of the societies in the region impoverished.[30] France's historic links in Aleppo had almost entirely been with the Catholic elements and involved little understanding of the concerns of the Muslims who comprised over 60 per cent of the city's population of 320,000 by 1943. (Still a dominant element among Christian communities in Aleppo, Catholics of all sects comprised 10 per cent of the city's population.) France thus spent the twenty years of its Mandate battling a tide of Arab nationalism which it preferred to interpret in confessional terms, failing to appreciate that France's own heavy hand was the greatest incentive encouraging the rise of national feeling which had been barely perceptible before 1920.

The jigsaw

A brief summation of these problems might help us better to interpret that future that lay ahead of Syria in the twentieth century. The pieces of this new jigsaw just didn't fit. No wonder; it was like trying to fit the incomplete pieces from three separate pictures into one frame. In the process, there could be no resolution of the anomalies which the sudden collapse of the Ottoman system had brought. Versailles had decided that the answer was to be a Mandate over the provinces of Arabistan soon to be defined as Iraq, Lebanon, Palestine, Trans-Jordan and Syria. In theory, the Mandate was high-handed paternalism of the most pernicious kind cloaked in the lofty wording of the League of Nations Covenant:

> Certain communities formerly belonging to the Turkish Empire have reached a stage of development where their existence as independent nationals can be provisionally recognised subject to the rendering of administrative advice and assistance by a Mandatory until such time as they are able to stand alone.[31]

In practice, it was even worse than this cynical paternalism indicated. Much might have been forgiven if it had been done adroitly or at least with an eye to consistency. The first obstacle the French had to clear was Faysal's kingdom. After the fall of Damascus and Aleppo in 1918, most Arabs had understood that an Arab kingdom would be the successor to Turkish rule in Arabistan, at least in Syria. Britain's winks and nods to Faysal were rapidly corrected. Such hints had been conveyed by T. E. Lawrence during his adventurous leadership of the Arab forces on their campaign up to Damascus. The Allied commander Allenby had even ensured that the city's subsequent 'fall' was stage-managed to give the Hashemite forces and Faysal at least a symbolic role in the victory.

Any lingering belief Faysal may have had, however, that the British occupation forces were to be under his final authority vanished when in November 1919 Britain withdrew its army from the inland provinces. Britain took no action to oppose France's ultimatum in July 1920 and handed over inland Syria to French authority. The successor power under the Treaty of Sèvres was to be a 'Mandate', formally inaugurated in 1923 in Syria on behalf of the League of Nations but in effect pursuing almost exclusively French interests. French-directed administrations were installed in Lebanon[32] and in Syria; Britain ruled in Palestine; and appointees of the Hashemite family were placed on the thrones confected in Iraq and Trans-Jordan. All were to be heavily overseen by Mandated advisors, French 'governors-general' in the case of Lebanon and Syria.

The big loser

French troops had already marched into Aleppo on 23 July 1920, garrisoning it with 18,000 troops in the face of an earlier attempt by local tribesmen to seize the city. The townspeople themselves came out to greet General Lamothe, the representative of the French High Commissioner, and a new administration of locals of conspicuous incapacity was installed under Kamil al-Qudsi, whose sole qualification seemed to be that he had headed the Ottoman secret service bureau in the city for twenty years.

Aleppo suffered the worst fate of any Syrian city in the new arrangements. The leading city of Ottoman Syria in economic terms now languished, poorly integrated into the new economy of Mandate Syria. Aleppo lost much of its natural economic hinterland to the north and east with the former Turkish sanjaks of Aintab (now Gaziantep) and Urfa reassigned to Turkey whose frontier was confirmed along the line of the Baghdad railway. Aleppo necessarily wondered who had won the war. The rewards of the conflict had gone to its defeated neighbour while much of the country to Aleppo's northwest in the Amanus range as well as to the west towards the Jebel Ansariye would be beset by turmoil for the next two years.

France now imposed a clumsy divide and rule approach to handling the complex ethnic and confessional Syrian picture. It hoped to do deals with minorities such as the Druze in the Hauran, south of Damascus, the Alawites

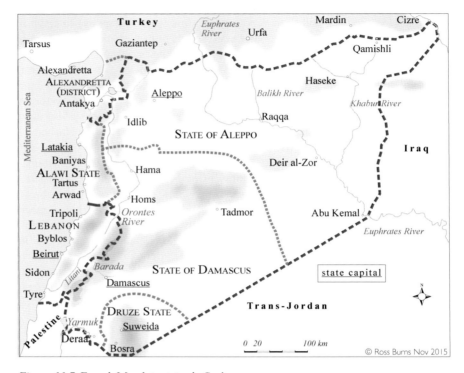

Figure 11.7 French Mandate states in Syria

of the coastal mountains and the ethnic Turk component of the province of Alexandretta. In addition, Lebanon was redefined in 1920 to embrace a collection of five previous Ottoman sanjaks. This expansion was intended to provide a Christian majority with sufficient hinterland to ensure the prosperity of the Maronite Catholic citadel, Mount Lebanon, that had long sought French protection. A game of divide and rule of an excessively clumsy and cynical kind had begun.

In granting these areas enhanced autonomy (for a time the Druze and the Alawites were also accorded status as separate 'states' under the Mandate), Aleppo increasingly felt that its voice as a remote inland town was marginalised in the new dispensation. All essential decisions seemed to be cast in response to sentiment in Beirut and Damascus. Many wondered if Aleppo might not have been better off in joining Turkey rather than an entity ruled from distant Damascus. Aleppo had enjoyed slightly closer ties with the cultural milieu of Istanbul than had the rest of Syria and the abrupt departure from the Ottoman realm had clearly brought severe dislocation. The fact that France settled for a deal with the Turkish Republic that sacrificed so much of its hinterland confirmed such perception of Aleppo's second rung status.

In less chaotic circumstances, French rule in Aleppo might have had an easier passage. Aleppo had a more heterogeneous population than the southern capital. The city had been slower than Damascus in responding to the rise of Arab nationalism in the late Ottoman years. In reality, Aleppo's transition was not an easy one, though distance preserved it from the direct effects of the insurrection that broke out in the Druze areas of the Hauran in 1925. For the first three years, however, French control could only be maintained through the conspicuous use of often deadly force, usually through its Senegalese or Moroccan troops. Much of the rebel activity was not urban-based, though there were some incidents directed again at Aleppo's poorer Christian quarters. In the region between Harim and Jisr al-Shugur on the middle Orontes, much of the unrest coordinated by Ibrahim Hananu had collapsed when the Turks reached agreement with France, recognising Turkish territorial claims in Cilicia in 1921 and depriving Hananu of covert Kemalist aid. Hananu fled to Jordan but was extradited in 1921 and subsequently released as the situation began to calm down.

Losing Antioch

The noose the new political geography had drawn around Aleppo would be tightened further when the Syrian province of Antioch passed in 1938 as a result of a rigged referendum from mandated Syria to Turkey. Kemalist Turkey had never reconciled itself to the inclusion of the sanjak of Alexandretta (including Antioch) in France's Syrian Mandate. Arab nationalists in Syria were even more suspicious of France's motives in earlier granting the area undefined 'autonomous' status that suggested its future was left open. The sanjak's population contained a higher proportion of Turks than other areas of northern Syria but probably not a majority. The rest of its Muslim population comprised Alawites (a community virtually an extension of those in the coastal mountains of Syria to the south) as well as a small number of Sunni Arabs. The loss of the most direct access to the Mediterranean deprived Aleppo of its closest port (as of 1938, 60–70 per cent of Aleppo's trade had used the ports of the Sanjak of Alexandretta including Antioch), a situation that had to be corrected in coming decades by developing its links to Latakia well to the south. Some 80 per cent of the sanjak's minorities emigrated in the two years after the referendum, further swelling the Christian population of Aleppo.

Terminating the Mandate

After the fall of France to Nazi Germany in May 1940, the Vichy French authorities promised Germany use of military facilities in Syria. Allied forces moved in to deprive the Germans of further access in June 1941 using Indian, Australian and Free French units stationed in Egypt and Iraq. The commander of the pro-Vichy forces in Syria sought an armistice on 10 July and Allied forces handed control of Syria to the Free French under General Catroux, who gave formal recognition to both Syria and Lebanon as independent nations.

In the confusion of war, the Mandate was not formally wound up; it was quietly allowed to expire from irrelevance. The Mandate experience may have had some merit in bringing Syria into an environment more advanced than the Ottomans had provided in their last years but it was deficient in almost all other respects. The Mandate was not France's preferred framework for its presence in Syria. It had contemplated a more paternalistic heavy hand along the lines of its Moroccan and Algerian experiences. Woodrow Wilsonian idealism fitted uneasily with France's determination to pursue tactics which set one community against another. France was more intent on blocking the path to democracy than smoothing it by building a consensual relationship with the growing forces of nationalism.

France, conflicted back home between left and right factions' approach to colonial adventures, seemed unable to make up its mind how to play this uneasy fit. The French sought above all to prevent the emergence of a Syria united politically within a framework of confessional tolerance but in the end found its best endeavours headed off by a wartime Allied occupation that made independence inevitable. France had failed to recognise that it was not enough to co-opt only a small segment of the notables (usually chosen among those who had served the Ottomans in high office). It largely failed to keep to a course that could work enthusiastically with the professional, middle class and other notable elements who sought a path to independence based not on conflict but on collaboration with France.

The fault was not entirely France's alone. The League of Nations framework allowed the old Sykes–Picot Agreement and Balfour Declaration mindsets to flourish even under the noses of the League of Nations idealistic framework. The fact that virtually the last act of the French was to unleash the shelling of Damascus in an attempt to terrorise the opposition underlined how impoverished the whole experience had been. French tutelage had proved an inadequate substitute even for the imperfect legitimacy the Ottoman Sultan/Caliph had managed to provide.

Aleppo's loss of innocence

For centuries, Aleppo had largely been a city of tolerance where communities learned to live alongside each other, conscious of difference but not seeking to make a point of it in daily life. In November 1947, the UN vote in favour of the creation of Israel touched off anti-Jewish riots whose consequences led to the demise of one of Aleppo's oldest communities whose origins probably went back to before the Roman period. Its ranks had been steadily augmented over the centuries, in particular with a wave of Sephardic Jews in the late fifteenth/sixteenth centuries. The Jewish population count was over 9000 in the 1908 census but may have subsequently fallen with the loss of Aleppo's regional markets after the First World War.

While it is not clear whether the riots had official encouragement, little was done to limit the damage as violence continued over two days, causing extensive property damage in the heavily Jewish Bandara and Bahsita quarters within the walls as well as the modern Jamaliya Quarter on the northwest edge. While figures of deaths by the score have been cited, it is noteworthy that the number was possibly as low as nil as numerous non-Jewish families gave protection to their Jewish neighbours while the rioting continued.[33] Specific official restrictions on the Jewish community followed, however, and within months more than half the Jews of Aleppo had emigrated. Aleppo had long been a centre of Jewish scholarship, one of the most active in the Middle East and the treasure of the Bandara Synagogue (the centre of much of the burning and looting) had been the Aleppo Codex. Details of the historical background to how the codex had arrived in Aleppo have never been clarified but it appears to reflect the scholarly community's intensive work since the sixteenth century to establish the earliest precise text of the Hebrew Bible.[34]

The Bandara Synagogue, though badly burnt out with the loss of some parts of the wooden sections of its largely stone structure and many of its fittings destroyed, contained a series of small chambers for the housing of the Torah scrolls[35] (see Figure 3.8 on page 65). The most precious item, the Aleppo Codex, however, was kept in a lower cave, the Cave of Elijah. Exactly what happened to the scroll during the rioting is disputed but claims that it was destroyed were clearly disproved in the coming years when it re-emerged in Jerusalem (where it is now housed in the Israel Museum). It would appear to have spent some years in the safe keeping of a local non-Jewish merchant before it was smuggled out via Turkey in 1958.

The creation of Israel would bring in its train numerous more murderous reactions across the Middle East for many decades but the Aleppo riots were the first time since the anti-Christian disturbances of 1850 that a single community among Aleppo's complex mix was singled out. It was a wake-up call that the consequences of the collapse of the Ottoman consensus, which had already brought more deadly consequences for many of the Christian communities to the north, were still to be absorbed.

Notes

1 'While the empire in the sixteenth and early seventeenth centuries had boasted men of integrity and calibre to match any in the known world, a century later those serving the state seemed to have been as venal and unimaginative as were ever produced anywhere' (Masters 1988: 189).
2 Locally recruited troops were known as *yerliyye* to distinguish them from *kapi kullari* out-posted from Istanbul (Hathaway 2008: 91).
3 David (2008: 338) on the janissaries.
4 De Chasseboeuf was elevated under Napoleon to the rank of Comte de Volney (Chasseboeuf 1959 [1787]: 271).
5 Chasseboeuf 1959 [1787]: 272–3.
6 Masters 2013: 47. Masters also examines the reluctance of the Arabs to accept that the Ottoman sultans could rightly be titled 'Caliph' when they were neither descendants of the Prophet's family nor even Arab (Masters 2013: 48–58).
7 The Maronites first came under the authority of the Holy See in 1215, their status formalised by a Papal Bull of Innocent III, *Quae divinae Sapientiae* (Heyberger 2013: 5). Masters notes that the Maronite community in Aleppo played an important role in

giving the church an 'urban face' at a time when their main body of adherents in Lebanon lived largely in rural environments, thus easing their transition to a European defined 'modernity' (Masters 2001: 44).

8 Masters puts emphasis on a number of other factors including the appeal of Catholic practices to women who, eager to move from the more segregationist approaches of Orthodox faiths, often switched allegiance ahead of their husbands or children (Masters 2001: 87).

9 David 1991: 189.

10 Barker 1876: I, 141–2.

11 This remarkably blunt report was unearthed by Bruce Masters in the Ottoman archives and quoted in Masters (2013: 146).

12 Marcus (1989: 339); Masters (1999: 65) has a slightly different range for the 1840s. Marcus' figures correct the considerably exaggerated population estimates of the foreign consuls and visitors.

13 Masters 2013: 172.

14 Masters 2001: 132.

15 Roded notes that those elected were rarely people of stature in their own communities with an emphasis on young and inexperienced deputies or men drawn from the Turkish administration (Roded 1984: 306).

16 Deringli 1998: 28–31.

17 D. Sourdel 'Dja'bar' *EI2*. When this part of the Euphrates Valley was to be inundated as part of a new Euphrates Dam in the 1970s, the tomb was moved to a site near another Euphrates crossing, northeast of Menbij and much closer to the Syrian/Turkish frontier. During the current Syrian conflict, the remains were moved again in a covert operation by Turkish solders in February 2015 to a new spot immediately north of the frontier. For a report on the events leading to the drowning, see Lindner (2007: 19–20).

18 Eich 'Abu'l-Huda al-Sayyadi' *EI3*.

19 Sirriyeh 2013: 76. Abu 'l-Huda built a family house in Aleppo on the eastern rim of the Citadel ditch. On his move to Istanbul, the building was expanded to house a *zawiya,* later converted to serve as a twentieth-century school for training in arts and crafts. The architecture was somewhat flashy and untraditional with features such as external windows and a double sweeping staircase ascending to the entrance.

20 After Syrian independence, the barracks were renamed after the local hero of the resistance to the French Mandate, Ibrahim Hananu – see pages 261–2.

21 For 'well-protected domains', see Deringil (1998).

22 Antonius 1938: ebook edition, loc. 1632.

23 Kayali 1997: 70.

24 McMeekin 2015: 234.

25 This is borne out by the separate exercise to expel the Armenians from their villages along the Syrian coast including in the Musa Dag hills north of Antioch (Sanjian 1965: 285–6). The extension of the massacres to the Syrian Orthodox villages of the Tur Abdin and towns of southeastern Turkey, where massacres were to persist for the next two years, is given long over-due coverage in de Courtois (2004).

26 Mango 1999: 181.

27 Khoury 1987: 219.

28 Antonius 1938: ebook loc. 3961.

29 The phrase is from the title of Fromkin's 1989 study.

30 Khoury (1987: 31) noted that France's trade with Syria was below the level of its European rivals in the market. French investment was mainly in the transport sector. Khoury (1987: 45) also notes the irony of France gaining the Mandate on the basis of its 'interests' while simultaneously being expected to act oblivious to those interests.

31 Article 22 of the Covenant of the League of Nations.

32 The Maronite enclave was enlarged in 1920 to embrace other parts of Syria including the Beqaʻa Valley and the south.
33 'No one was killed, raped, or even seriously hurt' (Friedman 2012: 38).
34 The date usually given for the compiling of the codex is the tenth century. It was subsequently brought to Aleppo, via Jerusalem and Cairo, as a result of the importance of the city's scholarly Jewish community in the sixteenth century.
35 With the departure of the Jewish community in the coming decades, the synagogue – the oldest continually functioning religious centre in the city – ceased to function and passed to the responsibility of the state. Some basic restoration work was carried out in the 1990s with assistance from the World Monuments Fund.

POSTSCRIPT

The town is as old as eternity yet it has never ceased to renew itself. . . .
When its kings depart, this wondrous city remains; they perish but the city
survives.

—Ibn Jubayr 2003: 260

Before the twenty-first century, Aleppo had been the great metropolis that had
grown over five thousand years from unprepossessing origins to replace upstart
Antioch as the most prosperous and creative centre in the wide region from Cilicia
across to Mesopotamia.

As I complete this account, this city of over four million reaches its fourth year
of involvement in a conflict more terrible than experienced by a major city of the
past seventy years. It is too soon to answer the question 'What went wrong?' but
this attempt at a history warrants drawing a few lessons from the city's past

Let us step back again for a moment. One of the unintended consequences
of the sudden collapse of the Ottoman order has been the loss of the concept of
a community embracing all subjects of the ruler. Some subjects might have
always had better access to the empire's benefits than others. The imperial entity
that in 1800 still contained a near majority of non-Muslims had morphed one
hundred years later into a consciously Turkish state. The terrible consequences
of the 'new think', Turkey for the Turks, was laid before the First World War
and were driven home with the massacres and expulsions meted out to the
Armenian and other Christian minorities of eastern Turkey in 1915. The process
of ethnic identification was carried forward during the subsequent Ottoman collapse and was further entrenched with the population exchanges between Greeks
and Turks in 1922.

After 1918, though, Aleppo remarkably turned itself into a refuge and a
microcosm of the old more tolerant order. True the model was threatened by the
anti-Jewish riots of November 1947 described earlier but Aleppines stepped in to
limit the casualties while the government, too slowly, restored order. Tolerance
was shakily rebuilt but the cost was the loss over the next twenty years of one of
the communities that had made up the city's mix over two millennia.

Boxed in

The post-First World War had presented many challenges for Aleppo. A city that had once virtually snaffled most of the region's transit trade was now cut off from its old arteries of commerce. The stranglehold on Aleppo only tightened further when it found after 1938 that its links westwards to the sea and to Antioch were cut off by an international border.

Second, Aleppo's agricultural zone of activity had correspondingly shrunk, exposing it more than ever to the hazards of its immediate marginal rainfall zone no longer complemented by access to more varied climatic environments around Antioch or in the foothills of the Anti-Taurus. In addition, its productive capacities were badly affected by an agricultural collectivisation programme that crippled farmers' access to fair prices by depriving them of the normal incentives and disciplines of markets.

Third, for a while it lost much of its capacity to make or transform things. As the Syrian state became increasingly centralised and many industries nationalised, the economic advantage moved increasingly towards Damascus.

Fighting back

Aleppo, though, had never been a city that resigned itself to slipping into a passive decline. It still had one advantage to exploit. Once again it looked to the lands spreading east. It was now constrained by an international frontier with Iraq that touched only briefly on the Tigris but at least spared for Syria command of much of the old Jazira and the waters of the mid-Euphrates and the Khabur system. This hinterland embracing Raqqa, Haseke, Qamishli and Deir al-Zor may not have evoked the prestige of the medieval centres of Islamic culture such as Aintab, Urfa, Mardin (let alone Mosul) but the assets the Syrian Jazira could offer were cotton, grain and (with the introduction of the Euphrates dam in the early 1980s) irrigation to help overcome the perennial uncertainties of weather. The second advantage Aleppines sought to revive was its capacity to make things. From the 1950s, Aleppo again became the centre of a textile industry, partly fed by the new cotton boom.

A setback, however, was experienced when the entrepreneurial spirit was further stifled both by the union with Egypt (1958–61) and by the subsequent Baathist coup (1963). The resulting concentration of decision making in Damascus blinded leaders to the consequences of the suppression of incentive in agriculture and in most other sectors on which Aleppo depended, notably transport and banking. Many Aleppan business people preferred to move their activities to Lebanon or Egypt, deserting an environment where it had become impossible to pursue entrepreneurial activities without access to capital or other essential inputs.

Living off the past

Aleppo fell back on making a virtue of its past. By the 1970s, the favoured image of Aleppo on overseas television clips was its addiction to flashy American vehicles of the 1950s and of huge dimensions. To journalists it became a Middle Eastern Cuba, a curio consigned to the past – even if by necessity rather than choice. It was an option made possible by the inventiveness of the city's Armenian mechanics whose ability to whip up replacement parts on backyard lathes was formidable.

The second favoured symbol of Aleppo's past was the Baron Hotel, a threadbare but compulsory stop on every visitor's checklist and which conveyed the sort of distressed charm that can only be achieved with serious shortage of funds and clientele. Already by the 1950s this gem, in the hands of the Mazloumian family since its opening in 1911, was believed to store as many memories of a glorious past as the Ritz in London or Raffles in Singapore. Its heyday had come when it was an obligatory stop for Allied officers on leave in the Second World War, for passengers occasionally stopping over on the seventy-seven hour flying boat haul to Australia or for storm-tossed lovers escaping Olivia Manning's Cairo. Its Edwardian stones had acquired just the right level of faded charm after less than fifty years when it was rescued from bankruptcy by the Syrian state. It was a fitting and for me a beloved metaphor for the passing of Aleppo's better days. Still living off its past – and its list of repeat visitors such as Agatha Christie or T. E. Lawrence – it reeked of 'Orient Express' romanticism; at least just enough to temper the impression of its musty rooms.

Figure 12.1 Baron Hotel (1911) said to have launched Aleppo as a destination on the Orient Express

A third milestone in Aleppo's discovery of its past was the creation of an archaeological museum of a stature able to rival the Damascus example. In 1931, a first museum had been built on the present site west of the city walls. This quickly proved to be too small given the large number of archaeological sites being explored in northern Syria and down the Euphrates, the major catchment zone assigned to the Aleppo collection. In 1966, the present museum building was opened.

Keeping a healthy distance

In the six and a half decades from Syrian independence until the outbreak of the civil conflict in 2011, Aleppo managed to exploit such symbols of nostalgia and remain a little apart from many of the tensions and distractions that beset the rest of the country. A series of revolving door attempts at democracy were punctuated by coups and confected intervals of 'civilian' rule based on a one-party model. Aleppo when I first got to know it in the 1980s liked to feel a bit different as if the events perturbing the rest of the country were not to be taken too seriously. Its population was more mixed both confessionally and ethnically and its atmosphere more conservative in its respect for past conventions. Aleppo's economic life too was more traditional: entrepreneurial and still revolving around its Medina, the most lively of the traditional Middle Eastern bazars. The separation between Aleppo and the more doctrinaire interpretation of Baathist economics in Damascus gave its entrepreneurs a little more breathing room as efforts to refashion the Syrian economy around Baathist 'socialism' faltered, easing the path to the crony capitalism of the late 1990s.

Syria had entered the new era of independence with the superficial trappings of a democracy but no means of embedding democratic traditions in a political milieu which had relied excessively on French meddling as a means of settling the jockeying for power. The two decades after 1946 were to see a constant process of turmoil with few levers that could be applied to temper the rivalries between competing confessional and regional factions. Aleppo and Damascus were often at loggerheads with their respective political leaderships sponsoring their own political parties. In Aleppo, the People's Party sought to arrest the southwards focus of government and reorient its links towards Iraq.

At the end of this period, the armed forces stepped in to quell the turmoil – in the process, of course, simply adding a new level of stress. The fact was the army itself was now perceived as a confessional player, its ranks (particularly at the officer level) heavily weighted towards the Alawi minority deriving from the coastal mountains southwest of Aleppo. The French creation there of the Latakia state had whetted the Alawis' enthusiasm for political influence. Policies encouraging their recruitment to the armed forces provided the vehicle for advancement for a confessional group which had long laboured as the serfs of the urban Sunnis of the main coastal and inland towns.

The Baathist 'Revolution'

The ideological framework to bolster a new alliance against the political notables of the majority Sunnis came through Baathism, enshrined in the Arab Socialist Baath Party in 1952. Based on a set of ideas loosely culled from European ideological movements of the 1920s and 1930s, it lacked a real basis at the popular level. This proved an advantage in suggesting to a wider audience, particularly among minorities, that the party's vaguely socialist, secularist aspirations were a suitable antidote to the potential rise of Islam as a political vehicle. Baathism under Hafez al-Assad, who first rose to political prominence in 1963 and held the post of president from 1969 to 2000, became the ill-defined doctrine smoothing the path of Alawis to higher office in the defence forces. In the end, Baathism was little more than a clubbish party structure able to promote the interests of fellow members with appeal mainly to non-Sunnis.

At one level, Baathism did much to address the problems of an ethnically and confessionally complex society and to spread the benefits of gradually rising prosperity to the massively underprivileged communities, particularly in the marginal agricultural areas. Its achievements in education and infrastructure were impressive but its poor understanding of economics was a brake on attracting the level of new investment in the private sector which was needed to absorb the rising number of those leaving school or university.

From 1969 to the time of writing, however, Baathism gradually became the plaything of the wider Assad family, manipulating power through increasingly ruthless means. It was the majority confession in Syria, the Sunnis, who now felt aggrieved. Though many in business remained aloof, or as individuals sought to do deals with the Assad family, others wanted the dismantling of the secular state. In 1982, the tensions between the Assad regime and the Islamist opposition focused on the Syrian branch of the Muslim Brotherhood whose local influence centred on the religious and merchant classes of the major cities. A series of massacres (initiated by an attack by Islamist forces on the army's artillery school near Aleppo in 1979) brought a pattern of acts of mutually assured destruction, culminating when the core merchant–mosque alliance in Hama rose up in open revolt in February 1982. For four weeks, the regime used the heights around the bowl-like centre of the city to pound Hama's historic core. The resulting casualties were in the thousands. So massively decisive was this display of repression that tensions between the government and the Islamist forces were driven underground again for another thirty years, partly due to an ever more efficient and brutal network of secret police and intelligence agencies.

Rescuing ancient Aleppo

Why had Aleppo in those barren political years been more successful than most Middle Eastern cities in retaining the flavour of its past, not just in terms of turning historic buildings into museum pieces but also in retaining much of the economic and social environment that preserved the city's Medina and walled city as a living entity? Much of the credit must go to the preservation of the historic endowments or waqfs as enduring legal instruments governing ownership and use of historic buildings. Whereas other centres outside Syria allowed the waqf system to lapse or permitted multiple ownership without any regard for the integrity of a building, most Syrian governments have managed to retain the right framework to enable the waqfs to serve their original purpose.

The second source of strength for the continuation of a traditional cityscape as a functional environment was the preservation of ancient crafts and their workshops. Although Aleppo had long been a centre for the production of things for external markets the lack of new investment and shortages of foreign currency

Figure 12.2 Regenerated streetscape in the street leading to Bab Qinnisrin

285

meant the old ways continued to prevail to meet the city's needs. The cloth and fabrics workshops had helped kick off the international trade of the boom years of the early Ottoman period, even if much of the trade was later replaced with a dominant role for imports in fine wool. The fabrics industry along with metal-working, tanneries, soap- and tent-making all endured into recent times and the Medina was still the most practical centre for selling the products of small-scale producers.

Town planning

There were still challenges but the city rallied to meet them. One of the positive aspects of Aleppo's absorption in its own past was the campaign to rescue the old city and environs from the clutches of an ambitious town planning programme that managed to combine insensitivity to the benefits of retaining the city's tra-ditional profile with a rush towards rebuilding in a consciously brutal attempt to be modern. The urge to 'open up' the old walled city to a greater traffic flow had originated in the last years of the Ottomans when urban economic revival was a major issue on the agenda of administrators including Jemal Pasha who liked to see themselves as new pharaohs. Under the French Mandate, the administration was to some extent influenced by the lure of 'urbanisme' but a consolidated plan to free the traffic flow to and around the Medina had been slow to develop. The authorities had already called in foreign expertise but in a context which still gave

Figure 12.3 Vaulted laneway in the Jdeide Quarter, also a target for the upgrading of services to regenerate an ancient quarter for modern uses

priority to vehicle flow rather than giving the ancient city a means of adapting within the bonds of its past. The appointment of the French Danger brothers to a supervisory role in urban planning led to the preparation of the first plan for Aleppo's regeneration in 1931 by René Danger.

The Dangers' approach continued the French idea of its '*mission civilisatrice*' in which the new concept of a global plan for a city became part of its mission, recalling to some extent the role of Sinan's studio under Suleiman the Magnificent. Instead of the post-seventeenth-century pattern of a series of individual projects unsupervised by a metropolitan planning body, the plan became part of France's civilising mission applied to the traditional fabric of the city, prioritising hygiene and accessibility.

The application of these planning ideas fortunately proceeded in parallel with the work of the remarkable band of historical researchers assembled in the Mandate's archaeological service.[1] The French architect Michel Ecochard was employed from 1934 to apply historical perspective to implementation of the Dangers' plan. Both Ecochard and his Arabist historian colleague Jean Sauvaget complemented the plan by informing the administration on what was there, its historical significance and what should be preserved. It is to their work that we owe many of the seminal studies which inform us still on the city's history.

Part of the Dangers' study emphasised the need to accommodate the city's expansion by extending into new quarters, each contributing a distinctly different phase in its urban history. Consequently, much of the city's regeneration in the Mandate period spared the old city and gravitated towards the neatly laid out grid of the Aziziye Quarter east of the now-old Jdeide Quarter. Here some success had been achieved in introducing the fruits of French pre- and inter-war architecture in a modified 'Belle Epoque' (but more often Art Deco influenced) style which still graces the spaces near the eastern banks of the Quweiq.

By the 1970s, Baathism brought a new taste for massive construction projects, usually assigned to one military-run construction behemoth, Milihouse. After the country took on a Baathist agenda from 1969, the first major project for Aleppo was the regeneration of the Banqusa and Bandara quarters badly run down after the 1947 riots. The new plan for this area involved high-rise and featureless office blocks deployed like gigantic gravestones. In spite of the increasingly oppressive Baathist clamp imposed on Syria, even Aleppo found this attempt to bulldoze many of the remains of two traditional quarters in the interests of progress sufficiently provocative to wake the city from its preference to remain aloof from government. In a society where dissent was often met with harsh repression, a groundswell developed by the early 1980s which saw the first stage of the project halted and eventually re-evaluated. Whereas elsewhere, Baathist determination to remake cities in a style reminiscent of Eastern Europe, or worse still North Korea, usually carried all before it, this time a genuinely popular reaction to preserve the city's stone-paved alleyways and wonky minarets developed.

In the Banqusa Quarter, the remaining historic buildings were retained and a new company set up with funding from Kuwait and German sources to train

Aleppines in the application of traditional crafts to the regeneration of old quarters. An alternative regeneration plan which had been devised by the local architect Adli Qudsi was adopted, a funding stream for the regeneration of utilities under the old city's streets was begun and loans supplied to local householders to bring their houses up to modern standards of comfort. To lock the new approach into place, the city was successfully placed on UNESCO's World Heritage List in 1986 and major refurbishment plans followed under several other schemes, most notably the Aga Khan Trust's impressive programme for the regeneration of the surrounds of the Citadel.

When the bonds of a semi-socialist system were eased in the 1990s, Aleppo rapidly overtook Damascus in the number of new industrial projects after 2000 when the Assad dynasty arranged a smooth transfer of the Baathist state from Hafez al-Assad to his son, Bashar, seen by many as more attuned to the economic realities of the time. By 2010, Aleppo seemed poised to gain a new entrepreneurial advantage over other parts of Syria. New industrial areas had opened and were rapidly filling.

One industry that readily recommended itself in Aleppo was tourism. By the 2010s it had become the third most important foreign exchange earner for Syria after expatriate earnings and exports of gas and some petroleum products. The preceding decade had shown how easy it was, once economic reform removed the shackles that had been holding back investment, for Aleppo to crank up its response to this market. Foreign investment in major new hotels took off, largely with Gulf money. Aleppo's stock of untouched historic homes could readily be converted to small hotels or restaurants; its extraordinary range of historic religious and civic buildings largely retained their original form and function. Above all, the Aleppines were bright, immensely proud of their country's historic heritage and adept at offering a hospitable environment.

2011

Then in April 2011 Syria hit the wall. The resulting conflagration was like an explosion that might have had numerous causes all building on the other but ready to respond to a single spark. It is too soon to assess how and when Syria's conflicts might be resolved. The trouble began as a protest movement in Dera'a, south of Damascus, which the regime claimed had been hijacked by Islamist forces deeply antagonistic to a secular-based leadership. It quickly earned the label 'civil war'. It did not initially resemble a sectarian conflict (though with the rise of self-styled 'Islamic state' it has now taken on that form in some parts) and sectarian violence between Syrians at a popular level has never attained the dimensions of the communal massacres of the Lebanese Civil War (though tensions between villages in the seam line between the Alawis and Sunni villages of the Orontes Valley for a time brought outbreaks of appalling violence). The multiplication of groups involved partly reflects tribal affiliations in some rural areas with ideological motivation a convenient tag for attracting outside funding.

Figure 12.4 Beit Wakil in the Jdeide Quarter of Aleppo regenerated as a tourist
hotel – the modern decor is a poor substitute for the magnificent panels
now in the Islamic Museum in Berlin

There is a large proportion of foreigners engaged on both sides and there is no
doubt that following its initial phase a major impetus to the spread and persistence
of the conflict is both outside funding and the ease of access for foreigners joining
the fighting elements.

For the first fifteen months, Aleppo continued to do what it did best, keep
its head down. Perhaps it could not see any point in getting involved. The still-
influential Christian and other minorities largely saw their interests as tied to the
regime's secular-based agenda and the Sunni business elite saw advantage in
looking beyond confessional horizons. Perhaps the lessons of living and working
together as a complex mixed society still had deep roots.

A war for (or against?) Aleppo

Fourteen months into the Syrian conflict, on 19 July 2012, the first clashes broke out between rebels of the 'Free Syrian Army' and regime forces. By January 2013 fighting had reached the Great Mosque and the zone of confrontation spread across the centre of the old city with rebel forces (now joined by numerous Islamist groups) attempting to wrest the Citadel from government hands. From then until the time of writing, the centre of the historic city remained an intense zone of confrontation with the regime forces maintaining their hold on the Citadel. The opposition controlled much of the Medina to the south along with the cluster of mosques facing the Citadel gateway in the Ayyubids' ceremonial zone.

Given the continuing confrontation as I close this account (mid 2017), it would be pointless here to try to describe the course of the fighting but the pattern was one in which the regime had clung to its hold on the Citadel which is joined to the western (regime-held) areas of the city by a zone that stretched across the northern side of the walled city via Jdeide. Virtually the whole of the historic city was therefore exposed to the damage from shellfire that ranges across the central monumental zone. The particularly heavy concentration was in the area between the Great Mosque, the suqs and the Citadel. Efforts by both sides to create a free fire zone along this interface turned parts of the main monumental area into a wasteland. Several buildings were sucked into the cavities created by enormous tunnel bombs set by Islamist forces keen to neutralise regime positions right up against the line of division.

Buildings of incomparable historic and religious significance simply vanished, including the burial mosque of the son of Saladin, Sultan al-Ghazi, the first Ottoman project in Aleppo (the Otrushiye Mosque, the work of the great court architect, Sinan) and later buildings including the 'Neo-Saracenic' Mandate-period Governor's Office (Serail) and the Ottoman National Hospital. There has also been major secondary damage to buildings of unique value such as the Hammam Yalbugha (the largest bath complex in Syria) and a group of khans. The singular loss in this area was the toppling in April 2013 of the minaret of the Great Mosque. The mosque itself had already suffered extensive damage when an electricity sub-station caught fire amid the fighting between regime and rebel forces in September 2012, setting off a wider conflagration. A library of important manuscripts held in the mosque's eastern wing was incinerated.

A monthly update listing the cumulative reports on the damage to monuments in Syria is given on my website at www.monumentsofsyria.com. To record only the situation at the time of writing, the table on p. 291 gives a readout on the number of monuments in Aleppo damaged in the first three categories of damage assessment (on a scale of five). Compiled from visual information posted on the internet and compared with pre-April 2011 photos in my own records.

If there is one building, however, that does symbolise the reckless abandon with which the fighting has been pursued on all sides it is the above-mentioned minaret of Aleppo's Great Mosque. To most outsiders reading reports of the building's

Degree of damage (first 3 categories on a scale of 5)	Cases
1 Structure destroyed or threatened	12
2 Major damage but structure could be saved	11
3 Conspicuous material damage	22
Total (all five categories)	78
Total monuments in Aleppo database	231

demise, it may be just another minaret. In fact its collapse under shellfire can only be compared to the loss of a building of the unique artistic value of, for example, the baptistery of the Florence Cathedral. Without this building – the only Seljuk monument in Syria and dated to the 1190s – we wipe out memory of a whole era.

Hussein's lost child

We have touched at several points above on the peculiar history of the Shrine of Muhassin which sits at the vantage point looking over Aleppo so frequently used by artists and photographers that it earned its familiar name *al-Dikka* or 'the Platform'.[2] It has a complex building history expertly unravelled in a recent pioneering study of Shi'i shrines in medieval Syria by Stephennie Mulder. In a city now plagued by tensions between Sunni and Shi'a, it has much to teach us. It was initially commemorated as the burial place of a premature child born to Fatima, wife of Hussein, fleeing the battle of Karbala in 680. The Shi'i-inclined Sayf al-Dawla rediscovered the legend in Hamdanid times (962) and identified this as the burial spot. In their siege of the city in 1124, the rampaging Crusaders destroyed much of the structure and provoked the retaliatory seizure by Qadi Ibn al-Khashshab of four Christian churches in Aleppo (see page 133). Rather than close down or re-purpose the shrine during the campaign to revive Sunnism, the Zengid and Ayyubid rulers of Aleppo in the following decades continued to honour it with new buildings and even an inscription praising the Shi'i imams. They probably hoped to persuade the city's remaining Shi'a that an accommodation could be found between the two traditions.[3] Even after the shrine was ransacked by the Mongols in 1260, the orthodox Sunni Baybars repaired it and probably endowed the beautiful painted wood panelling of the cenotaph that the shrine's guardian would let you inspect behind its grated and cloth-covered enclosure if you asked very nicely.

Another view from the platform

The Shrine of the Platform is a paradigm showing how Aleppo over the years has survived even the worst its enemies could bring. The nightmare that has descended on the city at the foot of the platform as I close this account is a reflection of another aspect of the city's story: its experience of mindless violence at

Figure 12.5 Outer entrance doorway to the Mashhad al-Hussein

the hands of conquerors and raiders from the Sasanians, through the Crusaders
to the Mongols or the Timurids. A companion Shiʻi shrine stands a little to the
north on Jebel Jawshan. This complex, begun well after Saif al-Dawla's project,
is the Shrine to Hussein (Mashhad al-Hussein). It has survived an even worse
event: it was blown up in 1920 by accident having been used by Faysal's forces
as a gunpowder store. The pulverised shrine was expertly rebuilt fifty years later
by the Syrian antiquities authorities who were able to take advantage of the
detailed drawings of the German-American scholar Ernst Herzfeld made during
his survey of Aleppo's epigraphy in 1908. A comparison of modern photos with
Herzfeld's make it difficult to fault the reconstruction supervised by the Syrian

archaeological official ʿAli Summaqiya.[4] We should also remember that Aleppo has always prided itself on the dexterity of its stonemasons, whose skill in conjuring from the crisp local limestone the most intricate shapes and twirls fascinated Gertrude Bell a century ago.

As of 2011, the great doorway to Hussein's mashhad stood proudly welcoming both locals and Shiʿi visitors from Iran. It has been variously described as 'the most beautiful architectural work in Aleppo', 'magnificent, a tour de force of Ayyubid architecture' or the 'most enigmatic religious monument in Ayyubid Aleppo'.[5] The shrine doorway (Figure 12.5), unprecedented in its ambitious height, enfolds those entering in a brilliant assemblage of muqarnas segments, strap decoration and a multi-lobed arch composed of nine massive blocks faced in contrasting stone crowning the opening. Described by Yasser Tabbaa as 'the most important medieval Shiʿi structure in all of Syria', the shrine was built under a string of Sunni rulers, beginning just after the death of Saladin to the end of the Ayyubids, though largely with public funding. Its completion was delayed by the need to raise the finance from the remaining Shʿi community.

These two shrines – their histories and their survival – therefore give us some glimmer of hope that Aleppo can recover this time too from a blight probably as bad as the Mongols in its savage intensity but which has already lasted much longer. The Ayyubids were convinced Sunnis but like most of Aleppo's successful rulers they encouraged the city's various communities to survive alongside each other, conscious of differences but able to minimise their sharp edges. The regime of Bashar al-Assad in 2011 did its best to forget this lesson, stoking the fires of popular demonstrations, initially no more deadly than the earlier popular manifestations in Tahrir Square, Cairo. They sought to turn the tensions into a signal to the Islamists that the lesson of Hama 1982 still applied: 'defy us and there is no end to the violence we are prepared to unleash'.

It would be foolhardy to identify prematurely any lessons that the Syrian conflict has for us given that it might well have a long course still to run. If Aleppo's history tells us anything, though, it is that the city was strong in the past when it practised co-existence. Its best rulers worked to soften the edges of sectarian confrontations. It often had to cope with a difficult wider environment as it stood right on the corridor between Central Asia, the Arab world and Europe in a complex overlay of Kurds, Persians, Turks, Turkmen, Armenians, Circassians and Europeans; heterodox and orthodox Christians; Sunni and Shiʿa; Ismaelis, Jews, Druze – all superimposed on an Arab base going back thousands of years.

A confected Doomsday

The wider Middle East now faces a different challenge. The failure after 1918, for multiple reasons, to effect a reasonable replacement for the Ottoman system has proved an impossible legacy. Too busy with settling their own internal rivalries, the European/American powers a century ago were content to see the Middle East reordered in line with their own colonial ambitions or their historical preoccupations.

The continuing experiments in redefinition of the Ottoman Empire's successor states as enclaves defined to reflect the interests of one privileged faith or ethnicity are still less than a hundred years old but the fallout gets worse by the decade. Thirty years after 1918, the creation of Israel in the absence of any understanding with its Arab and largely Muslim neighbours introduced a new dimension. In 2003, in a copybook repeat of the folly of the past, the complexities of local politics were brushed aside in the scenario devised for Saddam Hussein's fall. Iraq post-2003 has brought another state where a mosaic society virtually collapsed in a process stage-managed under Western auspices. The unintended consequences, exposing Iraq to Wahhabism gone wild, have spawned a Sunni revival of a uniquely savage kind. Syria, which had opted after the Second World War for the formula of a secular state, is a collateral victim of this attempt to overturn and find a new 'Year Zero'.

The confrontation between Shi'a and Sunni, of course, goes back much earlier than all these events. It has its roots in the genesis of the first Islamic dynasty in the seventh century but the recent eruption of a new form of Wahhabism has suddenly gone critical after centuries in which it was 'managed' by firm leadership or confined to the recesses of Arabia. Its re-emergence has recently threatened to bring a new quality of primal intensity to Syria's war which could have even worse consequences for the region. Let us hope that the history of Aleppo can teach us that there is a way back from this confected Doomsday that the twisted minds of 'Islamic state' wanted to bring on at Marj Dabiq on an otherwise insignificant plain 35 kilometres north of Aleppo.[6]

Notes

1 The service itself was set up in the context of France's civilising mission, as put frankly by Ernest Babelon to the first congress held to consider this aspect of France's mission in Syria (May 1919): 'France has to take on a glorious heritage in Syria/Palestine that all might envy but none can take from us. This tradition goes back at least to the Crusades and we would be guilty if we let it lapse' (quoted in Chevalier 2002: 283).
2 The shrine's Hamdanid origins are discussed in Chapter 5.
3 On the previously neglected issue of the survival of a Shi'a community in Aleppo well into Ayyubid times, see Eddé (1999: 436–46) and Mulder (2014: 268).
4 Yasser Tabbaa, however, has rightly pointed out that the meticulous restoration, a decade or so after its completion, has been forced to compete with a new intrusion – a massive canopy supported on a steel frame over the courtyard once open to the sky, denying the monument the play of light and shade across the façades (Tabbaa 1997: 110). This was presumably done in order to accommodate the waves of visitors who began to arrive by bus from Iran in the 1990s.
5 Quotes are, in order, from Sauvaget (1941: 125), Mulder (2014: 89) (referring to the doorway), Tabbaa (1997: 110).
6 It is no accident that 'Islamic state' calls its glossy monthly magazine *Dabiq*. On 'Islamic state' and its morbid fascination with Dabiq, see page 86 and Chapter 4, note 9.

APPENDIX – MAPS OF ALEPPO

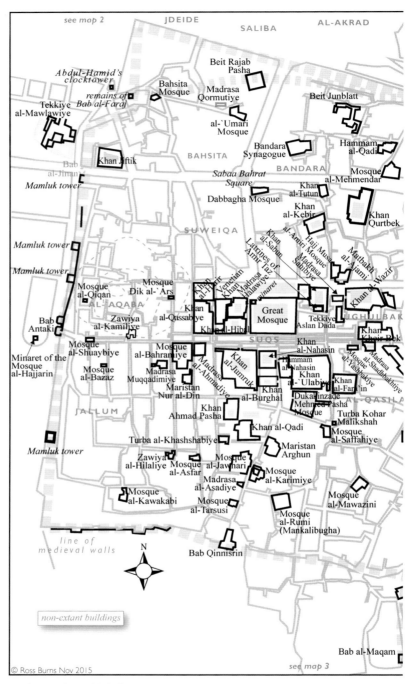

A.1 Aleppo, the walled city

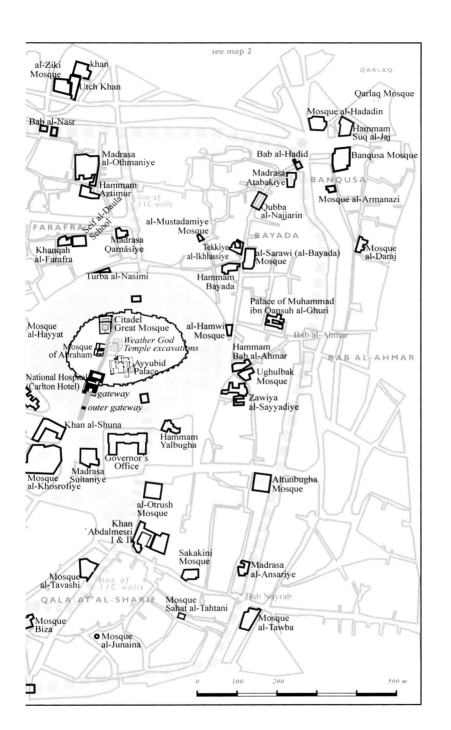

see map 2

QARLAQ

al-Ziki Mosque   khan
    Utch Khan

Qarlaq Mosque

Mosque al-Hadadin

Hammam
Suq al-Jaj

Bab al-Nasr

Madrasa
al-Othmaniye

Bab al-Hadid

Banqusa Mosque

Madrasa
Atabakiye

BANQUSA

Hammam
Aztimur

line of
IIC walls

Qubba
al-Najjarin

Mosque al-Armanazi

FARAFRA

al-Mustadamiye
Mosque

BAYADA

Madrasa
Qarnâsîye

Khanqah
al-Farafra

Tekkiye
al-Ikhlassiye

al-Sarawi (al-Bayada)
Mosque

Mosque
al-Daraj

Turba al-Nasimi

Hammam
Bayada

Palace of Muhammad
ibn Qansuh al-Ghuri

Mosque
al-Hayyat

Citadel
Great Mosque

al-Hamwi
Mosque

Weather God
Temple excavations

Bab al-Ahmar

Hammam
Bab al-Ahmar

BAB AL-AHMAR

Mosque
of Abraham

Ayyubid
Palace

Ughulbak
Mosque

National Hospital
(Carlton Hotel)

gateway

Zawiya
al-Sayyadiye

outer gateway

Khan al-Shuna

Hammam
Yalbugha

Governor's
Office

Mosque
al-Khosrofiye

Madrasa
Sultaniye

Altunbugha
Mosque

al-Otrush
Mosque

Khan
`Abdalmesri
I & II

Sakakini
Mosque

Madrasa
al-Ansariye

Mosque
al-Tavashi

line of
IIC walls

QALA'AT AL-SHARIF

Mosque
Sahat al-Tahtani

Bab Nayrab

Mosque
al-Tawba

Mosque
Biza

● Mosque
al-Junaina

0   100   200   500 m

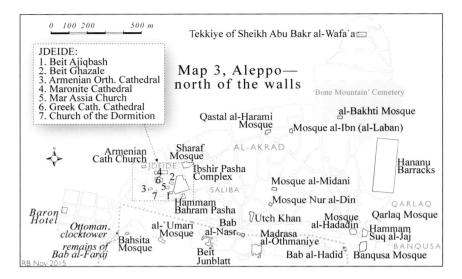

A.2 Aleppo, northern suburbs

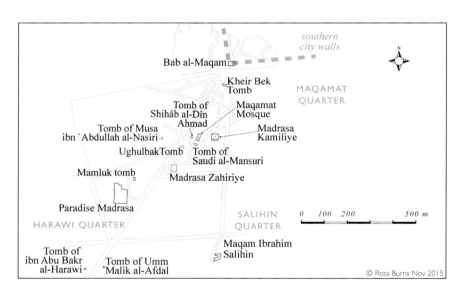

A.3 Aleppo, southern cemeteries

GLOSSARY

Though some Arabic plural forms are listed, in most cases in the text the plural is formed simply by adding '–s' to the singular form to avoid confusion, especially where the word is in reasonably common use in historical sources – hence *madrasa*, *madrasa*s, etc.

Terms which have only a single mention in the text (with parenthetical explanation) are not included.

ablaq (Arabic)   use of contrasting black and ochre stone for decorative effect on facades, doorways

abu (Arabic)   father of

agha (pl *aghawat*) (Turkish)   local militia leader, quarter boss

ahdath (Arabic)   urban youth gangs

ʿ*ain* (Arabic)   see ʿ*ayn*

ʿ**Alawi or Alawites** (Arabic)   followers of a sect resulting from a ninth-century split from Shiʿa Islam; sought refuge in coastal mountains of Syria

amir (*amir al-Hajj*) (Arabic)   commander (commander of the annual pilgrimage), prince

apse (Greek)   semi-circular space facing into a church and usually used to frame the altar

Arabistan (Turkish)   majority Arabic-speaking provinces of the Ottoman Empire

Artuqids (Turkish)   Turkic dynasties who maintained a precarious independence in the lands to the northeast of Aleppo in the twelfth to thirteenth centuries

asharif (pl *ashraf*), **Ashraf** (Arabic)   descendant of the family of the Prophet Muhammad

atabeg (Turkish)   Seljuk title indicating mentor, high dignitary or commander in chief of an army

aʿyan (pl of ʿ*ayn*) (Arabic)   notables, prominent figures favoured by Ottomans

ʿ*ayn* **or** ʿ*ain* (Arabic)   spring, source; eye; essence

bab (Arabic)   gate, door

barid (Arabic from Turkish)   postal service, usually restricted to official mail

basha   **see** pasha

basilica (Latin)   originally a Roman hall structure with two rows of columns positioned longitudinally and used for administrative purpose, later the typical form for Syrian churches

bayt, beit (Arabic)   house

bedestan (Turkish)   hall lined with shops, each lockable, the common space often covered by domes – see also *qaisariye*

bey (Turkish)   lord (Ottoman title)

bimaristan (Persian)   see *maristan*

bin (Arabic)   see *ibn* ('son of')

burj (Arabic)   tower

cadi (Arabic)   see *qadi*

Caliph (Arabic)   head of the Islamic community – Abu Bakr was appointed as Muhammad's successor in 632 with the title

Capitulations (Latin)   series of treaties signed between the Ottoman and European powers giving favourable treatment to European citizens in Ottoman lands and their local employees

caravanserai (Persian/Turkish)   caravan stop – hostel for travellers with provision for storage of their goods

Chalcedonian   follower of the churches which accepted the decisions of the Council of Chalcedon (451)

codex (Latin)   document in form of sheets bound between board covers

Corinthian (order) (Greek)   the most common treatment of Classical capitals in the Eastern provinces shaped by an elaborate cluster of acanthus leaves and stems

dar al-ʿadl (Arabic)   court of justice

dar al-Hadith (Arabic)   institution devoted to the study of approved texts commenting on Islamic tradition

dayr or *deir* (Arabic)   monastery

demos (Greek)   assembly of citizens of a city, limited to those who had the benefit of a Greek education

dervish (Persian)   member of a Sufi order, mystic

devşirme (*devshirme*) (Turkish)   process of recruiting or kidnapping youths for military training, usually from minority communities

dhimmi (Arabic)   non-Muslims from one of the communities of 'the Book' – Christian, Jew, Samaritan

diwan (**plural** *dawawin*) (Turkish/Arabic)   (1) office, ministry – the governor's *seraya*; (2) consultative body advising a governor

dragoman (Turkish)   local interpreter assisting a European consul or merchant

Druze (Arabic)   sect which broke away from Ismaeli mainstream under the third Fatimid Caliph, Hakim (r.996–1021); found in certain mountainous regions of Syria and Lebanon

East, Eastern   when capitalised, shorthand for the eastern provinces of the Classical world (usually Greek-speaking)

effendi (Turkish)   (originally) scribe or bureaucrat; Ottoman honorific title

emir (Arabic)   see *amir* (but 'emirate' is more commonly used in English for the territory controlled by an amir)

firman (Turkish)   Ottoman imperial decree

fondaco (Italian)   see *funduq*

funduq **(pl *fanadiq)*** (Greek/Arabic)   inn; factory housing merchant and his wares (from Greek *pandocheion*)

ghazi (Arabic)   Islamic warrior

hadith (Arabic)   recorded sayings or actions attributed to the Prophet Muhammad

Hajj (Arabic)   annual pilgrimage to Mecca

Hanafi (Arabic)   one of the four schools of Islamic jurisprudence – from teachings of Abu Hanifa al-Nu'man ibn Thabit (d.767) – developed in the mideighth century from Basra-Kufa tradition – emphasis on personal reflexion in decisions – favoured by Ottomans

Hanbali (Arabic)   one of the four schools of Islamic jurisprudence – from teachings of Ahmad ibn Hanbal (d.855) – most literal and rigorous, emphasis on the Koran and Sunna not speculation or mysticism – in vanguard of Sunni revival in tenth century – particularly strong under Mamluks

hammam (Arabic)   public steam bath

hara **(pl *harat)*** (Arabic)   quarter – e.g. Harat al-Jehud (Jewish quarters)

Hijaz (Arabic)   northern Arabia, location of the holy cities of Islam, Mecca and Medina

hijra (Arabic)   Muhammad's 'emigration' from Mecca to Medina (AD 622) – start of the Islamic era

hisba (Arabic)   the duty of every Muslim to promote 'good faith and prevent evil'

Ibn (Arabic)   son of (sometimes '*bin*')

Ikhshidids (Persian/Arabic)   Muhammad Ibn Tughj al-Ikhshid established a short-lived dynasty (935–69) which maintained Damascene independence against the rising power of the Arab principality of the Hamdanids in Aleppo

Ilkhans (Persian)   Mongol ruling dynasty in Persia, thirteenth–fourteenth centuries

imam (Arabic)   prayer leader

insula **(pl *insulae)*** (Latin)   city block in a Greek/Roman grid plan

iqta ' (Arabic)   grant entitling holder of military or administrative office to use tax revenues raised from an estate – unlike European feudalism, no permanent right to ownership of land was conferred

Ismaelis (Isma 'ilis) (Arabic)   branch of Shi 'a Islam, supporters of the claim of Isma 'il, son of Jafar as Sadiq (d.765), to the spiritual leadership of Islam

iwan (Arabic from Persian)   room with open side looking onto a courtyard and serving as a space for entertainment or instruction

jadid (Arabic)   new

jami 'a (Arabic)   congregational mosque

janissaries (Turkish)   Ottoman troops – both locally raised (*yerliyya*) and Istanbul-based (*kapikul*)

al-Jazira (Arabic)   literally 'island' – usually refers to the northeast of Syria or to lands between the Euphrates and Tigris Rivers

jebel (Arabic)   hill or mountain

jihad (Arabic)   'effort directed upon oneself for the attainment of moral and religious perfection' – by extension, 'military action with the object of the expansion of Islam' ('Djihad' in *Encyclopaedia of Islam*, second edition)

jizya (Arabic)   poll tax paid by non-Muslims

jund **(pl *ajnad*)** (Arabic)   governorate

kapikul **(pl *kapikuli*)** (Turkish)   Ottoman professional forces rotated from Istanbul (from Turkish *qapi qulu* – 'slave of the Porte')

khan **(pl *khanat*)** (Persian)   large courtyard complex combining provision for storage of goods and accommodation for merchants

khanqah (Arabic from Persian)   'monastery' for Sufi mystics, generally stricter than a *zawiya* and usually named after a benefactor

khatun (Persian)   'princess', woman of high rank

khirbet (Arabic)   ruin

Koran (*Qur'an*) (Arabic)   Muslim holy scripture as revealed to Muhammad

külliye (Turkish from Arabic)   complex of buildings fulfilling a range of religious and charitable purposes centred on a mosque/madrasa

Kurds   people of Iranian origin inhabiting eastern Turkey, parts of northern Syria and northern Iraq

limes (Latin)   areas on the frontier of the Roman and Byzantine Empires

madhhab (Arabic)   way of thinking, persuasion – i.e. the four schools of Islamic jurisprudence

madrasa **(pl *madaris*)** (Arabic)   residential school for Islamic instruction, usually funded by a charitable endowment (*waqf*)

maidan (Persian/Arabic)   open space for assembly or for equestrian training

majlis (Turkish)   council of representatives, usually of a local character

malik (Arabic)   'king' but more commonly used for any governor or prince of the Ayyubid or Mamluk realms

Maliki (Arabic)   one of the four schools of Islamic jurisprudence – developed in the eighth century from doctrines of Imam Malik ibn Anas (d.795) as an initiative by ʿAbbasid Caliph al-Mansur to unify Islamic law codes around the consensus and tradition of Medina – emphasis on moderation; opposed to mysticism – strong in Spain and North Africa

mamlaka (Arabic)   royal power, kingdom or governorate

mamluk **(pl *mamalik*)** (Arabic)   literally 'thing possessed', 'slave' – professional soldiers recruited in childhood from marginal lands (e.g. Central Asia, Balkans) and trained to serve a patron

maqam (Arabic)   sanctified area, usually a cemetery

maristan (Persian)   hospital and medical teaching institution *marj* (Arabic)   grazing area on the edge of cultivated land often used as rallying zones for invading armies

mashhad (Persian)   'place of witness', shrine (especially in Shi'i tradition)

masjid   mosque, usually smaller, neighbourhood version

Mawlawiye (Mevlevi) (Arabic/Turkish)   Sufi order – followers of Jalal al-Din Rumi (*Mawlana* – 'our master') died Konya 1273 – by reputation, syncretist with inclinations towards Shi'ism

al-Medina (Arabic)   literally 'the city' but often referring to the central market area

mihrab (Arabic)   niche or alcove in the *qibla* wall of a mosque indicating the direction of Mecca

millet (Turkish)   Ottoman system allowing a religious community to regulate personal law under the community's own rules

Mongols   Central Asia people whose original home was in the east of present-day Mongolia – their thirteenth–fourteenth-century empire attained its greatest extent under Genghis Khan

Monophysite (Greek)   term, now out of favour, for those opposed to the decision of the Council of Chalcedon (451) on the nature of Christ

muhtasib (Arabic)   supervisor of moral behaviour (see *'hisba'*), including in markets (*EI2 'hisba'*)

mujahid (Arabic)   warrior in the cause of Islam

muqaddam (Arabic)   leader of a militia or armed group

muqarnas (Arabic)   three dimensional decoration in Islamic architecture taking the shape of a triangular segment of a sphere

mutasalli, mutasarrif (Arabic/Turkish)   local official in the Ottoman system, usually ruler of a *sanjak* (or deputy to a governor of a *wilayat*)

nahr (Arabic)   river or canal

na'ib (pl *nuwwab*) (Arabic)   'substitute, delegate' – military governor or senior administrative official

Naqshbandi (Nakshbendi) (Turkish)   Sufi order – followers of Bahar al-Din Naqshband

narthex (Greek)   vestibule stretching across western end of a church

nawfara (Arabic)   spring, water source, fountain

Nusairis (French)   outdated and often derogatory term for *'Alawis* – followers of a Shi'ite sect

Ortuqids (Turkish)   see Artuqids

pasha (Turkish)   Ottoman title of high rank (in Arabic, *basha*)

polis (pl *poleis*) (Greek)   Greek institution of the city

Porte (French)   the 'Sublime Porte' was the name of the gateway by which foreign envoys approached the Ottoman court and was often used as a synonym for the imperial administration

procurator (Latin)   agent of the Roman government, especially for financial affairs – also used for official supervising minor provinces where no legions were stationed

propylaeum (Latin from Greek)   gateway marking entry to a sacred enclosure

qaʿa (Arabic)   formal reception room of an Arab house

qadi (Arabic)   judge, high religious official administering Islamic (*Shariʿa*) law

qaisariye (Arabic)   group of shops inside a bazaar complex which can be separately locked, usually for sale of precious items – see also *bedestan*

qalaʿa (t) (Arabic)   citadel or castle

qasr (Arabic)   palace or mansion

qibla (Arabic)   wall facing the direction of prayer, towards Mecca (in Aleppo, south)

qubba (kubbat) (Arabic)   dome (often covering a mausoleum or *turba*)

Qur'an (Arabic)   more accurate transliteration of 'Koran'

raʿis (plural ruʿasaʿ) (Arabic)   leader – e.g. of a local gang or militia; of a village; of a religious community

riwaq (Arabic)   colonnaded or arched space on the side of a courtyard

sabil (pl subul) (Arabic)   fountain; structure for dispensing water

sahn (Arabic)   courtyard

sanjak (Turkish)   'flag', 'standard' – in Ottoman administration, local administrative unit

Seljuk (Turkish)   Turkish dynasty which reached peak of its power in eleventh–twelfth centuries in Anatolia, Syria and Iran

seraya (Turkish/Persian)   governor's palace or headquarters

Shafeʿi (Arabic)   one of the four schools of Islamic jurisprudence – follow teachings of Imam al-Shafeʿi (d.820) – opposed to conformism; more emphasis on community consensus, on Sunna – strong in non-Fatimid Egypt and in Syria; the preferred code under the Ayyubids

shahid (Arabic)   martyr in the cause of Islam

sharʿ (Arabic)   street (often anglicised as 'sharia')

sharaf   **see** 'ashrif'

shari'a (Arabic)   Islamic traditional law (confusingly, also often anglicised as 'Sharia')

sheikh (Arabic)   dignitary or headman; spiritual leader of a group of mystics

shihna (Arabic)   prefect of a city (Ayyubid)

Shiʿi (Shiʿa) (Arabic)   movement for the recognition of the claim of the descendants of ʿAli. Originally particularly strong in southern Iraq, the Shiʿi tradition became a reaction to the dominance of the Sunni Turkish Seljuks in the ʿAbbasid Empire

stylite (Greek)   monastic holy men who spent their lives confined to the top of a column

Sublime Porte (French)   see *Porte*

Sufi (Arabic)   Islamic mystic – Sufis sought to establish, through piety and self-denial, personal contact with the Creator – emphasis on *gnosis* or personal knowledge rather than legal interpretation of the Koran and hadith (*EI2* 'Tasawwuf')

sultan (Arabic)   a term with various meanings but which implies that a person is appointed by a higher authority to hold temporal power – by Ayyubid times it was fairly loosely used and could be held by several princes simultaneously as a personal title

sultana (Arabic)   woman holding high office

Sunna **(hence 'Sunni')** (Arabic)   generally approved standard or practice introduced by the Prophet (*EI2*)

suq **(pl *aswaq*)** (Arabic)   market (see also *suwayqa*)

suwayqa (Arabic)   small local market for daily needs (diminutive of *suq*)

Tanzimat (Turkish)   literally 'reorganisation' – administrative reforms introduced by the Ottoman authorities between 1839 and 1876 to regularise and centralise the workings of the imperial administration

tekkiye (Turkish)   Sufi monastery

tell (Arabic)   hill or mound built up by prolonged human occupation

turba (Arabic)   mausoleum, tomb chamber, usually domed

Turkic (Turkish)   language family of Turkish-speaking people

Turkoman, Turkmen (Turkish)   Turkic tribes distributed over much of the Near and Middle East and Central Asia from medieval to modern times' ('Türkmen' in *EI2*)

Turks   people of Central Asian origin who moved into Anatolia and parts of Syria and Iraq from the ninth century; (modern) Turkish-speaking inhabitants of the Ottoman Empire and its successor

umma (Arabic)   community of believers (in Islam)

vali (Arabic/Turkish)   'governor' – responsible for civil administration

vilaya **(pl *vilayat*)** (Turkish)   governorate (Mamluk, Ottoman)

vizier or *vezir* (Turkish)   minister, high official – see also *wazir* or *wali*

voussoir (French)   stone forming segment of an arch

waqf **(*wakf*, pl *awqaf*)** (Arabic)   endowment tying income from a business enterprise to support a religious, charitable or educational institution

Wahhabis (Arabic)   Islamic fundamentalist sect in Arabia

wali (Arabic/Turkish)   see *vali*

wazir (Arabic/Turkish)   Ottoman rank usually corresponding to the status of a governor

wilaya (Arabic/Turkish)   see *vilaya*

yerliyye (Turkish)   Ottoman local forces, often hired from among descendants of janissaries (Turkish *yerlu* = 'local')

zakat (Arabic)   Islamic tax, a levy of capital to provide alms; major source of revenue

zawiya **(pl *Zawaya*)** (Arabic/Turkish)   Sufi hospice – informal school for Islamic studies, usually named after the sheikh whose followers gathered there

zuqaq (Arabic)   lane

BIBLIOGRAPHY

Note: Arabic article *al-* or *el-* is ignored for the purposes of establishing alphabetical order; *ibn* is considered part of the name

– 1986. *Bulletin d'études orientales – Études sur la Ville d'Alep*. Damascus.
– 1999. *Annales archéologiques arabes syriennes – Alep et la route du Soie*. Vol. 43. Damascus.
Abdel Nour, Antoine. 1982. *Introduction à l'histoire urbaine de la Syrie Ottomane (XVI–XVIIIᵉ siècle)*. Beirut.
al-'Adim, Ibn. 1956. *L'Histoire d'Alep d'Ibn al 'Adim* (ed. Sami Dahan). Damascus.
Aigen, Wolfgang. 1980. *Sieben Jahre in Aleppo (1656–1663) – Ein Abschnitt aus den 'Reiße-Beschreibungen' des Wolffgang Aigen* (ed. Andreas Tietze). Vienna.
Allen, Terry. 1983. 'Some Pre-Mamluk Portions of the Courtyard Facades of the Great Mosque of Aleppo', *Bulletin d'études orientales* 35: 7–12, plates I–IV.
——. 1986. *A Classical Revival in Islamic Architecture*. Wiesbaden.
Altounyan, Taqui. 1969. *In Aleppo Once*. London.
Ambrose, Gwilym. 1931. 'English Traders at Aleppo (1658–1756)', *The Economic History Review* 3 (2): 246–67.
Amitai-Preiss, Reuven. 1995. *Mongols and Mamluks – The Mamluk-Ilkhanid War 1260–1281*. Cambridge.
anon. 1976. *Lives of the Later Caesars (the Augustan History)*. London.
Antonius, George. 1938. *The Arab Awakening: The Story of the Arab National Movement* (republished as ebook 2015).
Appian. 1912. *Roman History II, The Syrian Wars* (trans. Horace White), Loeb Classical Texts. Cambridge, MA.
Arabshah, Ahmad Ibn Muhammad. 1936; orig. 1435. *Tamerlane or Timur the Great – Aja'ib al-Maqdur fi Nawa'ib al-Taymur (The Wonders of Destiny of the Ravages of Timur)* (trans. John Herne Sanders). London.
Arbel, Benjamin. 2004. 'The Last Decade of Venice's Trade with the Mamluks – Importations into Egypt and Syria', *Mamluk Studies Review* VIII (2): 37–86.
Aro, Sanna. 2010. 'Luwians in Aleppo?' in *ipamati kistamati pari tumatimis, Luwian and Hittite Studies Presented to J. David Hawkins on the Occasion of his 70th birthday*, ed. Itamar Singer, 1–9. Tel Aviv.
——. 2016. 'Dem Krieg trotzem—Die alte und aktuelle Situation der al-Qiqan Moschee in Aleppo und der Inschrift des Talmi- Šarruma an ihrer Wand' *Alter Orient* 14: 13–7.

Asbridge, Thomas S. 1997a. 'The Principality of Antioch and the Jabal as-Summaq', in *The First Crusade: Origins and Impact*, ed. Jonathan Phillips, 142–52. Manchester.
——. 1997b. 'The Significance and Causes of the Battle of the Field of Blood', *Journal of Medieval History* 23 (4): 301–16.
——. 2000. *The Creation of the Principality of Antioch, 1098–1130*. Woodbridge.
——. 2005. *The First Crusade – A New History*. London.
——. 2013. 'How the Crusades Could Have Been Won: King Baldwin II of Jerusalem's Campaigns Against Aleppo (1124–5) and Damascus (1129)', *Journal of Medieval Military History* 11: 73–93.
Asbridge, Thomas S. and Susan B. Edgington. 1999. *Walter the Chancellor's The Antiochene Wars: A Translation and Commentary* (Crusader Texts in Translation). Aldershot.
Ashtor, Eliyahu. 1983. *Levant Trade in the Later Middle Ages*. Princeton.
Astengo, Gregorio, 2016 'The Rediscovery of Palmyra and Its Dissemination in Philosophical Transactions' *Notes and Records (Royal Society)*: 1–22.
El-Azhari, Taef Kamal. 2005. 'The Role of Saljuqid Women in Medieval Syria', in *Egypt and Syria in the Fatimid, Ayyubid and Mamluk Eras IV*, ed. U. Vermeulen and J. van Steenbergen, 111–26. Louvain.
——. 2014. 'The Policy of Balak the Artukids against Muslims and Crusaders. A Turkmen Identity Dilemma in the Middle East 1090–1124', *International Journal of Humanities and Social Science* 4 (4): 286–93.
Baduel, P. R., ed. 1991. *Villes au Levant, Hommage à André Raymond*. Aix-en-Provence.
Baha' al-Din Ibn, see Ibn Shaddad (trans. Richards 2001).
al-Baladhuri. 1966; reprint of 1916 ed. *The Origins of the Islamic State* (trans. Philip K Hitti). Beirut (New York).
Balog, Paul. 1908. *The Coinage of the Ayyubids*. London.
Balty, Jean-Charles. 1977. 'Les grandes étapes de l'urbanisme d'Apamée-sur-l'Oronte', *Ktema* 3–16.
——. 1991. 'L'urbanisme de la Tétrapolis syrienne', in *Héllenisme au Proche-Orient (First International Meeting on History and Archaeology, Delphi 6–9 November 1986)*, ed. W. Lambrinoudakis, 203–29. Athens.
Barbié du Bocage, J. 1825. 'Notice sur la carte générale des paschaliks de Bagdad, Orfa et Hhaleb et sur le plan d'Hhaleb de M. Rousseau', in *Recueil de voyages et de mémoires publié par la Societé de Géographie*, vol. II, 194–244. Paris.
Barkan, Ömer Lutfi. 1957. 'Essai sur les données statistiques des registres de recensement dans l'empire Ottoman aux Xv^e et XVIe siècles', *Journal of Economic and Social History of the Orient* 1: 9–36.
Barker, Edward B. 1973; orig. 1876. *Syria and Egypt Under the Last Five Sultans of Turkey, Experiences During Fifty Years of Mr. Consul-General Barker, Chiefly from his Journals and Letters*. 2 vols. London.
Barr, James. 2011. *A Line in the Sand : Britain, France and the Struggle that Shaped the Middle East*. London.
Barton, Donald Richmond. 1955. *Once in Aleppo*. London.
Bates, Ülkü Ü. 1985. 'Two Ottoman Documents on Architects in Egypt', *Muqarnas* 3: 121–7.
Battuta, Ibn. 1956. *The Travels of Ibn Battuta A.D. 1325–1354*, vol. I (trans H. A. R. Gibb). London.
Beal, Richard H. 2013. 'Review of Hawkins *festschrift*, ed. Itamar Singer 2010', *Journal of the American Oriental Society* 133 (4): 747–50.

Behrens-Abouseif, Doris. 2007. *Cairo of the Mamluks – A History of the Architecture and Its Culture*. Cairo.

Bell, Gertrude Lowthian. 1911. *Amurath to Amurath*. London.

Bembo, Ambrosio and Anthony Welch, eds. 2007. *The Travels and Journals of Ambrosio Bembo* (trans. Clara Bargellini). Berkeley.

Beyazit, Deniz. 2004. 'Architectural Decoration of the Artuqids of Mardin During the 12th and 13th Centuries: Between Antique and Islamic Style', *Asiatische Studien Etudes Asiatiques* LVIII (4): 1013–30.

Bianca, Stefano. 1980. *The Conservation of the Old City of Aleppo*. Paris.

——. 2000. *Urban Form in the Arab World: Past and Present*. Zurich/London.

——. 2007. *Syria – Medieval Citadels Between East and West*. Turin.

Bianquis, Thierry. 1991. 'Pouvoirs arabes à Alep aux Xe et XIe siècles', *Revue du monde musulman et de la Méditerranée* 62: 49–59.

Biddulph, William. 1609. *The Travels of Certaine Englishmen into Africa, Asia, Troy, Bythinia, Thracia and to the Blacke Sea And into Syria, Cilicia, Pisidia, Mesopotamia, Damascus, Canaan, Galile, Samaria, Iudea, Palestina, Ierusalem, Iericho and to the Red Sea: and to sundry other places*. London.

Biddulph, William and Theophilus Lavender. 1609. *Travels of Certaine Englishmen Into Africa, Asia, Troy, Bythinia, Thracia and to the Blacke Sea: And Into Syria, Cilicia, Pisidia, Mesopotamia, Damascus, Canaan, Galile, Samaria, Iudea, Palestina, Jerusalem, Iericho and to the Red Sea: and to Sundry Other Places. Begunne in the Yeere of Iubile 1600. and by Some of Them Finished this Yeere 1608. The Others Not Yet Returned . . .* London.

Bikhazi, Ramzi Jibran. 1981. 'The Hamdanid Dynasty of Mesopotamia and North Syria 254–404/868–1014', PhD, University of Michigan.

Bloom, Jonathan M. and Sheila S. Blair. 2009. *Grove Encyclopedia of Islamic Art & Architecture*. 3 vols. New York.

Bodman, Herbert L. 1963. *Political Factions in Aleppo, 1760–1826*. Chapel Hill.

Boussac, Denoix, Thibaud Fournet and Bérangère Redon, eds. 2014. *Bain collectif en Orient*. Cairo.

Bowersock, Glen W. 1978. *Julian the Apostate*. Cambridge, MA.

Brett-James, Antony. 1962. 'The Levant Company's Factory in Aleppo', *History Today* 12 (11): 793–8.

Bryce, Trevor. 1998. *The Kingdom of the Hittites*. Oxford.

——. 2012. *The World of the Neo-Hittite Kingdoms, a Political and Military History*. Oxford.

Buckingham, James Silk. 1827. *Travels in Mesopotamia, including a journey from Aleppo, across the Euphrates to Orfah, (the Ur of the Chaldees,) through the plains of the Turcomans, to Diarbeker, in Asia Minor; from thence to Mardin, on the borders of the Great Desert and by the Tigris to Mousul and Bagdad; with researches on the ruins of Babylon, Nineveh, Arbela, Ctesiphon and Seleucia*. London.

Bulliet, Richard W. 1990. *The Camel and the Wheel*. Cambridge, MA.

Burns, Ross. 2005. *Damascus, a History*. London.

Burns, Thomas S. and John W. Eadie. 2001. *Urban Centers and Rural Contexts in Late Antiquity*. Chicago.

Butcher, Kevin. 2004. *Coinage in Roman Syria, Northern Syria, 64 BC–AD 253*. London.

——. 2013. 'Coins and Hoards (Chapter One)', in *Excavations at Zeugma conducted by Oxford Archaeology*, vol III, ed. W. Qylward, 1–92. Los Altos.

Butcher, Kevin and Matthew Ponting. 2009. 'The Silver Coinage of Roman Syria Under the Julio-Claudian Emperors', *Levant* 41 (1): 59–78.

Butler, Howard Crosby. 1912. *Syria – Publications of the Princeton University Archaeological Expedition to Syria (1904–5, 9) – Division II Ancient Architecture in Syria – Section B Northern Syria – Part 5 The Djebel Halakah.* Leiden.

Cahen, Claude. 1940. *La Syrie du Nord a l'époque des Croisades et la Principauté Franque d'Antioche* (Bibliothèque archéologique et historique). Paris.

———. 1955–7. 'La Chronique des Ayyoubides (Ibn al-Amid's *Akhbar al-Ayyubiyyun*)', *Bulletin d'études orientales* 15: 109–84.

———. 1969. 'The Turkish Invasion', in *The History of the Crusades vol 1 – The First Hundred Years*, ed. Kenneth M. Setton and Marshall W. Baldwin, 135–176. Madison.

Canard, Marius. 1953. *Histoire de la dynastie des H'amdanides de Jazira et de Syrie.* Paris.

Cantacuzino, Sherban. 1975. 'Aleppo', *The Architectural Review* 44: 241–50.

———. 1984. 'Aleppo: Bab al-Faraj – The Importance of Townscape in Reconstruction', *Mimar: Architecture in Development* 12: 24–31.

Capdetrey, Laurent. 2007. *Le pouvoir séleucide – territoire, administration, finances d'un royaume hellènistique, 312–129 avant J.-C, Histoire.* Rennes.

Carré, Barthélemy (Abbé). 1947. *The Travels of Abbé Carré, 1672–74* vol. I (trans. Lady Fawcett and ed. Sir Charles Fawcett with the assistance of Sir Richard Burn). London.

Carruthers, Douglas, ed. 1996. *The Desert Route to India – being the journal of four travellers by the Great Desert Route between Aleppo and Basra 1745–1751.* Delhi.

Çelebi, Evliyâ. 2011. *An Ottoman Traveller, Selections of the Book of Travels of Evliya Çelebi* (trans. Sooyong Kim and Robert Dankoff). London.

Chalabi, Rana. 1988. 'Al-Madrasa Al-Firdaus in Aleppo: A Chef-d'oeuvre of Ayyubid Architecture', MA these, American University in Cairo.

Chasseboeuf, Constantin-François (Comte de Volney). 1959. *Voyage en Egypte et en Syrie Pendant les Années 1783, 1784 & 1785.* Paris.

Chen, Bianca. 2009. 'Digging for Antiquities with Diplomats: Gisbert Cusper (1644–1716) and his Social Capital', *Republic of Letters* 1 (1): 1–16.

Chevalier, Nicole. 2002. *La recherche archéologique française au Moyen-Orient 1842–1947.* Paris.

Cholidis, Nadja and Lutz Martin, eds. 2010. *Tell Halaf V – Im Krieg zerstörte Denkmäler und ihre Restaurierung*, Vol. V. Berlin.

Cline, Eric H. 2014. *1177 BC, the Year Civilization Collapsed, Turning Points in Ancient History.* New Haven.

Cloarec, Françoise. 2003. *Le temps des Consuls – L'échelle d'Alep sous les Ottomans.* Paris.

Cobb, Paul Michael. 2014. *The Race for Paradise: An Islamic History of the Crusades.* Oxford.

Cohen, Getzel M. 2006. *The Hellenistic Settlements in Syria, the Red Sea Basin and North Africa.* Berkeley.

Corlu, M. Sencer *et al.* 2010. 'The Ottoman Palace School Enderun and the Man with Multiple Talents, Matrakçı Nasuh', *Journal of the Korean Society of Mathematical Education* 14 (1): 19–31.

Coulter, Charles Russell. 2013. *Encyclopedia of Ancient Deities.* London.

Crowfoot, J. W. 1937. *Churches at Bosra and Samaria-Sebaste.* London.

Dapper, Olfert. 1677. *Naukeurige beschryving van gantsch Syrie, en Palestyn of Heilige Lant.* Amsterdam.

d'Arvieux, Laurent. 1735. *Mémoires du chevalier d'Arvieux, envoyé extraordinaire du Roy à la Porte, Consul d'Alep, d'Alger, de Tripoli, et autres Echelles du Levant.* 6 vols. Paris.

Daviau, P. M., John W. Wevers and Michael Weigl, eds. 2000. *The World of the Aramaeans.* 3 vols. Sheffield.

David, Jean-Claude. 1975. 'Alep, dégradation et tentatives actuelles de réadaptation des structures urbaines traditionelles', *Bulletin d'études orientales* xxviii: 19–50.

——. 1990. 'L'espace des Chrétiens à Alep. Ségrégation et mixité, Stratégies communautaires (1750–1850)', *Revue du monde musulman et de la Méditerranée* 55–6: 150–70.

——. 1991. 'Domaines et limites de l'architecture d'empire dans une capitale provinciale', *Revue du monde musulman et de la Méditerranée* 62: 169–94.

——. 1993a. 'Architectures, Formes et Fonctions urbaines – Systèmes en évolution à Alep du XVIᵉ au XIXᵉ siècle', *Fondation Max van Berchem, Bulletin* 7: 1–4.

——. 1993b. 'La formation du tissu de la ville arabo-islamique, apport de l'étude de plans cadastraux d'Alep', *Environmental Design: Journal of the Islamic Environmental Design Research Centre* 1–2: 138–55.

——. 1994. 'Le patrimoine, architectures et espaces, pratiques et comportements – les souks et les khans d'Alep', *Revue du monde musulman et de la Méditerranée* 73–4: 189–205.

——. 1996a. 'Les territories des groupes à Alep à l'époque ottomane', *Revue du monde musulman et de la Méditerranée* 79: 225–54.

——. 1996b. 'Le consulat de France à Alep sous Louis XIV. Témoins architecturaux, descriptions par les consuls et les voyageurs', *Res Orientales* 8: 13–24.

——. 1998a. *La Suwayqat ʿAli à Alep.* Damascus.

——. 1998b. 'Une grande maison de la fin du XVIᵉ siècle à Alep', *Bulletin d'études orientales* 50: 61–96.

——. 2008. 'Aleppo: From the Ottoman Metropolis to the Syrian City', in *The City in the Islamic World*, ed. Salma K. Jayyusi, Renata Holod, Attilio Petruccioli and André Raymond, 329–56. Leiden.

David, Jean-Claude and Thierry Boissière. 2014a. 'La destruction du patrimoine culturel à Alep: banalité d'un fait de guerre?', *Confluences Méditerranée* 89 (2): 163–71.

——. 2014b. *Alep et ses territoires, fabrique et politique d'une ville 1868–2011.* Beirut.

David, Jean-Claude and Bruno Chauffert-Yvart. 1982. *Le waqf d'Ipsir Pasha à Alep (1063/1653): Étude d'urbanisme historique.* Damascus.

David, Jean-Claude and Gérard Degeorge. 2002. *Alep.* Paris.

——. 2009. *Palais et demeures d'Orient XVIᵉ–XIXᵉ siècles.* Paris.

David, Jean-Claude and Jean Grandin. 1994. 'L'habitat permanent des grands commerçants dans les khans d'Alep à l'époque ottomane', in *Les villes dans l'empire ottoman: activités et sociétés*, vol. 2, ed. Daniel Panzac, 84–124. Paris.

David, Jean-Claude and Dominique Hubert. 1982. 'Le dépérissement du hammam dans la ville : le cas d'Alep', *Cahiers de recherche architecturale* 10/11: 62–73.

Davis, Ralph. 1967. *Aleppo and Devonshire Square – English Traders in the Levant in the Eighteenth Century.* London.

Dawn, Ernest. 1962. 'The Rise of Arabism in Syria', *Middle East Journal* 16 (2): 145–68.

de Courtois, Sébastien. 2004. *The Forgotten Genocide: Eastern Christians, The Last Arameans.* Piscataway, NJ.

Del Fabbro, Roswitha. 2012. 'The Roads from and to Aleppo: Some Historical-geographical Considerations in Light of New Archaeological Data', in *Leggo!. Studies Presented to*

Frederick Mario Fales on the Occasion of His 65th Birthday, ed. Giovanni B. Lanfranci, Daniele Morandi Bonacossi, Cinzia Pappi and Simonetta Ponchia, 201–22. Wiesbaden.

della Valle, Pietro. 1650. *Viaggi Pietro Della Valle, Descritti da lui medesimo in Lettere familiari All'erudito suo Amico Mario Schipano*. Rome.

Deringil, Selim. 1998. *The Well-Protected Domains: Ideology and the Legitimation of Power in the Ottoman Empire, 1876–1909*. London.

de Wailly, Henri. 2006. *Syrie 1941: la guerre occultée – vichystes contre gaullistes*. Paris.

Dinning, Hector William. 1920. *Nile to Aleppo – With the Light-Horse in the Middle East*. London.

Dodgeon, Michael H. and Samuel N. C. Lieu. 1991. *The Roman Eastern Frontier & the Persian Wars (AD 226–363) – A Documentary History*. London.

Donner, Fred McGraw. 1981. *The Early Islamic Conquests*. Princeton.

Drummond, Alexander. 1754. *Travels Through the Different Parts of Germany, Italy, Greece and Parts of Asia*. London.

Eames, Andrew. 2004. *The 8:55 to Baghdad*. London.

Ebied, Rifaat Y. and M. J. L. Young. 1974. 'A List of Ottoman Governors of Aleppo A. H. 1002–1168', *Annali* 34 (new series XXIV): 103–8.

Ecochard, Michel. 1950. 'Notes sur un edifice chrétien d'Alep', *Syria*: 270–83.

Eddé, Anne-Marie. 1987–88, 'La prise d'Alep par les Mongols en 658/1260' *Quarderni di Studi Arabi* 5–6: 226–40.

——. 1999. *La principauté ayyoubide d'Alep (579/1183–658/1260)*. Stuttgart.

——. 2000. 'Alep', in *Grandes villes méditerranéennes du monde mussulman médiéval*, ed. Jean-Claude Garcin, 157–175. Paris.

——. 2006. 'Chrétiens d'Alep et de Syrie du nord à l'époque des Croisades: Crises et mutations', in *Mémorial Monseigneur Joseph Nasrallah*, ed. Pierre Canivet and Jean-Paul Rey-Coquais, 153–80. Damascus.

——. 2011. *Saladin* (trans. Jane Marie Todd). Cambridge, MA.

Eddé, Anne-Marie and Françoise Micheau. 1987. 'Sous les murailles d'Alep: assaillants et défenseurs de 351/962 à 658/1260', in *Actes des congrès de la Société des historiens médiévistes de l'enseignement supérieur public. 18e congrès, Montpellier, 1987*, 63–72.

——. 1987. 'Sous les murailles d'Alep: assaillants et défenseurs de 351/962 à 658/1260', *Actes des congrès de la Société des historiens médiévistes*, Montpelier 1987: 63–72.

Ehrenkreutz, Andrew S. 1972. *Saladin*. Albany.

*EI*2 and *EI*3 indicate the second and third editions of the *Encyclopaedia of Islam*. Leiden.

Eich, Thomas. 2001. 'Quest for a Phantom, Investigating Abu'l-Huda al-Sayyadi', *Newsletter of the International Institute for the Study of Islam in the Modern World (ISIM, Leiden)* 7 (1): 24.

Eldem, Edhem, Daniel Goffman and Bruce Masters. 1999. *The Ottoman City Between East and West – Aleppo, Izmir and Istanbul*. Cambridge.

Elisséeff, Nikita. 1949–51. 'Les monuments de Nür al-Din', *Bulletin d'études orientales* 13: 5–43.

——. 1967. *Nur ad-Din – un Grand prince Musulman de Syrie au Temps des Croisades (511-569 H/1118-1174)*. 3 vols. Damascus.

Emrence, Cem. 2011. *Remapping the Ottoman Middle East: Modernity, Imperial Bureaucracy and the Islamic State*. London.

Fangi, Gabriele and Wissam Wahbeh. 2013. 'The Destroyed Minaret of the Umayyad Mosque of Aleppo: The Survey of the Original State', *European Scientific Journal* (Dec): 403–9.

Findley, Carter Vaughan. 2004. *The Turks in World History*. Oxford.

Fleet, Kate. 2010. 'The Rise of the Ottomans', in *The New Cambridge History of Islam Volume 2: The Western Islamic World, Eleventh to Eighteenth Centuries*, ed. Maribel Fierro, 313–31. Cambridge.

Foster, Charles. 2004. *Travellers in the Near East*. London.

Freely, John. 1998. *The Eastern Mediterranean Coast of Turkey*. Istanbul.

Frenkel, Miriam. 2010. 'Constructing the Sacred: Holy Shrines in Aleppo and its Environs', in *Egypt and Syria in the Fatimid, Ayyubid and Mamluk Eras VI*, ed. U. Vermeulen and K. D'Huister, 63–79. Louvain.

Friedman, Matti. 2012. *The Aleppo Codex*. Melbourne.

Friès, Franck. 1996. 'Les plans d'Alep et de Damas, un banc d'essai pour l'urbanisme des frères Danger (1931-37)', *Revue du monde musulman et de la Méditerranée (REMMM)* 73–4: 311–26.

Fromkin, David. 1989. *A Peace to End All Peace: Creating the Modern Middle East – 1914–1922*. London.

Fuglestad-Aumeunier, Viviane, ed. 1991. *Alep et la Syrie du Nord, Revue de la Monde Musulman et de la Méditerranée*. Aix-en-Provence.

Gabriel, Albert. 1928. 'Les étapes d'une campagne des deux 'Irak' d'aprè un manuscrit turque du XVIe siècle', *Syria* IX (4): 328–49.

Gabrieli, Francesco. 1977. *Chroniques arabes des Croisades*. Paris.

Gangler, Annette. 1993. *Ein traditionelles Wohnviertel im Nordosten der Altstadt von Aleppo in Nordsyrien*. Tübingen.

Gangler, Annette and Heinz Gaube. 1992. 'A Quarter of Aleppo in the 19th and 20th Centuries. Some Socio-economical and Architectural Aspects', in *Alep et la Syrie du Nord*, ed. Viviane Fuglestad-Aumeunier, 159–68. Aix-en-Provence.

Garcin, Jean-Claude, ed. 2000. *Grandes villes méditerranéennes du monde musulman médiéval*. Paris.

Garrood, William. 2008. 'The Byzantine Conquest of Cilicia and the Hamdanids of Aleppo, 959–965', *Anatolian Studies* 58: 127–40.

Gaube, Heinz. 2000. 'Aleppo zwischen Alexander dem Grossen und der Arabischen Erobung', in *Damaskus – Aleppo: 5000 Jahre Stadtentwicklung in Syrien*, ed. Mamoun Fansa, 101–7. Mainz.

——. 2007. 'A History of the City of Aleppo', in *Syria – Medieval Citadels between East and West*, ed. Stefano Bianca, 73–102. Turin.

Gaube, Heinz and Mamoun Fansa, eds. 2000. *Damaskus – Aleppo: 5000 Jahre Stadtentwicklung in Syrien*. Mainz am Rhein.

Gaube, Heinz and Eugen Wirth, eds. 1984. *Aleppo – Historische und geographische Beiträge zur baulichen Gestaltung, zur sozialen Organisation und zur wirtschlichen Dynamik einer vorderasiatischen Fernhandelsmetropole*. 2 vols. Wiesbaden.

Gelin, Mathilde. 2002. *L'archéologie en Syrie et au Liban à l'époque du Mandat (1919–1946)*. Paris.

Gelvin, James L. 1998. *Divided Loyalties: Nationalism and Mass Politics in Syria at the Close of the Empire*. Berkeley.

Gharipour, Mohammad, ed. 2012. *The Bazaar in the Islamic City – Design, Culture and History*. Cairo.

Gibb, Hamilton A. R. 1969a. 'The Caliphate and the Arab States', in *A History of the Crusades – Volume 1, The First Hundred Years*, ed. Marshall W. Baldwin, 81–98. Madison.

——. 1969b. 'Zengi and the Fall of Edessa', in *A History of the Crusades – Volume 1, The First Hundred Years*, ed. Marshall W. Baldwin, 449–62. Madison.

——. 1980. *The Damascus Chronicle of the Crusades, Extracted and Translated from the Chronicle of Ibn al-Qalanisi*. London.

Gonnella, Julia. 1995. *Islamische Heiligenverehrung im urbanen Kontext am Beispiel von Aleppo (Syrien), Islamkundliche Untersuchungen*. Berlin.

——. 1996a. *Das Aleppo-Zimmer*. Mainz am Rhein.

——. 1996b. *Ein christlich-orientalisches Wohnhaus des 17. Jahrhunderts aus Aleppo (Syrien)*. Berlin.

——. 1999. 'The Citadel of Aleppo', *Proceedings of the 11th International Congress of Turkish Art (Utrecht 23–28 Aug 1999)* 22: 1–24.

——. 2001a. 'The Citadel of Aleppo', *Electronic Journal of Oriental* Studies IV: 1–24.

——. 2001b. 'La citadelle d'Alep: les périodes islamiques', *Archéologie islamique* 11: 188–94.

——. 2002. 'As-Sayyid Abu'l-Huda al-Sayyadi in Aleppo', in *The Empire in the City – Arab Provincial Capitals in the Late Ottoman Empire*, ed. Jens Hanssen, Thomas Philipp and Stefan Weber, 297–310. Würzburg (Beirut).

——. 2006. 'The Citadel of Aleppo: Recent Studies', in *Muslim Military Architecture in Greater Syria – From the Coming of Islam to the Ottoman Period*, ed. Hugh Kennedy, 165–75. Leiden.

——. 2008. *The Citadel of Aleppo: Description, History, Site Plan and Visitor Tour* (Aga Khan Trust for Culture and the Syrian Directorate, General of Antiquities and Museums). Aleppo.

——. 2010. 'Columns and Hieroglyphs: Magic Spolia in Medieval Islamic Architecture of Northern Syria', *Muqarnas* 27: 103–20.

Gonnella, Julia and Jens Kröger. 2008. *Angels, Peonies and Fabulous Creatures: The Aleppo Room in Berlin, International Symposium of the Museum für Islamische Kunst – Staatliche Museen zu Berlin 12–14 April 2002*. Münster.

Gonnella, Julia, Walid Khayyata and Kay Kohlmeyer. 2005. *Die Zitadelle von Aleppo und der Tempel des Wettergottes. Neue Forschungen und Entdeckungen*. Münster.

Goodwin, Godfrey. 1987. 'Sinan and City Planning', *Environmental Design: Journal of the Islamic Environmental Design Research Centre* (special issue on Mimar Sinan: The Urban Vision): 10–19.

Goyau, Georges. 1942. *Un précurseur: François Picquet – Consul de Louis XIV en Alep et Évêque de Babylone* (Institut français de Damas, Bibliothèque orientale). Paris.

Grabar, Oleg, Richard Ettinghausen, and Marilyn Jenkins-Madina. 2001. *The Art and Architecture of Islam 650–1250*. New Haven.

——. 1990. *The Great Mosque of Isfahan*. London.

Grainger, John D. 1990. *The Cities of Seleukid Syria*. Oxford.

——. 2013. *The Battle for Syria*. Woodbridge.

Graves, William 1999 (May–June). 'Preserving Old Aleppo', *Aramco World Magazine*, 39–43.

Green, Alberto Ravinell Whitney. 2003. *The Storm God in the Ancient Near East, Biblical and Judaic Studies*. Winona Lake.

Grousset, René. 1991. *Histoire des Croisades, vol. 1 – l'anarchie musulmane et la monarchie franque*. Paris.

Guest, John S. and Peter Gwynvay Hopkins. 1996. *The Ancient Road – From Aleppo to Baghdad in the Days of the Ottoman Empire*. London.

Guidetti, Mattia. 2014. 'Churches Attracting Mosques, Religious Architecture in Early Islamic Syria', in *Sacred Precincts: Non-Muslim Religious Architecture in the Islamic World*, ed. Mohammad Gharipour, 11–27. Leiden.

Guyer, Samuel. 1914. 'La Madrasa Hallawiya à Alep', *Bulletin de l'Institut français d'archéologie orientale*. XI: 217–231 plus 7 plates.

Gyselen, Rika, ed. 1996. *Sites et monuments disparus d'après les témoignages de voyageurs*. Vol. VIII, *Res Orientales*.

Hachicho, Mohamad Ali. 1964. 'English Travel Books about the Arab near East in the Eighteenth Century', *Die Welt des Islams (new series)* 9 (1/4): 1–206.

Hadjar, Abdallah. 2000. *Historical Monuments of Aleppo*. Aleppo.

———. 2006. *Historical Monuments of Aleppo*. 2nd edn. Aleppo.

Halifax, William. 1695a. 'A Relation of a Voyage from Aleppo to to Palmyra in Syria; Sent by the Reverend Mr. William Halifax to Dr. Edw. Bernard (Late) Savilian Professor of Astronomy in Oxford and by Him Communicated to Dr. Thomas Smith. Reg. Soc. S.', *Philosophical Transactions of the Royal Society* 19 (217): 83–110.

———. 1695b. 'An Extract of the Journals of Two Several Voyages of the English Merchants of the Factory of Aleppo, to Tadmor, Anciently Call'd Palmyra', *Philosophical Transactions of the Royal Society* 19 (218): 129–60.

Hammad, Manar. 2003. *Madrasat al-Firdaws*. Paris.

———. 2004. *Architecture Ayyoubides, le style austère à Alep*. Paris.

al-Harawi, 'Ali Ibn Abi Bakr (d.1215). 2004. *Lonely Wayfarer's Guide to Pilgrimage (Kitab al-Ishārāt ilā Ma'rifat al-Ziyārat)* (trans. Josef Meri). Princeton.

Hathaway, Jane. 2008. *The Arab Lands Under Ottoman Rule, 1516–1800*. Harlow.

Hawkins, J. David. 2009. 'Cilicia, the Amuq and Aleppo – New Light in a Dark Age', *Near Eastern Archaeology* 72 (4): 164–74.

———. 2011. 'The Inscriptions of the Aleppo Temple', *Anatolian Studies* 61: 35–54.

Heidemann, Stefan. 1994. *Das Aleppiner Kalifat (A.D. 1261). Vom Ende des Kalifates in Bagdad über Aleppo zu den Restaurationen in Kairo*. Vol. 6, *Islamic History and Civilization, Studies and Texts*. Leiden.

———. 2005. 'Numayrid ar-Raqqa. Archaeological and Historical Evidence for a 'Dimorphic State' in the Bedouin Dominated Fringes of the Fatimid Empire', in *Egypt and Syria in the Fatimid, Ayyubid and Mamluk Eras*, ed. U. Vermeulen and J. Van Steenbergen. Leiden.

Herzfeld, Ernst. 1943. 'Damascus: Studies in Architecture – II – The Cruciform Plan; Syrian Architecture, Period of Nur al-Din', *Ars Islamica* X: 16–70.

———. 1954–55. *Inscriptions et Monuments d'Alep – (Matériaux pour un Corpus Inscriptionum Arabicarum)*. 2 vols, plus volume of plates. Cairo.

Heyberger, Bernard. 1988. 'Les chrétiens d'Alep (Syrie) à travers les récits des conversions des missionnaires Carmes Déchaux (1657–1681)', *Mélanges de l'École française de Rome, Moyen-Age, Temps modernes* 100 (1): 461–99.

———. 2013. *Hindiyya, Mystic and Criminal, 1720–1798 – A Political and Religious Crisis in Lebanon*. Cambridge.

Hillenbrand, Carole. 1979. 'The History of the Jazira 1100–1150: The Contribution of Ibn al-Azraq al-Fariqi', PhD thesis, Edinburgh.

———. 1981. 'The Career of Najm al-Din Il-Ghazi', *Der Islam* 58 (2): 250–92.

———. 1985. 'The History of the Jazira, 1100–1250: A Short Introduction', in *The Art of Syria and the Jazira 1100–1250*, ed. Julian Raby, 9–20. Oxford.

——. 1997. 'The First Crusade: The Muslim Perspective', in *The First Crusade: Origins and Impact*, ed. Jonathan Phillips, 130–41. Manchester.

——. 1999. *The Crusades – Islamic Perspectives*. Edinburgh.

——. 2005. 'The Evolution of the Saladin Legend in the West', *Mélanges de l'Université Saint-Joseph*. 58: 1–13.

——. 2011. 'The Shīʿīs of Aleppo in the Zengid Period: Some Unexploited Textual and Epigraphic Evidence', in *Differenz und Dynamik im Islam – Festschrift für Heinz Halm zum 70. Geburtstag*, ed. Hinrich Biesterfeldt and Verena Klemm, 163–80. Würzburg.

Hillenbrand, Robert. 1985. 'Eastern Islamic Influences in Syria: Raqqa and Qalʿat Jaʿbar in the Later 12th Century,' in *The Art of Syria and the Jazira 1100–1250*, ed. Julian Raby, 21–48. Oxford.

——. 2001a. 'The Classical Heritage in Islamic Art: The Case of Medieval Architecture', in *Studies in Medieval Islamic Architecture I*, 225–242. London.

——. 2001b. *Hillenbrand, Studies in Medieval Islamic Architecture*. 2vols. London.

Holt, Peter Malcolm. 1957. 'The Study of Arabic Historians in Seventeenth Century England: The Background and the Work of Edward Pococke', *Bulletin of the School of Oriental and African Studies* 19 (3): 444–55.

Hoover, Oliver D. 2007. 'A Revised Chronology for the Late Seleucids at Antioch 121/0–64 BC', *Historia* 56 (3): 280–301.

Howard, Deborah. 2000. *Venice and the East – The Impact of the Islamic World on Venetian Architecture 1100–1500*. New Haven, CN.

Howard-Johnston, James D. 2010. *Witnesses to a World Crisis – Historians and Histories of the Middle East in the Seventh Century*. Oxford.

Hreitani, Mahmoud and Jean-Claude David. 1984. 'Souqs traditionelles et centre moderne: Espaces et pratiques à Alep (1930–1980)', *Bulletin d'Études orientales* 36: 1–78.

Humphreys, R. Stephen. 1977. *From Saladin to the Mongols: The Ayyubids of Damascus, 1193–1260*. Albany, NY.

——. 1994. 'Women as Patrons of Architecture in Ayyubid Damascus', *Muqarnas* 11: 35–54.

——. 1999. 'The Origins of the Ayyubid Confederation', *International Journal of Kurdish Studies* 13 (1): 63–103.

Ibn ach-Chihna. 1933. *Les Perles Choisies' d'Ibn ach-Chihna* (trans. Jean Sauvaget) (Matériaux pour servir à l'histoire de la ville d'Alep I). Damascus.

Ibn al-ʿAdim, Kamal al-Din. 1900. *Histoire d'Alep (Bughyat al-ṭalab fī tārīkh Ḥalab)* (trans E. Blochet). Paris.

Ibn al-Athir, ʿIzz al-Din Abu al-Hasan ʿAli. 2002. *Ibn Al ʿAthir, the Annals of the Saljuq Turks* (trans D. S. Richards). London.

——. 2008. *The Chronicle of Ibn al-Athir for the Crusading Periods from al-Kamil fi'l Ta'rikh* (trans D. S. Richards) (Crusader Texts in Translation). 3 vols. Abingdon.

Ibn Battuta 1956. *The Travels of Ibn Battuta A. D. 1325–1354, vol. I* (trans H. A. R. Gibb). London.

Ibn Jubayr. 2003. *The Travels of Ibn Jubayr* (trans. Broadhurst). London.

Ibn Khallikan. 1843. *Biographical Dictionary (1211–1282)* (trans. Mac Guckin de Slane). London.

Ibn al-Qalanisi see Gibb, Hamilton A. R. 1980.

Ibn Saddâd, Izz al-Dîn Muhammad Ibn ʿAli. 1984. *Description de la Syrie du nord. (Traduction annotée de Al-Aʿlaq Al-Hatira fi dikr Umarâ Al-Sâm wa l-Gazira – section II, North Syria excluding Aleppo)* (trans. Anne-Marie Eddé). Damascus.

Ibn Shaddad, Baha' al-Din. 2001. *The Rare and Excellent History of Saladin or al-Nawadir al-Sultaniyya wa'l-Mahasin al-Yusufiyya* (trans. D. S. Richards) (Crusader Texts in Translation). Aldershot.

Irwin, Robert. 1986. *The Middle East in the Middle Ages: The Early Mamluk Sultanate 1250–1382*, Carbondale.

Issa, Abed. 2010. *A Guide to the National Museum of Aleppo*. Damascus.

Issawi, Charles. 1988. *The Fertile Crescent, 1800–1914: A Documentary Economic History*. Oxford.

Jackson, Peter, 2017 *The Mongols and the Islamic World—From Conquest to Conversion*. New Haven.

Jayyusi, Salma K., Renata Holod, Attilio Petruccioli and André Raymond, eds. 2008. *The City in the Islamic World*. Leiden.

Josephus. 1927. *The Jewish War* – Books III–IV (trans. H. St J. Thackeray) (Loeb Classical Library). Cambridge, MA.

Julian the Apostate. 1913. *Letters*, vol. III (trans W. C Wright) (Loeb Classical Texts). Boston.

Kaegi, Walter E. 1992. *Byzantium and the Early Islamic Conquests*. Cambridge.

Kafescioğlu, Çiğdem. 1999. '"In the Image of Rum": Ottoman Architectural Patronage in Sixteenth Century Aleppo and Damascus', *Muqarnas* XVI: 70–96.

Kahn, Dan'el. 2007. 'The Kingdom of Arpad (Bit Agusi) and "All Aram": International Relations in Northern Syria in the Ninth and Eighth Centuries BCE', *Ancient Near Eastern Studies (ANES)* 44: 66–89.

Kaiser, Hilmar. 2010. 'Regional Resistance to Central Government Policies: Ahmed Djemal Pasha, the Governors of Aleppo and Armenian Deportees in the Spring and Summer of 1915', *Journal of Genocide Research* 12 (3/4): 173–218.

Kayali, Hasan. 1997. *Arabs and Young Turks: Ottomanism, Arabism and Islamism in the Ottoman Empire, 1908–1918*. Berkeley.

Kemal al-Din. 1884. *Chronicle of Aleppo*, vol. III (Recueil des historiens des Croisées, historiens orientaux). Paris.

Kennedy, Hugh. 1985. 'From Polis to Madina: Urban Change in Late Antique and Early Islamic Syria', *Past and Present* 106: 3–27.

——. 2004. *The Court of the Caliphs – The Rise and Fall of Islam's Greatest Dynasty*. London.

——. 2007. *The Great Arab Conquests – How the Spread of Islam Changed the World We Live in*. London.

Khairallah, Shereen. 1991. *Railways in the Middle East 1856–1948*. Beirut.

Khayyata, Wahid. nd. *National Museum of Aleppo, Museum Guide*. Aleppo.

——. 1977a. *Guide to the Old Oriental Department, National Museum of Aleppo*. Aleppo.

——. 1977b. *Guide to the Museum of Aleppo – Ancient Oriental Department*. Aleppo.

Khayyata, Wahid and Kay Kohlmeyer. 1998. 'Die Zitadelle von Aleppo – Vorläufiger Bericht über die Untersuchungen 1996 unds 1997', *Damaszener Mitteilungen* 10: 69–95.

Khoury, Philip S. 1987. *Syria and the French Mandate – The Politics of Arab Nationalism, 1920–45*. London.

Kidner, Frank L. 2001. 'Christianizing the Syrian Countryside: An Archaeological and Architectural Approach', in *Urban Centers and Rural Contexts in Late Antiquity*, ed. Thomas S. Burns and John W. Eadle. Chicago.

Knost, Stefan. 2009. *Die organisation des religiösen Raums in Aleppo – die Rolle der islamischen religiösen Stiftungen (auqāf) in der Gesellschaft einer Provinzhauptstadt des Osmanischen Reiches an der Wende zum 19. Jahrhundert* (Beirute Texte und Studien). Beirut.

Köhler, Michael A. 2013. *Alliances and Treaties between Frankish and Muslim Rulers in the Middle East, Cross-Cultural Diplomacy in the Period of the Crusades* (trans. Peter M. Holt). Leiden.

Kohlmeyer, Kay. 2000. *Der Tempel des Wettergottes von Aleppo*. Münster.

——. 2009. 'The Temple of the Storm God in Aleppo During the Late Bronze and Early Iron Ages', *Near Eastern Archaeology* 72 (4): 190–202.

The Koran 1983 (trans. N. J. Dawood). Harmondsworth.

Krey, August C., ed. 2012. *The First Crusade, The Accounts of Eye-Witnesses and Participants*, Fontes Mediaevalium. Merchantville NJ.

Lange, Christian and Songül Mecit, eds. 2011. *Seljuqs – Politics, Society and Culture*. Edinburgh.

Laor-Sirak, S. 2010. 'The Contribution of Armenian Architecture to the Origins of the Stone Muqarnas in Syria', in *Egypt and Syria in the Fatimid, Ayyubid and Mamluk Eras VI*, ed. U. Vermeulen and K. D'Huister, 27–44. Louvain.

Lauffray, Jean. 1953. 'Une madrasa ayyoubide de la Syrie du Nord: La Soultaniya d'Alep, étude architecturale', *Annales archéologiques arabes syriennes (AAAS)* 3: 49–68.

Lawler, Andrew. 2009. 'Temple of the Storm God', *Archaeology* 62 (2): 20–5.

Lawson, Fred H. 2004. 'The Northern Syrian Revolts of 1919–1921 and the Sharifian Regime: Congruence or Conflict of Interests?', in *From the Syrian Land to the States of Syria and Lebanon*, ed. Thomas Philipp and Christoph Schumann, 258–74. Würzburg.

Lefèvre, Raphaël. 2013. *Ashes of Hama, The Muslim Brotherhood in Syria*. Oxford.

le Strange, Guy. 1890. *Palestine Under the Moslems – A Description of Syria and the Holy Land from A.D. 650 to 1500*. London.

le Tourneau, Roger. 1952. *Damas de 1075 à 1134 (Traduction annotée d'un fragment d'une histoire d'Ibn Al-Qalanisi)*. Damascus.

Lightfoot, J. L. 2003. *Lucian, On the Syrian Goddess* (trans. and commentary). Oxford.

Lilie, Ralph-Johannes. 1993. *Byzantium & the Crusader States*. Oxford.

Lindner, Rudi Paul. 2007. *Explorations in Ottoman Prehistory*. Chicago.

Littmann, Enno. 1934. *Syria – Publications of the Princeton University Archaeological Expedition to Syria (1904–5, 9) – Division IV, Semitic Inscriptions in Syria, B – Syriac*. Leiden.

Llewelyn, Michael Gareth. 1945. *The Aleppo Merchant*. London.

Longrigg, Stephen Hemsley. 1968. *Syria and Lebanon Under French Mandate*. Beirut.

Lucas, Paul. 1704. *Voyage du Sieur Paul Lucas au Levant*. 2 vols. Paris.

Lucian, see Lightfoot, J. L.

Maalouf, Amin. 1984. *The Crusades Through Arab Eyes*. London.

Ma'oz, Moshe. 1966. 'Syrian Urban Politics in the Tanzimat Period between 1840 and 1861', *Bulletin of the School of Oriental and African Studies* 29 (2): 277–301.

Maclean, Gerald M. 2004. 'Strolling in Syria with William Biddulph', *Criticism* 46 (3): 415–39.

——. 2006. *The Rise of Oriental Travel: English Visitors to the Ottoman Empire, 1580–1720*. London.

Mango, Andrew. 1999. *Ataturk*. London.

Marchetti, Nicolo. 2014. *Karkemish, An Ancient Capital on the Euphrates* (OrientLab, Researches on the Archaeology of the Ancient Near East). Bologna.

Marcotte, Roxanne D. 2001. 'Suhrawardī al-Maqtūl, the Martyr of Aleppo', *Al-Qantara* XXII (2): 395–419.

Marcus, Abraham. 1989. *The Middle East on the Eve of Modernity: Aleppo in the Eighteenth Century*. New York.

Marozzi, Justin. 2014. *Baghdad – City of Peace, City of Blood*. London.

Masters, Bruce. 1987. 'Trading Diasporas and 'Nations': The Genesis of National Identities in Ottoman Aleppo', *The International History Review* 9 (3): 345–67.

——. 1988. *The Origins of Western Economic Dominance in the Middle East – Mercantilism and the Islamic Economy in Aleppo, 1600–1750*. New York.

——. 1990. 'The 1850 Events in Aleppo: An Aftershock of Syria's Incorporation into the Capitalist World System', *International Journal of Middle East Studies* 22: 3–20.

——. 1991. 'Power and Society in Aleppo in the 18th and 19th Centuries', in *Alep et la Syrie du Nord*, ed. Viviane Fuglestad-Aumeunier, 151–8. Aix-en-Provence.

——. 2001. *Christians and Jews in the Ottoman Arab World: The Roots of Sectarianism*. Cambridge.

——. 2013. *The Arabs of the Ottoman Empire, 1516–1918: A Social and Cultural History*. New York.

Mathers, John. 1981. *The River Qoueiq, Northern Syria and its Catchment – Studies from the Tell Rifa'at Survey 1977–79*. 2 vols. Oxford.

Matthews, Henry. 2010. *Mosques of Istanbul, Including the Mosques of Bursa and Edirne*. Istanbul.

Matthiae, Paolo. 2013. 'La déesse nue et le dieu au panache, Aux origines de l'iconographie d'Ishtar d'Ebla', in *Ritual, Religion and Reason, Studies in the Ancient World in Honour of Paolo Xella*, ed. Oswald Loretz, Sergio Ribichini, Wilfred G. E. Watson and José A. Zamora, 61–76. Münster.

Matthiae, Paolo and Nicolo Marchetti, eds. 2013. *Ebla and Its Landscape*. Walnut Creek.

Maundrell, Alexander. 1703. *A Journey from Aleppo to Jerusalem at Easter, AD MDCXCVII (1697)*. Oxford.

McCants, William. 2015. *The ISIS Apocalypse – the History, Strategy and Doomsday Vision of the Islamic State*. New York.

McHugo, John. 2014. *Syria, From the Great War to Civil War*. London.

McMeekin, Sean. 2010. *The Berlin-Baghdad Express: The Ottoman Empire and Germany's Bid for World Power*. London.

——. 2015. *The Ottoman Endgame – War, Revolution and the Making of the Modern Middle East 1908–1923*. London.

Méouchy, Nadine. 2014. 'Les temps et les territoires de la révolte du Nord (1919–1921)', in *Alep et ses territoires – fabrique et politique d'une ville 1868–2011*, ed. Jean-Claude David and Thierry Boissière, 81–104. Beirut.

Meri, Joseph W. 2004. *The Cult of Saints among Muslims and Jews in Medieval Syria*. Oxford.

Meriwether, Margaret L. 1999. *The Kin Who Count – Family and Society in Ottoman Aleppo 1770–1840*. Austin.

Michael the Syrian. 1899. *Chronique de Michel le Syrien, Patriarche Jacobite d'Antioche*. (trans. Chabot). Paris.

Millar, Fergus. 1993. *The Roman Near East, 31 BC–AD 337*. Cambridge, MA.

Mills, Simon. 2011. 'The English Chaplains at Aleppo: Exploration and Scholarship between England and the Ottoman Empire, 1620–1760', *Bulletin of the Council for British Research in the Levant* 6 (1): 13–20.

Miquel, André. 1960. 'Les portes d'Alep chez al-Muqaddasi', *Arabica* 7 (1): 60–71.

Miroglu, Ebru Aras. 2005. 'The Transformation of Urban Space at the Conjunction of the Old and New Districts: The City of Aleppo', MSc thesis, Middle East Technical University.

Mola, Luca. 2000. *The Silk Industry of Renaissance Venice*. Baltimore.

Morgan, David. 1986. *The Mongols*. Oxford.

——. 1994. *An Ayyubid Notable and his World: Ibn Al-ʿAdīm and Aleppo as Portrayed in His Biographical Dictionary of People Associated with the City, Islamic History and Civilization: Studies and Texts*. Leiden.

El-Mudarris, Hussein I. and Olivier Salmon. 2009. *Le Consulat de France à Alep au XVIIe siècle: Journal de Louis Gédoyn, Vie de François Picquet, Mémoires de Laurent d'Arvieux*. Paris.

——. 2010. *Mémoire sur la Syrie ou promenades d'un ingénieur géographe à Alep (1831–1832)*. Aleppo.

Mulder, Stephennie. 2014. *The Shrines of the ʿAlids in Medieval Syria: Sunnis, Shiʾis and the Architecture of Coexistence, Edinburgh Studies in Islamic Art*. Edinburgh.

Munro, John M. 1982. 'The Russells of Aleppo', *Saudi Aramco World* 33/1: 28–32

Necipoğlu, Gülru. 2005. *The Age of Sinan: Architectural Culture in the Ottoman Empire*. London.

Neglia, Giulia Annalinda. 2003. 'Città del Mediterraneo: Aleppo, forme e tipi della città intra moenia', PhD, Politecnico di Bari.

——. 2006. 'Bab Qinnisrin in Aleppo: Structure of the Urban Fabric', *Fondation Max van Berchem Bulletin* 20 (Dec): 3–4.

——. 2008. 'Some Historiographical Notes on the Islamic City with Particular Reference to the Visual Representation of the Built City', in *The City in the Islamic World*, vol. 1, ed. Salma K. Jayyusi, 3–47. Leiden.

——. 2009. *Aleppo, Processi di formazione della città medievale islamica (Aleppo: Processes of Formation of the Medieval Islamic City)*, vol. 6: *Archinauti: Monografie no. 6*. Bari.

——. 2010. 'The Forma Urbis of Aleppo (Syria) during the Middle Ages', in *Studies in the Archaeology of the Medieval Mediterranean*, ed. James Schryver, 115–53. Leiden.

——. 2014. 'The Permanence of Roman Layouts in the Urban Fabric of Aleppo'. http://web.mit.edu/akpia/www/articleneglia.pdf (accessed 18 Aug 2013).

Niebuhr, Carsten. 1778. *Reisebeschreibung nach Arabien und andern umliegenden Ländern*, vol II. Copenhagen.

Niehr, Herbert, ed. 2014. *The Aramaeans in Ancient Syria, Handbook of Oriental Studies, Section 1 – Ancient Near East*. Leiden.

Nigro, Lorenzo. 1999. 'Yamkhad/Aleppo: Investigating the Second Millennium BC Capital of Northern Syria through Islamic, Byzantine and Classical Towns', in *Environmental Design: Trails to the East, Essays in Memory of Paolo Cuneo (Journal of the Islamic Environmental Design Centre)*, ed. Paolo Cuneo, 46–55. Rome.

Nour, Antoine Abdel. 1982. *Introduction à l'histoire urbaine de la Syrie ottomane (XVIe–XVIIIe siècle)*. Beirut.

Peacock, A. C. S. 2015. *The Great Seljuk Empire*. Edinburgh.

Petry, Carl F. 1994. *Protectors or Praetorians? The Last Mamluk Sultans and Egypt's Waning as a Great Power*. Albany, NY.

Philipp, Thomas. 2010. 'The Economic Impact of the Ottoman Conquest on Bilad al-Sham', in *Syria and Bilad al-Sham under Ottoman Rule: Essays in Honour of Abdul-Karim Rafeq*, ed. Peter Sluglett and Stefan Weber, 101–14. Leiden.

Ploix de Rotrou, George. 2007. *La citadelle d'Alep et ses alentours* (text reprinted from *Comptes-rendus de l'Academie des Inscriptions et Belles-Lettres (CRAI) 1930*). Paris.

Pococke, Richard. 1745. *A Description of the East and Some Other Countries. Vol. II Part 1: Observations on Palaestine or the Holy Land, Syria, Mesopotamia, Cyprus and Candia*. London.

Popper, William. 1954. *History of Egypt, 1382–1469 A.D.* (2 parts, trans. William Popper from Annals of Abu l-Maḥâsin ibn Taghrî Birdî) (University of California Publications in Semitic Philology). Berkeley.

Prentice, William Kelly. 1914. *Syria – Publications of the Princeton University Archaeo-logical Expedition to Syria (1904–5, 9) – Division III Greek and Latin Inscriptions in Syria – Section B – Northern Syria – Part 5 The Djebel Halakah*. Leiden.

Procopius. 1914. *History of the Wars*, Books 1–2 (Persian War) (Loeb Classical Library). Cambridge, MA.

——. 1971. *Buildings* – Book VII (Loeb Classical Library). Cambridge, MA.

Rabbat, Nasser. 1993. 'Mamluk Throne Halls: "Qubba" or "Iwan"?', *Ars Orientalis* 23: 201–18.

——. 1997–8. 'The Mosaics of the Qubba al-Zahiriyya in Damascus: A Classical Syrian Medium Acquires a Mamluk Signature', *Aram* 9 (19): 227–39.

——. 2010. *Mamluk History Through Architecture – Monuments, Culture and Politics in Medieval Egypt and Syria, Library of Middle East History*. London.

Rabbath, Gabriel. 1931. 'Les portes d'Alep', *Revue archeologique syrienne*:

——. 1934. 'Les mosquées d'Alep – 1. Mosquée Al-Touté', *Revue archéologique syrienne* 3 (4): 87–91.

——. 1935a. 'Les mosquées d'Alep – 1I. la Grande Mosquée ou Mosquée al-Amaouy', *Revue archéologique syrienne* 5 (1): 1–9.

——. 1935b. 'Le nom et les origines de la ville d'Alep', *Revue archéologique syrienne* IV (Jan–Mar): 16–22.

Raby, Julian. 2004. 'Nur Al-Din, the Qastal al-Shuaybiyya and the Classical Revival', *Muqarnas*. 21: 289–310.

Raymond, André. 1979. 'Les grand waqfs et l'organisation de l'espace urbain à Alepo et au Caire à l'époque ottomane (XVIe–XVIIe siècles)', *Bulletin d'études orientales* 31: 113–28.

——. 1984. 'The Population of Aleppo in the 16th and 17th Centuries', *International Journal of Middle East Studies* 16 (1): 447–60.

——. 1990. 'Le déplacement des tanneries à Alep, au Caire et à Tunis à l'époque otto-mane: un "indicateur" de croissance urbaine', *Revue du monde musulman et de la Méditerranée (REMMM)* 55–6: 34–43.

——. 1991. 'Alep à l'époque ottomane (XVIe–XIXe s.)', *Revue du monde musulman et de la Méditerranée (REMMM)* 62: 93–109.

——. 1993. 'Cartographie et histoire des villes arabes: Quelques remarques generales', *Environmental Design: Journal of the Islamic Environmental Design Research Centre* 1–2: 22–31.

——. 1998. *La Ville Arabe – Alep, à l'époque ottomane (XVIe–XVIIIe siècles)*. Damascus.

——. 2008. 'Les chrétiens d'Alep dans la fabrication et le commerce des tissus aux XVIIᵉ et XVIIIᵉ siècles', *Rives méditerranéennes* 29: 53–60.

——. 2010. 'Aux origines du plan d'Alep par Rousseau: le plan de Vincent Germain de 1811', in *Syria and Bilad al-Sham under Ottoman Rule: Essays in Honour of Abdul-Karim Rafeq*, ed. Peter Sluglett and Stefan Weber, 499–512. Leiden.

Redford, Scott. 1993. 'The Seljuqs of Rum and the Antique', *Muqarnas* 10: 148–56.

Riis, T. 1999. 'Observations sur la population d'Alep au XIXᵉ siècle', *Bulletin d'études orientales* 51: 279–98.

Robson, Charles. 1628. *Newes from Aleppo, a Letter written to T. V[icars], B.D., Vicar of Cockfield in Southsex (Cockfield, Sussex) . . . containing many remarkeable Occurrences* (accessed via Early English Books Online).

Roded, Ruth Michal. 1984. *Tradition and Change in Syria During the Last Decades of Ottoman Rule: The Urban Elite of Damascus, Aleppo, Homs and Hama, 1876–1918.* Denver.

Roffé, Sarina. 2010. 'The Jews of Aleppo' (www.jewishgen.org/Sephardic/aleppojews.htm).

Rowan, Clare. 2007. 'Zeus Casios and the Baetyl of Sidon: Two New Coins at ACANS', *Journal of the Numismatic Association of Australia* 18: 35–9.

Roxburgh, David J., Nazan Olcer and Filiz Cagman, eds. 2005. *Turks: A Journey of a Thousand Years, 600–1600.* London.

Runciman, Steven. 1965. *A History of the Crusades.* 3 vols. Harmondsworth.

Russell, Alexander. 1756. *The Natural History of Aleppo and the Parts Adjacent, containing a Description of the City and the Principal Natural Productions in its Neighbourhood; together with an Account of the Climate, Inhabitants and Diseases, particularly of the Plague, with the Methods used by the Europeans for their Preservation.* London.

Russell, Alexander and Patrick Russell. 1794. *The Natural History of Aleppo and the Parts Adjacent, containing a Description of the City and the Principal Natural Productions in its Neighbourhood; together with an Account of the Climate, Inhabitants and Diseases, particularly of the Plague, with the Methods used by the Europeans for their Preservation* (reissued and expanded in 2 vols.). London.

Salati, Marco. 1990. 'Note sul waqf di Ipshir Pasha a Aleppo (1064/1654)', *Islam, Storia e Civiltà* (Unione Islamica in Occidente, Accademia della Cultura Islamica) 32 (3): 193–9.

Salmon, Olivier. 2011. *Alep dans la litérature de voyage européenne pendant la période ottomane (1516–1918).* 3 vols. Aleppo.

Sanderson, John, ed. 1931. *The Travels of John Sanderson in the Levant (1584–1602).* London.

Sanjian, Avedis K., ed. 1965. *The Armenian Communities in Syria under Ottoman Occupation.* Cambridge, MA.

Saouaf, Soubhi. 1974. *Enceintes et portes d'Alep.* Aleppo.

——. 1975a. *Alep – son histoire et ses monuments.* Aleppo.

——. 1975b. *La citadelle d'Alep.* Aleppo.

Saoud, Rabah. 2003. *Muslim Architecture Under Seljuk Patronage (1038–1327).* Manchester (e-publication at www.fstc.co.uk).

Saouf, Soubhi. 1954. *Aleppo, son Histoire, sa Citadelle, ses Monuments Antiques et son Musée – Guide des Visiteurs.* Aleppo.

——. 1972. *Alep dans sa plus ancienne Histoire.* Aleppo.

Sauvaget, Jean. 1928. 'Deux sanctuaires chiites d'Alep', *Syria* IX: 224–37.

———. 1931. 'Inventaire des monuments musulmans de la ville d'Alep', *Revue des études islamiques*. Paris.

———. 1935. 'Le plan de Laodicée-sur-mer', *Bulletin d'études orientales*. IV: 81–114.

———. 1936. 'Alep au temps de Sayf al-Dawla', in *Al Mutanabbî: recueil publié à l'occasion de son millénaire*, 19–30. Beirut.

———. 1938. 'La tombe de l'Ortokide Balak', *Ars Islamica* 5 (2): 207–15.

———. 1939. 'Le 'tell' d'Alep', in *Mélanges syriennes offerts à M. R. Dussaud*, 59–65. Paris.

———. 1941. *Alep, essai sur le développement d'une grande ville syrienne des origines au milieu du XIXe siècle – I Texte, II Album* (Bibliothèque archéologique et historique). Paris.

Schaeffer, Claude. 1938. 'Fouilles de Ras Shamra – Ugarit XIII – Fouilles sur le sommet du Jebel Akra et aux ruines du couvent de Saint-Barlaam', *Syria* XIX: 323–7.

Scharabi, Mohamed. 1980. 'Bemerkungen zur Bauform des Süqs von Aleppo', *Mitteilungen des Deutschen Archäologischen Instituts, Abteiling Kairo* 36: 391–410.

Schwemer, Daniel. 2008. 'The Storm-Gods of the Ancient Near East: Summary, Synthesis, Recent Studies', *Journal of Ancient Near Eastern Religions* 7 (2): 121–68.

Seale, Patrick. 1986. *The Struggle for Syria: A Study of Post-War Arab Politics 1945–1958*. London.

Searight, Sarah. 1994. 'Vision of the Middle East', *Saudi Aramco World* 45 (3): 32–9.

Setton, Kenneth M. and Marshall W. Baldwin, eds. 1969. *A History of the Crusades 1 – The First Hundred Years*. Madison and London.

Seyrig, Henri. 1958. 'Monnaies grecques des fouilles de Doura et d'Antioche', *Revue numismatique* 1: 171–81.

———. 1970. 'Antiquités syriennes – 92. Séleucus I et la fondation de la monarchie syrienne', *Syria* 47: 287–311.

Shalit, Yoram. 1996. *Nicht-Muslime und Fremde in Aleppo und Damaskus im 18. und in der ersten Hälfte des 19. Jahrhunderts*. Berlin.

———. 1999. 'European Foreigners in Damascus and Aleppo During the Late Ottoman Period', in *Modern Syria, From Ottoman Rule to Pivotal Role in the Middle East*, ed. Moshe Ma'oz, J. Ginat and Onn Wincler, 150–69. Brighton.

Shambrook, Peter A. 1998. *French Imperialism in Syria 1927–1936*. Reading.

Shields, Sarah D. 2011. *Fezzes in the River: Identity Politics and European Diplomacy in the Middle East on the Eve of World War II*. New York.

Sibt Ibn al-Ajami. 1950. *'Les Tresors d'Or' de Sibt Ibn al-'Ajami (1415–1479) – Kunūz ad-dahab fi tarih Halab* (trans. Jean Sauvaget, *Materiaux pour Servir à l'histoire de la ville d'Alep II*).

Sirriyeh, Elizabeth. 1984. 'The Memoires of a French Gentleman in Syria: Chevalier Laurent d'Arvieux (1635–1702)', *Bulletin of the Society for Middle Eastern Studies* 11 (2): 125–39.

———. 2013. *Sufis and Anti-Sufis: The Defence, Rethinking and Rejection of Sufism in the Modern World*. London.

Sluglett, Peter and Stefan Weber, eds. 2010. *Syria and Bilad Al-Sham Under Ottoman Rule: Essays in Honour of Abdul Karim Rafeq, The Ottoman Empire and its Heritage*. Leiden.

Smoor, Pieter. 1985. *Kings and Bedouins in the Palace of Aleppo as Reflected in Ma'arri's Works, Journal of Semitic Studies Monographs*. Manchester.

Sobernheim, Moritz. 1909. 'Das Heiligtum Shaikh Muhassin in Aleppo', in *Mélanges Hartwig Derenbourg (1844–1908)*, 379–90. Paris.

——. 1916. 'Der Shi'a in Aleppo', *Der Islam* 6: 95–7.

——. 1926. 'Die arabischen Inschriften von Aleppo. Mit 8 Abbildungen und X Tafeln', *Aufsätze und Berichte* 15: 161–241.

Sourdel, Dominique. 1949–51. 'Les professeurs de Madrasa à Alep aux XIIᵉ – XIIIᵉ siècles d'après Ibn Šaddād', *Bulletin d'études orientales* XIII: 85–115.

——. 1952. 'Esquisse topographique d'Alep intra-muros à l'époque ayyoubide', *Annales archéologiques arabes syriennes* 2: 109–29.

Sourdel-Thomine, Janine. 1970. 'La mosquée et la madrasa', *Cahiers de la civilisation médiévale* 13: 97–115.

Starkey, Janet C. M. 2003. 'Mercantile Gentlemen and Inquisitive Travellers – Constructing the Natural History of Aleppo', in *Travellers in the Near East*, ed. Charles Foster, 29–71. London.

——. 2012. 'The Continuity of Sacred Space: Khan al-Jumruk within the Bazaars of Aleppo', in *The Bazaar in the Islamic City – Design, Culture and History*, ed. Mohammad Gharipour, 115–48. Cairo.

Steensgaard, Niels. 1974. *The Asian Trade Revolution of the Seventeenth Century: The East India Companies and the Decline of the Caravan Trade*. Chicago.

Syrian, Michael the. 1899. *Chronique de Michel le Syrien, Patriarche Jacobite d'Antioche (1166–1199)*. 3 vols. Paris.

Tabbaa, Yasser. 1988. 'Geometry and Memory in the Design of the Madrasat al-Firdows in Aleppo', in *Theories and Principles of Design in the Architecture of Islamic Societies*, ed. Margaret Bentley Sevchenko. Cambridge, MA.

——. 1993a. 'Circles of Power: Palace, Citadel and City in Ayyubid Aleppo', *Ars Orientalis* 23: 181–200.

——. 1993b. 'Survivals and Archaisms in the Architecture of Northern Syria c980 – c1150', *Muqarnas* 8: 29–41.

——. 1997. *Constructions of Power and Piety in Medieval Aleppo, 1178–1260*. University Park, PA.

——. 2006. 'Defending Ayyubid Aleppo: The Fortifications of al-Zahir Ghazi (1186–1216)', in *Muslim Military Architecture in Greater Syria, From the Coming of Islam to the Ottoman Period*, ed. Hugh Kennedy, 176–85. Leiden.

Taghribirdi, see Popper, William.

Takieddine, Zena and Samer Abd al-Ghafour 'Madrasat al-Firdaws'. 2015. *Discover Islamic Art, Museum With No Frontiers* (www.discoverislamicart.org/database_item.php?id=monument;ISL;sy;Mon01;4;en&cp).

Talbot Rice, Tamara. 1961. *The Seljuks* (Ancient Peoples & Places series). London.

Talmon-Heller, Daniella. 2007. *Islamic Piety in Medieval Syria. Mosques, Cemeteries and Sermons Under the Zangids and Ayyūbids (1146–1260)* (Jerusalem Studies in Religion and Culture). Leiden.

Tate, Georges. 1991. 'Prosperité économique de la Syrie du Nord à l'époque byzantine (IVe–VIIIe s.)', in *Alep et la Syrie du Nord*, ed. Viviane Fuglestad-Aumeunier, 41–8. Aix-en-Provence.

Tawil, Hayim and Bernard Schneider. 2010. *Crown of Aleppo: The Mystery of the Oldest Hebrew Bible Codex*. Philadelphia.

Teixeira, Pedro. 1902. *The Travels of Pedro Teixeira* (trans. W. F. Sinclair). London.

Thorau, Peter. 1992. *The Lion of Egypt – Sultan Baybars I and the Near East in the Thirteenth Century*. London.

Toueir, Kassem. 1983. 'Heraqlah: a unique victory monument of Harun ar-Rashid', *World Archaeology* 14 (3): 296–304.

Tudela, Benjamin of. 1907. *The Itinerary of Benjamin of Tudela* (ed. Adler). London.

Uluengin, Mehmet Bengü. 2010. 'Secularizing Anatolia Tick by Tick: Clock Towers in the Ottoman Empire and the Turkish Republic', *International Journal of Middle East Studies* 42 (1): 17–36.

Vallet, Eric. 1999. *Marchands vénetiens en Syrie à la fin du XVᵉ siècle*. Paris.

van den Boogert, Maurits. 2010. 'Provocative Wealth: Non-Muslim Elites in Eighteenth-Century Aleppo', *Journal of Early Modern History* 14: 219–37.

Vârth, Gerhard. 1987. *Die Geschichte der artuqidischen Fürstentümer in Syrien und der Gazira 'l-Furatiya (496–812/1002–1409)* (Islamkundliche Untersuchungen). Berlin.

Watenpaugh, Heghnar Zeitlian. 2004. *The Image of an Ottoman City – Imperial Architecture and Urban Experience in Aleppo in the 16th and 17th Centuries*. Leiden.

——. 2005. 'Deviant Dervishes: Space, Gender and the Construction of Antinomian Piety in Ottoman Aleppo', *International Journal of Middle East Studies* 37: 535–65.

Watenpaugh, Keith David. 2006. *Being Modern in the Middle East – Revolution, Nationalism, Colonialsm and the Arab Middle Class*. Princeton.

Weingarten, Judith, 2016, 'The Mystery of the First Drawings of Palmyra,' *Zenobia, Empress of the East* (http://judithweingarten.blogspot.com.au/).

Wilkins, Charles L. 2010. *Forging Urban Solidarities: Ottoman Aleppo 1640–1700* (The Ottoman Empire and its Heritage). Leiden.

Wirth, Eugen. 1990. 'Alep et les courants commerciaux entre l'Europe et l'Asie du XIIᵉ au XVIᵉ siècles', *Revue du monde musulman et de la Méditerranée* 55/56: 44–56.

Woolley, Leonard. 1953. *A Forgotten Kingdom*. Harmondsworth.

Wood, Alfred Cecil. 1935. *A History of the Levant Company*. Oxford.

Wood, Robert. 1753. *The Ruins of Palmyra otherwise Tedmor in the Desart* (1971 reprint). Westmead, Hants.

Yanoski, Jean and Jules David. 1848. *Syrie ancienne et moderne, L'univers ou histoire et description de tous les peuples, de leurs religions, moeurs coutumes etc.* Paris.

Yerasimos, Stephane. 1991. *Les voyageurs dans l'empire ottoman (XIVᵉ–XVIᵉ siècles) – bibliographie, itinéraires et inventaire des lieux habités*. Ankara.

Zakkar, Suhayl. 1971. *The Emirate of Aleppo: 1004–1094*. Beirut.

Zenner, Walter P. 2000. *A Global Community: The Jews From Aleppo, Syria*. Detroit.

Ziadeh, Nicola A. 1997–98. 'Ottoman Occupation of Bilad al-Sham and its Immediate Results', *Aram* 9–10: 337–46.

INDEX

Italics indicate a reference to an illustration (figure no.)
In establishing alphabetical order—Arabic prefix 'al-' is disregarded; 'Ibn' ('son of') is
included *as* part of name